THE POEMS OF
WILLIAM DUNBAR

EDITED BY

W. MACKAY MACKENZIE
M.A., D.LITT.

FABER AND FABER LIMITED
24 RUSSELL SQUARE
LONDON

FIRST PUBLISHED IN 1932
BY FABER AND FABER LIMITED
24 RUSSELL SQUARE, LONDON, W.C.I
FIRST PUBLISHED IN THIS EDITION 1970
PRINTED IN GREAT BRITAIN BY
JOHN DICKENS AND CO. LTD., NORTHAMPTON
ALL RIGHTS RESERVED   ·
SBN 571 09239 X

THE POEMS OF WILLIAM DUNBAR

PREFACE

A RECENT enquiry through the bookshops of Edinburgh disclosed the fact that there was but one copy of Dunbar's poems for sale, and that a handsomely bound, and therefore costly, example of the first collected edition in two volumes. Such being the case in the capital and university city, it is not likely that, outside the big libraries, any other place had more to offer. It seemed that there was a gap to fill.

What made the undertaking further desirable was the material now available in the publication by the " Scottish Text Society " of trustworthy editions of the MS. collections in which the poems have been preserved. The Society readily consented to place these, as well as their own earlier editions of the poet's works, at the disposal of the editor and publishers, who would record here their grateful thanks for this courtesy. References to MS. sources are therefore to be understood as to the S.T.S. transcripts.

It is necessary, however, to say that the present edition is in no sense a reproduction of any other but the result of a fresh and independent survey of the material. Several considerations made that course desirable, and in this connection it is proper to express the debt which every student owes to the Scottish element in the *New English Dictionary*.

That a new treatment emerges in general handling and in many details is an individual responsibility. On such issues judgments will probably differ. That the issues should be raised, however, and should stimulate interest and enquiry, may be held to be an advantage. Necessarily, the scope of a single compact volume limits the field of exposition, but it is hoped that sufficient has been done to serve the needs of those in view.

W. M. M.

NOTE ON THE PRESENT EDITION

Dr. William Mackay Mackenzie's edition of the poems of William Dunbar was first published in 1932 and reprinted unchanged, by photolithography, in 1950. Two years later the editor died in his eightieth year. His work has stood the test of time and is now reprinted, again by photolithography, with no more than a few necessary additions and corrections.

Mackenzie graduated M.A. (with honours in classics) of Edinburgh in 1897 and taught for some years in Glasgow Academy. Though he produced good editions of Barbour's *Bruce* (1909), Dunbar, and *The Kingis Quair* (1939) he was primarily not a specialist in Middle Scots but in history and antiquities—a necessary basis for the competent editor of a medieval Scots text. Already in 1904 he had been elected to the Society of Antiquaries of Scotland and had published in 1907 a still useful *Outline of Scottish History . . . to the Disruption.* He was thus well qualified for the Secretaryship to the Royal Commission on Ancient and Historical Monuments and Constructions of Scotland, a post he held with distinction from 1913 till 1935. Between 1914 and 1933 there appeared under his editorship Volumes v–xi of the Commission's publications, covering a great part of the Scottish Lowlands as well as the Outer Hebrides, Skye and the Small Isles. The present writer has always regretted that Mackenzie's survey of the early history of the South of Scotland, designed as an introduction to the East Lothian volume, never passed beyond the galley-proof stage. As bye-products of his work for the Commission, he published Volume ii of *The Book of Arran* (History and Folklore) in 1914, and a series of Rhind Lectures which appeared in 1927 as *The Mediaeval Castle in Scotland.* The quality of his work was very high, and he was unlucky that a vacancy in the Edinburgh chair of Scottish History came too late to profit him. But from 1940 till 1943 he carried on the work of the department. In the latter year he was appropriately appointed to the Commission of which he had been Secretary, and he was still busy in 1945 when he gave a second series of Rhind Lectures, published in 1949 as *The Scottish Burghs.* He was already a D.Litt. of Edinburgh when in 1949 he received the honorary degree of LL.D. He retired to his native Cromarty, to which he was deeply attached, and died on 4th August, 1952.

Few scholars· have worked on so broad a front or have applied so keenly critical a mind to the problems of Scots history and literature, among them the much fought-over battles of Bannockburn and Flodden. The present writer, who went to Edinburgh as a young lecturer in 1919, remembers him with gratitude as a good friend and a most stimulating, as well as most salutary, critic.

Bruce Dickins

CONTENTS

* Titles within quotation points are from the headings or the
colophons of the poems.

CONTENTS

ALLEGORIES AND ADDRESSES

MORALISINGS

RELIGIOUS

SOME ATTRIBUTIONS

INTRODUCTION

I. THE SCOTTISH CHAUCERIANS

By the fifteenth century England was established as " the auld enemy " of Scotland. But political history leaves the tale, like that of Cambuscan, half told. The conquest of Scotland which could not be achieved in the feudal field was made in that of literature, when Geoffrey Chaucer, " father of English poetry, and his compatriots Gower and Lydgate drew the ungrudging admiration and discipleship of the Scottish " makars." Even the author of *The Wallace* could ease his bitterness against the " southron " with strains and measures modelled on those of the great southern poet.[1] Robert Henryson, the Dunfermline poet, read Chaucer by his winter fire and shows himself a not unworthy follower. As *The Wallace* was composed about 1470 and nothing of Chaucer was in print before 1476, while Henryson also was writing well before the former date, the English poems must have circulated in MS. among the literary group in Scotland.

Now all this is of deep significance. It is remarkable that so cordial a welcome should have been given to the work of poets far removed in a hostile country. So sure a literary judgment augurs the existence of a critical standard and therefore of a definite culture. Men who could appreciate on its merits the work of an extraneous poet, a poet, too, who wrote in a language that differed from their own as much, according to the Spanish ambassador, as Aragonese from Castilian, must have had a cultivated literary sense.[2]

---

[1] See for versification Bk. ii, ll. 171-359, and on the general question *The Wallace and The Bruce Restudied*, by J. T. T. Brown, pp. 43-6, 79.

[2] And that is the whole matter. A recent accomplished critic has pointed out that " nobody could call Dunbar a Nationalist. As a conscious poet he derived from England, etc." (*Dunbar*, by Rachel Annand Taylor, p. 29). It is not a question of nationalism, but of literary values. Chaucer is not the less English because he " derived " so much from France and Italy.

What, primarily, Chaucer had done was to establish the national tongue as a literary medium of equal standing with the hitherto prevailing Latin or French, just as Dante, earlier in the same century, had done for Italian. The English poet had found a country of dialects and made one of them a literary language, imparting to it the courtly grace and flow that marked the poetry of France and moulding it in attractive and musical metrical forms. In all this, indeed, he had a fellow-worker in John Gower, whose share, however, has been overshadowed by the genius of his greater contemporary. Chaucer, for Dunbar, was " in oure tong ane flour imperiall," and he, Gower, and Lydgate had " our rude langage . . . clere illumynate." Before their time

> " This Ile . . . was bare and desolate
> Off rethorike or lusty fresch endyte (poetry)."

This claim was perhaps pitched rather high, but it shows how clearly the Scottish poet appreciated what Chaucer had done—his success in enriching the common language with so much of what was best in mediaeval poetry. And Dunbar testified not for himself alone, but for his predecessor Robert Henryson as well as his successors Gavin Douglas and Sir David Lindesay, not to speak of the number of lesser men who obviously learned in the same school.

But this following was that of disciples, not of imitators. The Scottish poets absorbed in their degree the spirit and technique of their English models, but used these to their own ends. They admired to the full but they produced something different; in that lay their originality. Chaucer had done much by the infusion of a Latin vocabulary transformed through French ; his Scottish admirers went further by drawing on the same ancient source directly. Thence came their Latinised or " aureate " diction, more alien to our ears than to theirs, which were attuned to Latin as almost a second colloquial language in the Scotland of that time.[1] For courtly poets it was another way of escape from the more ignoble associations of the dialectal vernacular,

---

[1] The contemporary John of Ireland explains that he wrote his book, the *Meroure of Wysdome* (1490)," in the commoune langage of this cuntre. Bot in the tounge that I knaw bettir, that is, Latin, I maid, etc." (ed. S.T.S., p. 164).

an ingredient of the "grand style" suitable for the more lofty
themes,[1] and a means of smoothing the emphatic effect of the
native language. Gavin Douglas opens his translation of the
Aeneid with an apology to Virgil for venturing to render his
"sugurate sang" and "polyst termys" into the "bad harsk
spech" that was current Scots, and, while professing his intention
to use "our awin langage," yet held himself free to admit useful
words from "bastard Latin," English, or French. This
"aureate" diction, however, was mainly for noble company in
phrases like "the goldyn candill matutyne," while its abundance
in *Ane Ballat of Our Lady* is a sheer *tour de force* in language that
seeks to vie with the sonorous melody of the Latin hymns on the
same subject. Diction of this origin was, indeed, a literary
fashion for a time: it appears in Lydgate and other English
writers, while in France it took shape in the "Latial verbocina-
tion" satirised by Rabelais. But Dunbar realised its limits
and observed them. He had, as Lindesay said, "language at
large" and could not only embellish the vernacular, but also
shape it with effect:

> " He schewre his feddreme that was schene,
> And slippit owt of it full clene,
> And in a myre, up to the ene,
> Amang the glar did glyd."

But in this usage, too, he exercised poetic discretion. A
familiar word like "kemp" might do for a burlesqued "Gow
Mac Morn," but its associations called for the substitution of a
more dignified equivalent in "Our campioun Chryst." On such
lines did Dunbar and his compatriots work: they were "makers"
of a literary Scots.[2] Not, however, as theorists but as poets.
Long after them Robert Burns undertook a similar task. But
while they had made Chaucer and Latin their exemplars, Burns

[1] "Not shaped for heroic flights" is R. L. Stevenson's verdict in *Some
Aspects of Robert Burns* on the Scots "written colloquially" by poets of
a later period.

[2] Schipper argues (*William Dunbar, sein Leben und seine Gedichte*, p. 45)
that this "aureate" fashion originated partly from the need felt by the
Scots (*aus dem Bedürfniss der Schotten*) to free themselves from the English
in their literature as well as in their political position (*wie in ihrer politischen
Stellung so auch in ihrer Literatur*). But this supposition is unnecessary and
is not in accord with the utterances of the Scottish writers themselves.

took as his the eighteenth-century English poets.   Under this aspect a typical product of the earlier school is *The Goldyn Targe*; of that of Burns *The Cotter's Saturday Night*.

Another influence exerted by Chaucer was in metre and the use of the stanza.   He gave native vogue to the beautiful rhyme-royal,[1] or stanza of seven ten-syllabled lines, which Dunbar adopts in *The Thrissil and the Rois*.   On the other hand Chaucer's ten-syllabled couplet, so effective in narrative, Dunbar uses only in the short piece *In Prais of Wemen*, the *Freiris of Berwick* being certainly from a different hand.   The narrative of *The Tua Mariit Wemen and the Wedo* is couched, with a subtle sense of artistic humour, in a remarkably regular example of the older, rather uncouth, alliterative measure.   For the rest, in mere variety of stanza and metrical device, Dunbar outranges his master.   In regard to these he could, of course, draw on the common stock of mediaeval Latin poems as models, but it may be that he was guided by French examples, though in this respect, too, he for the most part avoids imitation and frames his own measures.   In *The Dregy* the responses are in triolets,[2] a specifically French form of stanza, and that form he may have got directly.   To the same source may be attributed his exceeding fondness for stanzas with a common refrain, many such compositions roughly resembling the French *ballade*, but not in observance of its stricter rules.   Nevertheless for this class Chaucer could quite well have provided the model.   The *kyrielle* [3] verse used in the *Lament for the Makaris*, in *All Erdly Joy Returnis in Pane*, and in a number of other cases, is no doubt an old French form, but its construction is simple and obvious and was widely practised.[4]

Certainly in view of Dunbar's acquaintance with Paris, suggested by passages in *The Flyting*, it is natural to look in his work for traces of familiarity with the poetic output there. Villon was not long dead (*c.* 1474), but nothing by Dunbar can be attributed directly to that source, nor indeed, specifically, to

[1] So called because it was used in *The Kingis Quair*.

[2] An eight-line stanza on two rhymes, in which the first line is repeated as the fourth and the first two lines appear as the seventh and eighth.

[3] Composed of four-line verses rhyming in couplets with a refrain.

[4] On Dunbar's versification and metres see the section by G. P. McNeill, LL.B., in S.T.S., vol. i, pp. clxxii-cxciii, with the references given there.

any other French example. Obviously *The Goldyn Targe* is but an offshoot from the great *Roman de la Rose* with its literary properties of the dream, the fair garden, the classical figures, and the action conducted by personifications of human attributes or impulses. The same is true of *The Thrissil and the Rois* and other poems cast in that mould. No doubt, too, *In Secret Place* is a " pastoral " (*pastourelle*) taken indoors, and *The Wowing of the King* a sort of " beast-fable " (*fabliau*), both in a very sophisticated setting. Other such possible links are noted on pp. xxx, xxxii. But it must be remembered that all these types had spread from France to the literature of other countries and were now familiar in literary circles. The *Roman de la Rose* had an extraordinary influence upon the general poetic output for centuries, and Chaucer had translated it as *The Romaunt of the Rose*. The English poets were in close touch with French literature, and all that seems French in Dunbar may have come through these secondary channels ; at least it is hard to differentiate anything that was taken directly. Had Dunbar been conscious of having done so, it seems probable that he would have been as ready to acknowledge his debt as in the case of the English poets.

II. LITERATURE AND THE COURT

It would probably not be far wrong to trace the acquaintance with Chaucer back to the connections set up by the long detention of King James I as a prisoner at the English court, where he was brought up and educated. James himself is reputed to be the author of that plainly Chaucerian composition *The Kingis Quair*. But while James I was still in England there was necessarily much coming and going of Scottish magnates and messengers, and among them there may well have been some fitted to convey knowledge of the poet who had but recently passed away. Certain Scottish barons, indeed, have come down as patrons of literary men. It was a Stewart of Rosyth who urged Walter Bower to expansion and continuation of the earlier historic work of John of Fordun in that Latin leviathan the *Scotichronicon*. Another Fife laird did the same service in the case of Andrew Wyntoun's *Orygynale Cronykyl*. The *Buke of the Howlat*, according to its author, Richard Holland, was written for the Countess of Moray. Henryson informs us that he composed his *Fables* at the "requeist and precept of ane Lord," whose name, however, he does not give ; while in Dunbar's own time it was a St. Clair of Roslin, "fader of bukis," who pressed Gavin Douglas to undertake the translation of the *Aeneid*. These few names, accidentally preserved, no doubt stand for a line of men with literary interests, who were not of the clerical or professional class.

It is usual to depict the court of the fourth James in attractive colours as a home of culture of all sorts, and the king himself as an accomplished patron of the arts. Dunbar, indeed, in his *Remonstrance* catalogues a highly varied crowd of royal "servitours"—soldiers, professional and scientific men, artists, musicians, and craftsmen. What is noteworthy is that he follows this statement with the plea that, though unworthy to be reckoned in their number—surely a satirical qualification—

> " Als lang in mynd my wark sall hald
> As ony of thair werkis all."

In face of this protestation it is hard to believe that the circumstances and atmosphere of the court were as favourable to literary effort as has been assumed. The oft-quoted report of Pedro de Ayala, the Spanish ambassador, speaks of James as well read in the Bible and some other devout books, and in Latin and French histories. This accords with the notices of books bought for him in Paris,[1] which are on solemn theological or scientific subjects and are now but shadowy names, and among which the only literary place is occupied by the bucolics and eclogues of Virgil. In this connection, then, it is well to consider the remark of George Buchanan, who was a boy of seven when the king fell at Flodden. In his history he speaks of James's great popularity, his kindness of disposition and many virtues, but adds that he was "without literary culture " (*ab literis inculto*). And this comment is borne out by the more general complaint of Hector Boece in comparing the conditions under James I with "the gret displesouris that fallis to us, for laik of letters and virtew in our princis.[2] ...

---

[1] *Accounts of Lord High Treasurer*, ii, pp. cxi-cxviii.

[2] " Princes," translating *magistratus sacri et urbani*—*i.e.* rulers in general, sacred and secular.

Nane rasit in dignite, office, honour, nor benefice, but maist unhappy and avaritious pepill, void of all virtew and gud maneris ; and sa gret ennimes to men of letteris,[1] that they may not suffer thame to rise in proffit, dignite or honnouris." [2] We gather that, on the whole, it was no very appreciative or bountiful time for men of letters as such. King James had many practical interests. He was active in administration and concerned with economic developments. He accumulated artillery and built warships. His emotional piety led him to patronise friars, go on frequent long pilgrimages, and project a crusade. But his special interest was in medicine and surgery, a fact spoken to by Buchanan and later emphasised by Pitscottie, while their testimonies are supported by entries in the *Treasurer's Accounts*, as in references to surgical operations in which the king showed interest,[3] to a present of money for being allowed to bleed a man,[4] and to a " sair leg quhilk the king helit." [5] It is not difficult to see that a " leech " meant more to the king than a poet.[6] The test case is that of John Damian, whom Bishop Leslie calls an Italian but who figures in the *Accounts* as " the French leech," who was also a deviser of dances, an experimenter in the chemical production of gold, and aviator in feathers. For Dunbar he was a complete charlatan .[7] Yet within three years of his arrival in Scotland this man had received the abbacy of Tongland, while Dunbar over a long period pleaded for some such recognition in vain. But Dunbar's unsparing ridicule of this personage cannot have been pleasing to Damian's royal patron. The poet's wrath, however, can be understood in view of such an example and in respect of a court where a " fals cairt " in the sleeve was

" Worthe all my ballattis undir the byrkis,"

[1] *Ingenti nisu omnibus literis obsistentes.*

[2] Bellenden's translation in 1536 of Boece's *Scotorum Historiae*, Paris, 1526, *Lib. xvi, fol. ccclv.*

[3] i, p. 305 ; ii, p. 102.   [4] i, p. 176.   [5] ii, p. 465.

[6] So many of these professed physicians had gifts from the king that in addition to those named by the treasurer there are entries for " the Ireland leich," " Anthon Fidanis leich," " the ald leich that James Douglas brocht," " the leich with the curland hair," " the leich with the yallow hair," etc. —*Treasurer's Accounts*, vol. ii, *passim.*

[7] Cf. No. 38.

B

and where a "Schir Johne Kirkpakar" could boast that his seven benefices will grow to eleven ere one go to "yone ballet makar."[1]

It is not our plea, of course, that being a poet was a qualification for a bishopric, though men were made bishops for worse reasons ; nor that being a king's "clerk" or member of the civil service entitled one to a benefice, though that was in the manner of the time.   But even a poet had to get his bread and butter, as Dunbar urges :

> "How suld I leif, and I not landit,
> Nor yit withe benefice am blandit."

In a court represented as so favourable to writers a claim of this kind might be expected to carry weight in respect of literary standing alone.   But not till he was well on in years did Dunbar's regular salary or pension begin, and then as the result of much solicitation :

> "Schir, yit remember as of befoir,
> How that my youthe is done forloir
> In your service, with pane and greiff ;
> Gud conscience cryis reward thairfoir."

It seems clear that, despite the comparatively generous terms of pension ultimately allowed to Dunbar, his literary merits were not appreciated as inevitably as has been assumed, and not with the readiness and generosity shown to a foreign dabbler in quasi-scientific fantasies.

James's court, then, with all its bustle and glitter, was not a forcing-house of literary merit.   No one can read the *Remonstrance* and hold that it was.   Dunbar and his fellow-writers, as such, owed little to courtly patronage.   It is the sense of this undervaluation that motives the bitter and satirical burden of so much of the poet's work, an element which has been misunderstood because its conditions have been misrepresented.

III. WILLIAM DUNBAR

The life-story of William Dunbar—or, as it is frequently written, Dumbar—is almost a blank.   What has been written

---

[1] Cf. Nos. 20, l. 68 ; 60, l. 86.

of it, with more or less confidence, is to a large extent conjecture. The only precise indication of his date of birth is the assertion by Kennedy in *The Flyting*, l. 489 : "Thou was consavit in the grete eclips." Such an eclipse occurred on 18th July, 1460, and the expression, taken loosely, would fix Dunbar's birth in that or the following year. This is a very suitable date, though, on the other hand, Kennedy may simply have been connecting his origin, abusively, with an unpleasant occurrence. Even so, he must have had some regard to chronology, and it is more probable that the allusion is roughly correct. The play made by the same writer with the name Dunbar, and his determination to link it with the traitorous Earls of Dunbar as the poet's "forebears," have led to the conclusion that he was connected with that family, and so to the conjecture by Mr. Laing that a William Dunbar, son of Sir Patrick Dunbar of Biel, East Lothian, on record in 1440, may have been his father or his uncle, that branch representing the old forfeited earls. On the other hand it is scarcely consistent with this immediate origin that Kennedy should speak of the poet as a "foundling" (l. 38). But the whole manner of this exercise in scurrility forbids us to take such pronouncements seriously ; it was enough for Kennedy that the surname should be one that he could blacken with infamous associations.[1] That Dunbar, however, knew himself to be of good birth may be inferred from several utterances—for example from the lines

> "I wes in youthe, on nureice (nurse's) kne
> Cald dandillie, bischop, dandillie,"

and generally from *The Complaint*, the burden of which is the unhappy rise of people of humble origin to places of honour and profit. Dunbar did not hold that "A man's a man for a' that."[2] That the poet was a native of Lothian might be

---

[1] In the same spirit the Italian writer Matteo Franco, in his "flyting" with Luigi Pulci, makes great play with the surname of his opponent : *pulce* = flea.

[2] Schipper, however, attributes to Dunbar's "sense of justice" (*Rechtsgefühl*) his references in *The Complaint* to what nobly born persons had to suffer from upstarts, while, on the strength of another couplet in the same poem with its reference to Adam and Eve, he claims that the poet was "a democrat through and through" (*ein Demokrat durch und durch*). But the lines in their context amount to no more than that the needy poet had to

hazarded even without his own solitary ambiguous reference to that district in *The Flyting*. Kennedy, indeed, expressly excludes him from any connection with the Dunbars of Westfield in Moray, but the name cannot have been uncommon.[1]

This last qualification further applies to its appearance in the Register of St. Andrews as that of a Determinant or Bachelor of Arts in 1477, who became a Master of Arts two years later. It is not certain that this was our William Dunbar any more than that the " venerable man " Robert Henryson, who was incorporated in the University of Glasgow in 1462, was the poet of that name. Nevertheless, as fifteen was a usual age for a student to enter the university, the dates given would fit in with that inferred for his birth, and this result is rather too neat to be explained as a coincidence. Further, the regular prefix of " Maister " to his name implies a " Master's " degree. The one possible allusion to St. Andrews by Dunbar may be his use of St. Salvator in one poem, the college and church so dedicated in that town having been founded just before Dunbar's time and this being the only outstanding dedication of its class in Scotland. On the other hand the alliteration with " silver " and " sorrow " may account for the choice of the saint.

Some uncertainty even attaches to the accepted conclusion that Dunbar had been a novice in the order of Grey Friars or Franciscans. The sole grounds for this belief are contained in the poem *How Dumbar wes Desyrd to be Ane Freir*. There the poet himself confesses to having, for a time, borne " the freiris style "—and in this dress to have wandered far, playing the trickster. But St. Francis, who was really the Devil in disguise, urges him :

> " Thow, that hes lang done Venus lawis teiche,
> Sall now be freir and in this abbeit preiche " ;

live like others of the human species. Dunbar's general frame of mind is not democratic. He complains :

> " Ane rebald to renoun dois rys
> And carlis of nobillis hes the cure " (21. 22-3).

His expressions of compassion for the poor do not necessitate Schipper's inference (cf. Schipper's *William Dunbar, sein Leben und seine Gedichte*, p. 382).

[1] A Precept of Legitimation of 1511 is in favour of six Dunbars, one of them named William.—*Reg. Sec. Sig.*, i, No. 2293.

to which he answers :

> " Bot thame to weir it nevir come in my mynd
>
> . . . .
>
> Gif evir my fortoun wes to be a freir,
> The dait thairof is past full mony a yeir."

These lines scarcely suggest an early adherence to the order. There is no reference to the novitiate, and, strictly, a novice was not entitled to wear the full dress of his order. Moreover his refusal after novitiate would have branded him as an " apostate," and indeed in one place Kennedy does apply to him this term, but in a way—" Pilate apostata " [1]—which robs it of special significance. It may also be noted that Dunbar accuses the *Fenyeit Freir of Tungland* of having secured a religious dress by slaying its wearer, all that he additionally required being the ability to read and write. Dunbar himself, as Schipper suggests, may have been guilty of a similar fraud in his own case. In *The Flyting* he is accused by Kennedy of having gone about in the Lowlands as a " pardoner " and, in other lines, of having played an " unhonest " part as a pilgrim, both being professions that lent themselves to extensive and profitable imposition. These may be reflections of Dunbar's exploits as a pretended friar, or may have no more reality than the retort that Kennedy made a practice of stealing fowls.

The years succeeding this episode down to 1500 have yielded scarce a grain of information to the most anxious investigators. That Dunbar had travelled at least as far as Picardy we learn from his own words. But there is no reason to accept, with the S.T.S. biographer, as " a fragment of biography," with suitable conclusions, the verse :

> " Nocht I say all be this cuntre,
> France, Ingland, Ireland, Almanie,
> Bot als be Italie and Spane ;
> Quhilk to consider is ane pane."

Clearly the poet is not suggesting that he had visited all these countries on the king's business, but that the abuses of which he complains were rampant there as well as in Scotland. Further

[1] We get " Julius apostata " with no personal reference in *Sir John Rowll's Cursing*.

while Kennedy accuses him of disgusting conduct on the ship *Katryne*—and we know, from the *Treasurer's Accounts*, that a vessel of that name carried ambassadors to France in July 1491—we need not infer that this was the occasion referred to, since it is further stated that Dunbar had to be landed at the Bass ; while the event is fixed twenty years before the composition of the verses, which were published in 1508. All that can be said of this part of the poet's career is that he must have for some time discharged services to the king or about the court—been his "servant," as he expresses it—since he so emphatically pleads these as a reason for consideration and reward. What these services may have been we do not actually know, but he possibly acted as a king's messenger abroad—a post almost indistinguishable from that of an ambassador—as Chaucer did in England, Boccaccio in Italy, and Des Champs in France. He certainly seems to have visited France on more than one occasion, and he was in England at the end of 1501, presumably in connection with the embassy that completed the treaty for the marriage of James IV with Margaret Tudor. This episode is dealt with in Appendix C. His work as a poet was thus reinforced by that as a royal official or civil servant. The remarkable thing is that, so far as his own works are concerned, the allusions to other countries than his own should be so very few.

It is in this connection that we reach the first certain milestone in Dunbar's life—a gift to him in August 1500 of a "pension" of £10 paid by the king for life, or until he should be provided with a benefice worth £40 a year.[1] " Pension " simply meant a fixed money payment or salary, and £10 was, roughly, a common one for a prebendary in a collegiate church. By November 1507 the pension had been increased to £20, and in August 1510 to £80, till he should be promoted to a benefice of £100 or more. Dunbar was thus, in the former case, nominally as well off as Chaucer on his final pension of £20, and latterly much better off than Hector Boece, whose stipend as Principal of King's College, Aberdeen, was 30 merks or £26 13s. 4d.[2]

[1] The entries of payments made to Dunbar, as they appear in the *Accounts of the Lord High Treasurer of Scotland* and other sources, are collected in the S.T.S. edition, i, pp. cliv-vi.

[2] David Laing (*Poems of William Dunbar,* i, p. 27) quite unnecessarily warns us that certain expressions of the poet " are not to be taken in too

In addition he was apparently entitled to a gift of clothing at Yule, as on 27th January, 1506, and again on 4th January, 1507, he is recorded to have received £5, a considerable sum, in place of "his goun." A neglect to supply this perquisite explains the composition of *The Petition of the Gray Horse, Auld Dunbar*. On 14th March, 1503, there is a further biographical item in Dunbar's first mass, on which occasion the king made an offering of seven French crowns or £4 14s.

Dunbar's pension figures in the *Accounts* down to 14th May, 1513, but from 8th August of that year to June 1515 there is a gap in the Register and, when the accounts start again, there is no entry of the pension. Either, then, the payment had lapsed, or the poet had at last received a benefice, or he was dead. It is hard to believe that, in the event of either of the first two alternatives having occurred, he would have remained silent, yet if he wrote the poem *Quhen the Governour Past in France*, an event of 1517, which is attributed to him in the solitary version of the *Maitland MS.*, he cannot have been left unprovided for. Hector Boece, whose complaint as to the distribution of benefices is in accord with that of Dunbar, did in his later years receive such a gift, and the poet may well have been similarly fortunate. But the poem of about 1520 beginning "We Lordis hes chosin a chiftane mervellous," though included in his works but denied by Professor Schipper, is anonymous, and its opening is not in the Dunbar manner, while the rest is much below it. In such dubiety ends, as it began, the biography of the poet: no date can be assigned for his death ; he simply drops out of record.

From such forms of address in *The Flyting* as "dirtfast dearch (dwarf)" and "myten," with the same meaning, it has been inferred that Dunbar was of short stature. But possibly this taunt is no more realistic than his own plain slandering of Kennedy's face as a "fowll front" comparable to the most abhorrent in history. It may be remarked, too, that in their *Flyting* Montgomerie applied the same terms to Polwart, calling

---

literal a sense ; for instance, '*I stand fastand in a nuik*' or, '*How glaid that ever I dyne or sowp*,' as if they implied a state of absolute want." But the first quotation (12. 7) refers only to being left without a benefice while others "swallow" such big ones, and the second (10. 45) is a purely general statement unlikely to mislead even a casual reader.

him " droich " and " mything." " Mytting," again, is applied
to the tailor in *The Flytting betuix the Sowtar and the Tailyour*
in the *Bannatyne MS*. (S.T.S. iii, p. 23). Such a contemptuous
description, indeed, seems to have been no more than a brickbat
from the current stock of abuse.

Some reason for the latter conclusion may perhaps be found in
the fact that the items in the *Treasurer's Accounts* relating to
Dunbar's " livery " or gifts of dress from the king, give these as
for a man of average height. Six ells and a quarter of Paris
black for a gown, when four to five was an ordinary quantity
and there might be a little more or less, do not suggest a small
man. Nor do the five quarters of scarlet, most probably for
hose, when, in some cases, less than that quantity had to serve.
That Dunbar, as has been suggested,[1] had anything to do with
the impersonation of what Bannatyne inaccurately entitled the
" droichis (dwarf's) part " in *The Manere of the Crying of a
Play*, is a fanciful conjecture. It is not even certain that he
wrote the piece ; if he did, it does not necessarily follow that he
spoke it ; while, if it had been his intention to do so, he is not
likely to have provided himself with an " Erse " or Gaelic
ancestry, his sentiments about that people being what they were.

IV. THE POEMS

An obvious but, for the time, a novel characteristic of Dun-
bar's verse is that his poems are never long. In distinction from
so much of the poetic manner both before and after he is neither
voluble nor shapeless. His longest effort, *The Tua Mariit
Wemen and the Wedo*, runs to but 530 lines, and most of his
poems are short and lyrical in fashion.

Further, he is novel in many of his themes, these including
not only personal grievances but also the occasion of a headache,
the condition of the streets of Edinburgh, the way in which a
certain Mure had treated one of his poems, the character of the
tailors' and shoemakers' crafts—any topic that lent itself to
emotional or satiric treatment in verse. And verse was still the
only medium proper to one aiming at literature.

These features, however, must not be taken to imply a
complete break with the literary past. His appeals on the

---

[1] Schipper, *William Dunbar*, etc., p. 208. Cf. here Appendix D.

matter of his benefice may fall within the established category of " Complaints." [1] Of another current type, however, the " Testament" (or Will),[1] there is but one example, and that in a burlesque vein. But several of the most pretentious efforts are cast in the form of " allegory," the poetic form which had supplanted the old long-drawn romance. Even in metre there may be a reversion. In *Kynd Kyttok*, if it really be by Dunbar, we have a comic use of the stanza of the later romance poems in rhyming alliterative verse,[2] while in *The Tua Mariit Wemen and the Wedo* the unrhymed alliterative lines repeat a very old convention, of which this is the last example, save one, in the language. More generally an apt alliteration is a feature of his rhythms throughout. But on all his compositions Dunbar imposes his own freedom of treatment, and he is indeed less fettered by mediaeval convention than his younger contemporary, Gavin Douglas.

Dunbar was, indeed, a technically accomplished, self-conscious artist. He quite often draws attention to his " writing," and the misfortune of his headache (No. 3) was that, when he set himself to write, " the sentence lay full evil to find." He was as anxious as Chaucer that no one should spoil his " meter," and his anger at an outrage of this kind, in the *Complaint Aganis Mure*, which was communicated to the royal court, indicates both one mode of circulation and the reputation of Dunbar, to whose supposed utterance so much importance could be attached.

This, too, is a point which should be considered in relation to his appeals for ecclesiastical preferment. One critic [3] has denied seriousness to such of his compositions, claiming that they have " all the unreality of these fifteenth-century exercises " on the part of other writers and that Dunbar " wrote with his tongue

---

[1] Chaucer has eight poems entitled " Compleynt " ; Henryson, " The Testament of Cresseid " ; Lindesay, a " Complaynt," a " Testament and Complaynt," etc. The " Complaint " (Lat. *planctus*) was originally a lament for a dead patron or lady friend, but was in time given a more general sense. See *Nouvelle Anthologie des Troubadours*, Audian and Lavand, Paris, 1928, p. 10.

[2] Used also by Gavin Douglas in the *Prologue* to Bk. viii of the *Aeneid*.

[3] *The Transition Period* (*Periods of European Literature*), G. Gregory Smith, p. 55.

in his cheek." This is hard to believe in face of the bitterness and passion which in so many places beat behind his words :

> " For owther man my hart to breik,
> Or with my pen I man me wreik."

Harder still, perhaps, in respect of his apologetic manner in addressing the king :

> " I say not, sir, yow to repreiff,
> But doutles I ga rycht neir hand it."

It does not appear how "merriment at His Majesty's Court" could be extracted from such strains. And Boece, when he wrote what has already been cited on this question (p. xvi), is serious enough.

It is more reasonable to hold that Dunbar's angry sarcasms could not have failed to sting, because they were so obviously true. It cannot have been amusing for engrossers of parish livings, bishops or abbots or others to hear :

> " Swa thay the kirk have in thair cuir,
> Thay fors (care) bot litill how it fuir,
>   Nor of the buikis, nor bellis quha rang thame ;
> Thai pans (think) nocht of the prochin (parish) pure,
>   Had thai the pelfe to pairt amang thame."

For the inferior clergy his contempt is unmistakable and, by all accounts, fully warranted. The clerical order must have been inhumanly callous to remain unruffled by Dunbar's lashings, and, in that case, their influence against him must have weighed heavily with a king, like James IV, so sensitive to their appeal. The friars cannot have loved Dunbar, yet with the king they were most powerful. And even the king personally cannot but have been pricked by the vicious satire on his Italian protégé, John Damian, or the scorn the poet poured upon the hangers-on at his court. Bitter contempt exudes even from the obscure terms and compounds which he finds necessary to characterise the upstarts, charlatans, and avaricious persons who benefited by patronage :

> "Soukaris, groukaris, gledaris, gunnaris ;
>
> "Gryt glaschew-hedit gorge-millaris.

Conscious, probably, of his outspoken manner and its effect he, in *The Dream*, puts these words in the mouth of " Ressoun," protesting that he has long been a servant to the king but

> " all his tyme nevir flatter couthe nor faine,
> Bot humblie into ballat wyse complaine."

At the same time it must be kept in mind that satire on the shortcomings of the clergy was always and everywhere a mediaeval practice, contributed to by many saintly censors as well as by mere laymen.

Yet it was the life of court and town that was most congenial to Dunbar. Action, colour, music, the dance, " sangis, ballatis, and playis," were the elements of environment proper to a temperament such as his, subject to fits of despondency as Burns was to melancholia. Particularly was he depressed by the winter season. For him, as for the mediaeval folk of his class, there were substantially but two seasons—winter with what he calls its " dark and drublie " days, its enforced restraint on outdoor activity, its confinement in crowded, draughty, and smoky apartments, its few indoor amusements :

> " My hairt for languor dois forloir
> For laik of symmer with his flouris." [1]

Yet delight in the season does not lead to any pronounced pleasure in the aspect of the open country or, least of all, to finding in its features any mystical suggestiveness. A rare reference to the Highlands is but a shudder at the " dully glennis."

Dunbar, indeed, like all the other poets of the time, was fascinated by the garden described in the great French poem translated by Chaucer (or another) as *The Romaunt of the Rose*. This model garden is the scene of *The Goldyn Targe* and of the allegories generally, as inevitably as the month of May is their time. Only occasionally, and not then with any appreciation, does a more local element appear, as when the May of *The Thrissil and the Rois* is first thought by the poet to be disfigured by " busteous blasts," so that the birds have more reason to

---

[1] Cf. in Chaucer's *Parlement of Foules*:

> " Now welcom, somer, with thy sonne softe,
> Thet hast this wintres weders overshake."

weep than to sing. But this was an intrusion of reality; in his dream the poet enters "a lusty gairding gent."

The landscape, in fact, must consort with the mood; [1] of itself it does not call for notice; and there is nothing in Dunbar to set beside such nature pictures of Gavin Douglas, as are wholly Scottish in detail. The devotion of poets to the garden was probably due to the feeling that it was the proper artistic setting, a Nature not spontaneous, wild, and formless but (in Pope's phrase) "Nature methodised" and made rational, Nature as it aimed to be or at its best. Such an outlook was in agreement with Aristotle's aesthetic theory and so with mediaeval idealism in general.

Another inheritance from the same French poem was the allegory, a form which has never died and once again blossomed on a great scale in Spenser's *Faery Queen*. It had a special appeal to the mediaeval mind with its interest in abstraction and symbol. For serious work it became as inevitable as the symphony in music. The poet dreams, and in his dream enters the property garden, to which repair the allegorical personages who are to carry out in action the poet's conception. To our minds the reality of the performance may be less concrete than to the mediaeval listener, who was already familiar with the personification of ideas in his stage plays or in pictorial art. Particularly is it so in such a case as *The Dance of the Sevin Deidly Synnis*, which also is set in the classical framework of the allegory, since the vision came to the poet "in a trance," in which, instead of the usual garden, he "saw baith hevin and hell." But the figures of "Pride," "Envy," "Gluttony," etc., were already defined for the mediaeval observer by artistic representation, and the transition was easy to those of "Reason," "Fair Having," "Dame Homeliness" and abstractions generally. The vital difference between the two fields of allegory was in the language. For the pleasant or didactic and dignified type there had to be chosen "dulce and redolent" terms of description—the "grand style." For the other class the poet could safely dredge all the resources of the native tongue. To the latter belongs *The Birth*

---

[1] Or, as Henryson puts it:

> "Ane doolie sessoun to ane cairfull dyte (*i.e.* sad poem)
> Suld correspond and be equivalent."

The Testament of Cresseid, ll. 1-2.

of Antichrist, where the traditional setting of the dream ("a swevying ") is used to express a violent satire on Dunbar's *bête noire*, the abbot of Tungland.

This Scots vocabulary, too, is the material of his more exuberant satires. In these no class quite escapes his censure, though there is perhaps some tenderness towards rank, but kirkmen, the law courts, " mediciners " or doctors, and certain crafts he does not spare. This sensitiveness to what he considered abuses and injustices need not be wholly attributed to a sourness of mind engendered by his fruitless longing for a benefice. For one thing, it was quite in the manner of his time. Further, he, latterly at least, in his handsome pension had most of what such preferment would give him, and with money in his purse he could not feel his disappointment continuously bitter—not, as he himself said,

> " quhill thair is gude wyne to sell."

It cannot have been because he was " poisoned with a grievance " [1] that he wrote the satire on Edinburgh, which is rather the expression of one whose aesthetic sense is offended. That the capital city, the seat of " the Court and the Session," should be noisy, smelly, and cluttered with beggars seemed to him shameful, but not less so that its houses should be darkened by forestairs and its minstrels should limit themselves to a couple of tunes. Moreover, if he chastened Edinburgh, it was because he loved " the mirry toun," as many allusions show. He emphasised its shortcomings not because of a realistic cynicism that is claimed to have distorted his perceptions,[2] but because he genuinely disliked them, just as he did the charlatanism of the *Fenyeit Freir*, the nature of the *Sevin Deidly Synnis*, and his Gaelic-speaking countrymen. Indeed, he mixes up the two latter groups, a confusion which some regard as an anti-climax but which is just Dunbar's fun, and shows how real to him were his allegorical personifications. The mediaeval poet, too, like the mediaeval artist generally, was better at sinners than at saints. With the same hilarious spirit he introduces himself into the *Dance in the Queenis Chalmer*, while a bold humour informs the *Dregy*, as it does also *The Testament of Mr. Andro Kennedy* and *Kynd Kyttok*.

---

[1] *Dunbar*, by Rachel Annand Taylor, p. 52.   [2] *Ibid*.

No great stress, however, need be laid on the fact that, in these latter poems, Dunbar seems to indulge a mocking, irreverent spirit ; in others a vein of physical grossness. To a social life like that of the Middle Ages, at once coarse and naïve, such pleasantries were not out of place. Since the mid-thirteenth century there had been a practice of parodying portions of the church services,[1] and a parody of Scripture in ridicule of the Scots and their leaders is one of the English memorials of the War of Independence.

A similar mingling of apparently discordant strains is to be observed in his treatment of love. Just as the mediaeval mind found room on the religious side for both abject devotion and indecorous gesture, so in the matter of love writers oscillated from an extreme idealisation of the female sex to an equally extreme defamation. Dunbar has examples of both fashions—not, indeed, to a greater extent than poets before and after him. Most of these poems are in a mode very similar to that of the allegory. In a certain season, on a certain day, and at a particular time the poet goes forth and overhears a lover or lovers, whose utterance or dialogue he records. That is the general type, and the numerous examples have been classed under the name of *Chansons d'Aventure*, France having been the origin of this mode as of so many others.[2] Thus we get Dunbar starting off with :

" In secreit place this hyndir nycht,
    I hard ane beyrne (man) say till ane bricht (maid),"

just as the writer of *The Murning Maidin*, an anonymous poem in the *Maitland MS.*, begins :

" Still undir the levis grene,
    This hindir day I went alone ;
I hard ane May sair murne and meyne,
    To the King of Luif scho maid hir mone."

[1] See *Die Parodie im Mittelalter*, Paul Lehmann, Munich, 1922, followed by *Parodistische Texte*, 1923. Prof. Lehmann, however, confines himself to examples in Latin, including the one from England to which reference is made and which may be found in *Proceedings of the Society of Antiquaries of Scotland*, xix (1884-5), pp. 167-184.

[2] On the whole subject see *The " Chanson d'Aventure " in Middle English*, by Helen Estabrook Sandison, Pennsylvania, 1913. The same conventional opening survives in Robert Fergusson's *Leith Races* and in Burns's *Holy Fair* and *Hallowe'en*.

Like the May morning, the beautiful garden, the river and the singing birds it is an established opening, of which *The Tua Mariit Wemen and the Wedo* gives a complete example. This poem, however, is of a particular species, that telling of unhappy marriage, usually on the part of a wife (*chanson à mal mariée*) but in some cases of a husband.[1] Despite the many French and English exercises in this class also, Dunbar's contribution is in several respects unique. The personages in number are unusual, and in their parts unlike those of any other example.[2] The work is too long for a *chanson*; it is a poem, while its elaborately alliterative unrhymed metre removes it still further from the general category. In its character as a satire it comes nearer to Chaucer's *Prologue* to *The Wife of Bath's Tale*.

The matter of the poem, too, goes beyond anything hitherto attempted on this line. "From the mysteries of religion," wrote Landor, "the veil is seldom to be drawn, from the mysteries of love never." Landor, however, was much too late with his admonition for Dunbar, and even since his time it has scarcely been honoured with strict observance. The author of the *Introduction* to the S.T.S. edition of the poems holds this one to be a picture, perhaps a caricature, of the "moral disease" of the time, which was to undergo the cure of the Reformation. Mrs. Taylor, on the contrary, describes it as "this very modern debate" and says that "the first lady's doctrine would suit a Bloomsbury novel to-day."[3] Professor Saintsbury contrasts the beautiful opening and close of the poem with its "ugly" content. As to expressions used here and in some other poems it is well to remember Macaulay's comment on Restoration Dramatists: "Whether a thing shall be designated by a plain noun substantive or by a circumlocution, is a mere matter of fashion." The brief

---

[1] For a specimen of each see the *Maitland Folio MS.* in the S.T.S. edition, p. 243: "Way wourthe maryage for evirmair"; and p. 244: "God gif I wer wedo now," the latter being that of a husband: the term "widow" was then applicable to either sex. The sentiments of the lady resemble those of Dunbar's "Wedo":

> "Luffairis bayth suld heir and se
> I suld luif thame that wald luif me."

[2] Cf. Miss Sandison, as cited, p. 13.

[3] *William Dunbar*, p. 50. The curious may consider a passage in *Don Juan in America*, by Eric Linklater (1931), p. 84.

moralising at the close is artistically an anti-climax, but something of the sort would be expected. On the poem as a whole Dunbar has obviously expended much pains.

Of all his compositions, however, the most bizarre to modern taste is *The Flyting* or " The Scolding," in which, of course, he is but one of the two protagonists. Yet this sort of verbal tournament *à outrance* as a form of literature has wide relationships. The *agōn* or " altercation " was one essential element of the Old Comedy of Greece, while in a more personal vein it has parallels in other literatures, Arabic, Italian, Provençal, Celtic. The Provençal *tenson,* or debate in alternate verses between troubadours, was of this class, but rarely exceeded half a dozen stanzas and, though often lively enough, was not of a scurrilous character. The contention of *The Merle and the Nychtingaill* is more of this type. It therefore cannot have served as a model, while the stimulus need not be searched out. Such a bout reflects a common human resort under passion to improvised personal abuse, a stray example of which may still crop up even in more polite times, as in the case of Tennyson's retort to " the padded man who wears the stays." But in the present or similar literary examples no impulse of real animosity need be assumed. King James V and Sir David Lindesay engaged in a *Flyting*, while King James VI included this exercise in his not unworthy treatise on poetical forms. Such a contest, indeed, seems to have caused amusement in the best circles.[1] Its psychology may be illustrated from a passage in a contemporary (1931) novel : " They were good friends, these two, so they called each other insulting names and explained how little they thought of each other." As regards the present " jocund and merrie " interchange of vigorous but often coarse abuse we are invited in one MS. to " juge quha gat the war (worse)."

Dunbar's moralising and religious poems are individually characteristic only in the metrical quality of certain examples. In the fifteenth century the Middle Ages were in their twilight ; there was a poverty of ideas, and a sententious preaching manner was popular. Reflections on the instability of life, on the certainty of death, and on man's subsequent destiny chimed in a particular harmony with the spirit of the time. For much of this

---

[1] See Montgomerie's *Poems,* Sonnet xxvii.

frame of mind the emotional teaching of the friars was answerable. Other results of the same influence were the new attitude towards such themes as the crucifixion of Christ and praise of the Virgin. In the former, Christ has become primarily the Suffering One, and there is an almost morbid tendency to dwell in detail on every incident of the Passion. Dunbar's poem on the subject opens in the conventional dream-form, and it is significant that the place is within a cloister of the friars, after which no harrowing feature of the tragedy is overlooked. In the practical precision of the details we further trace the ocular effects of the mystery plays. A similar particularity marks the triumphant outburst, *Done is a battell on the dragon blak*, with its march of vivid, sonorous lines. The conception of the Virgin, again, has reverted to the Byzantine figure of the Empress of Heaven—Villon's *haute déesse*, Dunbar's " Empryce of prys, imperatrice "—but now with an added significance as the protectress and " oratrice " of mankind.

All this, of course, was common at the time to Western Christendom, of which Scotland was just a part, and was expressed in the contemporary graphic arts as well as in literature. And Dunbar, though showing no profound spiritual quality, was devout in his observances. That he satirised the clergy is no discordance, for the reason already given (p. xxvii). Kennedy's gibe at him as " Lamp Lollardorum " is but topical abuse with no religious significance. Editors, however, have tended to agree in assigning the religious poems to the closing years of the poet's life. But, apart from a somewhat naïve psychology, there is no reason for such a conclusion. A temperament like that of Dunbar was open to religious impressionism and devotional outpouring at any period of life, though the more laboured efforts may well be taken to suggest a stage of failing power.

Over all, then, Dunbar is one of the poets who illuminate the life of their time but do not idealistically transform it. Robert Browning in an essay distinguishes the class of poet as "fashioner," or as the Scots, after the Greeks, would say, " makar," from that of the poet as " seer "—the objective from the subjective type. Dunbar is of the former class; he does not proffer " intuitions " as reflections of an " absolute mind," as Browning held himself to do. Poetry was for him a social art, not the functioning of a seer or diviner, the latter being an assumption which by now as surely dates itself as does Dunbar's "mellifluate" diction. This restriction may or may not be a disparagement, but other poets, from Aristophanes and Juvenal downwards, flourish in spite of it. Further, he is without the sentimentalism incident to Burns, though, like him, he tended to become, at times, "literary" in the prevailing fashion. Most poets carry dead weight of this character. But he and the rest of his school saved their share of the island literature from the blight [1] which fell upon the successors of Chaucer in the southern kingdom. And so they worthily repaid the debt they owed to that great master.

V. THE TEXTS

The individual text sources, as published by the "Scottish Text Society," are : (1) what remains of the Chepman and Myllar Print of several of the poems in 1508 (ed. Stevenson) ; (2) the *Asloan MS.* of a few years later (ed. Craigie) ; (3) the *Bannatyne MS.* of 1568 (ed. Tod Ritchie) ; (4) the *Maitland Folio MS.* of 1570-86 (ed. Craigie). In addition to these there is the *Reidpeth MS.* of 1623, which, however, has been copied from the *Maitland MS.* and is therefore of importance only as an aid to that collection, save in so far as it preserves eight poems now lost from its original and not found elsewhere. These have been printed in the second volume of the *Maitland Folio MS.* A few other sources for single poems are mentioned in the notes to these. In the case of one poem (No. 87), some additional verses are here included in a collected edition for the first time.

Since all these texts, with the exception of the printed tract, are but scribal copies, and we possess nothing in the poet's own handwriting, it may be considered that the versions of such poems as were printed in his lifetime, presumably from copy supplied by himself—even though he may not have corrected a proof—are the primary authority. This conclusion, however, is challenged by Professor Schipper, who gives his preference to the MS. versions of the poems in question. But the grounds for this judgment are not well founded, as is shown in Appendix A, and the Print is here accepted, with reasonable limitations, as prior in authority to the MSS. Next, in respect of date, being

---

[1] The word is that used in this connection by the late Professor W. P. Ker in *Form and Style in Poetry*, p. 82.

also contemporary with the poet, come the copies preserved in the *Asloan MS*. As between the *Bannatyne* and *Maitland MSS.*, a less definite pronouncement can be made. A few poems are found only in one or the other of these collections, and regarding them no question of choice arises. It is another matter in the case of poems which appear in two or more of the MSS. Differences of spelling may be disregarded, as the scribes probably were here influenced by individual preferences or by the practice of their own time ; the latter effect seems to be more apparent in the *Maitland MS*. Many variations of readings, too, are of little moment, but there is a residue that cannot be so dismissed.

It must be kept in mind that much the greater number of the poems circulated only in MS., that copies were made not only by scribes but probably by the poet himself, and that, as happened in the case of Burns, he might make verbal changes, while scribes could add their own contributions either by carelessness or, for reasons of their own, by altering what they found written. George Bannatyne confesses that, in compiling his invaluable collection of poems, he had to use copies which were " awld mankit (defective) and mutillait."

The present collection includes all poems which in one source or another have Dunbar's name attached to them. Three of these, however (Nos. 8, 28, 77), in one of the MSS. are attributed to other authors, and to these reference is made in the notes. Certain poems, which in no case bear Dunbar's name but have been assigned to him by editors, form a separate group of such attributions, where much the least probable is *The Freiris of Berwick*. Beyond these, however, other ten poems figure in collected editions as possibly the work of Dunbar— even when, as happens with Schipper, the editor refuses the claim. They are short and not particularly distinguished, while a connection with Dunbar is founded mainly on a similarity of theme or metre, which is in no case sufficient, and against which can be set serious novelties of vocabulary as well as other considerations. They have, accordingly, been omitted from the present collection.

The principles here followed have, as far as possible, been made objective. Thus the Print, for what it contains, and then the MS. earliest in date have been preferred. It is true that a later MS. may preserve a better copy, but, in the present case, this is hard to say.   In certain poems judgment has been in favour of the version which is complete, either as a whole or in respect of lines or words, uniformity in spelling being thus preserved.   Other things being equal there is a preference for MS. B. as against MS. M. ;   the two are practically contemporary, but the latter appears generally to have been more consciously worked upon.   The text chosen has, then, been strictly followed, except for cogent reasons, and only the most important differences find place in the notes.   The dangers attending a " conflate " text, such as Schipper constructs for certain passages, are illustrated with some examples on pp. 226 (77), 232.   For the minutiae of textual variations reference must be made to the large editions.

The following poems from two particular sections of the *Maitland MS.* are marked by peculiarities of spelling that in some cases are " almost illiterate " (Craigie): Nos. 5, 19, 22, 29, 31-5, 37, 66, 67.   On these see *The Maitland Folio Manuscript*, S.T.S., vol. ii, pp. 3, 6.

In reprinting the texts the following modifications have been made :

(1) The " thorn " letter (þ), often represented by *y* as in " ye " for " the," is expanded to its proper equivalent, *th*, as is done in the S.T.S. edition and in the less punctilious texts.

(2) The " yok " letter (ȝ), which later, from its resemblance to the letter written ȝ, passed into currency as *z*, is here transliterated as *y*, being but the representative of that sound as a consonant.   Thus it was sometimes written *yh*, and in this form it does appear in the C. and M. prints.   It is unnecessary, however, to insist on this, save perhaps in the case of " foryhet " = " forget," a form which actually does occur in *Ratis Raving*.

(3) The upright *s* with an ornamental curl (ß) is usually printed as *ss*.   This seems to be unjustifiable, and it is here represented by a single *s*.   If this results in such spellings as " pas," " las," " glaidnes," it must be added that it also spares us such as " thuss," " thiss," " wass," while " pas," " sadnes," and " glaydnes " do occur in these spellings both in MS. and in later printed texts, e.g. *Philotus* (1603), and we have a similar form in " princes " for " princess," while " wilfulnes " with the

final ornamental *s* in one MS. of a poem is in another spelled in the same way with an ordinary *s*. Where this form of the letter occurs initially, it can scarcely stand for *ss* and give "sservis" (5. 12). In two or three instances, however, the ornamental *s* seems to stand for *is*, e.g. 1. 16, 17.

(4) The letters *u*, *v*, *w* are given modern values, except in those cases which involve no ambiguity as to sound-value. Thus "haue" is changed to "have," but "suallow" remains; "wndir" or "vndir" becomes "under," but "trewth" stands; and so throughout. The modern values of *i* and *j* have also been discriminated.

Punctuation and the use of capitals have been adjusted to current usage.

VI. LANGUAGE

Some of the more important linguistic features of what is generally styled Middle Scots, as corresponding to Middle English, may be noted here : [1]

(1) For the long vowel with *i* or *y* see Appendix A. On a sound-value of *o(u)* see note on No. 44, line 29.

(2) After *ā* or *ō* the letter *l*, even though correct in etymology, may be elided in pronunciation, and the word so spelled e.g. "*Als* fresch *as* flouris," 56. 59. Or, whether displaced or not, it makes the preceding vowel a diphthong : both "wowf" and "wolf" occur in 27. 53, 57. In 77. 1, 2 "dreme" (pron. "drame") rhymes internally with "realme."

(3) Apparently by analogy, *l* is intruded, though not sounded, in words to which etymologically it does not belong, in order to indicate a long vowel or diphthong, a device characteristic of Middle Scots. Thus "awalk"=awake, "golk"=gowk, "chalmer"=Fr. *chambre* (where the *b* has been elided).

(4) Liquid *l* and *n* in words of French origin are represented by *ly*, *ny*—e.g. "tailyeour," "tailyour" (Fr. *tailleur*), "fenyeit" (cf. Fr. *feignant*), "Spanyie" (Fr. *Espagne*). These forms, too, are peculiar to Middle Scots.

(5) *f* or *ff* final=*v(e)*. *Ff* initial is printed as a single letter.

---

[1] For more detailed information see Murray's *Dialects of the Southern Counties of Scotland* ; Gregory Smith's *Selections from Middle Scots*.

(6) *h* initial is unsounded and dropped in "armony" (55. 7, etc.), "abbeit" ("habit," 4. 3, 6, etc.); prefixed but perhaps unsounded in "habound" (83. 154). *Quh=wh, qu* being a French symbol for the old *w*.

(7) Initial *s* becomes *sch=sh* in "schir," "schervice," "schervand." Conversely the southern *sh* in "shall," "should" is represented by "sall," "sould" or "suld," and "schedule" by "cedull" (6. 48).

(8) *v* medial between vowels disappears in pronunciation, as in "evir," "nevir" (2. 18, 19; 6. 200, etc.), "Devill" (58. 56, etc. Modern Scots "deil"), which are to be taken as monosyllables. So too with "evill"="ill," as in 17. 58.

Nouns. The plural is in *is*. "Gardingis" (56. 118)= "gardens"; "fludis," "wyndis" (56. 121, 122)="floods," "winds." The plural form is the same as that of the singular in cases like "sistir" (56. 83), "lef" (56. 27), "benefice" (12. 1), etc.

Adjectives. On the use of *ane* and *a* see Appendix A.

Pronouns. Thir is the usual plural for "these."

Verbs. (1) In the present tense indicative the conjugation, when each inflection is accompanied by its pronoun, is as in the modern language, save for the second person singular, which ends in *is*—*e.g.* "Thow callis the" (6. 97). When, however, the verb is separated from its personal pronoun, or its subject is some other pronoun—relative, interrogative, etc.—or other part of speech, all inflections end in *s* or *is*—*e.g.* "sum callis" (8. 8), "tungis that temis" (8. 39).

(2) The present participle ends properly in *and*—*e.g.* "spynnand" (36. 46); the gerund or verbal noun in *ing* or *yng*— *e.g.* "praying" (83. 37). But the latter form tends to encroach upon that of the participle, so that we may have gerund and participle spelled in the same way—*e.g.* "schyning" as participle in 47. 22 and as gerund in 53. 20.

(3) The past tense of weak verbs is in *it* or *yt*, representing the older *id* or *yd*. Strong verbs have their past in *in* or *yn*—*e.g.* "cumin," "cummyn," "haldin" (67. 35).

(4) The word *do* is used as an auxiliary with all parts of the verb—*e.g.* "The lork hes done the mirry day proclame" (55. 24).

Preposition. *Till* = " to " both as a simple preposition and in forming the infinitive.

Occasional forms such as " not " for " nocht," " sir " for " schir," and " ryght " for " rycht " are due to scribes or printers, or, with " to," " has," etc., may be reminiscences of his reading in the southern poets by the author himself.

Metathesis or transposition of *r*, characteristic of the northern dialects and common in Scots, appears in " brist " for " birst," " gers " for " gres," " Thirsill " (18. 22) for " Thrissil," etc.

ADDENDA AND CORRIGENDA

Pages xviii–xxiv. The most detailed biography is J. W. Baxter's *William Dunbar* (Edinburgh, 1952). M. P. McDiarmid (*Scottish Historical Review* xxxiii, 46–52) argues that the *Flyting* dates from about 1490.

Pages xxiv–xxxiv. Critical estimates can be found in general works, as by W. L. Renwick in *The Beginnings of English Literature to 1509*) (London, 1939 and 1952), C. S. Lewis, *English Literature in the Sixteenth Century* (Oxford, 1954), pp. 90–100, and James Kinsley in *Scottish Poetry: a Critical Survey* (London, 1955), pp. 14–16 and 24–32. More detailed studies are Janet M. Smith, *The French Background of Middle Scots Literature* (Edinburgh, 1934), pp. 47–77 and 164–6, Edwin Morgan's "Dunbar and the Language of Poetry" (*Essays in Criticism* II, 138–158), and Isabel Hyde's "Primary Sources and Associations of Dunbar's Aureate Imagery" (*Modern Language Review* LI, 481–492), with references cited in the last. Tom Scott, *Dunbar: A Critical Exposition of the Poems* (Edinburgh, 1966).

Pages xxxiv–xxxv. The Chepman and Myllar prints were published in facsimile by the Edinburgh Bibliographical Society in 1950, with an introduction by William Beattie.

NOTES

Page 201, on No. 6, v. 532. Aspasius, whose name alliterates with *eme*, ordered the martyrdom of the virgin St. Agnes (*Times Literary Supplement*, 20th Jan., 1945).

On No. 6, v. 538. Marcion of Sinope, who started the second-century Marcionite heresy, is a more promising candidate than the Roman emperor Marcian (*Times Literary Supplement*, 20th Jan., 1945).

On No. 6, v. 539. *Add:* The fragments of the fifteenth-century Scots Troy-Book amply explain the inclusion of *Antenor* and *Eneas* in Kennedy's list of unworthies (*Times Literary Supplement*, 20th Jan., 1945).

On No. 6, v. 541. *Add: Puttidew*, the Wandering Jew, who "pushed God roughly" on His Way to Calvary (*Times Literary Supplement*, 14th Dec., 1935).

Page 204, on No. 13, v. 62. *Calyecot.* Calicut on the Malabar coast, where Vasco da Gama, the first European to reach India by the Cape route, landed in 1498. He got back to Portugal in 1499—which gives the *terminus a quo* of the poem (*Modern Language Review* XXVIII, 506–7).

Page 213, on No. 39, vv. 31–32. Simon Magus tried to prove his magical powers to Nero by flying to heaven, but St. Peter prayed and he was dashed to the ground (*Medium Ævum*, XXVI, 196).

Page 216. On No. 47 see especially *Medium Ævum*, XXIII, 31 – 35.

Page 223, on No. 73 : *Add* There is a contemporary copy of this poem in Vol. 3 (unpaged) of the Register of Sasines in the Town Clerk's Office, Aberdeen (*Times Literary Supplement*, 8th April, 1939).

Page 229, on No. 86, v. 122. *Add* This identification was made in *Modern Language Notes*, LXIX, 479–480.

Page 231, on No. 90. *Add* : The ascription of this poem to Dunbar is strengthened in *The Times Literary Supplement*, 8th April, 1939.

Pages 242–4. On the subject of Appendix D see further W. H. Schofield, *Mythical Bards and the Life of William Wallace* (Cambridge, Mass., 1920).

1. TO THE KING

Sanct Salvatour ! send silver sorrow ;
It grevis me both evin and morrow,
Chasing fra me all cheritie ;
It makis me all blythness to borrow ;
My panefull purs so priclis me.   5

Quhen I wald blythlie ballattis breif,
Langour thairto givis me no leif ;
War nocht gud howp my hart uphie,
My verry corpis for cair wald cleif ;
My panefull purs so prikillis me.   10

Quhen I sett me to sing or dance,
Or go to plesand pastance,
Than pansing of penuritie
Revis that fra my remembrance ;
My panefull purs so prikillis me.   15

Quhen men that hes pursis in tone,
Pasis to drynk or to disjone,
Than mon I keip ane gravetic,
And say that I will fast quhill none ;
My panefull purs so priclis me.   20

My purs is maid of sic ane skyn,
Thair will na cors byd it within ;
Fra it as fra the Feynd thay fle.
Quha evir tyne, quha evir win ;
My panefull purs so prikillis me.   25

Had I ane man of ony natioun
Culd mak on it ane conjuratioun,

1

To gar silver ay in it be,
The Devill suld haif no dominatioun,
With pyne to gar it prickill me.   30

I haif inquyrit in mony a place,
For help and confort in this cace,
And all men sayis, My Lord, that ye
Can best remeid for this malice,
That with sic panis prickillis me.   35

2. ANE HIS AWIN ENNEMY

HE THAT hes gold and grit riches,
And may be into mirrynes,
And dois glaidnes fra him expell,
And levis in to wrechitnes,
He wirkis sorrow to him sell.   5

He that may be but sturt or stryfe,
And leif ane lusty plesand lyfe,
And syne with mariege dois him mell,
And bindis him with ane wicket wyfe,
He wirkis sorrow to him sell.   10

He that hes for his awin genyie
Ane plesand prop, but mank or menyie,
And schuttis syne at ane uncow schell,
And is forfairn with the fleis of Spenyie,
He wirkis sorrow to him sell.   15

And he that with gud lyfe and trewth,
But varians or uder slewth,
Dois evir mair with ane maister dwell,
That nevir of him will haif no rewth,
He wirkis sorrow to him sell.   20

Now all this tyme lat us be mirry,
And sett nocht by this warld a chirry;
Now, quhill thair is gude wyne to sell,
He that dois on dry breid wirry,
I gif him to the Devill of hell.   25

3. ON HIS HEID-AKE

My HEID did yak yester nicht,
This day to mak that I na micht,
   So sair the magryme dois me menyie,
   Perseing my brow as ony ganyie,
That scant I luik may on the licht.   5

And now, schir, laitlie, eftir mes,
To dyt thocht I begowthe to dres,
   The sentence lay full evill till find,
   Unsleipit in my heid behind,
Dullit in dulnes and distres.   10

Full oft at morrow I upryse,
Quhen that my curage sleipeing lyis,
   For mirth, for menstrallie and play,
   For din nor danceing nor deray,
It will nocht walkin me no wise.   15

4. HOW DUMBAR WES DESYRD TO BE ANE FREIR

This NYCHT, befoir the dawing cleir,
Me thocht Sanct Francis did to me appeir,
With ane religious abbeit in his hand,
And said, " In this go cleith the my servand ;
Reffus the warld, for thow mon be a freir."   5

With him and with his abbeit bayth I skarrit,
Lyk to ane man that with a gaist wes marrit :
Me thocht on bed he layid it me abone,
Bot on the flure delyverly and sone
I lap thairfra, and nevir wald cum nar it.   10

Quoth he, " Quhy skarris thow with this holy weid ?
Cleith the thairin, for weir it thow most neid ;
Thow, that hes lang done Venus lawis teiche,
Sall now be freir and in this abbeit preiche ;
Delay it nocht, it mon be done but dreid."   15

My brethir oft hes maid the supplicationis,
Be epistillis, sermonis, and relationis,
To tak the abyte, bot thow did postpone ;
But ony proces cum on thairfoir annone,
All sircumstance put by and excusationis.   20

Quod I, " Sanct Francis, loving be the till,
And thankit mot thow be of thy gude will
To me, that of thy clayis ar so kynd,
Bot thame to weir it nevir come in my mynd ;
Sweit Confessour, thow tak it nocht in ill.   25

In haly legendis haif I hard, allevin,
Ma sanctis of bischoppis nor freiris, be sic sevin ;
Off full few freiris that hes bene sanctis I reid ;
Quhairfoir ga bring to me ane bischopis weid,
Gife evir thow wald my sawle gaid unto Hevin.   30

Gif evir my fortoun wes to be a freir,
The dait thairof is past full mony a yeir ;
For into every lusty toun and place
Off all Yngland, frome Berwick to Kalice,
I haif in to thy habeit maid gud cheir.   35

In freiris weid full fairly haif I fleichit,
In it haif I in pulpet gon and preichit
In Derntoun kirk, and eik in Canterberry ;
In it I past at Dover our the ferry
Throw Piccardy, and thair the peple teichit.   40

Als lang as I did beir the freiris style,
In me, God wait, wes mony wrink and wyle ;
In me wes falset with every wicht to flatter,
Quhilk mycht be flemit with na haly watter ;
I wes ay reddy all men to begyle.   45

This freir that did Sanct Francis thair appeir,
Ane fieind he wes in liknes of ane freir ;
He vaneist away with stynk and fyrie smowk ;
With him me thocht all the hous end he towk,
And I awoik as wy that wes in weir.   50

5. COMPLAINT TO THE KING AGANIS MURE

SCHIR, I complane off injuris ;
A refing sonne off rakyng MURIS
Hes magellit my making, throw his malis,
And present it in to yowr palis :
 Bot, sen he plesis with me to pleid,   5
I sall him knawin mak hyne to Calis,
 Bot giff yowr Henes it remeid.

That fulle dismemberit hes my meter,
And poysonid it with strang salpeter,
With rycht defamows speiche off lordis,   10
Quhilk with my collouris all discordis :
 Quhois crewall sclander servis ded ;
And in my name all leis recordis,
 Your Grace beseik I of remeid.

He has indorsit myn indyting   15
With versis off his awin hand wryting ;
Quhairin baithe sclander is and tressoun :
Off ane wod fuill far owt off ressoun
 He wantis nocht bot a rowndit heid,
For he has tynt baith wit and ressoun :   20
 Your Grace beseik I off remeid.

Punes him for his deid culpabile,
Or gar deliver him ane babile,
That Cuddy Rig, the Drumfres fuill,
May him resave agane this Yuill,   25
 All roundit in to yallow and reid ;
That ladis may bait him lyk a buill,
 For that to me war sum remeid.

6. THE FLYTING OF DUNBAR AND KENNEDIE

Quod Dunbar to Kennedy

SCHIR JOHINE the Ros, ane thing thair is compild
 In generale be Kennedy and Quinting,
Quhilk hes thame self aboif the sternis styld ;

Bot had thay maid of mannace ony mynting
  In speciall, sic stryfe sould rys but stynting ;   5
Howbeit with bost thair breistis wer als bendit
As Lucifer, that fra the hevin descendit,
  Hell sould nocht hyd thair harnis fra harmis hynting.

The erd sould trymbill, the firmament sould schaik,
  And all the air in vennaum suddane stink,   10
And all the divillis of hell for redour quaik,
  To heir quhat I sould wryt with pen and ynk ;
  For and I flyt, sum sege for schame sould sink,
The se sould birn, the mone sould thoill ecclippis,
Rochis sould ryfe, the warld sould hald no grippis,   15
  Sa loud of cair the commoun bell sould clynk.

Bot wondir laith wer I to be ane baird,
  Flyting to use richt gritly I eschame ;
For it is nowthir wynning nor rewaird,
  Bot tinsale baith of honour and of fame,   20
  Incres of sorrow, sklander, and evill name ;
Yit mycht thay be sa bald, in thair bakbytting,
To gar me ryme and rais the feynd with flytting,
  And throw all cuntreis and kinrikis thame proclame.

Quod Kennedy to Dumbar

Dirtin Dumbar, quhome on blawis thow thy boist ?   25
  Pretendand the to wryte sic skaldit skrowis ;
Ramowd rebald, thow fall doun att the roist,
  My laureat lettres at the and I lowis ;
  Mandrag, mymmerkin, maid maister bot in mows,
Thrys scheild trumpir with ane threid bair goun,   30
Say Deo mercy, or I cry the doun,
  And leif thy ryming, rebald, and thy rowis.

Dreid, dirtfast dearch, that thow hes dissobeyit
  My cousing Quintene and my commissar,
Fantastik fule, trest weill thow salbe fleyit,   35
  Ignorant elf, aip, owll irregular,
  Skaldit skaitbird, and commoun skamelar ;
Wan-fukkit funling, that natour maid ane yrle,
Baith Iohine the Ros and thow sall squeill and skirle,
  And evir I heir ocht of your making mair.   40

Heir I put sylence to the in all pairtis,
　Obey and ceis the play that thow pretendis ;
Waik walidrag, and verlot of the cairtis,
　Se sone thow mak my commissar amendis,
　And lat him lay sax leichis on thy lendis,　　　　45
Meikly in recompansing of thi scorne,
Or thow sall ban the tyme that thow wes borne,
　For Kennedy to the this cedull sendis.

Quod Dumbar to Kennedy

Iersch brybour bard, vyle beggar with thy brattis,
　Cuntbittin crawdoun Kennedy, coward of kynd,　　50
Evill farit and dryit, as Denseman on the rattis,
　Lyke as the gleddis had on thy gule snowt dynd ;
　Mismaid monstour, ilk mone owt of thy mynd,
Renunce, rebald, thy rymyng, thow bot royis,
　Thy trechour tung hes tane ane heland strynd ;　　55
Ane lawland ers wald mak a bettir noyis.

Revin, raggit ruke, and full of rebaldrie,
　Scarth fra scorpione, scaldit in scurrilitie,
I se the haltane in thy harlotrie,
And in to uthir science no thing slie,　　　　60
　Off every vertew voyd, as men may sie ;
Quytclame clergie, and cleik to the ane club,
　Ane baird blasphemar in brybrie ay to be ;
For wit and wisdome ane wisp fra the may rub.

Thow speiris, dastard, gif I dar with the fecht ?　　65
　Ye dagone, dowbart, thairof haif thow no dowt !
Quhair evir we meit, thairto my hand I hecht
　To red thy rebald ryming with a rowt :
　Throw all Bretane it salbe blawin owt
How that thow, poysonit pelor, gat thy paikis ;　　70
　With ane doig leich I schepe to gar the schowt,
And nowther to the tak knyfe, swerd, nor aix.

Thow crop and rute of traitouris tressonable,
　The fathir and moder of morthour and mischeif,
Dissaitfull tyrand, with serpentis tung, unstable ;　　75
　Cukcald cradoun, cowart, and commoun theif ;
　Thow purpest for to undo our Lordis cheif,

In Paislay, with ane poysone that wes fell,
 For quhilk, brybour, yit sall thow thoill a breif;
Pelour, on the I sall it preif my sell.   80

Thocht I wald lie, thy frawart phisnomy
 Dois manifest thy malice to all men ;
Fy ! tratour theif; Fy ! glengoir loun, fy ! fy !
 Fy ! feyndly front, far fowlar than ane fen.
 My freyindis thow reprovit with thy pen !   85
Thow leis, tratour ! quhilk I sall on the preif,
 Suppois thy heid war armit tymis ten,
Thow sall recryat, or thy croun sall cleif.

Or thow durst move thy mynd malitius,
 Thow saw the saill abone my heid up draw ; 90
Bot Eolus full woid, and Neptunus,
 Mirk and moneless, wes met with wind and waw,
 And mony hundreth myle hyne cowd us blaw
By Holland, Seland, Yetland, and Northway coist,
 In desert quhair we wer famist aw ;   95
Yit come I hame, fals baird, to lay thy boist.

Thow callis the rethory with thy goldin lippis :
 Na, glowrand, gaipand fule, thow art begyld,
Thow art bot gluntow with thy giltin hippis,
 That for thy lounry mony a leisch hes fyld ; 100
 Wan wisaged widdefow, out of thy wit gane wyld,
Laithly and lowsy, als lathand as ane leik,
 Sen thow with wirschep wald sa fane be styld,
Haill, soverane senyeour ! Thy bawis hingis throw thy breik.

Forworthin fule, of all the warld reffuse,   105
 Quhat ferly is thocht thow rejoys to flyte ?
Sic eloquence as thay in Erschry use,
 In sic is sett thy thraward appetyte ;
 Thow hes full littill feill of fair indyte :
I tak on me ane pair of Lowthiane hippis   110
 Sall fairar Inglis mak, and mair parfyte,
Than thow can blabbar with thy Carrik lippis.

Bettir thow ganis to leid ane doig to skomer,
 Pynit pykpuirs pelour, than with thy maister pingill.
Thow lay full prydles in the peis this somer, 115

And fane at evin for to bring hame a single,
 Syne rubbit at ane uthir auld wyvis ingle ;
Bot now, in winter, for purteth thow art traikit ;
 Thow hes na breik to latt thy ballokis gyngill ;
Beg the ane club, for, baird, thow sall go naikit. 120

Lene larbar, loungeour, baith lowsy in lisk and lonye ;
 Fy ! skolderit skyn, thow art bot skyre and skrumple ;
For he that rostit Lawarance had thy grunye,
 And he that hid Sanct Johnis ene with ane womple,
 And he that dang Sanct Augustine with ane rumple, 125
Thy fowll front had, and he that Bartilmo flaid ;
 The gallowis gaipis eftir thy graceles gruntill,
As thow wald for ane haggeis, hungry gled.

Commirwald crawdoun, na man comptis the ane kers,
 Sueir swappit swanky, swynekeper ay for swaittis ; 130
Thy commissar Quintyne biddis the cum kis his ers,
 He luvis nocht sic ane forlane loun of laittis ;
 He sayis, thow skaffis and beggis mair beir and aitis
Nor ony cripill in Karrik land abowt ;
 Uther pure beggaris and thow ar at debaittis, 135
Decrepit karlingis on Kennedy cryis owt.

Mater annuche I haif, I bid nocht fenyie,
 Thocht thow, fowll trumpour, thus upoun me leid ;
Corruptit carioun, he sall I cry thy senyie ;
 Thinkis thow nocht how thow come in grit neid, 140
 Greitand in Galloway, lyk to ane gallow breid,
Ramand and rolpand, beggand koy and ox ;
 I saw the thair, in to thy wachemanis weid,
Quhilk wes nocht worth ane pair of auld gray sox.

Ersch Katherene, with thy polk breik and rilling, 145
 Thow and thy quene, as gredy gleddis, ye gang
With polkis to mylne, and beggis baith meill and schilling ;
 Thair is bot lys and lang nailis yow amang :
 Fowll heggirbald, for hennis thus will ye hang ;
Thow hes ane perrellus face to play with lambis ; 150
 Ane thowsand kiddis, wer thay in faldis full strang,
Thy lymmerfull luke wald fle thame and thair damis.

In till ane glen thow hes, owt of repair,
 Ane laithly luge that wes the lippir menis ;

C

With the ane sowtaris wyfe, off blis als bair,   155
   And lyk twa stalkaris steilis in cokis and hennis,
Thow plukkis the pultre, and scho pullis off the penis ;
All Karrik cryis, God gif this dowsy be drownd ;
   And quhen thow heiris ane guse cry in the glenis,
Thow thinkis it swetar than sacrand bell of sound.   160

Thow Lazarus, thow laithly lene tramort,
   To all the warld thow may example be,
To luk upoun thy gryslie peteous port,
   For hiddowis, haw, and holkit is thyne ee ;
   Thy cheik bane bair, and blaiknit is thy ble ;   165
Thy choip, thy choll, garris men for to leif chest ;
   Thy gane it garris us think that we mon de :
I conjure the, thow hungert heland gaist.

The larbar lukis of thy lang lene craig,
   Thy pure pynit thrott, peilit and owt of ply,   170
Thy skolderit skin, hewd lyk ane saffrone bag,
   Garris men dispyt thar flesche, thow Spreit of Gy :
   Fy ! feyndly front ; fy ! tykis face, fy ! fy !
Ay loungand, lyk ane loikman on ane ledder ;
   With hingit luik ay wallowand upone wry,   175
Lyke to ane stark theif glowrand in ane tedder.

Nyse nagus, nipcaik, with thy schulderis narrow,
   Thow lukis lowsy, loun of lownis aw ;
Hard hurcheoun, hirpland, hippit as ane harrow,
   Thy rigbane rattillis, and thy ribbis on raw,   180
Thy hanchis hirklis with hukebanis harth and haw,
Thy laithly lymis are lene as ony treis ;
   Obey, theif baird, or I sall brek thy gaw,
Fowll carrybald, cry mercy on thy kneis.

Thow purehippit, ugly averill,   185
   With hurkland banis, holkand throw thy hyd,
Reistit and crynit as hangitman on hill,
   And oft beswakkit with ane ourhie tyd,
   Quhilk brewis mekle barret to thy bryd ;
Hir cair is all to clenge thy cabroch howis,   190
   Quhair thow lyis sawsy in saphron, bak and syd,
Powderit with prymros, savrand all with clowis.

Forworthin wirling, I warne the it is wittin,
    How, skyttand skarth, thow hes the hurle behind ;
Wan wraiglane wasp, ma wormis hes thow heschittin   195
    Nor thair is gers on grund or leif on lind ;
    Thocht thow did first sic foly to my fynd,
Thow sall agane with ma witnes than I ;
    Thy gulsoch gane dois on thy back it bind,
Thy hostand hippis lattis nevir thy hos go dry.   200

Thow held the burch lang with ane borrowit goun,
    And ane caprowsy barkit all with sweit,
And quhen the laidis saw the sa lyk a loun,
    Thay bickerit the with mony bae and bleit :
    Now upaland thow leivis on rubbit quheit,   205
Oft for ane caus thy burdclaith ncidis no spredding,
    For thow hes nowthir for to drink nor eit,
Bot lyk ane berdles baird that had no bedding.

Strait Gibbonis air, that nevir ourstred ane hors,
    Bla berfute berne, in bair tyme wes thow borne ;   210
Thow bringis the Carrik clay to Edinburgh Cors
    Upoun thy botingis, hobland, hard as horne ;
    Stra wispis hingis owt, quhair that the wattis ar worne :
Cum thow agane to skar us with thy strais,
    We sall gar scale our sculis all the to scorne,   215
And stane the up the calsay quhair thow gais.

Off Edinburch the boyis as beis owt thrawis,
    And cryis owt ay, " Heir cumis our awin queir Clerk ! "
Than fleis thow lyk ane howlat chest with crawis,
    Quhill all the bichis at thy botingis dois bark :   220
    Than carlingis cryis, " Keip curches in the merk,
Our gallowis gaipis ; lo ! quhair ane greceles gais."
    Ane uthir sayis, " I se him want ane sark,
I reid yow, cummer, tak in your lynning clais."

Than rynis thow doun the gait with gild of boyis,   225
    And all the toun tykis hingand in thy heilis ;
Of laidis and lownis thair rysis sic ane noyis,
    Quhill runsyis rynis away with cairt and quheilis,
    And cager aviris castis bayth coillis and creilis,
For rerd of the and rattling of thy butis ;   230
    Fische wyvis cryis, Fy ! and castis doun skillis and skeilis ;
Sum claschis the, sum cloddis the on the cutis.

Loun lyk Mahoun, be boun me till obey,
   Theif, or in greif mischeif sall the betyd ;
Cry grace, tykis face, or I the chece and sley ;   235
   Oule, rare and yowle, I sall defowll thy pryd ;
   Peilet gled, baith fed and bred of bichis syd,
And lyk ane tyk, purspyk, quhat man settis by the !
   Forflittin, countbittin, beschittin, barkit hyd,
Clym ledder, fyle tedder, foule edder, I defy the.   240

Mauch muttoun, byt buttoun, peilit gluttoun, air to Hilhous ;
   Rank beggar, ostir dregar, foule fleggar in the flet ;
Chittirlilling, ruch rilling, lik schilling in the milhous ;
   Baird rehator, theif of natour, fals tratour, feyindis gett ;
   Filling of tauch, rak sauch, cry crauch, thow art our sett ; 245
Muttoun dryver, girnall ryver, yadswyvar, fowll fell the :
   Herretyk, lunatyk, purspyk, carlingis pet,
Rottin crok, dirtin dok, cry cok, or I sall quell the.

Quod Kennedy to Dumbar

Dathane devillis sone, and dragon dispitous,
   Abironis birth, and bred with Beliall ;   250
Wod werwoif, worme, and scorpion vennemous,
   Lucifers laid, fowll feyindis face infernall ;
   Sodomyt, syphareit fra sanctis celestiall,
Put I nocht sylence to the, schiphird knaif,
And thow of new begynis to ryme and raif,   255
   Thow salbe maid blait, bleir eit, bestiall.

How thy forbearis come, I haif a feill,
   At Cokburnispeth, the writ makis me war,
Generit betuix ane scho beir and a deill ;
   Sa wes he callit Dewlbeir and nocht Dumbar.   260
   This Dewlbeir, generit of a meir of Mar,
Wes Corspatrik, Erle of Merche ; and be illusioun
The first that evir put Scotland to confusioun
   Wes that fals tratour, hardely say I dar.

Quhen Bruce and Balioll differit for the croun,   265
   Scottis Lordis could nocht obey Inglis lawis ;
This Corspatrik betrasit Berwik toun,
   And slew sevin thousand Scottismen within thay wawis,
   The battall syne of Spottismuir he gart caus,

And come with Edwart Langschankis to the feild, 270
Quhair twelve thowsand trew Scottismen wer keild,
  And Wallace chest, as the Cornicle schawis.

Scottis Lordis chiftanis he gart hald and chessone
  In firmance fast, quhill all the feild wes done,
Within Dumbar, that auld spelunk of tressoun ; 275
  Sa Inglis tykis in Scotland wes abone,
  Than spulyeit thay the haly stane of Scone,
The Croce of Halyrudhous, and uthir jowellis.
He birnis in hell, body, banis, and bowellis,
  This Corspatrik that Scotland hes undone. 280

Wallace gart cry ane counsale in to Perth,
  And callit Corspatrik tratour be his style ;
That dampnit dragone drew him in diserth,
  And sayd, he kend bot Wallace, king in Kyle :
  Out of Dumbar that theif he maid exyle 285
Unto Edward and Inglis grund agane :
Tigris, serpentis, and taidis will remane
  In Dumbar wallis, todis, wolffis and beistis vyle.

Na fowlis of effect amangis thay binkis
  Biggis nor abydis, for no thing that may be ; 290
Thay stanis of tressone as the bruntstane stinkis.
  Dewlbeiris moder, cassin in by the se,
  The wariet apill of the forbiddin tre
That Adame eit, quhen he tynt Parradyce,
Scho eit invennomit lyk a cokkatryce, 295
  Syne merreit with the Divill for dignite.

Yit of new tressone I can tell the tailis,
  That cumis on nycht in visioun in my sleip ;
Archbald Dumbar betrasd the house of Hailis,
  Becaus the yung Lord had Dumbar to keip ; 300
  Pretendand throw that to thair rowmis to creip,
Rycht crewaly his castell he persewit,
Brocht him furth boundin and the place reskewit,
  Sett him in fetteris in ane dungeoun deip.

It war aganis bayth natur and gud ressoun, 305
  That Dewlbeiris bairnis were trew to God or man ;
Quhilkis wer baith gottin, borne, and bred with tressoun,

Belgebubbis oyis, and curst Corspatrikis clan :
Thow wes prestyt and ordanit be Sathan
For to be borne to do thy kin defame,   310
And gar me schaw thy antecessouris schame ;
Thy kin that leivis may wary the and ban.

Sen thow on me thus, lymmer, leis and trattillis,
And fyndis sentence foundit of invy,
Thy elderis banis ilk nycht rysis and rattillis,   315
Apon thy cors vengeance, vengeance ! thay cry,
Thow art the cause thay may not rest nor ly ;
Thow sadis for thame few psaltris, psalmis, or credis,
Bot geris me tell thair trentalis of mysdeidis,
And thair ald sin with new schame certify.   320

Insensuate sow, cesse, fals Eustase air !
And knaw, kene scald, I hald of Alathya,
And cause me nocht the cause lang to declare
Off thy curst kyn, Deulber and his allya :
Cum to the Croce, on kneis, and mak a crya ;   325
Confesse thy crime, hald Kenydy the king,
And with ane hauthorne scurge thy self and dyng ;
Thus dree thy penaunce wyth *Dereliquisti quia.*

Pas to my commissare, and be confest,
Cour befoir him on kneis, and cum in will ;   330
And syne ger Stobo for thy lyf protest ;
Renounce thy rymis, bath ban and birn thy bill ;
Heve to the hevyn thy handis, ande hald the still :
Do thou not thus, bogane, thou salbe brynt,
Wyth pik, fire, ter, gun puldre, or lint,   335
On Arthuris Sete, or on ane hyar hyll.

I perambalit of Pernaso the montayn,
Enspirit wyth Mercury fra his goldyn spere ;
And dulcely drank of eloquence the fontayne,
Quhen it was purifit wyth frost, and flowit cleir :   340
And thou come, Fule ! in Marche or Februere,
Thair till a pule, and drank the padok rod,
That gerris the ryme in to thy termis glod,
And blaberis that noyis mennis eris to here.

Thow lufis nane Irische, elf, I understand,   345
Bot it suld be all trew Scottis mennis lede ;

It was the gud langage of this land,
   And Scota it causit to multiply and sprede,
   Quhill Corspatrik, that we of tresoun rede,
Thy forefader, maid Irisch and Irisch men thin,   350
Throu his tresoun broght Inglise rumplis in,
   Sa wald thy self, mycht thou to him succede.

Ignorant fule ! in to thy mowis and mokis,
   It may be verifyit that thy wit is thin ;
Quhare thow writis Densmen dryit apon the rattis,   355
   Densmen of Denmark ar of the kingis kyn.
   The wit thou suld have had, was castin in
Evyn at thyne ers, bakwart, wyth a staf slong.
Herefore, fals harlot, hursone, hald thy tong :
   Deulbere ! thow devis the devill, thyne eme, wyth dyn.   360

Quhare as thou said that I stall hennis and lammys,
   I latt the witt, I have land, store and stakkis.
Thou wald be fayn to gnaw, lad, wyth thy gammys,
   Under my burd, smoch banis behynd doggis bakkis :
   Thow has a tome purs, I have stedis and takkis,   365
Thow tynt cultur, I have cultur and pleuch,
Substance and gere, thou has a wedy teuch,
   On Mount Falconn, about thy crag to rax.

And yit Mount Falconn gallowis is our fair
   For to be fylde with sik a fruteles face ;   370
Cum hame, and hyng on oure gallowis of Aire,
   To erd the under it I sall purchas grace ;
   To ete thy flesch the doggis sall have na space,
The ravyns sall ryve na thing bot thy tong rutis,
For thou sik malice of thy maister mutis,   375
   It is wele sett that thou sik barat brace.

Small fynance amang thy frendis thow beggit,
   To stanch the storm wyth haly muldis thou loste ;
Thou sailit to get a dowcare for to dreg it,
   It lyis closit in a clout on Seland cost :   380
   Sic reule gerris the be servit wyth cald rost,
And sitt unsoupit oft beyond the sey,
Criant *caritas* at duris *amore Dei*,
   Barefut, brekeles, and all in duddis updost.

Deulbere hes not ado wyth a Dunbar,   385
   The Erl of Murray bure that surname ryght,
That evyr trew to the King and constant ware,
   And of that kin come Dunbar of Westfelde knyght;
   That successione is hardy, wyse, and wycht,
And has na thing ado now with the devile,   390
Bot Deulbere is thy kyn, and kennis the wele,
   And has in hell for the a chaumir dicht.

Cursit croapand craw, I sall ger crop thy tong,
   And thou sall cry, *Cor mundum*, on thy kneis;
Duerch, I sall ding the, quhill thow dryte and dong,   395
   And thou sall lik thy lippis and suere thou leis:
   I sall degrade the, graceles, of thy greis;
Scaile the for scorne, and shere the of the scule,
Ger round the hede transforme the till a fule,
   And syne wyth tresone trone the to the treis.   400

Rawmowit ribald, renegate rehatour,
   My linage and forebearis war ay lele;
It cumis of kynde to the to be a traytoure,
   To ryde on nycht, to rug, to reve, and stele.
   Quhare thow puttis poysoun to me, I appelle   405
The in that part, preve it pelour wyth thy persone;
Clame not to clergy, I defy the, gersone,
   Thow sall by it dere wyth me, duerche, and thou dele.

In Ingland, oule, suld be thyne habitacione,
   Homage to Edward Langschankis maid thy kyn,   410
In Dunbar thai ressavit him, the falsc nacione,
   Thay suld be exilde Scotland mare and myn.
   A stark gallowis, a wedy, and a pyn,
The hede poynt of thyne elderis armes ar;
Wryttyn abone in poesie, Hang Dunbar,   415
   Quarter and draw, and mak that surname thin.

I am the kingis blude, his trew speciall clerk,
   That nevir yit ymaginit hym offense,
Constant in myn allegeance, word and werk,
   Onely dependand on his excellence;   420
   Traistand to have of his magnificence
Guerdoun, reward, and benefice bedene;
Quhen that the ravyns sal ryve out bath thine ene,
   And on the rattis salbe thy residence.

Fra Etrike Forest furthward to Drumfrese   425
    Thow beggit wyth a pardoun in all kirkis,
Collapis, cruddis, mele, grotis, grisis, and geis,
    And ondir nycht quhile stall thou staggis and stirkis.
    Because that Scotland of thy begging irkis,
Thow scapis in France to be a knycht of the felde ;   430
Thow has thy clamschellis and thy burdoun kelde,
    Unhonest wayis all, wolroun, that thou wirkis.

Thou may not pas Mount Barnard for wilde bestis,
    Nor wyn throw Mount Scarpre for the snawe ;
Mount Nycholas, Mount Godart thare arestis,   435
    Brigantis sik bois and blyndis thame wyth a blawe.
    In Parise wyth the maister buriawe
Abyde, and be his prentice nere the bank,
And help to hang the pece for half a frank,
    And, at the last, thy self sall thole the lawe.   440

Haltane harlot, the devill have gude thou hais !
    For fault of puissance, pelour, thou mon pak the ;
Thou drank thy thrift, sald and wedsett thy clais,
    Thare is na lorde that will in service tak the.
    A pak of flaskynnis, fynance for to mak the,   445
Thow sall ressave, in Danskyn, of my tailye ;
With *De profundis* fend the, and that failye,
    And I sall send the black Devill for to bak the.

Into the Katryne thou maid a foule cahute,
    For thow bedrate hir doune fra starn to stere ;   450
Apon hir sydis was sene thou coud schute,
    Thy dirt clevis till hir towis this twenty yere :
    The firmament na firth was nevir cler,
Quhill thou, Deulbere, devillis birth, was on the see,
The saulis had sonkin throu the syn of the,   455
    War not the peple maid sa grete prayere.

Quhen that the schip was saynit, and undir saile,
    Foul brow in holl thow preposit for to pas,
Thou schot, and was not sekir of thy tayle,
    Beschate the stere, the compas, and the glas ;   460
    The skippar bad ger land the at the Bas :
Thow spewit, and kest out mony a lathly lomp,
Fastar than all the marynaris coud pomp ;
    And now thy wame is wers than evir it was.

Had thai bene prouuait sa of schote of gune,   465
  By men of were but perile thay had past ;
As thou was louse and redy of thy bune,
  Thay mycht have tane the collum at the last ;
  For thou wald cuk a cartfull at a cast ;
Thair is na schip that wil the now ressave ;   470
Thou fylde faster than fyftenesum mycht lave,
  And myrit thaym wyth thy muk to the myd mast.

Throu Ingland, thef, and tak the to thy fute,
  And boune with the to have a fals botwand ;
A horse marschall thou call the at the mute,   475
  And with that craft convoy the throu the land :
  Be na thing argh, tak ferily on hand ;
Happyn thou to be hangit in Northumbir,
Than all thy kyn ar wele quyte of thy cumbir,
  And that mon be thy dome, I undirstand.   480

Hye Souverane Lorde, lat nevir this synfull sot
  Do schame, fra hame, unto your nacion !
That nevir nane sik ane be callit a Scot,
  A rottyn crok, louse of the dok, thare doune.
  Fra honest folk devoide this lathly lowne ;   485
In sum desert, quhare thare is na repaire,
For fylyng and infecking of the aire,
  Cary this cankerit corrupt carioun.

Thou was consavit in the grete eclips,
  A monstir maid be god Mercurius ;   490
Na hald agayn, na hoo is at thy hips,
  Infortunate, false, and furius,
  Evill schryvin, wan-thryvin, not clene na curius ;
A myten, full of flyting, flyrdom like,
A crabbit, scabbit, evill facit messan tyke ;   495
  A schit but wit, schyre and injurius.

Greit in the glaykis gude Maister Gilliam gukkis,
  Our imperfyte in poetry or in prose,
All clocis undir cloud of nycht thou cukkis ;
  Rymis thou of me of Rethory the Rose ;   500
  Lunatike, lymare, luschbald, louse thy hose,
That I may touch thy tone wyth tribulation,
In recompensing of thy conspiration,
  Or turse the out of Scotland : tak thy chose.

Ane benefice quha wald gyve sic ane beste,   505
  Bot gif it war to gyngill Iudas bellis ;
Tak the a fidill, or a floyte, and geste,
  Undought, thou art ordanyt to not ellis !
Thy cloutit cloke, thy skryp, and thy clamschellis,
Cleke on thy cors, and fare on in to France,   510
And cum thou nevir agayn but a mischance ;
  The fend fare wyth the forthwarde our the fellis.

Cankrit Caym, tryit trowane, Tutivillus,
  Marmaidyn, mymmerken, monstir of all men,
I sall ger bake the to the lard of Hillhouse,   515
  To suelly the in stede of a pullit hen.
  Fowmart, fasert, fostirit in filth and fen,
Foule fond, flend fule, apon thy phisnom fy !
Thy dok of dirt dreipis and will nevir dry,
  To tume thy tone it has tyrit carlingis ten.   520

Conspiratour, cursit cocatrice, hell caa,
  Turk, trumpour, traitour, tyran intemperate ;
Thow irefull attircop, Pilate apostata,
  Judas, jow, juglour, Lollard laureate ;
  Sarazene, symonyte provit, Pagane pronunciate,   525
Machomete, manesuorne, bugrist abhominabile,
Devill, dampnit dog, sodomyte insatiable,
  With Gog and Magog grete glorificate.

Nero thy nevow, Golyas thy grantsire,
  Pharao thy fader, Egipya thy dame,   530
Deulbere, thir ar thc causis that I conspire,
  Termygantis tempise the, and Vaspasius thine eme ;
  Belzebub thy full brothir will clame
To be thyne air, and Cayphas thy sectour ;
Pluto thy hede of kyn and protectour,   535
  To hell to lede the on lycht day and leme.

Herode thyne othir eme, and grete Egeas,
  Marciane, Machomete, and Maxencius,
Thy trew kynnismen, Antenor and Eneas,
  Throp thy nere nece, and austerne Olibrius,   540
  Puttidew, Baal, and Fyobulus ;
Thir fendis ar the flour of thy four branchis,
Sterand the potis of hell, and nevir stanchis,
  Dout not, Deulbere, *Tu es Dyabolus.*

Deulbere, thy spere of were, but feir, thou yelde,   545
   Hangit, mangit, eddir-stangit, strynde stultorum,
To me, maist hie Kenydie, and flee the felde,
   Pickit, wickit, convickit Lamp Lollardorum.
Defamyt, blamyt, schamyt, Primas Paganorum.
Out ! out ! I schout, apon that snowt that snevillis.   550
Tale tellare, rebellare, induellar wyth the devillis,
   Spynk, sink with stynk *ad Tertara Termagorum*.

7. LAMENT FOR THE MAKARIS

" Quhen He Wes Sek "

I THAT in heill wes and gladnes,
Am trublit now with gret seiknes,
And feblit with infermite ;
   Timor mortis conturbat me.

Our plesance heir is all vane glory,   5
This fals warld is bot transitory,
The flesche is brukle, the Fend is sle ;
   Timor mortis conturbat me.

The stait of man dois change and vary,
Now sound, now seik, now blith, now sary,   10
Now dansand mery, now like to dee ;
   Timor mortis conturbat me.

No stait in erd heir standis sickir ;
As with the wynd wavis the wickir,
Wavis this warldis vanite ;   15
   Timor mortis conturbat me.

On to the ded gois all Estatis,
Princis, Prelotis, and Potestatis,
Baith riche and pur of al degre ;
   Timor mortis conturbat me.   20

He takis the knychtis in to feild,
Anarmit under helme and scheild ;
Victour he is at all mellie ;
   Timor mortis conturbat me.

That strang unmercifull tyrand 25
Takis, on the moderis breist sowkand,
The bab full of benignite ;
    Timor mortis conturbat me.

He takis the campion in the stour,
The capitane closit in the tour, 30
The lady in bour full of bewte ;
    Timor mortis conturbat me.

He sparis no lord for his piscence,
Na clerk for his intelligencc ;
His awfull strak may no man fle ; 35
    Timor mortis conturbat me.

Art-magicianis, and astrologgis,
Rethoris, logicianis, and theologgis,
Thame helpis no conclusionis sle ;
    Timor mortis conturbat me. 40

In medicyne the most practicianis,
Lechis, surrigianis, and phisicianis,
Thame self fra ded may not supple ;
    Timor mortis conturbat me.

I se that makaris amang the laif 45
Playis heir ther pageant, syne gois to graif ;
Sparit is nocht ther faculte ;
    Timor mortis conturbat me.

He hes done petuously devour,
The noble Chaucer, of makaris flour, 50
The Monk of Bery, and Gower, all thre ;
    Timor mortis conturbat me.

The gude Syr Hew of Eglintoun,
And eik Heryot, and Wyntoun,
He hes tane out of this cuntre ; 55
    Timor mortis conturbat me.

That scorpion fell hes done infek
Maister Johne Clerk, and James Afflek,
Fra balat making and tragidie ;
    Timor mortis conturbat me. 60

Holland and Barbour he hes berevit ;
Allace ! that he nocht with us levit
Schir Mungo Lokert of the Le ;
   Timor mortis conturbat me.

Clerk of Tranent eik he hes tane,   65
That maid the Anteris of Gawane ;
Schir Gilbert Hay endit hes he ;
   Timor mortis conturbat me.

He hes Blind Hary and Sandy Traill
Slaine with his schour of mortall haill,   70
Quhilk Patrik Johnestoun myght nocht fle ;
   Timor mortis conturbat me.

He hes reft Merseir his endite,
That did in luf so lifly write,
So schort, so quyk, of sentence hie ;   75
   Timor mortis conturbat me.

He hes tane Roull of Aberdene,
And gentill Roull of Corstorphin ;
Two bettir fallowis did no man se ;
   Timor mortis conturbat me.   80

In Dumfermelyne he hes done roune
With Maister Robert Henrisoun ;
Schir Johne the Ros enbrast hes he ;
   Timor mortis conturbat me.

And he hes now tane, last of aw,   85
Gud gentill Stobo and Quintyne Schaw,
Of quham all wichtis hes pete :
   Timor mortis conturbat me.

Gud Maister Walter Kennedy
In poynt of dede lyis veraly,   90
Gret reuth it wer that so suld be ;
   Timor mortis conturbat me.

Sen he hes all my brether tane,
He will nocht lat me lif alane,
On forse I man his nyxt pray be ;   95
   Timor mortis conturbat me.

Sen for the deid remeid is none,
Best is that we for dede dispone,
Eftir our deid that lif may we ;
    Timor mortis conturbat me.   100

8. OF DEMING

MUSING ALLONE this hinder nicht,
Of mirry day quhen gone was licht,
Within ane garth undir a tre,
I hard ane voce that said on hicht,
May na man now undemit be.   5

For thocht I be ane crownit king,
Yit sall I not eschew deming ;
Sum callis me guid, sum sayis thai le,
Sum cravis of God to end my ring,
So sall I not undemit be.   10

Be I ane lord, and not lord lyk,
Than every pelour and purspyk
Sayis, " Land war bettir warit on me " ;
Thocht he dow not to leid a tyk,
Yit can he not lat deming be.   15

Be I ane lady fresche and fair,
With gentillmen makand repair,
Than will thay say, baith scho and hie,
That I am jaipit lait and air ;
Thus sall I not undemit be.   20

Be I ane courtman or ane knycht,
Honestly cled that cumis me richt,
Ane prydfull man than call thay me ;
Bot God send thame a widdy wicht,
That can not lat sic demyng be.   25

Be I bot littill of stature,
Thay call me catyve createure ;
And be I grit of quantetie,
Thay call me monstrowis of nature ;
Thus can I not undemit be.   30

And be I ornat in my speiche,
Than Towsy sayis I am sa streiche,
I speik not lyk thair hous menyie.
Suppois hir mowth misteris a leiche,
Yit can I not undemit be.   35

Bot wist thir folkis, that uthir demis,
How that thair sawis to uthir semis,
Thair vicious wordis and vanitie,
Thair tratling tungis that all furth temis,
Sum wald lat thair demyng be.   40

War nocht the mater wald grow mair,
To wirk vengeance on ane demair,
But dout I wald caus mony de,
And mony catif end in cair,
Or sum tym lat thair deming be.   45

Gude James the Ferd, our nobill king,
Quhen that he was of yeiris ying,
In sentens said full subtillie,
" Do weill, and sett not by demying,
For no man sall undemit be."   50

And so I sall, with Goddis grace,
Keip his command in to that cace ;
Beseiking ay the Trinitie,
In hevin that I may haif ane place,
For thair sall no man demit be.   55

9. HOW SALL I GOVERNE ME

How sould I rewill me or in quhat wys,
I wald sum wyse man wald devys ;
Sen I can leif in no degre,
Bot sum my maneris will dispys.
Lord God, how sould I governe me ?   5

Giff I be lustye, galland and blythe,
Than will thai say on me full swythe,
Yon man out of his mynd is he,

Or sum hes done him confort kythe.
Lord God, how sould I governe me ?   10

Giff I be sorrowfull and sad,
Than will thai say that I am mad ;
I do bot drowpe as I wald die,
So will thai deyme bayth man and lad.
Lord God, how sall I governe me ?   15

Be I liberall, gentill, and kynd,
Thocht I it tak of nobill strynd,
Yit will thai say, baythe he and he,
Yon man is lyke out of his mynd :
Lord God, how sall I governe me ?   20

Giff I be lustie in myne array,
Than lufe I paramoris say thai,
Or in my mynd is prowd and hie,
Or ellis I haif it sum wrang way.
Lord God, how sall I governe me ?   25

And gif I be not wele besene,
Than twa and twa sayis thame betwene,
Evill gydit is yon man par de ;
Be his clething it may be sene.
Lord God, how sould I governe me ?   30

Gif I be sene in court our lang,
Than will thai quhispir thame amang,
My freindis ar not worthe ane fle,
That I sa lang but gwerdon gang.
Lord God, how sould I governe me ?   35

In court rewaird than purches I,
Than have thai malice and invy,
And secreitly on me thai lie,
And dois me sklandir privaly.
Lord God, how sould I governe me ?   40

How sould my gyding be devysit :
Giff I spend litle I am dispysit ;
Be I courtas, nobill, and fre,
A prodigall man than am I prysit.
Lord God, how sould I governe me ?   45

Sen all is jugit, bayth gud and ill,
And no mannis toung I may had still,
To do the best my mynd salbe;
Lat everie man say quhat he will,
The gratious God mot governe me.   50

10. MEDITATIOUN IN WYNTIR

In to thir dirk and drublie dayis,
Quhone sabill all the hevin arrayis
    With mystie vapouris, cluddis, and skyis,
    Nature all curage me denyis
Off sangis, ballattis, and of playis.   5

Quhone that the nycht dois lenthin houris,
With wind, with haill, and havy schouris,
    My dule spreit dois lurk for schoir,
    My hairt for languor dois forloir
For laik of symmer with his flouris.   10

I walk, I turne, sleip may I nocht,
I vexit am with havie thocht;
    This warld all ouir I cast about,
    And ay the mair I am in dout,
The mair that I remeid have socht.   15

I am assayit on everie syde:
Dispair sayis ay, " In tyme provyde
    And get sum thing quhairon to leif,
    Or with grit trouble and mischeif
Thow sall in to this court abyd."   20

Than Patience sayis, " Be not agast:
Hald Hoip and Treuthe within the fast,
    And lat Fortoun wirk furthe hir rage,
    Quhome that no rasoun may assuage,
Quhill that hir glas be run and past."   25

And Prudence in my eir sayis ay,
" Quhy wald thow hald that will away?
    Or craif that thow may have no space,
    Thow tending to ane uther place,
A journay going everie day?"   30

And than sayis Age, " My freind, cum neir,
And be not strange, I the requeir :
   Cum, brodir, by the hand me tak,
   Remember thow hes compt to mak
Off all thi tyme thow spendit heir."   35

Syne Deid castis upe his yettis wyd,
Saying, " Thir oppin sall the abyd ;
   Albeid that thow wer never sa stout,
   Undir this lyntall sall thow lowt :
Thair is nane uther way besyde."   40

For feir of this all day I drowp ;
No gold in kist, nor wyne in cowp,
   No ladeis bewtie, nor luiffis blys,
   May lat me to remember this,
How glaid that ever I dyne or sowp.   45

Yit, quhone the nycht begynnis to schort,
It dois my spreit sum pairt confort,
   Off thocht oppressit with the schowris.
   Cum, lustie symmer ! with thi flowris,
That I may leif in sum disport.   50

11. QUHONE MONY BENEFICES VAKIT

Schir, at this feist of benefice,
Think that small partis makis grit service,
   And equale distributioun
   Makis thame content that hes ressoun ;
And quha hes nane ar plesit na wyis.   5

Schir, quhiddir is it mereit mair
To gif him drink that thristis sair,
   Or fill a fow man quhill he brist,
   And lat his fallow de a thrist,
Quhilk wyne to drynk als worthie war ?   10

It is no glaid collatioun
Quhair ane makis myrrie, ane uther lukis doun ;
   Ane thristis, ane uther playis cop out :
   Lat anis the cop ga round about,
And wyn the covanis banesoun.   15

12. TO THE KING

Off BENEFICE, Schir, at everie feist,
Quha monyast hes makis maist requeist ;
   Get thai nocht all, thai think ye wrang thame :
Ay is the ouir word of the geist,
   Giff thame the pelffe to pairt amang thame.   5

Sum swelleis swan, sum swelleis duke,
And I stand fastand in a nuke,
   Quhill the effect of all thai fang thame :
Bot, Lord ! how petewouslie I luke,
   Quhone all the pelfe thay pairt amang thame.   10

Off sic hie feistis of sanctis in glorie,
Baithe of commoun and propir storie,
   Quhair lairdis war patronis, oft I sang thame
Charitas pro Dei amore ;
   And yit I gat na thing amang thame.   15

This blynd warld ever so payis his dett,
Riche befoir pure spreidis ay thair nett,
   To fische all watiris dois belang thame :
Quha na thing hes, can na thing gett,
   Bot ay as syphir set amang thame.   20

Swa thai the kirk have in thair cure,
Thay fors bot litill how it fure,
   Nor of the buikis, or bellis quha rang thame :
Thai pans nocht of the prochin pure,
   Hed thai the pelfe to pairt amang thame.   25

So warryit is this warldis rent,
That nane thairof can be content,
   Off deathe quhill that the dragoun stang thame ;
Quha maist hes than sall maist repent,
   With largest compt to pairt amang thame.   30

13. OF THE WARLDIS INSTABILITIE

This WAVERAND warldis wretchidnes,
The failyeand and frutless bissines,
The mispent tyme, the service vane,
   For to considder is ane pane.

The slydand joy, the glaidnes schort,   5
The feynyeid luif, the fals confort,
The sweit abayd, the slichtfull trane,
   For to considder is ane pane.

The sugurit mouthis with myndis thairfra,
The figurit speiche with faceis tua,   10
The plesand toungis with hartis unplane,
   For to considder is ane pane.

The liell labour lost and liell service,
The lang availl on humill wyse,
And the lytill rewarde agane,   15
   For to considder is ane pane.

Nocht I say all be this cuntre,
France, Ingland, Ireland, Almanie,
Bot als be Italie and Spane;
   Quhilk to considder is ane pane.   20

The change of warld fro weill to wo,
The honourable use is all ago,
In hall and bour, in burgh and plane;
   Quhilk to considder is ane pane.

Beleif dois liep, traist dois nocht tarie,   25
Office dois flit, and courtis dois vary,
Purpos dois change as wynd or rane;
   Quhilk to considder is ane pane.

Gude rewle is banist our the Bordour,
And rangat ringis but ony ordour,   30
With reird of rebaldis and of swane;
   Quhilk to considder is ane pane.

The pepill so wickit ar of feiris,
The frutles erde all witnes beiris,
The ayr infectit and prophane;   35
   Quhilk to considder is ane pane.

The temporale stait to gryp and gather,
The sone disheris wald the father,

And as ane dyvour wald him demane ;
  Quhilk to considder is ane pane.   40

Kirkmen so halie ar and gude,
That on thair conscience, rowme and rude,
May turne aucht oxin and ane wane ;
  Quhilk to considder is ane pane.

I knaw nocht how the kirk is gydit,   45
Bot beneficis ar nocht leill devydit ;
Sum men hes sevin, and I nocht ane ;
  Quhilk to considder is ane pane.

And sum, unworthy to browk ane stall,
Wald clym to be ane cardinall,   50
Ane bischoprik may nocht him gane ;
  Quhilk to considder is ane pane.

Unwourthy I, amang the laif,
Ane kirk dois craif and nane can have ;
Sum with ane thraif playis passage plane ;   55
  Quhilk to considder is ane pane.

It cumis be king, it cumis be quene,
Bot ay sic space is us betwene,
That nane can schut it with ane flane ;
  Quhilk to considder is ane pane.   60

It micht have cumin in schortar quhyll
Fra Calyecot and the new fund Yle,
The partis of Transmeridiane ;
  Quhilk to considder is ane pane.

It micht, be this, had it bein kynd,   65
Cumin out of the desertis of Ynde,
Our all the grit se occeane ;
  Quhilk to considder is ane pane.

It micht have cumin out of all ayrtis,
Fra Paris, and the Orient partis,   70
And fra the Ylis of Aphrycane ;
  Quhilk to considder is ane pane.

It is so lang in cuming me till,
I dreid that it be quyt gane will,
Or bakwart it is turnit agane ;   75
   Quhilk to considder is ane pane.

Upon the heid of it is hecht
Bayth unicornis and crownis of wecht,
Quhen it dois cum all men dois frane ;
   Quhilk to considder is ane pane.   80

I wait [it] is for me provydit,
Bot sa done tyrsum it is to byd it,
It breikis my hairt and birstis my brane ;
   Quhilk to considder is ane pane.

Greit abbais grayth I nill to gather,   85
Bot ane kirk scant coverit with hadder ;
For I of lytill wald be fane ;
   Quhilk to considder is ane pane.

And for my curis in sindrie place,
With help, Sir, of your nobill Grace,   90
My sillie saule sall never be slane,
   Na for sic syn to suffer pane.

Experience dois me so inspyr,
Of this fals failyeand warld I tyre,
That evermore flytis lyk ane phane ;   95
   Quhilk to considder is ane pane.

The formest hoip yit that I have
In all this warld, sa God me save,
Is in your Grace, bayth crop and grayne,
   Quhilk is ane lessing of my pane.   100

14. OF DISCRETIOUN IN ASKING

Off every asking followis nocht
Rewaird, bot gif sum caus war wrocht ;
And quhair caus is, men weill ma sie,
And quhair nane is, it wilbe thocht :
In asking sowld discretioun be.   5

Ane fule, thocht he haif caus or nane,
Cryis ay, " Gif me ", in to a rane ;
And he that dronis ay as ane bee
Sowld haif ane heirar dull as stane :
In asking sowld discretioun be.   10

Sum askis mair than he deservis ;
Sum askis far les than he servis ;
Sum schames to ask, as braidis of me,
And all withowt reward he stervis :
In asking sowld discretioun be.   15

To ask but service hurtis gud fame ;
To ask for service is not to blame ;
To serve and leif in beggartie
To man and maistir is baith schame :
In asking sowld discretion be.   20

He that dois all his best servyis
May spill it all with crakkis and cryis,
Be fowll inoportunitie ;
Few wordis may serve the wyis :
In asking sowld discretioun be.   25

Nocht neidfull is men sowld be dum ;
Na thing is gottin but wordis sum ;
Nocht sped but diligence we se ;
For nathing it allane will cum :
In asking sowld discretioun be.   30

Asking wald haif convenient place,
Convenient tyme, lasar, and space,
But haist or preis of grit menyie,
But hairt abasit, but toung rekles :
In asking sowld discretion be.   35

Sum micht haif ' ye ' with littill cure,
That hes oft ' nay ' with grit labour ;
All for that tyme not byd can he,
He tynis baith eirand and honour :
In asking sowld discretion be.   40

Suppois the servand be lang unquit,
The lord sumtyme rewaird will it;
Gife he dois not, quhat remedy ?
To fecht with fortoun is no wit :
In asking sowld discretioun be.   45

15. OF DISCRETIOUN IN GEVING

To SPEIK of gift or almous deidis ;
Sum gevis for mereit and for meidis ;
Sum warldly honour to uphie
Gevis to thame that no thing neidis :
In geving sowld discretioun be.   5

Sum gevis for pryd and glory vane ;
Sum gevis with grugeing and with pane ;
Sum gevis in practik for supple ;
Sum gevis for twyis als gud agane :
In geving sowld discretioun be.   10

Sum gevis for thank, sum for threit ;
Sum gevis money, and sum gevis meit ;
Sum gevis wordis fair and sle ;
Giftis fra sum ma na man treit :
In giving sowld discretioun be.   15

Sum is for gift sa lang requyrd,
Quhill that the crevar be so tyrd
That, or the gift deliverit be,
The thank is frustrat and expyrd :
In geving suld discretioun be.   20

Sum gevis to littill full wretchitly,
That his giftis ar not set by,
And for a huidpyk haldin is he,
That all the warld cryis on him, Fy :
In geving sowld discretioun be.   25

Sum in his geving is so large,
That all ourlaidin is his berge ;

Than vyce and prodigalite
Thairof his honour dois dischairge :
In geving sowld discretioun be.   30

Sum to the riche gevis geir,
That micht his giftis weill forbeir ;
And thocht the peur for falt sowld de,
His cry nocht enteris in his eir :
In geving sowld discretioun be.   35

Sum givis to strangeris with face new,
That yisterday fra Flanderis flew,
And to awld serwandis list not se,
War thay nevir of sa grit vertew :
In geving sowld discretioun be.   40

Sum gevis to thame can craftlie plenyie ;
Sum gevis to thame can flattir and fenyie ;
Sum gevis to men of honestie,
And haldis all janglaris at disdenyie :
In geving sowld discretioun be.   45

Sum gettis giftis and riche arrayis,
To sweir all that his maister sayis,
Thocht all the contrair weill knawis he ;
Ar mony sic now in thir dayis :
In geving sowld discretioun be.   50

Sum gevis gud men for thair thewis ;
Sum gevis to trumpouris and to schrewis ;
Sum gevis to knaiffis awtoritie ;
Bot in thair office gude fundin few is :
In geving sowld discretioun be.   55

Sum givis parrochynnis full wyd,
Kirkis of Sanct Barnard and Sanct Bryd,
To teiche, to rewill, and to ouirsie,
That hes na wit thame selffe to gyd :
In geving sowld discretioun be.   60

Eftir geving I speik of taking,
Bot littill of ony gud forsaiking.
Sum takkis our littill awtoritie,
And sum our mekle, and that is glaiking :
In taking sowld discretioun be.   5

The clerkis takis beneficis with brawlis,
Sum of Sanct Petir, and sum of Sanct Pawlis ;
Tak he the rentis, no cair hes he,
Suppois the divill tak all thair sawlis :
In taking sowld discretioun be.   10

Barronis takis fra the tennentis peure
All fruct that growis on the feure,
In mailis and gersomes rasit ouirhie,
And garris thame beg fra dur to dure :
In taking sowld discretioun be.   15

[Thir merchandis takis unlesum win,
Quhilk makis thair pakkis oftymes full thin ;
Be thair successioun ye may see
That ill won geir riches not the kin :
In taking suld discretioun be.]   20

Sum takis uthir menis takkis,
And on the peure oppressioun makkis,
And nevir remembris that he mon die,
Quhill that the gallowis gar him rax :
In taking sowld discretioun be.   25

Sum takis be sie and be land,
And nevir fra taking can hald thair hand,
Quhill he be tit up to ane tre ;
And syne they gar him undirstand
In taking sowld discretioun be.   30

Sum wald tak all his nychbouris geir,
Had he of man als littill feir
As he hes dreid that God him see ;
To tak than sowld he nevir forbeir :
In taking sowld discretioun be   35

[Stude I na mair aw of man nor God,
Than suld I tak bayth evin and od,
Ane end of all thing that I see ;
Sic justice is not worth ane clod :
In taking suld discretioun be.]   40

Sum wald tak all this warldis breid,
And yit not satisfeit of thair neid,
Throw hairt unsatiable and gredie ;
Sum wald tak littill, and can not speid :
In taking sowld discretioun be.   45

Grit men for taking and oppressioun
Ar sett full famous at the Sessioun,
And peur takaris ar hangit hie,
Schamit for evir and thair successioun :
In taking sowld discretioun be.   50

17. REMONSTRANCE TO THE KING

SCHIR, YE have mony servitouris
And officiaris of dyvers curis ;
Kirkmen, courtmen, and craftismen fyne ;
Doctouris in jure, and medicyne ;
Divinouris, rethoris, and philosophouris,   5
Astrologis, artistis, and oratouris ;
Men of armes, and vailyeand knychtis,
And mony uther gudlie wichtis ;
Musicianis, menstralis, and mirrie singaris :
Chevalouris, cawandaris, and flingaris ;   10
Cunyouris, carvouris, and carpentaris,
Beildaris of barkis and ballingaris ;
Masounis lyand upon the land,
And schipwrichtis hewand upone the strand ;
Glasing wrichtis, goldsmythis, and lapidaris,   15
Pryntouris, payntouris, and potingaris ;
And all of thair craft cunning,
And all at anis lawboring ;
Quhilk pleisand ar and honorable,
And to your hienes profitable,   20
And richt convenient for to be

With your hie regale majestie ;
Deserving of your grace most ding
Bayth thank, rewarde, and cherissing.
    And thocht that I, amang the laif,   25
Unworthy be ane place to have,
Or in thair nummer to be tald,
Als lang in mynd my wark sall hald,
Als haill in everie circumstance,
In forme, in mater, and substance,   30
But wering, or consumptioun,
Roust, canker, or corruptioun,
As ony of thair werkis all,
Suppois that my rewarde be small.
    Bot ye sa gracious ar and meik,   35
That on your hienes followis eik
Ane uthir sort, more miserabill,
Thocht thai be nocht sa profitable :
Fenyeouris, fleichouris, and flatteraris ;
Cryaris, craikaris, and clatteraris ;   40
Soukaris, groukaris, gledaris, gunnaris ;
Monsouris of France, gud clarat-cunnaris ;
Innopportoun askaris of Yrland kynd ;
And meit revaris, lyk out of mynd ;
Scaffaris, and scamleris in the nuke,   45
And hall huntaris of draik and duik ;
Thrimlaris and thristaris, as thay war woid,
Kokenis, and kennis na man of gude ;
Schulderaris, and schowaris, that hes no schame,
And to no cunning that can clame ;   50
And can non uthir craft nor curis
Bot to mak thrang, Schir, in your duris,
And rusche in quhair thay counsale heir,
And will at na man nurtir leyr :
In quintiscence, eik, ingynouris joly,   55
That far can multiplie in folie ;
Fantastik fulis, bayth fals and gredy,
Off toung untrew, and hand evill deidie :
Few dar, of all this last additioun,
Cum in tolbuyth without remissioun.   60
    And thocht this nobill cunning sort,
Quhom of befoir I did report,
Rewardit be, it war bot ressoun,
Thairat suld no man mak enchessoun :

Bot quhen the uther fulis nyce,   65
That feistit at Cokelbeis gryce,
Ar all rewardit, and nocht I,
Than on this fals world I cry, Fy !
My hart neir bristis than for teyne,
Quhilk may nocht suffer nor sustene   70
So grit abusioun for to se,
Daylie in court befoir myn E !
   And yit more panence wald I have,
Had I rewarde amang the laif,
It wald me sumthing satisfie,   75
And les of my malancolie,
And gar me mony falt ouerse,
That now is brayd befoir myn E :
My mind so fer is set to flyt,
That of nocht ellis I can endyt ;   80
For owther man my hart to breik,
Or with my pen I man me wreik ;
And sen the tane most nedis be,
In to malancolie to de,
Or lat the vennim ische all out,   85
Be war, anone, for it will spout,
Gif that the tryackill cum nocht tyt
To swage the swalme of my dispyt !

18. TO THE KING

THAT HE WAR JOHNE THOMOSUNIS MAN

SCHIR, FOR your Grace bayth nicht and day,
Richt hartlie on my kneis I pray,
With all devotioun that I can,
   God gif ye war Johne Thomsounis man !

For war it so, than weill war me,   5
But benefice I wald nocht be ;
My hard fortoun wer endit than :
   God gif ye war Johne Thomsounis man !

Than wald sum reuth within yow rest,
For saik of hir, fairest and best   10
In Bartane, sen hir tyme began ;
   God gif ye war Johne Thomsounis man !

For it micht hurt in no degre,
That one, so fair and gude as sche,
Throw hir vertew sic wirschip wan,   15
   As yow to mak Johne Thomsounis man.

I wald gif all that ever I have
To that conditioun, sa God me saif,
That ye had vowit to the Swan
   Ane yeir to be Johne Thomsounis man.   20

The mersy of that sweit meik Rois
Suld soft yow, Thirbill, I suppois,
Quhois pykis throw me so reuthles ran ;
   God gif ye war Johne Thomsounis man !

My advocat, bayth fair and sweit,   25
The hale rejosing of my spreit,
Wald speid in to my erand than ;
   And ye war anis Johne Thomsounis man.

Ever quhen I think yow harde or dour,
Or mercyles in my succour,   30
Than pray I God and sweit Sanct An,
   Gif that ye war Johne Thomsounis man !

19. COMPLAINT TO THE KING

Complane I wald, wist I quhome till,
Or unto quhome darett my bill ;
Quhidder to God, that all thing steiris,
All thing seis, and all thing heiris,
And all thing wrocht in dayis seveyne ;   5
Or till his Moder, Quein off Heveyne ;
Or unto wardlie prince heir downe,
That dois for justice weir a crownne ;
Off wrangis, and off gryt injuris
That nobillis in thar dayis induris,   10
And men of vertew and cuning,
Of wit, and wysdome in gydding,
That nocht cane in this cowrt conquys
For lawte, luiff, nor lang servys.

Bot fowll, jow-jowrdane-hedit jevellis,   15
Cowkin-kenseis, and culroun kevellis ;
Stuffettis, strekouris, and stafische strummellis ;
Wyld haschbaldis, haggarbaldis, and hummellis ;
Druncartis, dysouris, dy[v]owris, drevellis,
Misgydit memberis of the devellis ;   20
Mismad mandragis off mastis strynd,
Crawdones, couhirttis, and theiffis of kynd ;
Blait-mowit bladyeanes with bledder cheikis,
Club-facet clucanes with clutit breikis,
Chuff-midding churllis, cumin off cart-fillaris,   25
Gryt glaschew-hedit gorge-millaris,
Evill horrible monsteris, fals and fowll.
Sum causles clekis till him ane cowll,
Ane gryt convent fra syne to tys,
And he him-selff exampill of vys :   30
Enterand for geir and no devocioun,
The devill is glaid of his promocioun.
Sum ramyis ane rokkat fra the roy
And dois ane dastart destroy ;
And sum that gaittis ane personage,   35
Thinkis it a present for a page,
And on no wayis content is he,
My lord quhill that he callit be.

Bot quhow is he content or nocht,
Deme ye abowt in to yowr thocht,   40
The lerit sone off erll or lord,
Upone this ruffie to remord,
That with all castingis hes him cled
His erandis for to ryne and red ?
And he is maister native borne   45
And all his eldaris him beforne,
And mekle mair cuning be sic thre
Hes to posseid ane dignite,
Saying his odius ignorance
Panting ane prelottis countenance,   50
Sa far above him set at tabell
That wont was for to muk the stabell :
Ane pykthank in a prelottis clais,
With his wavill feit and wirrok tais,
With hoppir hippis and henches narrow,   55
And bausy handis to beir a barrow ;
With lut schulderis and luttard bak,

Quhilk natur maid to beir a pak ;
With gredy mynd and glaschane gane,
Mell-hedit lyk ane mortar stanc,   60
Fenyeing the feris off ane lord,
And he ane strumbell, I stand for'd ;
And ever moir as he dois rys,
Nobles off bluid he dois dispys,
And helpis for to hald thame downe,   65
That they rys never to his renowne.
    Thairfoir, O Prince maist honorable !
Be in this meter merciabill,
And to auld servandis hatt ane E,
That lang hes lipinit into the ;   70
Gif I be ane off tha my sell,
Throw all regiones hes bein hard tell,
Off quhilk my wrytting witnes beris ;
And yete thy danger ay me deris :
Bot eftir danger cumis grace,   75
As hes bein herd in mony plece.

20. TO THE KING

SCHIR, YIT remembir as of befoir,
How that my youthe is done forloir
In your service, with pane and greiff ;
Gud conscience cryis reward thairfoir :
Exces of thocht dois me mischeif.   5

Your clarkis ar servit all aboute,
And I do lyke ane rid halk schout,
To cum to lure that hes na leif,
Quhair my plumis begynnis to mowt :
Exces of thocht dois me mischeif.   10

Foryhet is ay the falcounis kynd,
Bot ever the myttell is hard in mynd ;
Quhone the gled dois the peirtrikis preiff,
The gentill goishalk gois undynd :
Exces of thocht dois me mischeif.   15

The pyat withe the pairtie cote
Feynyeis to sing the nychtingale note,

D

Bot scho can not the corchet cleiff,
For harsknes of hir carleche throte :
Exces of thocht dois me mischeif.   20

Ay fairast feddiris hes farrest foulis ;
Suppois thay have no sang bot yowlis,
In sylver caiges thai sit at cheif ;
Kynd natyve nestis dois clek bot owlis :
Exces of thocht dois me mischeif.   25

O gentill egill ! how may this be ?
Quhilk of all foulis dois heast fle,
Your leggis quhy do ye nocht releif,
And chirreis thame eftir thair degre ?
Exces of thocht dois me mischeif.   30

Quhone servit is all uther man,
Gentill and sempill of everie clan,
Kyne of Rauf Colyard and Johine the Reif,
No thing I gett nor conqueis can :
Exces of thocht dois me mischeif.   35

Thocht I in courte be maid refuse,
And have few vertewis for to ruse,
Yit am I cum of Adame and Eve,
And fane wald leif as utheris dois ;
Exces of thocht dois me mischeif.   40

Or I suld leif in sic mischance,
Giff it to God war na grevance,
To be ane pykthank I wald preif,
For thay in warld wantis na plesance :
Exces of thocht dois me mischeif.   45

In sum pairt of my selffe I pleinye,
Quhone utheris dois flattir and feynye ;
Allace ! I can bot ballattis breif,
Sic barneheid leidis my brydill reynye :
Exces of thocht dois me mischeif.   50

I grant my service is bot lycht ;
Thairfoir of mercye, and not of rycht,
I ask you, sir, no man to greiff,

Sum medecyne gif that ye mycht :
Exces of thocht dois me mischeif.   55

Nane can remeid my maledie
Sa weill as ye, sir, veralie ;
With ane benefice ye may preiff,
And gif I mend not haistalie,
Exces of thocht lat me mischeif.   60

I wes in youthe, on nureice kne,
Cald dandillie, bischop, dandillie,
And quhone that age now dois me greif,
A sempill vicar I can not be :
Exces of thocht dois me mischeif.   65

Jok, that wes wont to keip the stirkis,
Can now draw him ane cleik of kirkis,
With ane fals cairt in to his sleif,
Worthe all my ballattis under the byrkis :
Exces of thocht dois me mischeif.   70

Twa curis or thre hes uplandis Michell,
With dispensationis in ane knitchell,
Thocht he fra nolt had new tane leif ;
He playis with *totum* and I with *nychell* :
Exces of thocht dois me mischeif.   75

How suld I leif and I not landit,
Nor yit withe benefice am blandit ?
I say not, sir, yow to repreiff,
Bot doutles I go rycht neir hand it :
Exces of thocht dois me mischeif.   80

As saule in to purgatorie,
Leifand in pane with hoip of glorie,
So is my selffe ye may beleiff
In hoip, sir, of your adjutoric :
Exces of thocht dois me mischeif.   85

21. NONE MAY ASSURE IN THIS WARLD

QUHOM TO sall I compleine my wo,
And kythe my cairis ane or mo ?
I knaw not, amang riche or pure,
Quha is my freind, quha is my fo ;
For in this warld may non assure.   5

Lord, how sall I my dayis dispone ?
For lang service rewarde is none,
And schort my lyfe may heir indure,
And losit is my tyme bygone :
In to this warld may none assure.   10

Oft falsatt rydis with a rowtt,
Quhone treuthe gois on his fute about,
And laik of spending dois him spure ;
Thus quhat to do I am in doutt :
In to this warld may none assure.   15

Nane heir bot rich men hes renown,
And pure men ar plukit doun,
And nane bot just men tholis injure ;
Swa wit is blyndit and ressoun ;
For in this warld may none assure.   20

Vertew the court hes done dispys ;
Ane rebald to renoun dois rys,
And carlis of nobillis hes the cure,
And bumbardis brukis benefys ;
So in this warld may none assure.   25

All gentrice and nobilite
Ar passit out of hie degre ;
On fredome is led foirfalture ;
In princis is thair no petie ;
So in this warld may none assure.   30

Is non so armit in to plait
That can fra trouble him debait ;
May no man lang in welthe indure,
For wo that lyis ever at the wait ;
So in this warld may none assure.   35

Flattrie weiris ane furrit goun,
And falsate with the lordis dois roun,
And trewthe standis barrit at the dure,
Exylit is honour of the toun ;
So in this warld may none assure.   40

Fra everie mouthe fair wordis procedis ;
In everie harte deceptioun bredis ;
Fra everie E gois lukis demure,
Bot fra the handis gois few gud deidis ;
Sa in this warld may none assure.   45

Towngis now are maid of quhite quhale bone,
And hartis ar maid of hard flynt stone,
And eyn ar maid of blew asure,
And handis of adamant laithe to dispone ;
So in this warld may none assure.   50

Yit hart and handis and body all
Mon anser dethe, quhone he dois call
To compt befoir the juge future :
Sen al ar deid or de sall,
Quha sould in to this warld assure ?   55

No thing bot deithe this schortlie cravis,
Quhair fortoun ever, as fo, dissavis
Withe freyndlie smylingis lyk ane hure,
Quhais fals behechtis as wind hyne wavis ;
So in this warld may none assure.   60

O ! quho sall weild the wrang possessioun,
Or gadderit gold with oppressioun,
Quhone the angell blawis his bugill sture,
Quhilk onrestorit helpis no confessioun ?
Into this warld may none assure.   65

Quhat help is thair in lordschips sevin,
Quhone na hous is bot hell and hevin,
Palice of lycht, or pit obscure,
Quhair yowlis ar with horrible stevin ?
In to this warld may none assure.   70

Vbi ardentes anime,
Semper dicentes sunt Ve! Ve!
Sall cry Allace! that women thame bure,
O quante sunt iste tenebre!
In to this warld may none assure.   75

Than quho sall wirk for warldis wrak,
Quhone flude and fyre sall our it frak,
And frelie frustir feild and fure,
With tempest keyne and thundir crak?
In to this warld may none assure.   80

Lord! sen in tyme sa sone to cum
De terra surrecturus sum,
Rewarde me with na erthlie cure,
Bot me ressave *in regnum tuum.*
Sen in this warld may non assure.   85

22. THE PETITION OF THE GRAY HORSE, AULD DUNBAR

Now LUFFERIS cummis with larges lowd,
Quhy sould not palfrayis thane be prowd,
Quhen gillettis wil be schomd and schroud,
That ridden ar baith with lord and lawd?
 Schir, lat it nevir in toun be tald,   5
 That I suld be ane Youllis yald!

Quhen I was young and into ply,
And wald cast gammaldis to the sky,
I had beine bocht in realmes by,
Had I consentit to be sauld.   10
 Schir, lett it nevir in toun be tauld,
 That I suld be ane Youllis yald!

With gentill hors quhen I wald knyp,
Thane is thair laid on me ane quhip,
To colleveris than man I skip,   15
That scabbit ar, hes cruik and cald.
 Schir, lett it nevir in toun be tald,
 That I suld be ane Youllis yald!

Thocht in the stall I be not clappit,
As cursouris that in silk beine trappit,   20
With ane new hous I wald be happit,
Aganis this Crysthinmes for the cald.
   Schir, lett it nevir in toun be tald,
   That I suld be ane Yuillis yald !

Suppois I war ane ald yaid aver,   25
Schott furth our clewch to squische the clever,
And hed the strenthis off all Strenever,
I wald at Youll be housit and stald,
   Schir, lat it never in toune be tald,
   That I suld be ane Yuillis yald !   30

I am ane auld hors, as ye knaw,
That ever in duill dois drug and draw ;
Great court hors puttis me fra the staw,
To fang the fog be firthe and fald.
   Schir, lat it never in toune be tald,   35
   That I suld be ane Yuillis yald !

I heff run lang furth in the feild
On pastouris that ar plane and peld ;
I mycht be now tein in for eild,
My bekis ar spruning he and bald.   40
   Schir, lat it never in toun be tald,
   That I suld be ane Yuillis yald !

My maine is turned in to quhyt,
And thair off ye heff all the wyt !
Quhen uthair hors hed brane to byt   45
I gat bot gris, grype giff I wald.
   Schir, lat it never in towne be tald,
   That I suld be ane Yuillis yald !

I was never dautit in to stabell,
My lyff hes bein so miserabell,   50
My hyd to offer I am abell,
For evill schoud strae that I reiv wald.
   Schir, lat it never in towne be tald,
   That I suld be ane Yuillis yald !

And yett, suppois my thrift be thyne,   55
Gif that I die your aucht within,
Lat nevir the soutteris have my skin,
With uglie gumes to be gnawin.
 Schir, lat it nevir in toun be tald,
 That I suld be ane Yuillis yald !   60

The court hes done my curage cuill,
And maid me ane forriddin muill ;
Yett, to weir trapperis at the Yuill,
I wald be spurrit at everie spald.
 Schir, lat it nevir in toun be tald,   65
 That I suld be ane Yuillis yald !

Respontio Regis

Efter our wrettingis, thesaurer,
Tak in this gray hors, Auld Dumbar,
Quhilk in my aucht with service trew
In lyart changeit is in hew.   70
Gar hows him now aganis this Yuill,
And busk him lyk ane bischopis muill,
For with my hand I have indost
To pay quhatevir his trappouris cost.

23. OF FOLKIS EVILL TO PLEIS

Four MANER of folkis ar evill to pleis ;
Ane is that riches hes and eis,
Gold, silver, cattell, cornis, and ky,
And wald have part fra utheris by.

Ane uther is of land and rent   5
So great ane Lord and ane potent,
That may nother rewll nor gy,
Yet he wald have fra utheris by.

Ane is that hes of nobill bluid
Ane nobill lady fair and guid,   10
Boith verteous, wyse, and womanly,
And yett wald have ane uther by.

Ane uther dois so dourlie drink,
And aill and wyne within him sink,
Quhill in his wame no roume be dry,   15
Bot he wald have fra utheris by.

In earth no wicht I can perseav
Of guid so great aboundance have,
Nor in this world so welthfull wy
Bot he wald have frome utheris by.   20

Bot yitt of all this gold and guid,
Or uthir cunyie to concluid,
Quha evir it have, it is not I,
It goes frome me to utheris by.

And nemlie at this Chrystis mes   25
Quharevir Schir Gold made his regres,
Of him I will no larges cry,
He yeid fra me till utheris by.

24. WELCOME TO THE LORD TREASURER

I THOCHT lang quhill sum lord come hame,
Fra quhom faine kyndnes I wald clame ;
His name of confort I will declair,
    Welcom, my awin Lord Thesaurair !

Befoir all raik of this regioun,   5
Under our roy of most renoun,
Of all my mycht, thocht it war mair,
    Welcom, my awin Lord Thesaurair.

Your nobill payment I did assay,
And ye hecht sone without delay,   10
Againe in Edinburgh till repair ;
    Welcom, my awin Lord Thesaurair !

Ye keipit tryst so winder weill,
I hald yow trew as ony steill ;
Neidis nane your payment till dispair ;   15
    Welcom, my awin Lord Thesaurair !

Yett in a pairt I was agast,
Or ye the narrest way had past,
Fra toun of Stirling to the air :
    Welcom, my awin Lord Thesaurair !   20

Thane had my dyt beine all in duill,
Had I my wage wantit quhill Yuill,
Quhair now I sing with heart onsair,
    Welcum, my awin Lord Thesaurair !

Welcum, my benefice, and my rent,   25
And all the lyflett to me lent ;
Welcum, my pensioun most preclair ;
    Welcum, my awin Lord Thesaurair !

Welcum, als heartlie as I can,
My awin dear maister, to your man,   30
And to your servand singulair,
    Welcum, my awin Lord Thesaurair !

25. TO THE LORDIS OF THE KINGIS CHALKER

My Lordis of Chalker, pleis yow to heir
My coumpt, I sall it mak yow cleir,
    But ony circumstance or sonyie ;
    For left is nether corce nor cunyie
Off all that I tuik in the yeir.   5

For rekkyning of my rentis and roumes,
Ye neid nocht for to tyre your thowmes ;
    Na for to gar your countaris clink,
    Nor paper for to spend nor ink,
In the ressaveing of my soumes.   10

I tuik fra my Lord Thesaurair
Ane soume of money for to wair :
    I cannot tell yow how it is spendit,
    Bot weill I waitt that it is endit ;
And that me think ane coumpt our sair !   15

I trowit the tyme quhen that I tuik it,
That lang in burgh I sould have bruikit,
   Now the remanes are eith to turs ;
  I have na preiff heir bot my purs,
Quhilk wald nocht lie and it war luikit.   20

26. A NEW YEAR'S GIFT TO THE KING

My PRINCE, in God gif the guid grace,
Joy, glaidnes, confort, and solace,
Play, pleasance, myrth, and mirrie cheir,
   In hansill of this guid new yeir.

God gif to the ane blissed chance,   5
And of all vertew aboundance,
And grace ay for to perseveir,
   In hansill of this guid new yeir.

God give the guid prosperitie,
Fair fortoun and felicitie,   10
Evir mair in earth quhill thow ar heir,
   In hansell of this guid new yeir.

The heavinlie Lord his help the send,
Thy realme to reull and to defend,
In peace and justice it to steir,   15
   In hansell of this guid new yeir.

God gif the blis quharevir thow bownes,
And send the many Fraunce crownes,
Hie liberall heart and handis not sweir,
   In hansell of this guid new yeir.   20

27. THE WOWING OF THE KING QUHEN HE WES IN DUMFERMELING

This HINDIR nycht in Dumfermeling,
To me wes tawld ane windir thing ;
That lait ane tod wes with ane lame,

And with hir playit, and maid gud game,
Syne till his breist did hir imbrace,   5
And wald haif riddin hir lyk ane rame :
And that me thocht ane ferly cace.

He braisit hir bony body sweit,
And halsit hir with fordir feit ;
Syne schuk his taill, with quhinge and yelp,   10
And todlit with hir lyk ane quhelp ;
Syne lowrit on growfe and askit grace ;
And ay the lame cryd, " Lady, help ! "
And that me thocht ane ferly cace.

The tod wes nowder lene nor skowry,   15
He wes ane lusty reid haird lowry,
Ane lang taild beist and grit with all ;
The silly lame wes all to small
To sic ane tribbill to hald ane bace :
Scho fled him nocht ; fair mot hir fall !   20
And that me thocht ane ferly cace.

The tod wes reid, the lame wes quhyte,
Scho wes ane morsall of delyte ;
He lovit na yowis auld, tuch, and sklender :
Becaus this lame wes yung and tender,   25
He ran upoun hir with a race,
And scho schup nevir for till defend hir :
And this me thocht ane ferly cace.

He grippit hir abowt the west,
And handlit hir as he had hest ;   30
This innocent, that nevir trespast,
Tuke hert that scho wes handlit fast,
And lute him kis hir lusty face ;
His girnand gamis hir nocht agast :
And that me thocht ane ferly cace.   35

He held hir till him be the hals,
And spak full fair, thocht he wes fals ;
Syne said and swoir to hir be God,
That he suld nocht tuich hir prenecod ;
The silly thing trowd him, allace !   40
The lame gaif creddence to the tod :
And that me thocht ane ferly cace.

I will no lesingis put in vers,
Lyk as thir jangleris dois rehers,
Bot be quhat maner thay war mard,   45
Quhen licht wes owt and durris wes bard ;
I wait nocht gif he gaif hir grace,
Bot all the hollis wes stoppit hard :
And that me thocht ane ferly cace.

Quhen men dois fleit in joy maist far,   50
Sone cumis wo, or thay be war ;
Quhen carpand wer thir two most crows,
The wolf he ombesett the hous,
Upoun the tod to mak ane chace ;
The lamb than cheipit lyk a mows :   55
And that me thocht ane ferly cace.

Throw hiddowis yowling of the wowf,
This wylie tod plat doun on growf,
And in the silly lambis skin,
He crap als far as he micht win,   60
And hid him thair ane weill lang space ;
The yowis besyd thay maid na din :
And that me thocht ane ferly cace.

Quhen of the tod wes hard no peip,
The wowf went all had bene on sleip ;   65
And, quhill the bell had strikkin ten,
The wowf hes drest him to his den,
Protestand for the secound place :
And this report I with my pen,
How at Dumfermling fell the cace.   70

28. IN SECREIT PLACE THIS HYNDIR NYCHT

In secreit place this hyndir nycht,
I hard ane beyrne say till ane bricht,
" My huny, my hart, my hoip, my heill,
I have bene lang your luifar leill,
And can of yow get confort nane ;   5
How lang will ye with danger deill ?
Ye brek my hart, my bony ane ! "

His bony beird was kemmit and croppit,
Bot all with cale it was bedroppit,
And he wes townysche, peirt, and gukit;   10
He clappit fast, he kist, and chukkit,
As with the glaikis he wer ouirgane;
Yit be his feirris he wald have fukkit;
Ye brek my hart, my bony ane!

Quod he, " My hairt, sweit as the hunye,   15
Sen that I borne wes of my mynnye,
I nevir wowit weycht bot yow;
My wambe is of your lufe sa fow,
That as ane gaist I glour and grane,
I trymble sa, ye will not trow;   20
Ye brek my hart, my bony ane!"

" Tehe!" quod scho, and gaif ane gawfe,
" Be still my tuchan and my calfe,
My new spanit howffing fra the sowk,
And all the blythnes of my bowk;   25
My sweit swanking, saif yow allane
Na leyd I luiffit all this owk;
Fow leis me that graceles gane."

Quod he, " My claver, and my curldodie,
My huny soppis, my sweit possodie,   30
Be not oure bosteous to your billie,
Be warme hairtit and not ewill willie;
Your heylis, quhyt as quhalis bane,
Garris ryis on loft my quhillelillie;
Ye brek my hart, my bony ane!"   35

Quod scho, " My clype, my unspaynit gyane,
With moderis mylk yit in your mychane,
My belly huddrun, my swete hurle bawsy,
My huny gukkis, my slawsy gawsy,
Your musing waild perse ane harte of stane,   40
Tak gud confort, my grit heidit slawsy,
Fow leis me that graceles gane."

Quod he, " My kyd, my capirculyoun,
My bony baib with the ruch brylyoun,
My tendir gyrle, my wallie gowdye,   45

My tyrlie myrlie, my crowdie mowdie ;
Quhone that oure mouthis dois meit at ane,
My stang dois storkyn with your towdie ;
Ye brek my hairt, my bony ane ! "

Quod scho, " Now tak me be the hand,   50
Welcum ! my golk of Marie land,
My chirrie and my maikles munyoun,
My sowklar sweit as ony unyoun,
My strumill stirk, yit new to spane,
I am applyit to your opunyoun ;   55
I luif rycht weill your graceles gane."

He gaiff to hir ane apill rubye ;
Quod scho, " Gramercye ! my sweit cowhubye."
And thai twa to ane play began,
Quhilk men dois call the dery dan ;   60
Quhill that thair myrthis met baythe in ane.
" Wo is me ! " quod scho, " quhair will ye, man ?
Bot now I luif that graceles gane."

29. AGANIS THE SOLISTARIS IN COURT

Be divers wyis and operatiounes
Men makis in court thair solistationes :
Sum be service and diligence,
Sum be continuall residence ;
Sum one his substance dois abyd,   5
Quhill fortoune do for him provyd ;
Sum singis, sum dances, sum tellis storyis,
Sum lait at evin bringis in the moryis ;
Sum flirdis, sum fenyeis, and sum flatteris,
Sum playis the fule and all owt clatteris ;   10
Sum man, musand be the waw,
Luikis as he mycht nocht do with aw ;
Sum standis in a nuk and rownes,
For covetyce ane uthair neir swownes ;
Sum beris as he wald ga wud   15
For hait desyr off warldis gud ;
Sum at the mes leves all devocion,

And besy labouris for premocione ;
Sum hes thair advocattis in chalmir,
And takis thame selff thairoff no glawmir.   20
   My sempillnes amang the laiff
Wait off na way, sa God me saiff !
Bot, with ane humill cheir and face,
Refferis me to the Kyngis grace :
Me think his graciows countenance   25
In ryches is my sufficiance.

30. THE DREGY OF DUNBAR

We that ar heir in hevins glory,
To yow that ar in purgatory,
Commendis us on our hairtly wyis ;
I mene we folk in parradyis,
In Edinburch with all mirrines,   5
To yow of Strivilling in distres,
Quhair nowdir plesance nor delyt is,
For pety this epistell wrytis.
O ! ye heremeitis and hankersaidilis,
That takis your pennance at your tablis,   10
And eitis nocht meit restorative,
Nor drynkis no wyn confortative,
Nor aill bot that is thyn and small,
With few coursis into your hall,
But cumpany of lordis and knychtis,   15
Or ony uder gudly wichtis,
Solitar walkand your allone,
Seing no thing bot stok and stone ;
Out of your panefull purgatory,
To bring yow to the blis and glory   20
Off Edinburgh, the mirry toun,
We sall begyn ane cairfull soun,
Ane dergy devoit and meik,
The Lord of blis doing beseik
Yow to delyver out of your noy,   25
And bring yow sone to Edinburgh joy,
For to be mirry amang us ;
And sa the dergy begynis thus.

Lectio prima.

The Fader, the Sone, and Haly Gaist,
The mirthfull Mary virgene chaist,   30
Of angellis all the ordouris nyne,
And all the hevinly court devyne,
Sone bring yow fra the pyne and wo
Of Strivilling, every court manis fo,
Agane to Edinburghis joy and blis,   35
Quhair wirschep, welth, and weilfar is,
Pley, plesance, and eik honesty :
Say ye amen for cheritie.

Responsio, Tu autem Domine.

Tak consolatioun In your pane,
In tribulatioun Tak consolatioun,   40
Out of vexatioun Cum hame agane,
Tak consolatioun In your pane.

Jube Domine benedicere.

Oute of distres of Strivilling toun
To Edinburch blis, God mak yow boun.

Lectio secunda.

Patriarchis, profeitis, and appostillis deir,   45
Confessouris, virgynis, and marteris cleir,
And all the saitt celestiall,
Devotely we upoun thame call,
That sone out of your panis fell,
Ye may in hevin heir with us dwell,   50
To eit swan, cran, pertrik, and plever,
And every fische that swymis in rever ;
To drynk with us the new fresche wyne,
That grew upoun the rever of Ryne,
Fresche fragrant clairettis out of France,   55
Of Angers and of Orliance,
With mony ane cours of grit dyntie :
Say ye amen for cheritie.

Responsorium, Tu autem Domine.

God and Sanct Jeill Heir yow convoy
Baith sone and weill, God and Sanct Jeill   60

To sonce and seill, Solace and joy,
God and Sanct Geill Heir yow convoy.

Jube Domine benedicere.

Out of Strivilling panis fell,
In Edinburch ioy sone mot ye dwell.

Lectio tertia

We pray to all the Sanctis of hevin,   65
That ar aboif the sterris sevin,
Yow to deliver out of your pennance,
That ye may sone play, sing, and dance
Heir in to Edinburch and mak gude cheir,
Quhair welth and weilfair is but weir ;   70
And I that dois your panis discryve
Thinkis for to vissy yow belyve ;
Nocht in desert with yow to dwell,
Bot as the angell Sanct Gabriell
Dois go betwene fra hevinis glory   75
To thame that ar in purgatory,
And in thair tribulatioun
To gif thame consolatioun,
And schaw thame quhen thair panis ar past
They sall till hevin cum at last ;   80
And how nane servis to haif sweitnes
That nevir taistit bittirnes,
And thairfoir how suld ye considdir
Of Edinburch bliss, quhen ye cum hiddir,
Bot gif ye taistit had befoir   85
Of Strivilling toun the panis soir ;
And thairfoir tak in patience
Your pennance and your abstinence,
And ye sall cum, or Yule begyn,
Into the bliss that we ar in ;   90
Quhilk grant the glorius Trinitie !
Say ye amen for cheritie.

Responsorium.

Cum hame and dwell No moir in Strivilling ;
Frome hiddous hell Cum hame and dwell,
Quhair fische to sell Is non bot spirling ;   95
Cum hame and dwell No moir in Strivilling.

Et ne nos inducas in temptationem de Strivilling :
Sed libera nos a malo illius.
Requiem Edinburgi dona eiis, Domine,
Et lux ipsius luceat eiis.   100
A porta tristitie de Strivilling,
Erue, Domine, animas et corpora eorum.
Credo gustare statim vinum Edinburgi,
In villa viventium.
Requiescant Edinburgi.   Amen.   105

Deus qui iustos et corde humiles
Ex omni eorum tribulatione liberare dignatus es,
Libera famulos tuos apud villam de Stirling versantes
A penis et tristitiis eiusdem,
Et ad Edinburgi gaudia eos perducas,   110
Ut requiescat Strivilling.   Amen.

31. TO THE QUENE

MADAM, YOUR men said thai wald ryd
And latt this Fasterrennis evin ower slyd ;
   Bott than thair wyffis cam furth in flockis,
And baid tham betteis som abyd
   Att haem and lib tham of the pockis.   5

Nou propois thai, sen ye dwell still,
Off Venus feest to fang ane fill,
   Bott in the felde preiff thai na cockis ;
For till heff riddin had bein les ill
   Nor latt thair wyffis breid the pockis.   10

Sum of your men sic curage hed,
Dame Venus fyre sa hard tham sted,
   Thai brak up durris and raeff up lockis,
To get ane pamphelet on a pled
   That thai mycht lib thame of the pockis.   15

Sum, that war ryatous as rammis,
Ar nou maid tame lyk ony lammis,
   And settin down lyk sarye crockis,
And hes forsaekin all sic gammis,
   That men callis libbin of the pockis.   20

Sum thocht tham selffis stark, lyk gyandis,
Ar nou maid waek lyk willing wandis,
    With schinnis scharp and small lyk rockis ;
And gottin thair bak in bayth thair handis,
    For ower offt libbin of the pockis.   25

I saw coclinkis me besyd
The young men to thair howses gyd,
    Had bettir ligget in the stockis ;
Sum fra the bordell wald nocht byd,
    Quhill that thai gatt the Spanyie pockis.   30

Thairfor, all young men, I you pray,
Keip you fra harlottis nycht and day ;
    Thay sall repent quhai with tham yockis ;
And be war with that perrellous play,
    That men callis libbin of the pockis.   35

32. OF A DANCE IN THE QUENIS CHALMER

Sir Jhon Sinclair begowthe to dance,
For he was new cum owt of France ;
For ony thing that he do mycht,
The ane futt yeid ay onrycht,
    And to the tother wald not gree.   5
Quod ane, " Tak up the Quenis knycht : "
    A mirrear dance mycht na man see.

Than cam in Maistir Robert Scha :
He leuket as he culd lern tham a ;
Bot ay his ane futt did waver,   10
He stackeret lyk ane strummall aver,
    That hopschackellt war aboin the kne :
To seik fra Sterling to Stranaver,
    A mirrear daunce mycht na man see.

Than cam in the Maister Almaser,   15
Ane hommiltye jommeltye juffler,
Lyk a stirk stackarand in the ry ;
His hippis gaff mony hoddous cry.
    John Bute the Fule said, " Waes me !
He is bedirtin,—Fye ! fy ! "   20
    A mirrear dance mycht na man se.

Than cam in Dunbar the Mackar ;
On all the flure thair was nane frackar,
And thair he dancet the dirrye dantoun ;
He hoppet lyk a pillie wanton,   25
    For luff of Musgraeffe, men tellis me ;
He trippet, quhill he tint his panton :
    A mirrear dance mycht na man se.

Than cam in Maesteres Musgraeffe ;
Scho mycht heff lernit all the laeffe ;   30
Quhen I schau hir sa trimlye dance,
Hir guid convoy and contenance,
    Than, for hir saek, I wissitt to be
The grytast erle or duk in France :
    A mirrear dance mycht na man see.   35

Than cam in Dame Dounteboir ;
God waett gif that schou louket sowr !
Schou maid sic morgeownis with hir hippis,
For lachtter nain mycht hald thair lippis ;
    Quhen schou was danceand bisselye,   40
Ane blast of wind son fra hir slippis :
    A mirrear dance mycht na man see.

Quhen thair was cum in fyve or sax,
The Quenis Dog begowthe to rax,
And of his band he maid a bred,   45
And to the danceing soin he him med ;
    Quhou mastevlyk about yeid he !
He stinckett lyk a tyk, sum saed :
    A mirrear dance mycht na man se.

33. OF JAMES DOG, KEPAR OF THE QUENIS WARDROP

To the Quene

THE WARDRAIPPER of Venus boure,
To giff a doublett he is als doure,
As it war off ane futt syd frog :
    Madame, ye heff a dangerous Dog !

Quhen that I schawe to him your markis,   5
He turnis to me again and barkis,
As he war wirriand ane hog :
    Madame, ye heff a dangerous Dog !

Quhen that I schawe to him your wrytin,
He girnis that I am red for bytin ;   10
I wald he had ane havye clog :
    Madame, ye heff ane dangerous Dog !

Quhen that I speik till him freindlyk,
He barkis lyk ane midding tyk,
War chassand cattell throu a bog :   15
    Madam, ye heff a dangerous Dog !

He is ane mastive, mekle of mycht,
To keip your wardroippe ouer nycht
Fra the grytt Sowdan Gog-ma-gog :
    Madam, ye heff a dangerous Dog !   20

He is owre mekle to be your messan,
Madame, I red you get a less ane,
His gang garris all your chalmeris schog :
    Madam, ye heff a dangerous Dog !

34. OF THE SAME JAMES, QUHEN HE HAD PLESETT HIM

O GRACIOUS Princes, guid and fair,
Do weill to James your Wardraipair ;
Quhais faythfull bruder maist freind I am :
    He is na Dog ; he is a Lam.

Thocht I in ballet did with him bourde,   5
In malice spack I nevir ane woord,
Bot all, my Dame, to do your gam :
    He is na Dog ; he is a Lam.

Your Hienes can nocht gett ane meter
To keip your wardrope, nor discreter   10

To rewle your robbis and dres the sam :
  He is na Dog ; he is a Lam.

The wyff that he had in his innis,
That with the taingis wald braek his schinnis,
I wald schou drownet war in a dam :   15
  He is na Dog ; he is a Lam.

The wyff that wald him kuckald mak,
I wald schou war, bayth syd and back,
Weill hatteret with ane barrou tram :
  He is na Dog ; he is ane Lam.   20

He hes sa weill doin me obey
In till all thing, thairfoir I pray
That nevir dolour mak him dram :
  He is na Dog ; he is a Lam.

35. OF SIR THOMAS NORNY

Now LYTHIS off ane gentill knycht,
Schir Thomas Norny, wys and wycht,
  And full off chevelry ;
Quhais father was ane giand keyne,
His mother was ane Farie Queyne,   5
  Gottin be sossery.

Ane fairar knycht nor he was ane,
On ground may nothair ryd nor gane,
  Na beire buklar nor brand ;
Or com in this court but dreid ;   10
He did full mony valyeant deid
  In Rois and Murray land.

Full many catherein hes he chaist,
And cummerid mony Helland gaist,
  Amang thay dully glennis :   15
Off the Clen Quhettane twenti scoir
He drave as oxin him befoir ;
  This deid thocht na man kennis.

At feastis and brydallis upaland
He wan the gre and the garland ;   20
  Dansit non so on deis :
He hes att werslingis bein ane hunder,
Yet lay his body never at under :
  He knawis giff this be leis.

Was never wyld Robein under bewch,   25
Nor yet Roger off Clekniskleuch,
  So bauld a berne as he ;
Gy off Gysburne, na Allan Bell,
Na Simonis sonnes off Quhynfell,
  At schot war never so slie.   30

This anterous knycht, quhar ever he went,
At justing and at tornament,
  Evermor he wan the gre ;
Was never off halff so gryt renowne
Sir Bevis the knycht off Southe Hamptowne :   35
  I schrew him giff I le.

Thairfoir Quenetyne was bot a lurdane,
That callit him ane full plum Jurdane,
  This wyse and worthie knycht ;
He callit him fowlar than a full,   40
He said he was ane licherus bull,
  That croynd baith day and nycht.

He wald heff maid him Curris kneff ;
I pray God better his honour saiff,
  Na to be lychtleit sua !   45
Yet this far furth I dar him prais,
He fyld never sadell in his dais,
  And Curry befyld tua.

Quhairfoir, ever at Pesche and Yull,
I cry him Lord of evere full,   50
  That in this regeone duellis ;
And, verralie, that war gryt rycht :
For, off ane hy renowned knycht,
  He wanttis no thing bot bellis.

36. EPETAPHE FOR DONALD OWRE

In vice most vicius he excellis,
That with the vice of tressone mellis ;
   Thocht he remissioun
   Haif for prodissioun,
   Schame and susspissioun   5
     Ay with him dwellis.

And he evir odious as ane owle,
The falt sa filthy is and fowle ;
   Horrible to natour
   Is ane tratour,   10
   As feind in fratour
     Undir a cowle.

Quha is a tratour or ane theif,
Upoun him selff turnis the mischeif ;
   His frawdfull wylis   15
   Him self begylis,
   As in the ilis
     Is now a preiff.

The fell strong tratour, Donald Owyr,
Mair falsett had nor udir fowyr   20
   Round ylis and seyis ;
   In his suppleis,
   On gallow treis
     Yitt dois he glowir.

Falsett no feit hes, nor deffence,   25
Be power, practik, nor puscence ;
   Thocht it fra licht
   Be smord with slicht,
   God schawis the richt
     With soir vengence.   30

Off the fals fox dissimulatour,
Kynd hes every theiff and tratour ;
   Eftir respyt
   To wirk dispyt
   Moir appetyt   35
     He hes of natour.

War the fox tane a thousand fawd,
And grace him gevin als oft for frawd,
   War he on plane
   All war in vane,   40
Frome hennis agane
   Micht non him hawd.

The murtherer ay murthour mais,
And evir quhill he be slane he slais;
   Wyvis thus makis mokkis   45
   Spynnand on rokkis;
   " Ay rynnis the fox
     Quhill he fute hais."

37. OF ANE BLAK-MOIR

Lang heff I maed of ladyes quhytt,
Nou of ane blak I will indytt,
   That landet furth of the last schippis;
Quhou fain wald I descryve perfytt,
   My ladye with the mekle lippis.   5

Quhou schou is tute mowitt lyk ane aep,
And lyk a gangarall onto gaep;
   And quhou hir schort catt nois up skippis;
And quhou scho schynes lyk ony saep;
   My ladye with the mekle lippis.   10

Quhen schou is claid in reche apparrall,
Schou blinkis als brycht as ane tar barrell;
   Quhen schou was born, the son tholit clippis,
The nycht be fain faucht in hir querrell:
   My ladye with the mekle lippis.   15

Quhai for hir saek, with speir and scheld,
Preiffis maest mychttelye in the feld,
   Sall kis and withe hir go in grippis;
And fra thyne furth hir luff sall weld:
   My ladye with the mekle lippis.   20

And quhai in felde receaves schaem,
And tynis thair his knychtlie naem,
  Sall cum behind and kis hir hippis,
And nevir to uther confort claem :
  My ladye with the mekle lippis.   25

38. THE FENYEIT FREIR OF TUNGLAND

As YUNG Awrora, with cristall haile,
In orient schew hir visage paile,
A swevyng swyth did me assaile,
  Off sonis of Sathanis seid ;
Me thocht a Turk of Tartary   5
Come throw the boundis of Barbary,
And lay forloppin in Lumbardy
  Full lang in waithman weid.
Fra baptasing for to eschew,
Thair a religious man he slew,   10
And cled him in his abeit new,
  For he cowth wryte and reid.
Quhen kend was his dissimulance,
And all his cursit govirnance,
For feir he fled and come in France,   15
  With littill of Lumbard leid.
To be a leiche he fenyt him thair,
Quhilk mony a man micht rew evirmair,
For he left nowthir seik nor sair
  Unslane, or he hyne yeid.   20
Vane organis he full clenely carvit,
Quhen of his straik so mony starvit,
Dreid he had gottin that he desarvit,
  He fled away gud speid.

In Scotland than the narrest way   25
He come, his cunnyng till assay ;
To sum man thair it was no play
  The preving of his sciens.
In pottingry he wrocht grit pyne,
He murdreist mony in medecyne ;   30
The jow was of a grit engyne,
  And generit was of gyans

In leichecraft he was homecyd;
He wald haif, for a nicht to byd,
A haiknay and the hurt manis hyd,   35
    So meikle he was of myance.
His irnis was rude as ony rawchtir,
Quhair he leit blude it was no lawchtir,
Full mony instrument for slawchtir
    Was in his gardevyance.   40

He cowth gif cure for laxatyve,
To gar a wicht hors want his lyve,
Quha evir assay wald, man or wyve,
    Thair hippis yeid hiddy giddy.
His practikis nevir war put to preif   45
But suddane deid, or grit mischeif;
He had purgatioun to mak a theif
    To dee withowt a widdy.
Unto no mes pressit this prelat,
For sound of sacring bell nor skellat;   50
As blaksmyth bruikit was his pallatt
    For battering at the study.
Thocht he come hame a new maid channoun,
He had dispensit with matynnis cannoun,
On him come nowther stole nor fannoun   55
    For smowking of the smydy.

Me thocht seir fassonis he assailyeit,
To mak the quintessance, and failyeit;
And quhen he saw that nocht availyeit,
    A fedrem on he tuke,   60
And schupe in Turky for to fle;
And quhen that he did mont on he,
All fowill ferleit quhat he sowld be,
    That evir did on him luke.
Sum held he had bene Dedalus,   65
Sum the Menatair marvelus,
Sum Martis blaksmyth Vulcanus,
    And sum Saturnus kuke.
And evir the cuschettis at him tuggit,
The rukis him rent, the ravynis him druggit,   70
The hudit crawis his hair furth ruggit,
    The hevin he micht not bruke.

The myttane, and Sanct Martynis fowle,
Wend he had bene the hornit howle,
Thay set aupone him with a yowle,   75
    And gaif him dynt for dynt.
The golk, the gormaw, and the gled,
Beft him with buffettis quhill he bled ;
The sparhalk to the spring him sped,
    Als fers as fyre of flynt.   80
The tarsall gaif him tug for tug,
A stanchell hang in ilka lug,
The pyot furth his pennis did rug,
    The stork straik ay but stynt.
The bissart, bissy but rebuik,   85
Scho was so cleverus of hir cluik,
His bawis he micht not langer bruik,
    Scho held thame at ane hint.

Thik was the clud of kayis and crawis,
Of marleyonis, mittanis, and of mawis,   90
That bikkrit at his berd with blawis
    In battell him abowt.
Thay nybbillit him with noyis and cry,
The rerd of thame rais to the sky,
And evir he cryit on Fortoun, Fy !   95
    His lyfe was in to dowt.
The ja him skrippit with a skryke,
And skornit him as it was lyk ;
The egill strong at him did stryke,
    And rawcht him mony a rowt.   100
For feir uncunnandly he cawkit,
Quhill all his pennis war drownd and drawkit,
He maid a hundreth nolt all hawkit
    Beneth him with a spowt.

He schewre his feddreme that was schene,   105
And slippit owt of it full clene,
And in a myre, up to the ene,
    Amang the glar did glyd.
The fowlis all at the fedrem dang,
As at a monster thame amang,   110
Quhill all the pennis of it owsprang
    In till the air full wyde.

And he lay at the plunge evirmair,
So lang as any ravin did rair ;
The crawis him socht with cryis of cair   115
    In every schaw besyde.
Had he reveild bene to the ruikis,
Thay had him revin all with thair cluikis :
Thre dayis in dub amang the dukis
    He did with dirt him hyde.   120
The air was dirkit with the fowlis,
That come with yawmeris and with yowlis,
With skryking, skrymming, and with scowlis,
    To tak him in the tyde.
I walknit with the noyis and schowte,   125
So hiddowis beir was me abowte ;
Sensyne I curs that cankerit rowte,
    Quhair evir I go or ryde.

39. THE BIRTH OF ANTICHRIST

Lucina schynnyng in silence of the nicht,
The hevin being all full of sternis bricht,
To bed I went, bot thair I tuke no rest,
With havy thocht I wes so soir opprest,
That sair I langit eftir dayis licht.   5

Off Fortoun I complenit hevely,
That scho to me stude so contrariowsly ;
And at the last, quhen I had turnyt oft,
For weirines on me ane slummer soft
Come with ane dremyng and a fantesy.   10

Me thocht Deme Fortoun with ane fremmit cheir
Stude me beforne and said on this maneir,
Thow suffer me to wirk gif thow do weill,
And preis the nocht to stryfe aganis my quheill,
Quhilk every warldly thing dois turne and steir.   15

Full mony ane man I turne unto the hicht,
And makis als mony full law to doun licht ;
Up on my staigis or that thow ascend,
Trest weill thy truble neir is at ane end,
Seing thir taikinis, quhairfoir thow mark thame rycht.   20

Thy trublit gaist sall neir moir be degest,
Nor thow in to no benifice beis possest,
Quhill that ane abbot him cleith in ernis pennis,
And fle up in the air amangis the crennis,
And as ane falcone fair fro eist to west. 25

He sall ascend as ane horrebble grephoun,
Him meit sall in the air ane scho dragoun ;
Thir terrible monsteris sall togidder thrist,
And in the cludis gett the Antechrist,
Quhill all the air infeck of thair pusoun. 30

Under Saturnus fyrie regioun
Symone Magus sall meit him, and Mahoun,
And Merlyne at the mone sall him be bydand,
And Jonet the weido on ane bussome rydand,
Off wichis with ane windir garesoun. 35

And syne thay sall discend with reik and fyre,
And preiche in erth the Antechrystis impyre,
Be than it salbe neir this warldis end.
With that this lady sone fra me did wend ;
Sleipand and walkand wes frustrat my desyre. 40

Quhen I awoik, my dreme it was so nyce,
Fra every wicht I hid it as a vyce ;
Quhill I hard tell be mony suthfast wy,
Fle wald ane abbot up in to the sky,
And all his fethreme maid wes at devyce. 45

Within my hairt confort I tuke full sone ;
" Adew," quod I, " My drery dayis ar done ;
Full weill I wist to me wald nevir cum thrift,
Quhill that twa monis wer sene up in the lift,
Or quhill ane abbot flew aboif the mone." 50

40. THE TESTAMENT OF MR. ANDRO KENNEDY

I, MAISTER ANDRO KENNEDY,
    Curro quando sum vocatus,
Gottin with sum incuby,
    Or with sum freir infatuatus ;

In faith I can nought tell redly,   5
    Unde aut ubi fui natus,
Bot in treuth I trow trewly,
    Quod sum dyabolus incarnatus.

Cum nichill sit certius morte,
    We mon all de, quhen we haif done,   10
Nescimus quando vel qua sorte,
    Na blind Allane wait of the mone,
Ego pacior in pectore,
    This night I myght nocht sleip a wink ;
Licet eger in corpore,   15
    Yit wald my mouth be wet with drink.

Nunc condo testamentum meum,
    I leiff my saull for evermare,
Per omnipotentem Deum,
    In to my lordis wyne cellar ;   20
Semper ibi ad remanendum,
    Quhill domisday without dissever,
Bonum vinum ad bibendum,
    With sueit Cuthbert that luffit me nevir.

Ipse est dulcis ad amandum,   25
    He wald oft ban me in his breith,
Det michi modo ad potandum,
    And I forgif him laith and wraith :
Quia in cellario cum cervisia,
    I had lever lye baith air and lait,   30
Nudus solus in camesia,
    Na in my Lordis bed of stait.

A barell bung ay at my bosum,
    Of warldis gud I bad na mair ;
Corpus meum ebriosum,   35
    I leif on to the toune of Air ;
In a draf mydding for ever and ay
    Ut ibi sepeliri queam,
Quhar drink and draff may ilka day
    Be cassyne super faciem meam :   40

I leif my hert that never wes sicir,
    Sed semper variabile,

That never mair wald flow nor flicir,
   Consorti meo Iacobe :
Thought I wald bynd it with a wicir,   45
   Verum Deum renui ;
Bot and I hecht to teme a bicker,
   Hoc pactum semper tenui.

Syne leif I the best aucht I bocht,
   Quod est Latinum propter caupe,   50
To hede of kyn, bot I wait nought
   Quis est ille, than I schrew my scawpe :
I callit my Lord my heid, but hiddill,
   Sed nulli alii hoc dixerunt,
We weir als sib as seve and riddill,   55
   In una silva que creverunt.

Omnia mea solacia,
   Thay wer bot lesingis all and ane,
Cum omni fraude et fallacia
   I leif the maistter of Sanct Antane ;   60
Willelmo Gray, sine gratia,
   Myne awne deir cusing, as I wene,
Qui nunquam fabricat mendacia,
   Bot quhen the holyne growis grene.

My fenyening and my fals wynyng   65
   Relinquo falsis fratribus ;
For that is Goddis awne bidding,
   Dispersit, dedit pauperibus.
For menis saulis thay say thai sing,
   Mencientes pro muneribus ;   70
Now God gif thaim ane evill ending,
   Pro suis pravis operibus.

To Iok Fule, my foly fre
   Lego post corpus sepultum ;
In faith I am mair fule than he,   75
   Licet ostendit bonum vultum :
Of corne and catall, gold and fe,
   Ipse habet valde multum,
And yit he bleris my lordis E
   Fingendo eum fore stultum.   80

To Master Johne Clerk syne,
  Do et lego intime,
Goddis malisone and myne;
  Ipse est causa mortis mee.
War I a dog and he a swyne,   85
  Multi mirantur super me,
Bot I suld ger that lurdane quhryne,
  Scribendo dentes sine de.

Residuum omnium bonorum
  For to dispone my Lord sall haif,   90
Cum tutela puerorum,
  Ade, Kytte, and all the laif.
In faith I will na langar raif:
  Pro sepultura ordino
On the new gys, sa God me saif,   95
  Non sicut more solito.

In die mee sepulture
  I will nane haif bot our awne gyng,
Et duos rusticos de rure
  Berand a barell on a styng;   100
Drynkand and playand cop out, evin,
  Sicut egomet solebam;
Singand and gretand with hie stevin,
  Potum meum cum fletu miscebam.

I will na preistis for me sing,   105
  Dies illa, Dies ire;
Na yit na bellis for me ring,
  Sicut semper solet fieri;
Bot a bag pipe to play a spryng,
  Et unum ail wosp ante me;   110
In stayd of baneris for to bring
  Quatuor lagenas cervisie,
Within the graif to set sic thing,
  In modum crucis juxta me,
To fle the fendis, than hardely sing   115
  De terra plasmasti me.

To DWELL in court, my freind, gife that thow list,
For gift of fortoun invy thow no degre ;
Behold and heir, and lat thy tung tak rest,
In mekle speic[h]e is pairt of vanitie ;
And for no malyce preis the nevir to lie ;   5
Als trubill nevir thy self, sone, be no tyd,
Uthiris to rewill, that will not rewlit be :
He rewlis weill, that weill him self can gyd.

Bewar quhome to thy counsale thow discure,
For trewth dwellis nocht ay for that trewth appeiris :   10
Put not thyne honour into aventeure ;
Ane freind may be thy fo as fortoun steiris :
In cumpany cheis honorable feiris,
And fra vyle folkis draw the far on syd ;
The Psalme sayis, *Cum sancto sanctus eiris* :   15
He rewlis weill, that weill him self can gyd.

Haif pacience thocht thow no lordschip posseid,
For hie vertew may stand in law estait ;
Be thow content, of mair thow hes no neid ;
And be thow nocht, desyre sall mak debait   20
Evirmoir, till deth say to the than chakmait :
Thocht all war thyne this warld within so wyd,
Quha can resist the serpent of dispyt ?
He rewlis weill, that weill him self can gyd.

Fle frome the fallowschip of sic as ar defamit,   25
And fra all fals tungis fulfild with flattry,
Als fra all schrewis, or ellis thow art eschamit ;
Sic art thow callit as is thy cumpany :
Fle perrellus taillis foundit of invy ;
With wilfull men, son, argown thow no tyd,   30
Quhome no ressone may seis nor pacify :
He rewlis weill, that weill him self can gyd.

And be thow not ane roundar in the nuke,
For, gif thow be, men will hald the suspect :
Be nocht in countenance ane skornar, nor by luke,   35
Bot dowt siclyk sall stryk the in the neck :

Be war also to counsall or coreck
Him that extold hes far him self in pryd :
Quhair parrell is but proffeit or effect,
He rewlis weill, that weill him self can gyd.   40

And sen thow seyis mony thingis variand,
With all thy hart treit bissines and cure ;
Hald God thy freind, evir stabill be him stand,
He will the confort in all misaventeur ;
And be no wayis dispytfull to the peure,   45
Nor to no man to wrang at ony tyd :
Quho so dois this, sicker I yow asseure,
He rewlis weill, that sa weill him can gyd.

42. THE DEVILLIS INQUEST

This nycht in my sleip I wes agast,
Me thocht the Devill wes tempand fast
The peple with aithis of crewaltie ;
Sayand as throw the mercat he past,
" Renunce thy God and cum to me."   5

Me thocht as he went throw the way,
Ane preist sweirit be God verey,
Quhilk at the alter ressavit he ;
" Thow art my clerk," the Devill can say,
" Renunce thy God and cum to me."   10

Than swoir ane courtyour, mekle of pryd,
Be Chrystis windis bludy and wyd,
And be his harmes wes rent on tre ;
Than spak the Devill hard him besyd,
" Renunce thy God and cum to me."   15

Ane goldsmyth said, " The gold is sa fyne,
That all the workmanschip I tyne,
The Feind ressaif me gif I le ;"
" Think on," quod the Devill, " that thow art myne,
Renunce thy God and cum to me."   20

Dremand me thocht that I did heir
The commowne people bane and sueir,

Blasfemiand Godis majestie ;
The Devill ay rowndand in thair eir,
" Renunce your God, and cum to me."   25

The marchand sweiris mony aithe,
That never man saw better clayth,
Na fynnar silk cum owr the se.
" To sweir," quod Sathan, " be nocht layth,
To sell my geir I will have thee."   30

The tailyour sayis, " In all this toun
Be thair ane better schappin gown,
I gif me to the Feynd all fre ; "
" Grant mercy, talyour," quod Mahowne,
" Renunce your God and cum to me."   35

The sowter sayis, in gud effek
The Devill mot hang him be the nek,
Gif better butis of ledder ma be ;
The Feind sayis, " Fy ! thow saris of blek,
Ga wysche the weill, syne cum to me."   40

The bakstar sayis, " I forsak God,
And all his werkis evin and od,
That better breid did na man se ; "
The Devill said, and on him cowld nod,
" With thy licht levis cum unto me."   45

Ane fleschour swoir be Godis woundis,
Come nevir sic beif into thir bowndis,
Na fattar mottoune can nocht be ;
" Fals," quod the feind, and till him rowndis,
" Renunce thy God and cum to me."   50

" Be Goddis blud," quod the tavernneir,
" Thair is sic wyine in my selleir
Hes never come in this cuntrie."
" Yit," quod the Devill, " thou sellis our deir,
With thy fals met cum downe to me."   55

The maltman sais, " I God forsaik,
And that the Devill of hell me taik
Gif ony bettir malt may be,

And of this kill I haif inlaik ; "
Renunce thy God and cum to me.   60

Ane browstar swoir " The malt wes ill,
Bath reid and reikit on the kill,
That it will be na aill for me,
Ane boll will nocht sex gallonis fill ; "
Renunce thy God and cum to me.   65

The smyth swoir " Be rude and raip,
In till a gallowis mot I gaip,
Gif I ten dayis wan pennyis thre,
For with that craft I can nocht thraip ; "
Renunce thy God and cum to me.   70

The menstrall sayis, " That ever I thryve
Gif I do oucht bot drink and swyve ; "
The Devill sayis, " Than I counsall the,
Excers that craft in all thy lyve ;
Syn cum and play ane spring to me."   75

Ane dysour said with wirdis of stryfe,
The Devill mot stik him with a knyfe,
Bot he kest up fair syisis thre ;
The Devill said, " Endit is thy lyfe,
Renunce thy God and cum to me."   80

The fiche wyfis flet and swoir thair menis
And to the Feind gaif flesche and banis,
Sa did the hukstaris hailellie
The Devil said, " Welcum all at anis,
Renunce your God and cum to me."   85

The rest of craftis grit ethis swair
Thair wark and craft had na compair,
Ilk ane into thar qualitie ;
The Devill said then, withouttin mair,
" Renunce you God and cum to me."   90

[The theif sayis, " That ever I scaip,
Na ane stark widdie gar me gaip,
Bot I in hell for geir wald be ; "
The Devil sayis, " Welcum in a raip,
Renunce your God and cum to me."   95

The cowrt man did grit aithis sweir,
He wald serve Sathan for sevin yeir
For fair claythis and gold plaintie ;
The Devill said, " Thair is sum for geir
Wald renunce God and duell with me."   100

To bane and sweir na staittis stud a,
Man or woman grit or sma,
Ryche and pur nor the clargie ;
The Devill said then, " Of commown la
All mensworne folk man cum to me."]   105

Me thocht the Devillis, als blak as pik,
Solistand wer as beis thik,
Ay tempand folk with wayis sle ;
Rownand to Robene and to Dik,
" Renunce thy God and cum to me."   110

43. TYDINGIS FRA THE SESSIOUN

ANE MURLANDIS man of uplandis mak
At hame thus to his nychtbour spak,
" Quhat tydingis gossep, peax or weir ? "
The tother rownit in his eir,
" I tell yow this undir confessioun,   5
Bot laitly lichtit of my meir
I come of Edinburch fra the Sessioun."

" Quhat tythingis hard ye thair, I pray yow ? "
The tother answerit, " I sall say yow,
Keip this all secreit, gentill brother ;   10
Is na man thair that trestis ane uther :
Ane commoun doar of transgressioun
Of innocent folkis prevenis a futher :
Sic tydingis hard I at the Sessioun."

Sum with his fallow rownis him to pleis,   15
That wald for invy byt of his neis ;
His fa sum by the oxstar leidis ;
Sum patteris with his mowth on beidis,

That hes his mynd all on oppressioun ;
Sum beckis full law and schawis bair heidis,   20
Wald luke full heich war not the Sessioun.

Sum bydand the law layis land in wed ;
Sum super expendit gois to his bed ;
Sum speidis, for he in court hes menis ;
Sum of parcialitie complenis,   25
How feid and favour flemis discretioun ;
Sum speiks full fair, and falsly fenis :
Sic tythingis hard I at the Sessioun.

Sum castis summondis, and sum exceptis ;
Sum standis besyd and skaild law keppis ;   30
Sum is continuit, sum wynnis, sum tynis ;
Sum makis him mirry at the wynis ;
Sum is put owt of his possessioun ;
Sum herreit, and on creddens dynis :
Sic tydingis hard I at the Sessioun.   35

Sum sweiris and forsaikis God ;
Sum in ane lambskin is ane tod ;
Sum in his toung his kyndnes tursis ;
Sum cuttis throttis, and sum pykis pursis ;
Sum gois to gallous with processioun ;   40
Sum sanis the Sait, and sum thame cursis :
Sic tydingis hard I at the Sessioun.

Religious men of divers placis
Cumis thair to wow and se fair facis ;
Baith Carmeleitis and Cordilleris   45
Cumis thair to genner and get ma freiris,
And ar unmyndfull of thair professioun ;
The yungar at the eldar leiris :
Sic tydingis hard I at the Sessioun.

Thair cumis yung monkis of he complexioun,   50
Of devoit mynd, luve, and affectioun,
And in the courte thair hait flesche dantis,
Full faderlyk, with pechis and pantis ;
Thay ar so humill of intercessioun,
All mercyfull wemen thair eirandis grantis :   55
Sic tydingis hard I at the Sessioun.

Quhy will ye, merchantis of renoun,
Lat Edinburgh, your nobill toun,
For laik of reformatioun
The commone proffeitt tyine and fame ?
    Think ye not schame,   5
That onie uther regioun
Sall with dishonour hurt your name !

May nane pas throw your principall gaittis
For stink of haddockis and of scattis,
For cryis of carlingis and debaittis,   10
For fensum flyttingis of defame :
    Think ye not schame,
Befoir strangeris of all estaittis
That sic dishonour hurt your name !

Your stinkand Scull, that standis dirk,   15
Haldis the lycht fra your parroche kirk ;
Your foirstairis makis your housis mirk,
Lyk na cuntray bot heir at hame :
    Think ye not schame,
Sa litill polesie to wirk   20
In hurt and sklander of your name !

At your hie Croce, quhar gold and silk
Sould be, thair is bot crudis and milk ;
And at your Trone bot cokill and wilk,
Pansches, pudingis of Jok and Jame :   25
    Think ye not schame,
Sen as the world sayis that ilk
In hurt and sclander of your name !

Your commone menstrallis hes no tone
Bot " Now the day dawis," and " Into Joun " ;   30
Cunningar men man serve Sanct Cloun,
And nevir to uther craftis clame :
    Think ye not schame,

To hald sic mowaris on the moyne,
In hurt and sclander of your name !   35

Tailyouris, soutteris, and craftis vyll,
The fairest of your streitis dois fyll ;
And merchandis at the Stinkand Styll
Ar hamperit in ane hony came :
   Think ye not schame,   40
That ye have nether witt nor wyll
To win yourselff ane bettir name !

Your burgh of beggeris is ane nest,
To schout thai swentyouris will not rest ;
All honest folk they do molest,   45
Sa piteuslie thai cry and rame :
   Think ye not schame,
That for the poore hes nothing drest,
In hurt and sclander of your name !

Your proffeit daylie dois incres,   50
Your godlie workis les and les ;
Through streittis nane may mak progres
For cry of cruikit, blind, and lame :
   Think ye not schame,
That ye sic substance dois posses,   55
And will nocht win ane bettir name !

Sen for the Court and the Sessioun,
The great repair of this regioun
Is in your burgh, thairfoir be boun
To mend all faultis that ar to blame,   60
   And eschew schame ;
Gif thai pas to ane uther toun
Ye will decay, and your great name !

Thairfoir strangeris and leigis treit,
Tak not ouer meikle for thair meit,   65
And gar your merchandis be discreit,
That na extortiounes be proclame
   All fraud and schame :
Keip ordour, and poore nighbouris beit,
That ye may gett ane bettir name !   70

Singular proffeit so dois yow blind,
The common proffeit gois behind :
I pray that Lord remeid to fynd,
That deit into Jerusalem,
   And gar yow schame !   75
That sum tyme ressoun may yow bind,
For to [   ] yow guid name.

45. IN PRAIS OF WEMEN

Now of wemen this I say for me,
Off erthly thingis nane may bettir be ;
Thay suld haif wirschep and grit honoring
Off men, aboif all uthir erthly thing ;
Rycht grit dishonour upoun him self he takkis   5
In word or deid quha evir wemen lakkis ;
Sen that of wemen cumin all ar we,
Wemen ar wemen and sa will end and de.
Wo wirth the fruct wald put the tre to nocht,
And wo wirth him rycht so that sayis ocht   10
Off womanheid that may be ony lak,
Or sic grit schame upone him for to tak.
Thay us consaif with pane, and be thame fed
Within thair breistis thair we be boun to bed ;
Grit pane and wo, and murnyng mervellus,   15
Into thair birth thay suffir sair for us ;
Than meit and drynk to feid us get we nane,
Bot that we sowk out of thair breistis bane.
Thay ar the confort that we all haif heir,
Thair may no man be till us half so deir ;   20
Thay ar our verry nest of nurissing ;
In lak of thame quha can say ony thing,
That fowll his nest he fylis, and for thy
Exylit he suld be of all gud cumpany ;
Thair suld na wyis man gif audience,   25
To sic ane without intelligence.
Chryst to his fader he had nocht ane man ;
Se quhat wirschep wemen suld haif than.
That Sone is Lord, that Sone is King of kingis,
In hevin and erth his majestie ay ringis.   30
Sen scho hes borne him in hir halines,

And he is well and grund of all gudnes,
All wemen of us suld haif honoring,
Service and luve, aboif all uthir thing.

46. THE TWA CUMMERIS

RYCHT AIRLIE on Ask Weddinsday,
Drynkand the wyne satt cumeris tway ;
The tane cowth to the tother complene,
Graneand and suppand cowd scho say,
" This lang Lentern makis me lene."   5

On cowch besyd the fyre scho satt,
God wait gif scho wes grit and fatt,
Yit to be feble scho did hir fene,
And ay scho said, " Latt preif of that,
This lang Lentern makis me lene."   10

" My fair, sweit cummer," quod the tuder,
" Ye tak that nigertnes of your muder ;
All wyne to test scho wald disdane
Bot mavasy, scho bad nane uder ;
This lang Lentern makis me lene."   15

" Cummer, be glaid both evin and morrow,
Thocht ye suld bayth beg and borrow,
Fra our lang fasting ye yow refrene,
And latt your husband dre the sorrow ;
This lang Lentern makis me lene.   20

" Your counsale, cummer, is gud," quod scho,
" All is to tene him that I do,
In bed he is nocht wirth a bene ;
Fill fow the glass and drynk me to ;
This lang Lentern makis me lene."   25

Off wyne owt of ane choppyne stowp,
They drank twa quartis, sowp and sowp,
Off drowth sic exces did thame strene ;
Be than to mend thay had gud howp
That Lentrune suld nocht mak thame lene.   30

47. THE TRETIS OF THE TUA MARIIT WEMEN AND THE WEDO

APON THE Midsummer evin, mirriest of nichtis,
I muvit furth allane, neir as midnicht wes past,
Besyd ane gudlie grein garth, full of gay flouris,
Hegeit, of ane huge hicht, with hawthorne treis ;
Quhairon ane bird, on ane bransche, so birst out hir notis   5
That never ane blythfullar bird was on the beuche harde :
Quhat throw the sugarat sound of hir sang glaid,
And throw the savour sanative of the sueit flouris,
I drew in derne to the dyk to dirkin efter mirthis ;
The dew donkit the daill and dynnit the feulis.   10

I hard, under ane holyn hevinlie grein hewit,
Ane hie speiche, at my hand, with hautand wourdis ;
With that in haist to the hege so hard I inthrang
That I was heildit with hawthorne and with heynd leveis :
Throw pykis of the plet thorne I presandlie luikit,   15
Gif ony persoun wald approche within that plesand garding.

I saw thre gay ladeis sit in ane grene arbeir,
All grathit in to garlandis of fresche gudlie flouris ;
So glitterit as the gold wer thair glorius gilt tressis,
Quhill all the gressis did gleme of the glaid hewis ;   20
Kemmit was thair cleir hair, and curiouslie sched
Attour thair schulderis doun schyre, schyning full bricht ;
With curches, cassin thair abone, of kirsp cleir and thin :
Thair mantillis grein war as the gress that grew in May sessoun,
Fetrit with thair quhyt fingaris about thair fair sydis :   25
Off ferliful fyne favour war thair faceis meik,
All full of flurist fairheid, as flouris in June ;
Quhyt, seimlie, and soft, as the sweit lillies
New upspred upon spray, as new spynist rose ;
Arrayit ryallie about with mony rich vardour,   30
That nature full nobillie annamalit with flouris
Off alkin hewis under hevin, that ony heynd knew,
Fragrant, all full of fresche odour fynest of smell.
Ane cumlie tabil coverit wes befoir tha cleir ladeis,
With ryalle cowpis apon rawis full of ryche wynis.   35
And of thir fair wlonkes, tua weddit war with lordis,
Ane wes ane wedow, I wis, wantoun of laitis.
And, as thai talk at the tabill of many taill sindry,

Thay wauchtit at the wicht wyne and waris out wourdis ;
And syne thai spak more spedelie, and sparit no matiris.   40

   Bewrie, said the Wedo, ye woddit wemen ying,
Quhat mirth ye fand in maryage, sen ye war menis wyffis ;
Reveill gif ye rewit that rakles conditioun ?
Or gif that ever ye luffit leyd upone lyf mair
Nor thame that ye your fayth hes festinit for ever ?   45
Or gif ye think, had ye chois, that ye wald cheis better ?
Think ye it nocht ane blist band that bindis so fast,
That none undo it a deill may bot the deith ane ?

   Than spak ane lusty belyf with lustie effeiris ;
It, that ye call the blist band that bindis so fast,   50
Is bair of blis, and bailfull, and greit barrat wirkis.
Ye speir, had I fre chois, gif I wald cheis better ?
Chenyeis ay ar to eschew ; and changeis ar sueit :
Sic cursit chance till eschew, had I my chois anis,
Out of the chenyeis of ane churle I chaip suld for evir.   55
God gif matrimony were made to mell for ane yeir !
It war bot merrens to be mair, bot gif our myndis pleisit :
It is agane the law of luf, of kynd, and of nature,
Togiddir hairtis to strene, that stryveis with uther :
Birdis hes ane better law na bernis be meikill,   60
That ilk yeir, with new joy, joyis ane maik,
And fangis thame ane fresche feyr, unfulyeit, and constant,
And lattis thair fulyeit feiris flie quhair thai pleis.
Cryst gif sic ane consuetude war in this kith haldin !
Than weill war us wemen that evir we war fre ;   65
We suld have feiris as fresche to fang quhen us likit,
And gif all larbaris thair leveis, quhen thai lak curage.
My self suld be full semlie in silkis arrayit,
Gymp, jolie, and gent, richt joyus, and gent[ryce].
I suld at fairis be found new faceis to se ;   70
At playis, and at preichingis, and pilgrimages greit,
To schaw my renone, royaly, quhair preis was of folk,
To manifest my makdome to multitude of pepill,
And blaw my bewtie on breid, quhair bernis war mony ;
That I micht cheis, and be chosin, and change quhen me lykit.   75
Than suld I waill ane full weill, our all the wyd realme,
That suld my womanheid weild the lang winter nicht ;
And when I gottin had ane grome, ganest of uther,
Yaip, and ying, in the yok ane yeir for to draw ;

Fra I had preveit his pitht the first plesand moneth,   80
Than suld I cast me to keik in kirk, and in markat,
And all the cuntre about, kyngis court, and uther,
Quhair I ane galland micht get aganis the nixt yeir,
For to perfurneis furth the werk quhen failyeit the tother ;
A forky fure, ay furthwart, and forsy in draucht,   85
Nother febill, nor fant, nor fulyeit in labour,
But als fresche of his forme as flouris in May ;
For all the fruit suld I fang, thocht he the flour burgeoun.

I have ane wallidrag, ane worme, ane auld wobat carle,
A waistit wolroun, na worth bot wourdis to clatter ;   90
Ane bumbart, ane dron bee, ane bag full of flewme,
Ane skabbit skarth, ane scorpioun, ane scutarde behind ;
To see him scart his awin skyn grit scunner I think.
Quhen kissis me that carybald, than kyndillis all my sorow ;
As birs of ane brym bair, his berd is als stif,   95
Bot soft and soupill as the silk is his sary lume ;
He may weill to the syn assent, bot sakles is his deidis.
With goreis his tua grym ene ar gladderrit all about,
And gorgeit lyk twa gutaris that war with glar stoppit ;
Bot quhen that glowrand gaist grippis me about,   100
Than think I hiddowus Mahowne hes me in armes ;
Thair ma na sanyne me save fra that auld Sathane ;
For, thocht I croce me all cleine, fra the croun doun,
He wil my corse all beclip, and clap me to his breist.
Quhen schaiffyne is that ald schalk with a scharp rasour,   105
He schowis one me his schevill mouth and schedis my lippis ;
And with his hard hurcheone skyn sa heklis he my chekis,
That as a glemand gleyd glowis my chaftis ;
I schrenk for the scharp stound, bot schout dar I nought,
For schore of that auld schrew, schame him betide !   110
The luf blenkis of that bogill, fra his blerde ene,
As Belzebub had on me blent, abasit my spreit ;
And quhen the smy one me smyrkis with his smake smolet,
He fepillis like a farcy aver that flyrit one a gillot.
    Quhen that the sound of his saw sinkis in my eris,   115
Than ay renewis my noy, or he be neir cumand :
Quhen I heir nemmyt his name, than mak I nyne crocis,
To keip me fra the cummerans of that carll mangit,
That full of eldnyng is and anger and all evill thewis.
I dar nought luke to my luf for that lene gib,   120
He is sa full of jelusy and engyne fals ;

Ever ymagynyng in mynd materis of evill,
Compasand and castand casis a thousand
How he sall tak me, with a trawe, at trist of ane othir :
I dar nought keik to the knaip that the cop fillis,   125
For eldnyng of that ald schrew that ever one evill thynkis ;
For he is waistit and worne fra Venus werkis,
And may nought beit worth a bene in bed of my mystirs.
He trowis that young folk I yerne yeild, for he gane is,
Bot I may yuke all this yer, or his yerd help.   130

Ay quhen that caribald carll wald clyme one my wambe,
Than am I dangerus and daine and dour of my will ;
Yit leit I never that larbar my leggis ga betueene,
To fyle my flesche, na fumyll me, without a fee gret ;
And thoght his pene purly me payis in bed,   135
His purse pays richely in recompense efter :
For, or he clym on my corse, that carybald forlane,
I have conditioun of a curche of kersp allther fynest,
A goun of engranyt claith, right gaily furrit,
A ring with a ryall stane, or other riche jowell,   140
Or rest of his rousty raid, thoght he wer rede wod :
For all the buddis of Johne Blunt, quhen he abone clymis,
Me think the baid deir aboucht, sa bawch ar his werkis ;
And thus I sell him solace, thoght I it sour think :
Fra sic a syre, God yow saif, my sueit sisteris deir !   145
Quhen that the semely had said her sentence to end,
Than all thai leuch apon loft with latis full mery,
And raucht the cop round about full of riche wynis,
And ralyeit lang, or thai wald rest, with ryatus speche.

The wedo to the tothir wlonk warpit ther wordis ;   150
Now, fair sister, fallis yow but fenyeing to tell,
Sen man ferst with matrimony yow menskit in kirk,
How haif ye farne be your faith ? confese us the treuth :
That band to blise, or to ban, quhilk yow best thinkis ?
Or how ye like lif to leid in to leill spousage ?   155
And syne my self ye exeme one the samyn wise,
And I sall say furth the south, dissymyland no word.

The plesand said, I protest, the treuth gif I schaw,
That of your toungis ye be traist. The tothir twa grantit ;
With that sprang up hir spreit be a span hechar.   160
To speik, quoth scho, I sall nought spar ; ther is no spy neir :
I sall a ragment reveil fra rute of my hert,

A roust that is sa rankild quhill risis my stomok ;
Now sall the byle all out brist, that beild has so lang ;
For it to beir one my brist wes beirdin our hevy :   165
I sall the venome devoid with a vent large,
And me assuage of the swalme, that suellit wes gret.

   My husband wes a hur maister, the hugeast in erd,
Tharfor I hait him with my hert, sa help me our Lord !
He is a young man ryght yaip, bot nought in youth flouris ;   170
For he is fadit full far and feblit of strenth :
He wes as flurising fresche within this few yeris,
Bot he is falyeid full far and fulyeid in labour ;
He has bene lychour so lang quhill lost is his natur,
His lume is waxit larbar, and lyis in to swonne :   175
Wes never sugeorne wer set na one that snaill tyrit,
For efter vii oulkis rest, it will nought rap anys ;
He has bene waistit apone wemen, or he me wif chesit,
And in adultre, in my tyme, I haif him tane oft :
And yit he is als brankand with bonet one syde,   180
And blenkand to the brichtest that in the burgh duellis,
Alse curtly of his clething and kemmyng of his hair,
As he that is mare valyeand in Venus chalmer ;
He semys to be sumthing worth, that syphyr in bour,
He lukis as he wald luffit be, thocht he be litill of valour ; 185
He dois as dotit dog that damys on all bussis,
And liftis his leg apone loft, thoght he nought list pische ;
He has a luke without lust and lif without curage ;
He has a forme without force and fessoun but vertu,
And fair wordis but effect, all fruster of dedis ;   190
He is for ladyis in luf a right lusty schadow,
Bot in to derne, at the deid, he salbe drup fundin ;
He ralis, and makis repet with ryatus wordis,
Ay rusing him of his radis and rageing in chalmer ;
Bot God wait quhat I think quhen he so thra spekis,   195
And how it settis him so syde to sege of sic materis.
Bot gif him self, of sum evin, myght ane say amang thaim,
Bot he nought ane is, bot nane of naturis possessoris.

   Scho that has ane auld man nought all is begylit ;
He is at Venus werkis na war na he semys :   200
I wend I josit a gem, and I haif geit gottin ;
He had the glemyng of gold, and wes bot glase fundin.
Thought men be ferse, wele I fynd, fra falye ther curage,
Thar is bot eldnyng or anger ther hertis within.
Ye speik of berdis one bewch : of blise may thai sing,   205

That, one Sanct Valentynis day, ar vacandis ilk yer ;
Hed I that plesand prevelege to part quhen me likit,
To change, and ay to cheise agane, than, chastite, adew !
Than suld I haif a fresch feir to fang in myn armes :
To hald a freke, quhill he faynt, may foly be calit.   210

    Apone sic materis I mus, at mydnyght, full oft,
And murnys so in my mynd I murdris my selfin ;
Than ly I walkand for wa, and walteris about,
Wariand oft my wekit kyn, that me away cast
To sic a craudoune but curage, that knyt my cler bewte,   215
And ther so mony kene knyghtis this kenrik within :
Than think I on a semelyar, the suth for to tell,
Na is our syre be sic sevin ; with that I sych oft :
Than he ful tenderly dois turne to me his tume person,
And with a yoldin yerd dois yolk me in armys,   220
And sais, " My soverane sueit thing, quhy sleip ye no betir ?
Me think ther haldis yow a hete, as ye sum harme alyt."
Quoth I, " My hony, hald abak, and handill me nought sair ;
A hache is happinit hastely at my hert rut."
With that I seme for to swoune, thought I na swerf tak ;   225
And thus beswik I that swane with my sueit wordis :
I cast on him a crabit E, quhen cleir day is cummyn,
And lettis it is a luf blenk, quhen he about glemys,
I turne it in a tender luke, that I in tene warit,
And him behaldis hamely with hertly smyling.   230

    I wald a tender peronall, that myght na put thole,
That hatit men with hard geir for hurting of flesch,
Had my gud man to hir gest ; for I dar God suer,
Scho suld not stert for his straik a stray breid of erd.
And syne, I wald that ilk band, that ye so blist call,   235
Had bund him so to that bryght, quhill his bak werkit ;
And I wer in a beid broght with berne that me likit,
I trow that bird of my blis suld a bourd want.

    Onone, quhen this amyable had endit hir speche,
Loudly lauchand the laif allowit hir mekle :   240
Thir gay Wiffis maid game amang the grene leiffis ;
Thai drank and did away dule under derne bewis ;
Thai swapit of the sueit wyne, thai swanquhit of hewis,
Bot all the pertlyar in plane thai put out ther vocis.

    Than said the Weido, I wis ther is no way othir ;   245
Now tydis me for to talk ; my taill it is nixt :
God my spreit now inspir and my speche quykkin,

And send me sentence to say, substantious and noble ;
Sa that my preching may pers your perverst hertis,
And mak yow mekar to men in maneris and condituounis.   250
    I schaw yow, sisteris in schrift, I wes a schrew evir,
Bot I wes schene in my schrowd, and schew me innocent ;
And thought I dour wes, and dane, dispitous, and bald,
I wes dissymblit suttelly in a sanctis liknes :
I semyt sober, and sueit, and sempill without fraud,   255
Bot I couth sexty dissaif that suttillar wer haldin.
    Unto my lesson ye lyth, and leir at me wit,
Gif you nought list be forleit with losingeris untrew :
Be constant in your governance, and counterfeit gud maneris,
Thought ye be kene, inconstant, and cruell of mynd ;   260
Thought ye as tygris be terne, be tretable in luf,
And be as turtoris in your talk, thought ye haif talis brukill ;
Be dragonis baith and dowis ay in double forme,
And quhen it nedis yow, onone, note baith ther strenthis ;
Be amyable with humble face, as angellis apperand,   265
And with a terrebill tail be stangand as edderis ;
Be of your luke like innocentis, thoght ye haif evill myndis ;
Be courtly ay in clething and costly arrayit,
That hurtis yow nought worth a hen ; yowr husband pays for all.
    Twa husbandis haif I had, thai held me baith deir,   270
Thought I dispytit thaim agane, thai spyit it na thing :
Ane wes ane hair hogeart, that hostit out flewme ;
I hatit him like a hund, thought I it hid preve :
With kissing and with clapping I gert the carll fone ;
Weil couth I keyth his cruke bak, and kemm his cowit noddill,
And with a bukky in my cheik bo on him behind,   276
And with a bek gang about and bler his ald E,
And with a kynd contynance kys his crynd chekis ;
In to my mynd makand mokis at that mad fader,
Trowand me with trew lufe to treit him so fair.   280
This cought I do without dule and na dises tak,
Bot ay be mery in my mynd and myrth full of cher.
    I had a lufsummar leid my lust for to slokyn,
That couth be secrete and sure and ay saif my honour,
And sew bot at certayne tymes and in sicir placis ;   285
Ay when the ald did me anger, with akword wordis,
Apon the galland for to goif it gladit me agane.
I had sic wit that for wo weipit I litill,
Bot leit the sueit ay the sour to gud sesone bring.
Quhen that the chuf wald me chid, with girnand chaftis,   290

I wald him chuk, cheik and chyn, and cheris him so mekill,
That his cheif chymys he had chevist to my sone,
Suppos the churll wes gane chaist, or the child wes gottin :
As wis woman ay I wrought and not as wod fule,
For mar with wylis I wan na wichtnes of handis.   295

    Syne maryit I a marchand, myghti of gudis :
He was a man of myd eld and of mene statur ;
Bot we na fallowis wer in frendschip or blud,
In fredome, na furth bering, na fairnes of persoune,
Quhilk ay the fule did foryhet, for febilnes of knawlege,   300
Bot I sa oft thoght him on, quhill angrit his hert,
And quhilum I put furth my voce and Pedder him callit :
I wald ryght tuichandly talk be I wes tuyse maryit,
For endit wes my innocence with my ald husband :
I wes apperand to be pert within perfit eild ;   305
Sa sais the curat of our kirk, that knew me full ying :
He is our famous to be fals, that fair worthy prelot ;
I salbe laith to lat him le, quhill I may luke furth.
I gert the buthman obey, ther wes no bute ellis ;
He maid me ryght hie reverens, fra he my rycht knew :   310
For, thocht I say it my self, the severance wes mekle
Betuix his bastard blude and my birth noble.
That page wes never of sic price for to presome anys
Unto my persone to be peir, had pete nought grantit.
Bot mercy in to womanheid is a mekle vertu,   315
For never bot in a gentill hert is generit ony ruth.
I held ay grene in to his mynd that I of grace tuk him,
And for he couth ken him self I curtasly him lerit :
He durst not sit anys my summondis, for, or the secund charge,
He wes ay redy for to ryn, so rad he wes for blame.   320
Bot ay my will wes the war of womanly natur ;
The mair he loutit for my luf, the les of him I rakit ;
And eik, this is a ferly thing, or I him faith gaif,
I had sic favour to that freke, and feid syne for ever,
    Quhen I the cure had all clene and him ourcummyn haill, 325
I crew abone that craudone, as cok that wer victour ;
Quhen I him saw subject and sett at myn bydding,
Than I him lichtlyit as a lowne and lathit his maneris.
Than woxe I sa unmerciable to martir him I thought,
For as a best I broddit him to all boyis laubour :   330
I wald haif ridden him to Rome with raip in his heid,
Wer not ruffill of my renoune and rumour of pepill.

And yit hatrent I hid within my hert all ;
Bot quhilis it hepit so huge, quhill it behud out :
Yit tuk I nevir the wosp clene out of my wyde throte,   335
Quhill I oucht wantit of my will or quhat I wald desir.
Bot quhen I severit had that syre of substance in erd,
And gottin his biggingis to my barne, and hie burrow landis,
Than with a stew stert out the stoppell of my hals,
That he all stunyst throu the stound, as of a stele wappin.   340
Than wald I, efter lang, first sa fane haif bene wrokin,
That I to flyte wes als fers as a fell dragoun.
I had for flattering of that fule fenyeit so lang,
Mi evidentis of heritagis or thai wer all selit,
My breist, that wes gret beild, bowdyn wes sa huge,   345
That neir my baret out brist or the band makin.
Bot quhen my billis and my bauchles wes all braid selit,
I wald na langar beir on bridill, bot braid up my heid ;
Thar mycht na molet mak me moy, na hald my mouth in :
I gert the renyeis rak and rif into sondir ;   350
I maid that wif carll to werk all womenis werkis,
And laid all manly materis and mensk in this eird.
Than said I to my cumaris in counsall about,
" Se how I cabeld yone cout with a kene brydill !
The cappill, that the crelis kest in the caf mydding,   355
Sa curtasly the cart drawis, and kennis na plungeing,
He is nought skeich, na yit sker, na scippis nought one syd : "
And thus the scorne and the scaith scapit he nothir.
    He wes no glaidsum gest for a gay lady,
Tharfor I gat him a game that ganyt him bettir ;   360
He wes a gret goldit man and of gudis riche ;
I leit him be my lumbart to lous me all misteris,
And he wes fane for to fang fra me that fair office,
And thoght my favoris to fynd through his feill giftis.
He grathit me in a gay silk and gudly arrayis,   365
In gownis of engranyt claith and gret goldin chenyeis,
In ringis ryally set with riche ruby stonis,
Quhill hely raise my renoune amang the rude peple.
Bot I full craftely did keip thai courtly wedis,
Quhill eftir dede of that drupe, that dotht nought in chalmir : 370
Thought he of all my clathis maid cost and expense,
Ane othir sall the worschip haif, that weildis me eftir ;
And thoght I likit him bot litill, yit for luf of otheris,
I wald me prunya plesandly in precius wedis,
That luffaris mycht apone me luke and ying lusty gallandis, 375

That I held more in daynte and derer be ful mekill
Ne him that dressit me so dink : full dotit wes his heyd.
Quhen he wes heryit out of hand to hie up my honoris,
And payntit me as pako, proudest of fedderis,
I him miskennyt, be Crist, and cukkald him maid ;   380
I him forleit as a lad and lathlyit him mekle :
I thoght my self a papingay and him a plukit herle ;
All thus enforsit he his fa and fortifyit in strenth,
And maid a stalwart staff to strik him selfe doune.

    Bot of ane bowrd in to bed I sall yow breif yit :   385
Quhen he ane hail year was hanyt, and him behuffit rage,
And I wes laith to be loppin with sic a lob avoir,
Alse lang as he wes on loft, I lukit on him never,
Na leit never enter in my thoght that he my thing persit,
Bot ay in mynd ane other man ymagynit that I haid ;   390
Or ellis had I never mery bene at that myrthles raid.
Quhen I that grome geldit had of gudis and of natur,
Me thought him gracelese one to goif, sa me God help :
Quhen he had warit all one me his welth and his substance,
Me thoght his wit wes all went away with the laif ;   395
And so I did him despise, I spittit quhen I saw
That super spendit evill spreit, spulyeit of all vertu.
For, weill ye wait, wiffis, that he that wantis riches
And valyeandnes in Venus play, is ful vile haldin :
Full fruster is his fresch array and fairnes of persoune,   400
All is bot frutlese his effeir and falyeis at the up with.

    I buskit up my barnis like baronis sonnis,
And maid bot fulis of the fry of his first wif.
I banyst fra my boundis his brethir ilkane ;
His frendis as my fais I held at feid evir ;   405
Be this, ye belief may, I luffit nought him self,
For never I likit a leid that langit till his blude :
And yit thir wisemen, thai wait that all wiffis evill
Ar kend with ther conditionis and knawin with the samin.

    Deid is now that dyvour and dollin in erd :   410
With him deit all my dule and my drery thoghtis ;
Now done is my dolly nyght, my day is upsprungin,
Adew dolour, adew ! my daynte now begynis :
Now am I a wedow, I wise and weill am at ese ;
I weip as I were woful, but wel is me for ever ;   415
I busk as I wer bailfull, bot blith is my hert ;
My mouth it makis murnyng, and my mynd lauchis ;
My clokis thai ar caerfull in colour of sabill,

Bot courtly and ryght curyus my corse is ther undir :
I drup with a ded luke in my dule habit,   420
As with manis daill [I] had done for dayis of my lif.
    Quhen that I go to the kirk, cled in cair weid,
As foxe in a lambis fleise fenye I my cheir ;
Than lay I furght my bright buke one breid one my kne,
With mony lusty letter ellummynit with gold ;   425
And drawis my clok forthwart our my face quhit,
That I may spy, unaspyit, a space me beside :
Full oft I blenk by my buke, and blynis of devotioun,
To se quhat berne is best brand or bredest in schulderis,
Or forgeit is maist forcely to furnyse a bancat   430
In Venus chalmer, valyeandly, withoutin vane ruse :
And, as the new mone all pale, oppressit with change,
Kythis quhilis her cleir face through cluddis of sable,
So keik I through my clokis, and castis kynd lukis
To knychtis, and to cleirkis, and cortly personis.   435
    Quhen frendis of my husbandis behaldis me one fer,
I haif a watter spunge for wa, within my wyde clokis,
Than wring I it full wylely and wetis my chekis,
With that watteris myn ene and welteris doune teris.
Than say thai all, that sittis about, " Se ye nought, allace ! 440
Yone lustlese led so lelely scho luffit hir husband :
Yone is a pete to enprent in a princis hert,
That sic a perle of plesance suld yone pane dre ! "
I sane me as I war ane sanct, and semys ane angell ;
At langage of lichory I leit as I war crabit :   445
I sich, without sair hert or seiknes in body ;
According to my sable weid I mon haif sad maneris,
Or thai will se all the suth ; for certis, we wemen
We set us all fra the syght to syle men of treuth :
We dule for na evill deid, sa it be derne haldin.   450
    Wise wemen has wayis and wonderfull gydingis
With gret engyne to bejaip ther jolyus husbandis ;
And quyetly, with sic craft, convoyis our materis
That, under Crist, no creatur kennis of our doingis.
Bot folk a cury may miscuke, that knawledge wantis,   455
And has na colouris for to cover thair awne kindly fautis ;
As dois thir damysellis, for derne dotit lufe,
That dogonis haldis in dainte and delis with thaim so lang,
Quhill all the cuntre knaw ther kyndnes and faith :
Faith has a fair name, bot falsheid faris bettir :   460
Fy one hir that can nought feyne her fame for to saif !

Yit am I wise in sic werk and wes all my tyme ;
Thoght I want wit in warldlynes, I wylis haif in luf,
As ony happy woman has that is of hie blude :
Hutit be the halok las a hunder yeir of eild !   465
    I have ane secrete servand, rycht sobir of his toung,
That me supportis of sic nedis, quhen I a syne mak :
Thoght he be sympill to the sicht, he has a tong sickir ;
Full mony semelyar sege wer service dois mak :
Thought I haif cair, under cloke, the cleir day quhill nyght,   470
Yit haif I solace, under serk, quhill the sone ryse.
    Yit am I haldin a haly wif our all the haill schyre,
I am sa peteouse to the pur, quhen ther is personis mony.
In passing of pilgrymage I pride me full mekle,
Mair for the prese of peple na ony perdoun wynyng.   475
    Bot yit me think the best bourd, quhen baronis and knychtis,
And othir bachilleris, blith blumyng in youth,
And all my luffaris lele, my lugeing persewis,
And fyllis me wyne wantonly with weilfair and joy :
Sum rownis ; and sum ralyeis ; and sum redis ballatis ;   480
Sum raiffis furght rudly with riatus speche ;
Sum plenis, and sum prayis ; sum prasis mi bewte,
Sum kissis me ; sum clappis me ; sum kyndnes me proferis ;
Sum kerffis to me curtasli ; sum me the cop giffis ;
Sum stalwardly steppis ben, with a stout curage,   485
And a stif standand thing staiffis in my neiff ;
And mony blenkis ben our, that but full fer sittis,
That mai, for the thik thrang, nought thrif as thai wald.
Bot, with my fair calling, I comfort thaim all :
For he that sittis me nixt, I nip on his finger ;   490
I serf him on the tothir syde on the samin fasson ;
And he that behind me sittis, I hard on him lene ;
And him befor, with my fut fast on his I stramp ;
And to the bernis far but sueit blenkis I cast :
To every man in speciall speke I sum wordis   495
So wisly and so womanly, quhill warmys ther hertis.
    Thar is no liffand leid so law of degre
That sall me luf unluffit, I am so loik hertit ;
And gif his lust so be lent into my lyre quhit,
That he be lost or with me lig, his lif sall nocht danger.   500
I am so mercifull in mynd, and menys all wichtis,
My sely saull salbe saif, quhen sa bot all jugis.
Ladyis leir thir lessonis and be no lassis fundin :
This is the legeand of my lif, thought Latyne it be nane.

Quhen endit had her ornat speche, this eloquent wedow,   505
Lowd thai lewch all the laif, and loffit hir mekle ;
And said thai suld exampill tak of her soverane teching,
And wirk efter hir wordis, that woman wes so prudent.
Than culit thai thair mouthis with confortable drinkis ;
And carpit full cummerlik with cop going round.   510

Thus draif thai our that deir nyght with danceis full noble,
Quhill that the day did up daw, and dew donkit flouris ;
The morow myld wes and meik, the mavis did sing,
And all remuffit the myst, and the meid smellit ;
Silver schouris doune schuke as the schene cristall,   515
And berdis schoutit in schaw with thair schill notis ;
The goldin glitterand gleme so gladit ther hertis,
Thai maid a glorius gle amang the grene bewis.
The soft sowch of the swyr and soune of the stremys,
The sueit savour of the sward and singing of foulis,   520
Myght confort ony creatur of the kyn of Adam,
And kindill agane his curage, thocht it wer cald sloknyt.
Than rais thir ryall roisis, in ther riche wedis,
And rakit hame to ther rest through the rise blumys ;
And I all prevely past to a plesand arber,   525
And with my pen did report thair pastance most mery.

Ye auditoris most honorable, that eris has gevin
Oneto this uncouth aventur, quhilk airly me happinnit ;
Of thir thre wantoun wiffis, that I haif writtin heir,
Quhilk wald ye waill to your wif, gif ye suld wed one ?   530

48. OF THE LADYIS SOLISTARIS AT COURT

THIR LADYIS fair, That makis repair
And in the court ar kend,
Thre dayis thair Thay will do mair
Ane mater for till end,
Than thair gud men Will do in ten,   5
For ony craft thay can,
So weill thay ken Quhat tyme and quhen
Thair menes thay sowld mak than.

With littill noy Thay can convoy
Ane mater fynaly,   10
Richt myld and moy, And keip it coy,
On evyns quyetly.
Thay do no mis, Bot gif thay kis,
And keipis collatioun,
Quhat rek of this ?   Thair mater is   15
Brocht to conclusioun.

Wit ye weill, Thay haif grit feill
Ane mater to solist,
Trest as the steill, Syne nevir a deill
Quhen thay cum hame ar mist.   20
Thir lairdis ar, Methink, richt far
Sic ladeis behaldin to,
That sa weill dar Go to the bar,
Quhen thair is ocht ado.

Thairfoir I reid, Gif ye haif pleid,   25
Or mater in to pley,
To mak remeid, Send in your steid
Your ladeis grathit up gay.
Thay can defend Evin to the end
Ane mater furth expres ;   30
Suppois thay spend, It is unkend,
Thair geir is nocht the les.

In quyet place, Thocht thay haif space
Within les nor twa howris,
Thay can, percaice, Purches sum grace   35
At the compositouris.
Thair compositioun, With full remissioun,
Thair fynaly is endit,
With expeditioun And full conditioun,
And thairto seilis appendit.   40

Alhaill almoist, Thay mak the coist
With sobir recompens,
Richt littill loist, Thay get indoist
Alhaill thair evidens.
Sic ladyis wyis Thay ar to pryis,   45
To say the veretie,
Swa can devyis, And none suppryis
Thame nor thair honestie.

49. TO A LADYE

SWEIT ROIS of vertew and of gentilnes,
Delytsum lyllie of everie lustynes,
   Richest in bontie and in bewtie cleir,
   And everie vertew that is [held most] deir,
Except onlie that ye ar mercyles.   5

In to your garthe this day I did persew,
Thair saw I flowris that fresche wer of hew;
   Baith quhyte and reid moist lusty wer to seyne,
   And halsum herbis upone stalkis grene;
Yit leif nor flour fynd could I nane of rew.   10

I dout that Merche, with his caild blastis keyne,
Hes slane this gentill herbe that I of mene,
   Quhois petewous deithe dois to my hart sic pane
   That I wald mak to plant his rute agane,
So confortand his levis unto me bene.   15

50. QUHONE HE LIST TO FEYNE

MY HARTIS tresure, and swete assured fo,
   The finale endar of my lyfe for ever;
The creuell brekar of my hart in tuo,
   To go to deathe, this I deservit never:
   O man slayar! quhill saule and life dissever   5
Stynt of your slauchter; Allace! your man am I,
A thowsand tymes that dois yow mercy cry.

Have mercie, luif! have mercie, ladie bricht!
   Quhat have I wrocht aganis your womanheid,
That ye [suld] murdir me, a sakles wicht,   10
   Trespassing never to yow in word nor deid?
   That ye consent thairto, O God forbid!
Leif creuelte, and saif your man for schame,
Or throucht the warld quyte losit is your name.

My deathe chasis my lyfe so besalie
   That wery is my goist to fle so fast;
Sic deidlie dwawmes so mischeifaislie

Ane hundrithe tymes hes my hairt ouirpast;
Me think my spreit rynnis away full gast,
Beseikand grace on kneis yow befoir,   20
Or that your man be lost for evermoir.

Behald my wod intollerabill pane,
For evermoir quhilk salbe my dampnage!
Quhy, undir traist, your man thus have ye slane?
Lo! deithe is in my breist with furious rage,   25
Quhilk may no balme nor tryacle asswage,
Bot your mercie, for laik of quhilk I de:
Allace! quhair is your womanlie petie!

Behald my deidlie passioun dolorous!
Behald my hiddows hew and wo, allace!   30
Behald my mayne and murning mervalous,
Withe sorrowfull teris falling frome my face!
Rewthe, luif, is nocht, helpe ye not in this cace,
For how sould ony gentill hart indure
To se this sycht on ony creature!   35

Quhyte dow, quhair is your sobir humilnes?
Swete gentill turtour, quhair is your pete went?
Quhair is your rewthe? the frute of nobilnes,
Off womanheid the tresour and the rent;
Mercie is never put out of meik intent,   40
Nor out of gentill hart is fundin petie,
Sen mercyles may no weycht nobill be.

In to my mynd I sall yow mercye cry,
Quhone that my toung sall faill me to speik,
And quhill that nature me my sycht deny,   45
And quhill my ene for pane incluse and steik,
And quhill the dethe my hart in sowndir breik,
And quhill my mynd may think and towng may steir;
And syne, fair weill, my hartis Ladie deir!

51. INCONSTANCY OF LUVE

Quha will behald of luve the chance,
With sueit dissavyng countenance,
In quhais fair dissimulance
            May none assure;

Quhilk is begun with inconstance,   5
And endis nocht but variance,
Scho haldis with continuance
            No serviture.

Discretioun and considerance
Ar both out of hir govirnance ;   10
Quhairfoir of it the schort plesance
            May nocht indure ;
Scho is so new of acquentance,
The auld gais fra remembrance ;
Thus I gife our the observans   15
            Of luvis care.

It is ane pount of ignorance
To lufe in sic distemperance,
Sen tyme mispendit may avance
            No creature ;   20
In luve to keip allegance,
It war als nys an ordinance,
As quha wald bid ane deid man dance
            In sepulture.

52. OF LUVE ERDLY AND DIVINE

Now CULIT is Dame Venus brand ;
Trew luvis fyre is ay kindilland,
And I begyn to undirstand,
In feynit luve quhat foly bene :
Now cumis aige quhair yewth hes bene,   5
And trew luve rysis fro the splene.

Quhill Venus fyre be deid and cauld,
Trew luvis fyre nevir birnis bauld ;
So as the ta lufe waxis auld,
The tothir dois incres moir kene :   10
Now cumis aige quhair yewth hes bene,
And trew lufe rysis fro the splene.

No man hes curege for to wryte
Quhat plesans is in lufe perfyte,
That hes in fenyeit lufe delyt,   15

Thair kyndnes is so contrair clene :
Now cumis aige quhair yewth hes bene,
And trew lufe rysis fro the splene.

Full weill is him that may imprent,
Or onywayis his hairt consent,   20
To turne to trew luve his intent,
And still the quarrell to sustene :
Now cumis aige quhair yewth hes bene,
And trew lufe rysis fro the splene.

I haif experience by my sell ;   25
In luvis court anis did I dwell,
Bot quhair I of a joy cowth tell,
I culd of truble tell fyftene :
Now cumis aige quhair yewth hes bene,
And trew lufe rysis fro the splene.   30

Befoir quhair that I wes in dreid,
Now haif I confort for to speid ;
Quhair I had maugre to my meid,
I trest rewaird and thankis betuene :
Now cumis aige quhair yewth hes bene,   35
And trew lufe rysis fro the splene.

Quhair lufe wes wont me to displeis,
Now find I in to lufe grit eis ;
Quhair I had denger and diseis,
My breist all confort dois contene :   40
Now cumis aige quhair yewth hes bene,
And trew lufe rysis fro the splene.

Quhair I wes hurt with jelosy,
And wald no luver wer bot I,
Now quhair I lufe I wald all wy,   45
Als weill as I, luvit I wene :
Now cumis aige quhair yewth hes bene,
And trew lufe rysis fro the splene.

Befoir quhair I durst nocht for schame
My lufe discure, nor tell hir name ;   50
Now think I wirschep wer and fame,

To all the warld that it war sene :
Now cumis aige quhair yewth hes bene,
And trew lufe rysis fro the splene.

Befoir no wicht I did complene,   55
So did hir denger me derene ;
And now I sett nocht by a bene
Hir bewty nor hir twa fair ene :
Now cumis aige quhair yewth hes bene,
And trew lufe rysis fro the splene.   60

I haif a luve farar of face,
Quhome in no denger may haif place,
Quhilk will me guerdoun gif and grace,
And mercy ay quhen I me mene :
Now cumis aige quhair yewth hes bene,   65
And trew lufe rysis fro the splene.

Unquyt I do no thing nor sane,
Nor wairis a luvis thocht in vane ;
I salbe als weill luvit agane,
Thair may no jangler me prevene :   70
Now cumis aige quhair yewth hes bene,
And trew luve rysis fro the splene.

Ane lufe so fare, so gud, so sueit,
So riche, so rewthfull, and discreit,
And for the kynd of man so meit,   75
Nevir moir salbe nor yit hes bene :
Now cumis aige quhair yewth hes bene,
And trew lufe rysis fro the splene.

Is none sa trew a luve as he,
That for trew luve of us did de ;   80
He suld be luffit agane, think me,
That wald sa fane our luve obtene :
Now cumis aige quhair yewth hes bene,
And trew luve rysis fro the splene.

Is non but grace of God I wis,   85
That can in yewth considdir this ;
This fals dissavand warldis blis,

So gydis man in flouris grene :
Now cumis aige quhair yewth hes bene,
And trew luve rysis fro the splene.   90

53. DUNBAR AT OXINFURDE

To SPEIK of science, craft, or sapience,
   Off vertew, morall cunnyng, or doctrene ;
Off jure, of wisdome, or intelligence ;
   Off everie study, lair, or disciplene ;
   All is bot tynt or reddie for to tyne,   5
Nocht using it as it sould usit be,
   The craift exerceing, considdering not the fyne :
A paralous seiknes is vane prosperite.

The curious probatioun logicall,
   The eloquence of ornat rethorie,   10
The naturall science philosophicall,
   The dirk apperance of astronomie,
   The theologis sermoun, the fablis of poetrie,
Without gud lyfe all in the selfe dois de,
   As Maii flouris dois in September dry :   15
A paralous lyfe is vane prosperite.

Quhairfoir, ye clarkis and grittest of constance,
   Fullest of science and of knawlegeing,
To us be myrrouris in your governance,
   And in our darknes be lampis in schyning,   20
   Or than in frustar is your lang leirning ;
Giff to your sawis your deidis contrair be,
   Your maist accusar salbe your awin cunning :
A paralus seiknes is vane prosperitie.

54. BEWTY AND THE PRESONEIR

SEN THAT I am a presoneir
Till hir that farest is and best,
I me commend, fra yeir till yeir,
In till hir bandoun for to rest.

I govit on that gudliest,   5
So lang to luk I tuk laiseir,
Quhill I wes tane withouttin test,
And led furth as a presoneir.

Hir sweit having, and fresche bewte,
Hes wondit me but swerd or lance,   10
With hir to go commandit me
Ontill the castell of pennance.
I said, " Is this your govirnance,
To tak men for thair luking heir ? "
Bewty sayis, " Ya, schir, perchance   15
Ye be my ladeis presoneir."

Thai had me bundin to the yet,
Quhair Strangenes had bene portar ay,
And in deliverit me thairat,
And in thir termis can thai say,   20
" Do wait, and lat him nocht away ; "
Quo Strangenes unto the porteir,
" Ontill my lady, I dar lay,
Ye be to pure a presoneir."

Thai kest me in a deip dungeoun,   25
And fetterit me but lok or cheyne ;
The capitane, hecht Comparesone,
To luke on me he thocht greit deyne.
Thocht I wes wo I durst nocht pleyne,
For he had fetterit mony a feir ;   30
With petous voce thus cuth I sene,
Wo is a wofull presoneir.

Langour wes weche upoun the wall,
That nevir sleipit bot evir wouke ;
Scorne wes bourdour in the hall,   35
And oft on me his babill schuke,
Lukand with mony a dengerous luke :
" Quhat is he yone, that methis us neir ?
Ye be to townage, be this buke,
To be my ladeis presoneir ".   40

Gud Houp rownit in my eir,
And bad me baldlie breve a bill ;

F

With Lawlines he suld it beir,
With Fair Service send it hir till.
I wouk, and wret hir all my will;   45
Fair Service fur withouttin feir,
Sayand till hir with wordis still,
" Haif pety of your presoneir."

Than Lawlines to Petie went,
And said till hir in termis schort,   50
" Lat we yone presoneir be schent,
" Will no man do to us support;
Gar lay ane sege unto yone fort."
Than Petie said, " I sall appeir; "
Thocht sayis, " I hecht, com I ourthort,   55
I houp to lows the presoneir."

Than to battell thai war arreyit all,
And ay the vawart kepit Thocht;
Lust bur the benner to the wall,
And Bissines the grit gyn brocht.   60
Skorne cryis out, sayis, " Wald ye ocht? "
Lust sayis, " We wald haif entre heir; "
Comparisone sayis, " That is for nocht,
Ye will nocht wyn the presoneir."

Thai thairin schup for to defend,   65
And thai thairfurth sailyeit ane hour;
Than Bissines the grit gyn bend,
Straik doun the top of the foir tour.
Comparisone began to lour,
And cryit furth, " I yow requeir,   70
Soft and fair and do favour,
And tak to yow the presoneir."

Thai fyrit the yettis deliverly
With faggottis wer grit and huge;
And Strangenes, quhair that he did ly,   75
Wes brint in to the porter luge.
Lustely thay lakit bot a juge,
Sik straikis and stychling wes on steir,
The semeliest wes maid assege,
To quhome that he wes presoneir.   80

Thrucht Skornes nos thai put a prik,
This he wes banist and gat a blek ;
Comparisone wes crdit quik,
And Langour lap and brak his nek.
Thai sailyeit fast, all the fek,   85
Lust chasit my ladeis chalmirleir,
Gud Fame wes drownit in a sek ;
Thus ransonit thai the presoneir.

Fra Sklandir hard Lust had undone,
His enemeis, him aganis,   90
Assemblit ane semely sort full sone,
And rais and rowttit all the planis.
His cusing in the court remanis,
Bot jalous folkis and geangleiris,
And fals Invy that no thing lanis,   95
Blew out on Luvis presoneir.

Syne Matremony, that nobill king,
Wes grevit, and gadderit ane grit ost,
And all enermit, without lesing,
Chest Sklander to the west se cost.   100
Than wes he and his linege lost,
And Matremony, withowttin weir,
The band of freindschip hes indost,
Betuix Bewty and the presoneir.

Be that of eild wes Gud Famis air,   105
And cumyne to continuatioun,
And to the court maid his repair,
Quhair Matremony than woir the crowne.
He gat ane confirmatioun,
All that his modir aucht but weir,   110
And baid still, as it wes resone,
With Bewty and the presoneir.

55. THE THRISSIL AND THE ROIS

Quhen Merche wes with variand windis past,
And Appryll had, with hir silver schouris,
Tane leif at nature with ane orient blast ;

And lusty May, that muddir is of flouris,
Had maid the birdis to begyn thair houris   5
Amang the tendir odouris reid and quhyt,
Quhois armony to heir it wes delyt ;

In bed at morrow, sleiping as I lay,
Me thocht Aurora, with hir cristall ene,
In at the window lukit by the day,   10
And halsit me, with visage paill and grene ;
On quhois hand a lark sang fro the splene,
Awalk, luvaris, out of your slomering,
Se how the lusty morrow dois up spring.

Me thocht fresche May befoir my bed upstude,   15
In weid depaynt of mony divers hew,
Sobir, benyng, and full of mansuetude,
In brycht atteir of flouris forgit new,
Hevinly of color, quhyt, reid, broun, and blew,
Balmit in dew and gilt with Phebus bemys,   20
Quhill all the hous illumynit of hir lemys.

" Slugird," scho said, " awalk annone for schame,
And in my honour sum thing thow go wryt ;
The lork hes done the mirry day proclame,
To rais up luvaris with confort and delyt,   25
Yit nocht incresis thy curage to indyt,
Quhois hairt sum tyme hes glaid and blisfull bene,
Sangis to mak undir the levis grene."

" Quhairto," quod I, " sall I uprys at morrow,
For in this May few birdis herd I sing ?   30
Thai haif moir caus to weip and plane thair sorrow,
Thy air it is nocht holsum nor benyng ;
Lord Eolus dois in thy sessone ring ;
So busteous ar the blastis of his horne,
Amang thy bewis to walk I haif forborne."   35

With that this lady sobirly did smyll,
And said, " Uprys, and do thy observance ;
Thow did promyt, in Mayis lusty quhyle,
For to discryve the Ros of most plesance.
Go se the birdis how thay sing and dance,   40
Illumynit our with orient skyis brycht,
Annamyllit richely with new asur lycht."

Quhen this wes said, depairtit scho, this quene,
And enterit in a lusty gairding gent;
And than, me thocht, full hestely besene,   45
In serk and mantill [eftir hir] I went
In to this garth, most dulce and redolent
Off herb and flour and tendir plantis sueit,
And grene levis doing of dew doun fleit.

The purpour sone, with tendir bemys reid,   50
In orient bricht as angell did appeir,
Throw goldin skyis putting up his heid,
Quhois gilt tressis schone so wondir cleir,
That all the world tuke confort, fer and neir,
To luke upone his fresche and blisfull face,   55
Doing all sable fro the hevynnis chace.

And as the blisfull sonne of cherarchy
The fowlis song throw confort of the licht;
The birdis did with oppin vocis cry,
O, luvaris fo, away thow dully nycht,   60
And welcum day that confortis every wight;
Haill May, haill Flora, haill Aurora schene,
Haill princes Natur, haill Venus luvis quene.

Dame Nature gaif ane inhibitioun thair
To fers Neptunus, and Eolus the bawld,   65
Nocht to perturb the wattir nor the air,
And that no schouris, nor blastis cawld,
Effray suld flouris nor fowlis on the fold;
Scho bad cik Juno, goddes of the sky,
That scho the hevin suld keip amene and dry.   70

Scho ordand eik that every bird and beist
Befoir hir hienes suld annone compeir,
And every flour of vertew, most and leist,
And every herb be feild fer and neir,
As thay had wont in May, fro yeir to yeir,   75
To hir thair makar to mak obediens,
Full law inclynnand with all dew reverens.

With that annone scho send the swyft Ro
To bring in beistis of all conditioun;
The restles Suallow commandit scho also   80

To feche all fowll of small and greit renown ;
And, to gar flouris compeir of all fassoun,
Full craftely conjurit scho the Yarrow,
Quhilk did furth swirk als swift as ony arrow.

All present wer in twynkling of ane e,   85
Baith beist, and bird, and flour, befoir the quene,
And first the Lyone, gretast of degre,
Was callit thair, and he, most fair to sene,
With a full hardy contenance and kene,
Befoir dame Natur come, and did inclyne,   90
With visage bawld and curage leonyne.

This awfull beist full terrible wes of cheir,
Persing of luke, and stout of countenance,
Rycht strong of corpis, of fassoun fair but feir,
Lusty of schaip, lycht of deliverance,   95
Reid of his cullour, as is the ruby glance ;
On feild of gold he stude full mychtely,
With flour delycis sirculit lustely.

This lady liftit up his cluvis cleir,
And leit him listly lene upone hir kne,   100
And crownit him with dyademe full deir
Off radyous stonis, most ryall for to se ;
Saying, " The King of Beistis mak I the,
And the cheif protector in woddis and schawis ;
Onto thi leigis go furth, and keip the lawis.   105

Exerce justice with mercy and conscience,
And lat no small beist suffir skaith na skornis
Of greit beistis that bene of moir piscence ;
Do law elyk to aipis and unicornis,
And lat no bowgle, with his busteous hornis,   110
The meik pluch ox oppress, for all his pryd,
Bot in the yok go peciable him besyd."

Quhen this was said, with noyis and soun of joy,
All kynd of beistis in to thair degre,
At onis cryit lawd, " Vive le Roy ! "   115
And till his feit fell with humilite,
And all thay maid him homege and fewte ;
And he did thame ressaif with princely laitis,
Quhois noble yre is *parcere prostratis*.

Syne crownit scho the Egle King of Fowlis,   120
And as steill dertis scherpit scho his pennis,
And bawd him be als just to awppis and owlis,
As unto pacokkis, papingais, or crennis,
And mak a law for wycht fowlis and for wrennis ;
And lat no fowll of ravyne do efferay,   125
Nor devoir birdis bot his awin pray.

Than callit scho all flouris that grew on feild,
Discirnyng all thair fassionis and effeiris ;
Upon the awfull Thrissill scho beheld,
And saw him kepit with a busche of speiris ;   130
Concedring him so able for the weiris,
A radius croun of rubeis scho him gaif,
And said, " In feild go furth, and fend the laif ;

And, sen thow art a king, thow be discreit ;
Herb without vertew thow hald nocht of sic pryce   135
As herb of vertew and of odor sueit ;
And lat no nettill vyle, and full of vyce,
Hir fallow to the gudly flour delyce ;
Nor latt no wyld weid, full of churlichenes,
Compair hir till the lilleis nobilnes.   140

Not hald non udir flour in sic denty
As the fresche Ros of cullour reid and quhyt ;
For gife thow dois, hurt is thyne honesty,
Conciddering that no flour is so perfyt,
So full of vertew, plesans, and delyt,   145
So full of blisfull angeilik bewty,
Imperiall birth, honour and dignite."

Than to the Ros scho turnyt hir visage,
And said, " O lusty dochtir most benyng,
Aboif the lilly, illustare of lynnage,   150
Fro the stok ryell rysing fresche and ying,
But ony spot or macull doing spring ;
Cum blowme of joy with jemis to be cround,
For our the laif thy bewty is renownd."

A coistly croun, with clarefeid stonis brycht,   155
This cumly quene did on hir heid inclois,
Quhill all the land illumynit of the licht ;
Quhairfoir me thocht all flouris did rejos,

Crying attonis, " Haill be, thow richest Ros !
Haill, hairbis empryce, haill, freschest quene of flouris,   160
To the be glory and honour at all houris."

Thane all the birdis song with voce on hicht,
Quhois mirthfull soun wes mervelus to heir ;
The mavys song, " Haill, Rois most riche and richt,
That dois up flureis undir Phebus speir ;   165
Haill, plant of yowth, haill, princes dochtir deir,
Haill, blosome breking out of the blud royall,
Quhois pretius vertew is imperiall."

The merle scho sang, " Haill, Rois of most delyt,
Haill, of all flouris quene and soverane ; "   170
The lark scho song, " Haill, Rois, both reid and quhyt,
Most plesand flour, of michty cullouris twane ; "
The nychtingaill song, " Haill, naturis suffragene,
In bewty, nurtour, and every nobilnes,
In riche array, renown, and gentilnes."   175

The commoun voce uprais of birdis small,
Apone this wys, " O blissit be the hour
That thow wes chosin to be our principall ;
Welcome to be our princes of honour,
Our perle, our plesans, and our paramour,   180
Our peax, our play, our plane felicite,
Chryst the conserf frome all adversite."

Than all the birdis song with sic a schout,
That I annone awoilk quhair that I lay,
And with a braid I turnyt me about   185
To se this court, bot all wer went away :
Than up I lenyt, halflingis in affrey,
And thus I wret, as ye haif hard to forrow,
Off lusty May upone the nynt morrow.

56. THE GOLDYN TARGE

Ryght as the stern of day begouth to schyne,
Quhen gone to bed war Vesper and Lucyne,
    I raise and by a rosere did me rest ;
Up sprang the goldyn candill matutyne,
With clere depurit bemes cristallyne,   5

Glading the mery foulis in thair nest ;
Or Phebus was in purpur cape revest
Up raise the lark, the hevyns menstrale fyne
In May, in till a morow myrthfullest.

Full angellike thir birdis sang thair houris   10
Within thair courtyns grene, in to thair bouris
   Apparalit quhite and red wyth blomes suete ;
Anamalit was the felde wyth all colouris,
The perly droppis schake in silvir schouris,
    Quhill all in balme did branch and levis flete ;   15
   To part fra Phebus did Aurora grete,
Hir cristall teris I saw hyng on the flouris,
    Quhilk he for lufe all drank up wyth his hete.

For mirth of May, wyth skippis and wyth hoppis,
The birdis sang upon the tender croppis,   20
   With curiouse note, as Venus chapell clerkis :
The rosis yong, new spreding of thair knopis,
War powderit brycht with hevinly beriall droppis,
    Throu bemes rede birnyng as ruby sperkis ;
   The skyes rang for schoutyng of the larkis,   25
The purpur hevyn, our scailit in silvir sloppis,
    Ourgilt the treis, branchis, lef, and barkis.

Doune throu the ryce a ryvir ran wyth stremys,
So lustily agayn thai lykand lemys,
   That all the lake as lamp did leme of licht,   30
Quhilk schadowit all about wyth twynkling glemis ;
That bewis bathit war in secund bemys
    Throu the reflex of Phebus visage brycht ;
   On every syde the hegies raise on hicht,
The bank was grene, the bruke was full of bremys,   35
    The stanneris clere as stern in frosty nycht.

The cristall air, the sapher firmament,
The ruby skyes of the orient,
   Kest beriall bemes on emerant bewis grene ;
The rosy garth depaynt and redolent,   40
With purpur, azure, gold, and goulis gent
    Arayed was, by dame Flora the quene,
   So nobily, that joy was for to sene ;
The roch agayn the rivir resplendent
    As low enlumynit all the leves schene.   45

Quhat throu the mery foulys armony,
And throu the ryveris soune rycht ran me by,
  On Florais mantill I slepit as I lay,
Quhare sone in to my dremes fantasy
I saw approch, agayn the orient sky,   50
  A saill, als quhite as blossum upon spray,
  Wyth merse of gold, brycht as the stern of day,
Quhilk tendit to the land full lustily,
  As falcoune swift desyrouse of hir pray.

And hard on burd unto the blomyt medis,   55
Amang the grene rispis and the redis,
  Arrivit sche, quhar fro anone thare landis
Ane hundreth ladyes, lusty in to wedis,
Als fresch as flouris that in May up spredis,
  In kirtillis grene, withoutyn kell or bandis :   60
  Thair brycht hairis hang gletering on the strandis
In tressis clere, wyppit wyth goldyn thredis ;
  With pappis quhite, and mydlis small as wandis.

Discrive I wald, bot quho coud wele endyte
How all the feldis wyth thai lilies quhite   65
  Depaynt war brycht, quhilk to the hevyn did glete :
Noucht thou, Omer, als fair as thou coud wryte,
For all thine ornate stilis so perfyte ;
  Nor yit thou, Tullius, quhois lippis suete
  Off rethorike did in to termes flete :   70
Your aureate tongis both bene all to lyte,
  For to compile that paradise complete.

Thare saw I Nature and Venus, quene and quene,
The fresch Aurora, and lady Flora schene,
  Juno, Appollo, and Proserpyna,   75
Dyane the goddesse chaste of woddis grene,
My lady Cleo, that help of makaris bene,
  Thetes, Pallas, and prudent Minerva,
  Fair feynit Fortune, and lemand Lucina,
Thir mychti quenis in crounis mycht be sene,   80
  Wyth bemys blith, bricht as Lucifera.

There saw I May, of myrthfull monethis quene,
Betuix Aprile and June, her sistir schene,
  Within the gardyng walking up and doun,

Quham of the foulis gladdith al bedene ;   85
Scho was full tender in hir yeris grene.
   Thare saw I Nature present hir a goune
   Rich to behald and nobil of renoune,
Off eviry hew under the hevin that bene
   Depaynt, and broud be gude proporcioun.   90

Full lustily thir ladyes all in fere
Enterit within this park of most plesere,
   Quhare that I lay our helit wyth levis ronk ;
The mery foulis, blisfullest of chere,
Salust Nature, me thoucht, on thair manere,   95
   And eviry blome on branch, and eke on bonk,
   Opnyt and spred thair balmy levis donk,
Full low enclynyng to thair Quene so clere,
   Quham of thair nobill norising thay thonk.

Syne to dame Flora, on the samyn wyse,   100
Thay saluse, and thay thank a thousand syse ;
   And to dame Venus, lufis mychti quene,
Thay sang ballettis in lufe, as was the gyse,
With amourouse notis lusty to devise,
   As thay that had lufe in thair hertis grene ;   105
   Thair hony throtis, opnyt fro the splene,
With werblis suete did perse the hevinly skyes,
   Quhill loud resownyt the firmament serene.

Ane othir court thare saw I consequent,
Cupide the king, wyth bow in hand ybent,   110
   And dredefull arowis grundyn scharp and square ;
Thare saw I Mars, the god armypotent,
Aufull and sterne, strong and corpolent ;
   Thare saw I crabbit Saturn ald and haire,
   His luke was lyke for to perturb the aire ;   115
Thare was Mercurius, wise and eloquent,
   Of rethorike that fand the flouris faire ;

Thare was the god of gardingis, Priapus ;
Thare was the god of wildernes, Phanus ;
   And Janus, god of entree delytable ;   120
Thare was the god of fludis, Neptunus ;
Thare was the god of wyndis, Eolus,
   With variand luke, rycht lyke a lord unstable ;

Thare was Bacus the gladder of the table ;
Thare was Pluto, the elrich incubus,   125
  In cloke of grene, his court usit no sable.

And eviry one of thir, in grene arayit,
On harp or lute full merily thai playit,
  And sang ballettis with michty notis clere :
Ladyes to dance full sobirly assayit,   130
Endlang the lusty ryvir so thai mayit,
  Thair observance rycht hevynly was to here ;
  Than crap I throu the levis, and drew nere,
Quhare that I was rycht sudaynly affrayit,
  All throu a luke, quhilk I have boucht full dere.   135

And schortly for to speke, be lufis quene
I was aspyit, scho bad hir archearis kene
  Go me arrest ; and thay no time delayit ;
Than ladyes fair lete fall thair mantillis grene,
With bowis big in tressit hairis schene,   140
  All sudaynly thay had a felde arayit ;
  And yit rycht gretly was I noucht affrayit,
The party was so plesand for to sene,
  A wonder lusty bikkir me assayit.

And first of all, with bow in hand ybent,   145
Come dame Beautee, rycht as scho wald me schent ;
  Syne folowit all hir dameselis yfere,
With mony diverse aufull instrument,
Unto the pres, Fair Having wyth hir went,
  Fyne Portrature, Plesance, and lusty Chere.   150
  Than come Resoun, with schelde of gold so clere,
In plate and maille, as Mars armypotent,
Defendit me that nobil chevallere.

Syne tender Youth come wyth hir virgyns ying,
Grene Innocence, and schamefull Abaising,   155
  And quaking Drede, wyth humble Obedience ;
The Goldyn Targe harmyt thay no thing ;
Curage in thame was noucht begonne to spring ;
  Full sore thay dred to done a violence :
  Suete Womanhede I saw cum in presence,   160
Of artilye a warld sche did in bring,
  Servit wyth ladyes full of reverence.

Sche led wyth hir Nurture and Lawlynes,
Contenence, Pacience, Gude Fame, and Stedfastnes,
   Discrecioun, Gentrise, and Considerance,   165
Levefell Company, and Honest Besynes,
Benigne Luke, Mylde Chere, and Sobirnes :
   All thir bure ganyeis to do me grevance ;
   But Resoun bure the Targe wyth sik constance,
Thair scharp assayes mycht do no dures   170
   To me, for all thair aufull ordynance.

Unto the pres persewit Hie Degree,
Hir folowit ay Estate, and Dignitee,
   Comparisoun, Honour, and Noble Array,
Will, Wantonnes, Renoun, and Libertee,   175
Richesse, Fredome, and eke Nobilitee :
   Wit ye thay did thair baner hye display ;
   A cloud of arowis as hayle schour lousit thay.
And schot, quhill wastit was thair artilye,
   Syne went abak reboytit of thair pray.   180

Quhen Venus had persavit this rebute,
Dissymilance scho bad go mak persute,
   At all powere to perse the Goldyn Targe ;
And scho, that was of doubilnes the rute,
Askit hir choise of archeris in refute.   185
   Venus the best bad hir go wale at large ;
   Scho tuke Presence, plicht ankers of the barge,
And Fair Callyng, that wele a flayn coud schute,
   And Cherising for to complete hir charge.

Dame Hamelynes scho tuke in company,   190
That hardy was and hende in archery,
   And broucht dame Beautee to the felde agayn ;
With all the choise of Venus chevalry
Thay come and bikkerit unabaisitly :
   The schour of arowis rappit on as rayn ;   195
   Perilouse Presence, that mony syre has slayne,
The bataill broucht on bordour hard us by,
   The salt was all the sarar suth to sayn.

Thik was the schote of grundyn dartis kene ;
Bot Resoun, with the Scheld of Gold so schene,   200
   Warly defendit quho so evir assayit ;

The aufull stoure he manly did sustene,
Quhill Presence kest a pulder in his ene,
    And than as drunkyn man he all forvayit :
    Quhen he was blynd, the fule wyth hym thay playit,   205
And banyst hym amang the bewis grene ;
    That sory sicht me sudaynly affrayit.

Than was I woundit to the deth wele nere,
And yoldyn as a wofull prisonnere
    To lady Beautee, in a moment space ;   210
Me thoucht scho semyt lustiar of chere,
Efter that Resoun tynt had his eyne clere,
    Than of before, and lufliare of face :
    Quhy was thou blyndit, Resoun ? quhi, allace !
And gert ane hell my paradise appere,   215
    And mercy seme, quhare that I fand no grace.

Dissymulance was besy me to sile,
And Fair Calling did oft apon me smyle,
    And Cherising me fed wyth wordis fair ;
New Acquyntance enbracit me a quhile,   220
And favouryt me, quhill men mycht go a myle,
    Syne tuk hir leve, I saw hir nevir mare :
    Than saw I Dangere toward me repair,
I coud eschew hir presence be no wyle.
    On syde scho lukit wyth ane fremyt fare,   225

And at the last departing coud hir dresse,
And me delyverit unto Hevynesse
    For to remayne, and scho in cure me tuke.
Be this the Lord of Wyndis, wyth wodenes,
God Eolus, his bugill blew I gesse,   230
    That with the blast the levis all to-schuke ;
    And sudaynly, in the space of a luke,
All was hyne went, thare was bot wildernes,
    Thare was no more bot birdis, bank, and bruke.

In twynkling of ane eye to schip thai went,   235
And swyth up saile unto the top thai stent,
    And with swift course atour the flude thay frak ;
Thay fyrit gunnis wyth powder violent,
Till that the reke raise to the firmament,
    The rochis all resownyt wyth the rak,   240

For rede it semyt that the raynbow brak ;
Wyth spirit affrayde apon my fete I sprent
   Amang the clewis, so carefull was the crak.

And as I did awake of my sueving,
The joyfull birdis merily did syng   245
   For myrth of Phebus tendir bemes schene ;
Suete war the vapouris, soft the morowing,
Halesum the vale, depaynt wyth flouris ying ;
   The air attemperit, sobir, and amene ;
   In quhite and rede was all the felde besene,   250
Throu Naturis nobil fresch anamalyng,
   In mirthfull May, of eviry moneth Quene.

O reverend Chaucere, rose of rethoris all,
As in oure tong ane flour imperiall,
   That raise in Britane evir, quho redis rycht,   255
Thou beris of makaris the tryumph riall ;
Thy fresch anamalit termes celicall
   This mater coud illumynit have full brycht :
   Was thou noucht of oure Inglisch all the lycht,
Surmounting eviry tong terrestriall,   260
   Alls fer as Mayis morow dois mydnycht ?

O morall Gower, and Ludgate laureate,
Your sugurit lippis and tongis aureate,
   Bene to oure eris cause of grete delyte ;
Your angel mouthis most mellifluate   265
Oure rude langage has clere illumynate,
   And faire ourgilt oure speche, that imperfyte
   Stude, or your goldyn pennis schupe to wryte ;
This Ile before was bare and desolate
   Off rethorike or lusty fresch endyte.   270

Thou lytill Quair, be evir obedient,
Humble, subject, and symple of entent,
   Before the face of eviry connyng wicht :
I knaw quhat thou of rethorike hes spent ;
Off all hir lusty rosis redolent   275
   Is none in to thy gerland sett on hicht ;
   Eschame thar of, and draw the out of sicht.
Rude is thy wede, disteynit, bare, and rent,
   Wele aucht thou be aferit of the licht.

Off Februar the fyiftene nycht,
Full lang befoir the dayis lycht,
I lay in till a trance ;
And then I saw baith hevin and hell :
Me thocht, amangis the feyndis fell,   5
Mahoun gart cry ane dance
Off schrewis that wer nevir schrevin,
Aganis the feist of Fasternis evin
To mak thair observance ;
He bad gallandis ga graith a gyis,   10
And kast up gamountis in the skyis,
That last came out of France.

" Lat se," quod he, " Now quha begynnis ; "
With that the fowll Sevin Deidly Synnis
Begowth to leip at anis.   15
And first of all in dance wes Pryd,
With hair wyld bak and bonet on syd,
Lyk to mak waistie wanis ;
And round abowt him, as a quheill,
Hang all in rumpillis to the heill   20
His kethat for the nanis :
Mony prowd trumpour with him trippit,
Throw skaldand fyre ay as thay skippit
Thay gyrnd with hiddous granis.

Heilie harlottis on hawtane wyis   25
Come in with mony sindrie gyis,
Bot yit luche nevir Mahoun,
Quhill preistis come in with bair schevin nekkis,
Than all the feyndis lewche and maid gekkis,
Blak Belly and Bawsy Brown.   30

Than Yre come in with sturt and stryfe ;
His hand wes ay upoun his knyfe,
He brandeist lyk a beir :
Bostaris, braggaris, and barganeris,
Eftir him passit in to pairis,   35
All bodin in feir of weir ;

In jakkis, and stryppis and bonettis of steill,
Thair leggis wer chenyeit to the heill,
Frawart wes thair affeir :
Sum upoun udir with brandis beft,   40
Sum jaggit uthiris to the heft,
With knyvis that scherp cowd scheir.

Nixt in the dance followit Invy,
Fild full of feid and fellony,
Hid malyce and dispyte ;   45
For pryvie hatrent that tratour trymlit.
Him followit mony freik dissymlit,
With fenyeit wirdis quhyte ;
And flattereris in to menis facis ;
And bakbyttaris in secreit places,   50
To ley that had delyte ;
And rownaris of fals lesingis ;
Allace ! that courtis of noble kingis
Of thame can nevir be quyte.

Nixt him in dans come Cuvatyce,   55
Rute of all evill and grund of vyce,
That nevir cowd be content ;
Catyvis, wrechis, and ockeraris,
Hud-pykis, hurdaris, and gadderaris,
All with that warlo went :   60
Out of thair throttis thay schot on udder
Hett moltin gold, me thocht a fudder,
As fyreflawcht maist fervent ;
Ay as thay tomit thame of schot,
Feyndis fild thame new up to the thrott   65
With gold of allkin prent.

Syne Sweirnes, at the secound bidding,
Come lyk a sow out of a midding,
Full slepy wes his grunyie :
Mony sweir bumbard belly huddroun,   70
Mony slute daw and slepy duddroun,
Him servit ay with sounyie ;

He drew thame furth in till a chenyie,
And Belliall, with a brydill renyie,
Evir lascht thame on the lunyie :   75
In dance thay war so slaw of feit,
Thay gaif thame in the fyre a heit,
And maid thame quicker of counyie.

Than Lichery, that lathly cors,
Come berand lyk a bagit hors,   80
And Ydilnes did him leid ;
Thair wes with him ane ugly sort,
And mony stynkand fowll tramort,
That had in syn bene deid.
Quhen thay wer entrit in the dance,   85
Thay wer full strenge of countenance,
Lyk turkas birnand reid ;
All led thay uthir by the tersis,
Suppois thay fyllt with thair ersis,
It mycht be na remeid.   90

Than the fowll monstir Glutteny,
Off wame unsasiable and gredy,
To dance he did him dres :
Him followit mony fowll drunckart,
With can and collep, cop and quart,   95
In surffet and exces ;
Full mony a waistles wallydrag,
With wamis unweildable, did furth wag,
In creische that did incres ;
" Drynk ! " ay thay cryit, with mony a gaip,   100
The feyndis gaif thame hait leid to laip,
Thair lovery wes na les.

Na menstrallis playit to thame but dowt,
For glemen thair wer haldin owt,
Be day and eik by nycht ;   105
Except a menstrall that slew a man,
Swa till his heretage he wan,
And entirt be breif of richt.

Than cryd Mahoun for a Heleand padyane ;
Syne ran a feynd to feche Makfadyane,   110
Far northwart in a nuke ;
Be he the correnoch had done schout,
Erschemen so gadderit him abowt,
In Hell grit rowme thay tuke.
Thae tarmegantis, with tag and tatter,   115
Full lowd in Ersche begowth to clatter,
And rowp lyk revin and ruke :
The Devill sa devit wes with thair yell,
That in the depest pot of hell
He smorit thame with smuke.   120

58. THE SOWTAR AND TAILYOURIS WAR

NIXT THAT a turnament wes tryid,
That lang befoir in hell wes cryid,
In presens of Mahoun ;
Betuix a telyour and ane sowtar,
A prick lous and ane hobbell clowttar,   5
The barres wes maid boun.
The tailyeour, baith with speir and scheild,
Convoyit wes unto the feild
With mony lymmar loun,
Off seme byttaris and beist knapparis,   10
Off stomok steillaris and clayth takkaris,
A graceles garisoun.

His baner born wes him befoir,
Quhairin wes clowttis ane hundreth scoir,
Ilk ane of divers hew ;   15
And all stowin out of sindry webbis,
For, quhill the greit sie flowis and ebbis,
Telyouris will nevir be trew.
The tailyour on the barres blent,
Allais ! he tynt all hardyment,   20
For feir he chaingit hew :
Mahoun come furth and maid him knycht,
Na ferly thocht his hart wes licht,
That to sic honor grew.

The tailyeour hecht befoir Mahoun   25
That he suld ding the sowtar doun,
Thocht he wer strang as mast ;
Bot quhen he on the barres blenkit,
The telyoris hairt a littill schrenkit,
His hairt did all ourcast.   30
Quhen to the sowtar he did cum,
Off all sic wirdis he wes full dum,
So soir he wes agast ;
In harte he tuke yit sic ane scunner,
Ane rak of fartis, lyk ony thunner,   35
Went fra him, blast for blast.

The sowtar to the feild him drest,
He wes convoyid out of the west,
As ane defender stout :
Suppois he had na lusty varlot,   40
He had full mony lowsy harlott
Round rynnand him aboute.
His baner wes of barkit hyd,
Quhairin Sanct Girnega did glyd
Befoir that rebald rowt :   45
Full sowttarlyk he wes of laitis,
For ay betuix the harnes plaitis
The uly birstit out.

Quhen on the telyour he did luke,
His hairt a littill dwamyng tuke,   50
He mycht nocht rycht upsitt ;
In to his stommok wes sic ane steir,
Off all his dennar, quhilk he coft deir,
His breist held deill a bitt.
To comfort him, or he raid forder,   55
The Devill off knychtheid gaif him order,
For sair syne he did spitt,
And he about the Devillis nek
Did spew agane ane quart of blek,
Thus knychtly he him quitt.   60

Than fourty tymis the Feynd cryd, Fy !
The sowtar rycht effeiritly
Unto the feild he socht :

Quhen thay wer servit of thair speiris,
Folk had ane feill be thair effeiris,   65
Thair hairtis wer baith on flocht.
Thay spurrit thair hors on adir syd,
Syne thay attour the grund cowd glyd,
Than thame togidder brocht ;
The tailyeour that wes nocht weill sittin,   70
He left his sadill all beschittin,
And to the grund he socht.

His harnas brak and maid ane brattill,
The sowtaris hors scart with the rattill,
And round about cowd reill ;   75
The beist that frayit wes rycht evill,
Ran with the sowtar to the Devill,
And he rewardit him weill.
Sum thing frome him the Feynd eschewit,
He went agane to bene bespewit,   80
So stern he wes in steill :
He thocht he wald agane debait him,
He turnd his ers and all bedret him,
Evin quyte from nek till heill.

He lowsit it of with sic a reird,   85
Baith hors and man he straik till eird,
He fartit with sic ane feir ;
" Now haif I quitt the," quod Mahoun ;
Thir new maid knychtis lay bayth in swoun,
And did all armes mensweir.   90
The Devill gart thame to dungeoun dryve,
And thame of knychtheid cold depryve,
Dischairgeing thame of weir ;
And maid thame harlottis bayth for evir,
Quhilk style to keip thay had fer levir,   95
Nor ony armes beir.

I had mair of thair werkis writtin,
Had nocht the sowtar bene beschittin
With Belliallis ers unblist ;
Bot that sa gud ane bourd me thocht,   100
Sic solace to my hairt it rocht,
For lawchtir neir I brist ;

Quhairthrow I walknit of my trance.
To put this in rememberance,
Mycht no man me resist, 105
For this said justing it befell
Befoir Mahoun, the air of hell :
Now trow this gif ye list.

59. THE AMENDIS TO THE TELYOURIS AND SOWTARIS
FOR THE TURNAMENT MAID ON THAME

BETUIX TWELL houris and ellevin,
I dremed ane angell came fra Hevin
With plesand stevin sayand on hie,
Telyouris and Sowtaris, blist be ye.

In Hevin hie ordand is your place, 5
Aboif all sanctis in grit solace,
Nixt God grittest in dignitie :
Tailyouris and Sowtaris, blist be ye.

The caus to yow is nocht unkend,
That God mismakkis ye do amend, 10
Be craft and grit agilitie :
Tailyouris and Sowtaris, blist be ye.

Sowtaris, with schone weill maid and meit,
Ye mend the faltis of ill maid feit,
Quhairfoir to Hevin your saulis will fle ; 15
Telyouris and Sowtaris, blist be ye.

Is nocht in all this fair a flyrok,
That hes upoun his feit a wyrok,
Knowll tais, nor mowlis in no degrie,
Bot ye can hyd thame : blist be ye. 20

And ye tailyouris, with weil maid clais
Can mend the werst maid man that gais,
And mak him semely for to se :
Telyouris and Sowtaris, blist be ye.

Thocht God mak ane misfassonit man,   25
Ye can him all schaip new agane,
And fassoun him bettir he sic thre :
Telyouris and Sowtaris, blist be ye.

Thocht a man haif a brokin bak,
Haif he a gude telyour, quhatt rak,   30
That can it cuver with craftis slie :
Telyouris and Sowtaris, blist be ye.

Off God grit kyndnes may ye clame,
That helpis his peple fra cruke and lame,
Supportand faltis with your supple :   35
Tailyouris and Sowtaris, blist be ye.

In erd ye kyth sic mirakillis heir,
In Hevin ye salbe sanctis full cleir,
Thocht ye be knavis in this cuntre :
Telyouris and Sowtaris, blist be ye.   40

60. THE DREAM

THIS HINDER nycht, halff sleiping as I lay,
Me thocht my chalmer in ane new aray
   Was all depent with many divers hew,
   Of all the nobill storyis ald and new,
Sen oure first father formed was of clay.   5

Me thocht the lift all bricht with lampis lycht,
And thairin enterrit many lustie wicht,
   Sum young, sum old, in sindry wyse arayit,
   Sum sang, sum danceit, on instrumentis sum playit,
Sum maid disportis with hartis glaid and lycht.   10

Thane thocht I thus, this is ane felloun phary,
Or ellis my witt rycht woundrouslie dois varie ;
   This seimes to me ane guidlie companie,
   And gif it be ane freindlie fantasie,
Defend me Jhesu and his moder Marie !   15

Thair pleasant sang, nor yett thair pleasant toun,
Nor yett thair joy did to my heart redoun ;
 Me thocht the drerie damiesall Distres,
 And eik hir sorie sister Hivines,
Sad as the leid, in baid lay me abone.   20

And Langour satt up at my beddis heid,
With instrument full lamentable and deid ;
 Scho playit sangis so duilfull to heir,
 Me thocht ane houre seimeit ay ane yeir ;
Hir hew was wan and wallowed as the leid. 25

Thane com the ladyis danceing in ane trace,
And Nobilnes befoir thame come ane space,
 Saying, withe cheir bening and womanly,
 " I se ane heir in bed oppressit ly,
My sisteris, go and help to get him grace." 30

With that anon did start out of a dance
Twa sisteris callit Confort and Pleasance,
 And with twa harpis did begin to sing,
 Bot I thairof mycht tak na rejoseing,
My heavines opprest me with sic mischance. 35

Thay saw that I not glader wox of cheir,
And thairof had thai winder all but weir,
 And said ane lady, that Persaveing hecht,
 " Of Hevines he fiellis sic a wecht,
Your melody he pleisis nocht till heir, 40

Scho and Distres hir sister dois him greve."
Quod Nobilnes, " Quhow sall he thame eschev ? "
 Thane spak Discretioun, ane lady richt bening,
 " Wirk eftir me, and I sall gar him sing,
And lang or nicht gar Langar tak hir leve." 45

And then said Witt, " Gif thai work nocht be the,
But onie dout thai sall not work be me."
 Discretioun said, " I knaw his malady,
 The strok he feillis of melancholie,
And Nobilnes, [his] lecheing lyis in the. 50

Or evir this wicht at heart be haill and feir,
Both thow and I most in the court appeir,
 For he hes lang maid service thair in vane :
 With sum rewaird we mane him quyt againe,
Now in the honour of this guid new yeir."   55

" Weill worth the, sister," said Considerance,
" And I sall help for to mantene the dance."
 Than spak ane wicht callit Blind Effectioun,
 " I sall befoir yow be, with myne electioun,
Of all the court I have the governance."   60

Thane spak ane constant wycht callit Ressoun
And said, " I grant yow hes beine lord a sessioun
 In distributioun, bot now the tyme is gone,
 Now I may all distribute myne alone ;
Thy wrangous deidis did evir mane enschesoun. 65

For tyme war now that this mane had sum thing,
That lange hes bene ane servand to the king,
 And all his tyme nevir flatter couthe nor faine,
 Bot humblie into ballat wyse complaine,
And patientlie indure his tormenting.   70

I counsall him be mirrie and jocound,
Be Nobilnes his help mon first be found."
 " Weill spokin, Ressoun, my brother," quoth Discretioun,
 " To sett on dies with lordis at the cessioun,
Into this realme yow war worth mony ane pound." 75

Thane spak anone Inoportunitie,
" Ye sall not all gar him speid without me,
 For I stand ay befoir the kingis face ;
 I sall him deiff or ellis my self mak hace,
Bot gif that I befoir him servit be.   80

Ane besy askar soonner sall he speid
Na sall twa besy servandis out of dreid,
 And he that askis nocht tynes bot his word,
 Bot for to tyne lang service is no bourd,
Yett thocht I nevir to do sic folie deid." 85

Than com anon ane callit Sir Johne Kirkpakar,
Off many cures ane michtie undertaker,
   Quod he, " I am possest in kirkis sevin,
   And yitt I think thai grow sall till ellevin,
Or he be servit in ane, yone ballet maker.   90

And then Sir Bet-the-kirk, " Sa mot I thryff,
I haif of busie servandis foure or fyve,
   And all direct unto sindrie steidis,
   Ay still awaitting upoun kirkmenes deidis,
Fra quham sum tithingis will I heir belyff."   95

Quod Ressoun than, " The ballance gois unevin,
That thow, allace, to serff hes kirkis sevin,
   And sevin als worth kirk nocht haifand ane,
   With gredines I sie this world ourgane,
And sufficience dwellis nocht bot in heavin."   100

" I have nocht wyt thairof," quod Temperance,
" For thocht I hald him evinlie the ballance,
   And but ane cuir full micht till him wey,
   Yett will he take ane uther and gar it suey :
Quha best can rewll wald maist have governance.   105

Patience to me, " My friend," said, " mak guid cheir,
And on the prince depend with humelie feir,
   For I full weill dois knaw his nobill intent ;
   He wald not for ane bischopperikis rent
That yow war unrewairdit half ane yeir."   110

Than as ane fary thai to duir did frak,
And schot ane gone that did so ruidlie rak,
   Quhill all the air did raird the ranebow under,
   On Leith sandis me thocht scho brak in sounder,
And I anon did walkin with the crak.   115

61. THE BALLADE OF LORD BERNARD STEWART, LORD OF AUBIGNY

Renownit, ryall, right reverend, and serene
   Lord, hie tryumphing in wirschip and valoure,
Fro kyngis downe, most Cristin knight and kene,
   Most wyse, most valyeand, moste laureat hie victour,

Onto the sterris upheyt is thyne honour ;   5
In Scotland welcum be thyne Excellence
  To King, Queyne, lord, clerk, knight and servatour,
Withe glorie and honour, lawde and reverence.

Welcum, in stour most strong, incomparable knight,
  The fame of armys, and floure of vassalage ;   10
Welcum, in were moste worthi, wyse, and wight ;
  Welcum, the soun of Mars of moste curage ;
  Welcum, moste lusti branche of our linnage,
In every realme oure scheild and our defence ;
  Welcum, our tendir blude of hie parage,   15
With glorie and honour, lawde and reverence.

Welcum, in were the secund Julius,
  The prince of knightheyd, and flour of chevalry ;
Welcum, most valyeant and victorius ;
  Welcum, invincible victour moste wourthy ;   20
  Welcum, our Scottis chiftane most dughti ;
Wyth sowne of clarioun, organe, song, and sence,
  To the atonis, Lord, Welcum all we cry ;
With glorie and honour, lawde and reverence.

Welcum, oure indeficient adjutorie,   25
  That evir our naceoun helpit in thare neyd ;
That never saw Scot yit indigent nor sory,
  Bot thou did hym suport with thi gud deid ;
  Welcum, therfor, abufe all livand leyd,
Withe us to live and to maik recidence,   30
  Quhilk never sall sunye for thy saik to bleid :
To quham be honour, lawde and reverence.

Is none of Scotland borne faithfull and kynde,
  Bot he of naturall inclinacioune
Dois favour the, withe all his hert and mynde,   35
  Withe fervent, tendir, trew intencioun ;
  And wald of inwart hie effectioun,
Bot dreyd of danger, de in thi defence,
  Or dethe, or schame, war done to thi persoun ;
To quham be honour, lawde and reverence.   40

Welcum, thow knight moste fortunable in feild ;
  Welcum, in armis moste aunterus and able,

Undir the soune that beris helme or scheild ;
    Welcum, thou campioun in feght unourcumable ;
    Welcum, most dughti, digne, and honorable,   45
And moist of lawde and hie magnificence,
    Nixt undir kingis to stand incomparable ;
To quham be honour, lawde, and reverence.

Throw Scotland, Ingland, France, and Lumbardy,
    Fleys on weyng thi fame and thi renoune ;   50
And our all cuntreis undirnethe the sky,
    And our all strandis fro the sterris doune ;
    In every province, land, and regioune,
Proclamit is thi name of excellence,
    In every cete, village, and in toune,   55
Withe glorie and honour, lawde and reverence.

O feyrse Achill in furius hie curage !
    O strong invincible Hector undir scheild !
O vailyeant Arthur in knyghtli vassalage !
    Agamenon in governance of feild !   60
    Bold Henniball in batall to do beild !
Julius in jupert, in wisdom and expence !
    Most fortunable chiftane bothe in yhouth and eild,
To the be honour, lawde and reverence !

At parlament thow suld be hye renownit,   65
    That did so mony victoryse opteyn ;
Thi cristall helme with lawry suld be crownyt,
    And in thi hand a branche of olyve greyn ;
    The sueird of conquis and of knyghtheid keyn
Be borne suld highe before the in presence,   70
    To represent sic man as thou has beyn ;
With glorie and honour, lawde and reverence.

Hie furius Mars, the god armipotent,
    Rong in the hevin at thyne nativite ;
Saturnus doune, withe fyry eyn, did blent,   75
    Throw bludy visar, men manasing to gar de ;
    On the fresche Venus keist hir amourouse E ;
On the Marcurius furtheyet his eloquence ;
    Fortuna Maior did turn hir face on the ;
With glorie and honour, lawde and reverence.   80

Prynce of fredom and flour of gentilnes,
  Sweyrd of knightheid and choise of chevalry,
This tyme I lefe, for grete prolixitnes,
  To tell quhat feildis thou wan in Pikkardy,
  In France, in Bertan, in Naplis, and Lumbardy ;   85
As I think eftir, withe all my diligence,
  Or thow departe, at lenthe for to discry ;
With glorie and honour, lawde and reverence.

B, in thi name, betaknis batalrus ;
  A, able in feild ; R, right renoune most hie ;   90
N, nobilnes ; and A, for aunterus ;
  R, ryall blude ; for dughtines, is D ;
  V, valyeantnes ; S, for strenewite ;
Quhoise knyghtli name, so schynyng in clemence,
  For wourthines in gold suld writtin be ;   95
With glorie and honour, lawde and reverence.

62. ELEGY ON THE DEATH OF BERNARD STEWART, LORD OF AUBIGNY

Illuster Lodovick, of France most Cristin king,
  Thow may complain with sighis lamentable
The death of Bernard Stewart, nobill and ding,
  In deid of armis most anterous and abill,
  Most mychti, wyse, worthie, and confortable,   5
Thy men of weir to governe and to gy :
  For him, allace ! now may thow weir the sabill,
Sen he is gone, the flour of chevelrie.

Complaine sould everie nobill valiant knycht
  The death of him that douchtie was in deid,   10
That many ane fo in feild hes put to flight,
  In weiris wicht, be wisdome and manheid.
  To the Turk sey all land did his name dreid,
Quhois force all France in fame did magnifie ;
  Of so hie price sall nane his place posseid,   15
For he is gon, the flour of chevelrie.

O duilfull death ! O dragon dolorous !
  Quhy hes thow done so dulfullie devoir

The prince of knychtheid, nobill and chevilrous,
  The witt of weiris, of armes and honour,   20
  The crop of curage, the strenth of armes in stour,
The fame of France, the fame of Lumbardy,
  The chois of chiftanes, most awfull in airmour,
The charbuckell, cheif of every chevelrie !

Pray now for him all that him loveit heir !   25
  And for his saull mak intercessioun
Unto the Lord, that hes him bocht so deir,
  To gif him mercie and remissioun ;
  And namelie we of Scottis natioun,
Intill his lyff quhom most he did affy,   30
  Foryhett we nevir into our orisoun
To pray for him, the flour of chevelrie.

63. THE MERLE AND THE NYCHTINGAILL

In MAY as that Aurora did upspring,
With cristall ene chasing the cluddis sable,
I hard a merle with mirry notis sing
A sang of lufe, with voce rycht comfortable,
Agane the orient bemis amiable,   5
Upone a blisfull brenche of lawry grene ;
This wes hir sentens sueit and delectable,
A lusty lyfe in luves service bene.

Undir this brench ran doun a revir bricht,
Of balmy liquour, cristallyne of hew,   10
Agane the hevinly aisur skyis licht,
Quhair did, upone the tother syd, persew
A nychtingall, with suggurit notis new,
Quhois angell fedderis as the pacok schone ;
This wes hir song, and of a sentens trew,   15
All luve is lost bot upone God allone.

With notis glaid and glorious armony,
This joyfull merle so salust scho the day,
Quhill rong the widdis of hir melody,
Saying, " Awalk, ye luvaris, O, this May.   20

Lo, fresche Flora hes flurest every spray,
As natur hes hir taucht, the noble quene,
The felld bene clothit in a new array ,
A lusty lyfe in luvis service bene.

Nevir suetar noys wes hard with levand man,   25
Na maid this mirry gentill nychtingaill,
Hir sound went with the rever as it ran,
Outthrow the fresche and flureist lusty vaill.
" O merle," quod scho, " O fule, stynt of thy taill,
For in thy song gud sentens is thair none,   30
For boith is tynt the tyme and the travaill
Of every luve bot upone God allone."

" Seis," quod the merle, " thy preching, nychtingale,
Sall folk thair yewth spend in to holines ?
Of yung sanctis growis auld feyndis but faill ;   35
Fy, ypocreit, in yeiris tendirness,
Agane the law of kynd thow gois expres,
That crukit aige makis on with yewth serene,
Quhome natur of conditionis maid dyvers ;
A lusty life in luves service bene."   40

The nychtingaill said, " Fule, remembir the,
That both in yewth and eild, and every hour,
The luve of God most deir to man suld be,
That him of nocht wrocht lyk his awin figour,
And deit him self fro deid him to succour.   45
O, quhithir wes kythit thair trew lufe or none ?
He is most trew and steidfast paramour ;
All luve is lost bot upone him allone."

The merle said, " Quhy put God so grit bewte
In ladeis, with sic womanly having,   50
Bot gife he wald that thay suld luvit be ?
To luve eik natur gaif thame inclynnyng ;
And He, of natur that wirker wes and king,
Wald no thing frustir put, nor lat be sene,
In to his creature of his awin making :   55
A lusty lyfe in luves service bene."

The nychtingall said, " Nocht to that behufe
Put God sic bewty in a ladeis face,

That scho suld haif the thank thairfoir or lufe,
Bot He, the wirker, that put in hir sic grace   60
Off bewty, bontie, riches, tyme or space,
And every gudnes that bene to cum or gone,
The thank redoundis to him in every place ;
All luve is lost bot upone God allone."

" O nychtingall, it wer a story nyce,   65
That luve suld nocht depend on cherite,
And gife that vertew contrair be to vyce,
Than lufe mon be a vertew, as thinkis me ;
For ay to lufe invy mone contrair be :
God bad eik lufe thy nychtbour fro the splene,   70
And quho than ladeis suetar nychbouris be ?
A lusty lyfe in lufes service bene."

The nychtingaill said, " Bird, quhy dois thow raif ?
Man may tak in his lady sic delyt,
Him to foryhet that hir sic vertew gaif,   75
And for his hevin rassaif hir cullour quhyt ;
Hir goldin tressit hairis redomyt,
Lyk to Appollois bemis thocht thay schone,
Suld nocht him blind fro lufe that is perfyt ;
All lufe is lost bot upone God allone."   80

The merle said, " Lufe is caus of honour ay,
Luve makis cowardis manheid to purchas,
Luve makis knychtis hardy at assey,
Luve makis wrechis full of lergenes,
Luve makis sueir folkis full of bissines,   85
Luve makis sluggirdis fresche and weill besene,
Luve changis vyce in vertewis nobilnes ;
A lusty lyfe in luvis service bene."

The nychtingaill said, " Trew is the contrary ;
Sic frustir luve, it blindis men so far,   90
In to thair myndis it makis thame to vary ;
In fals vane glory thai so drunkin ar,
Thair wit is went, of wo thai ar nocht war,
Quhill that all wirchip away be fro thame gone,
Fame, guddis, and strenth ; quhairfoir weill say I dar,   95
All luve is lost bot upone God allone."

Than said the merle, " Myn errour I confes ;
This frustir luve all is bot vanite ;
Blind ignorance me gaif sic hardines,
To argone so agane the varite ;   100
Quhairfoir I counsall every man, that he
With lufe nocht in the feindis net be tone,
Bot luve the luve that did for his lufe de ;
All lufe is lost bot upone God allone."

Than sang thay both with vocis lowd and cleir ;   105
The merle sang, " Man, lufe God that hes the wrocht : "
The nychtingall sang, " Man, lufe the Lord most deir,
That the and all this warld maid ot nocht : "
The merle said, " Luve him that thy lufe hes socht
Fra hevin to erd, and heir tuk flesche and bone : "   110
The nychtingall sang, " And with his deid the bocht ;
All lufe is lost bot upone him allone."

Thane flaw thir birdis our the bewis schene,
Singing of lufe amang the levis small,
Quhois ythand pleid yit maid my thochtis grene,   115
Bothe sleping, walking, in rest and in travall ;
Me to reconfort most it dois availl
Agane for lufe, quhen lufe I can find none,
To think how song this merle and nychtingaill,
All lufe is lost bot upone God allone.   120

64. TO ABERDEIN

BLYTH ABERDEANE, thow beriall of all tounis,
    The lamp of bewtie, bountie, and blythnes ;
Unto the heaven [ascendit] thy renoun is
    Off vertew, wisdome, and of worthines ;
    He nottit is thy name of nobilnes,   5
Into the cuming of oure lustie Quein,
    The wall of welth, guid cheir, and mirrines :
Be blyth and blisfull, burgh of Aberdein.

And first hir mett the burges of the toun
    Richelie arrayit, as become thame to be,   10
Of quhom they cheset four men of renoun,
    In gounes of velvot, young, abill, and lustie,

G

To beir the paill of velves cramase
Abone hir heid, as the custome hes bein ;
　　Gryt was the sound of the artelyie :　　　　　　15
Be blyth and blisfull, burgh of Aberdein.

Ane fair processioun mett hir at the Port,
　　In a cap of gold and silk, full pleasantlie,
Syne at hir entrie, with many fair disport,
　　Ressaveit hir on streittis lustilie ;　　　　　　20
　　Quhair first the Salutatioun honorabilly
Of the sweitt Virgin guidlie mycht be seine ;
　　The sound of menstrallis blawing to the sky :
Be blyth and blisfull, burgh of Aberdein.

And syne thow gart the orient kingis thrie　　　　25
　　Offer to Chryst, with benyng reverence,
Gold, sence, and mir, with all humilitie,
　　Schawand him king with most magnificence ;
　　Syne quhow the angill, with sword of violence,
Furth of the joy of paradice putt clein　　　　　30
　　Adame and Ev for innobedience :
Be blyth and blisfull, burcht of Aberdein.

And syne the Bruce, that evir was bold in sto[u]r,
　　Thow gart as roy cum rydand under croun,
Richt awfull, strang, and large of portratour,　　35
　　As nobill, dreidfull, michtie campioun :
　　The [nobill Stewarts] syne, of great renoun,
Thow gart upspring, with branches new and greine,
　　Sa gloriouslie, quhill glaidid all the toun :
Be blyth and blisfull, burcht of Aberdein.　　　　40

Syne come thair four and tuentie madinis ying,
　　All claid in greine of mervelous bewtie,
With hair detressit, as threidis of gold did hing,
　　With quhyt hattis all browderit rycht brav[elie,]
　　Playand on timberallis and syngand rycht sweitlie ;　45
That seimlie sort, in ordour weill besein,
　　Did meit the Quein, hir [saluand] reverentlie :
Be blyth and blisfull, burcht of Aberdein.

The streittis war all hung with tapestrie,
　　Great was the pres of peopill dwelt about,　　　　50

And pleasant padgeanes playit prattelie ;
   The legeis all did to thair Lady loutt,
   Quha was convoyed with ane royall routt
Off gryt barrounes and lustie ladyis [schene] ;
   Welcum, our Quein ! the commones gaif ane schout : 55
Be blyth and blisfull, burcht of Aberdein.

At hir cuming great was the mirth and joy,
   For at thair croce aboundantlie rane wyne ;
Untill hir ludgeing the toun did hir convoy ;
   Hir for to treit thai sett thair haill ingyne,   60
   Ane riche present thai did till hir propyne,
Ane costlie coup that large thing wald contene,
   Coverit and full of cunyeitt gold rycht fyne :
Be blyth and blisfull, burcht of Aberdein.

O potent princes, pleasant and preclair,   65
   Great caus thow hes to thank this nobill toun,
That, for to do the honnour, did not spair
   Thair geir, riches, substance, and persoun,
   The to ressave on maist fair fasoun ;
The for to pleis thay socht all way and mein ;   70
   Thairfoir, sa lang as Quein thow beiris croun,
Be thankfull to this burcht of Aberdein.

65. QUHEN THE GOVERNOUR PAST IN FRANCE

Thow that in hevin, for our salvatioun,
   Maid justice, mercie, and pietie, to aggre ;
And Gabriell send with the salutatioun
   On to the mayd of maist humilite ;
   And maid thy sone to tak humanite,   5
For our demeritis to be of Marie borne ;
   Have of us pietie and our protectour be !
For, but thy help, this kynrik is forlorne.

O hie supernale Father of sapience,
   Quhilk of thy vertew dois everie folie chais,   10
Ane spark of thy hie excellent prudence
   Giff us, that nowther wit nor ressoun hes !

In quhais hertis no prudence can tak place,
Exemple, nor experience of beforne ;
    To us, synnaris, ane drop send of thy grace !   15
For, but thy help, this kynrik is forlorne.

We are so beistlie, dull, and ignorant,
    Our rudnes may nocht lichtlie be correctit ;
Bot thow, that art of mercy militant,
    Thy vengeance seis on us to syn subjectit,   20
    And gar thy justice be with reuth correctit ;
For quyt away so wyld fra us is worne,
    And in folie we ar so fer infectit,
At, but thy help, this kingrik is forlorne.

Thow, that on rude us ransounit and redemit,   25
    Rew on our syn, befoir your sicht decydit ;
Spair our trespas, quhilk may nocht be expremit,
    For breif of justice, for we may nocht abyd it,
    Help this pure realme in partiis all devydit !
Us succour send, that war the croun of thorne,   30
    That with the gift of grace it may be gydit !
For, but thy help, this kinrik is forlorne.

Lord ! hald thy hand, that strikken hes so soir ;
    Have of us pietie eftir our punytioun ;
And gif us grace the to greif no moir,   35
    And gar us mend with pennance and contritioun ;
    And to thy vengeance mak non additioun,
As thow that of michtis may to morne ;
    Fra cair to confort thow mak restitutioun,
For, but thy help, this kynrik is forlorne.   40

66. OF THE CHANGES OF LYFE

I seik about this warld unstabille
To find ane sentence convenabille,
    Bot I can nocht in all my wit
    Sa trew ane sentence fynd off it,
As say, it is dessaveabille.   5

For yesterday, I did declair
Quhow that the seasoun, soft and fair,
  Com in alo fresche as pako fedder;
  This day it stangis lyk ane edder,
Concluding all in my contrair.   10

Yisterday fair up sprang the flouris,
This day thai ar all slane with schouris;
  And fowllis in forrest that sang cleir,
  Now walkis with a drery cheir,
Full caild ar baith thair beddis and bouris.   15

So nixt to summer winter bein;
Nixt efter confort cairis kein;
  Nixt dirk mednycht the mirthefull morrow;
  Nixt efter joy aye cumis sorrow:
So is this warld and ay hes bein.   20

67. OF COVETYCE

Fredome, honour, and nobilnes,
Meid, manheid, mirth, and gentilnes
Ar now in cowrt reput as vyce,
And all for caus of cuvetice.

All weilfair, welth, and wantones   5
Ar chengit into wretchitnes,
And play is sett at littill price;
And all for caus of covetyce.

Halking, hunting, and swift hors rynning
Ar chengit all in wrangus wynnyng;   10
Thair is no play bot cartis and dyce;
And all for caus of covetyce.

Honorable houshaldis ar all laid doun;
Ane laird hes with him bot a loun,
That leidis him eftir his devyce;   15
And all for caus of covetyce.

In burghis, to landwart and to sie,
Quhair was plesour and grit plentie,
Vennesoun, wyld fowill, wyne, and spyce,
Ar now decayid thruch covetyce.   20

Husbandis that grangis had full grete,
Cattell and corne to sell and ete,
Hes now no beist bot cattis and myce ;
And all thruch caus of covettyce.

Honest yemen in every toun   25
War wont to weir baith reid and broun,
Ar now arrayit in raggis with lyce ;
And all thruch caus of covetyce.

And lairdis in silk harlis to the heill,
For quhilk thair tennentis sald somer meill,   30
And leivis on rutis undir the ryce ;
And all thruch caus of covetyce.

Quha that dois deidis of petie,
And leivis in pece and cheretie,
Is haldin a fule, and that full nyce ;   35
And all thruch caus of covetyce.

And quha can reive uthir menis rowmis,
And upoun peur men gadderis sowmis,
Is now ane active man and wyice ;
And all thruch caus of covetyce.   40

Man, pleis thy makar and be mirry,
And sett not by this warld a chirry ;
Wirk for the place of paradyce,
For thairin ringis na covettyce.

68. GUDE COUNSALE

Be ye ane luvar, think ye nocht ye suld
Be weill advysit in your governing ?
Be ye nocht sa, it will on yow be tauld ;
Bewar thairwith for dreid of misdemyng.

Be nocht a wreche, nor skerche in your spending,   5
Be layth alway to do amis or schame ;
Be rewlit rycht and keip this doctring,
Be secreit, trew, incressing of your name.

Be ye ane lear, that is werst of all,
Be ye ane tratlar, that I hald als evill ;   10
Be ye ane janglar, and ye fra vertew fall,
Be nevir mair on to thir vicis thrall ;
Be now and ay the maistir of your will,
Be nevir he that lesing sall proclame ;
Be nocht of langage quhair ye suld be still,   15
Be secreit, trew, incressing of your name.

Be nocht abasit for no wicket tung,
Be nocht sa set as I haif said yow heir ;
Be nocht sa lerge unto thir sawis sung,
Be nocht our prowd, thinkand ye haif no peir ;   20
Be ye so wyis that uderis at yow leir,
Be nevir he to sklander nor defame ;
Be of your lufe nor prechour as a freir,
Be secreit, trew, incressing of your name.

69. BEST TO BE BLYTH

FULL OFT I mus and hes in thocht
How this fals warld is ay on flocht,
Quhair no thing ferme is nor degest ;
And quhen I haif my mynd all socht,
For to be blyth me think is best.   5

This warld evir dois flicht and vary ;
Fortoun sa fast hir quheill dois cary,
Na tyme bot turne can it tak rest ;
For quhois fals change suld none be sary ;
For to be blyth me thynk it best.   10

Wald man in mynd considdir weill,
Or fortoun on him turn hir quheill,
That erdly honour may nocht lest,
His fall les panefull he suld feill ;
For to be blyth me think it best.   15

Quha with this warld dois warsill and stryfe,
And dois his dayis in dolour dryfe,
Thocht he in lordschip be possest,
He levis bot ane wrechit lyfe ;
For to be blyth me think it best.   20

Off wardlis gud and grit riches,
Quhat fruct hes man but mirines ?
Thocht he this warld had eist and west,
All wer povertie but glaidnes ;
For to be blyth me thynk it best.   25

Quho suld for tynsall drowp or de
For thyng that is bot vanitie,
Sen to the lyfe that evir dois lest
Heir is bot twynklyng of ane E ;
For to be blyth me think it best.   30

Had I for warldis unkyndnes
In hairt tane ony havines,
Or fro my plesans bene opprest,
I had bene deid langsyne, dowtles ;
For to be blyth me think it best.   35

How evir this warld do change and vary
Lat us in hairt nevir moir be sary,
Bot evir be reddy and addrest
To pas out of this frawdfull fary ;
For to be blyth me think it best.   40

70. OF CONTENT

Quho thinkis that he hes sufficence,
Off gudis hes no indigence ;
    Thocht he have nowder land nor rent,
Grit mycht, nor hie magnificence,
    He hes anewch that is content.   5

Quho had all riches unto Ynd,
And wer not satefeit in mynd,

With povertie I hald him schent ;
Off covatyce sic is the kynd :
   He hes anewch that is content.   10

Thairfoir I pray yow, bredir deir,
Not to delyt in daynteis seir ;
   Thank God of it is to the sent,
And of it glaidlie mak gud cheir :
   He hes anewch that is content.   15

Defy the warld, feynyeit and fals,
With gall in hart and huny in hals :
   Quha maist it servis maist sall repent :
Off quhais surcharge sour is the sals :
   He hes aneuch that is content.   20

Gif thow hes mycht, be gentill and fre ;
And gif thow standis in povertie,
   Off thine awin will to it consent,
And riches sall returne to the :
   He hes aneuch that is content.   25

And ye and I, my bredir all,
That in this lyfe hes lordschip small,
   Lat languour not in us imprent ;
Gif we not clym we tak no fall :
   He hes aneuch that is content.   30

For quho in warld moist covatus is
In world is purast man, I wis,
   And moist neidy of his intent ;
For of all gudis no thing is his
   That of no thing can be content.   35

71. ALL ERDLY JOY RETURNIS IN PANE

Off Lentren in the first mornyng,
Airly as did the day up spring,
Thus sang ane bird with voce upplane,
" All erdly joy returnis in pane."

" O man ! haif mynd that thow mon pas ;   5
Remembir that thow art bot as,
And sall in as return agane :
All erdly joy returnis in pane."

" Haif mynd that eild ay followis yowth ;
Deth followis lyfe with gaipand mowth,   10
Devoring fruct and flowring grane :
All erdly joy returnis in pane."

" Welth, warldly gloir, and riche array
Ar all bot thornis laid in thy way,
Ourcowerd with flouris laid in ane trane :   15
All erdly joy returnis in pane."

" Come nevir yit May so fresche and grene,
Bot Januar come als wod and kene ;
Wes nevir sic drowth bot anis come rane :
All erdly joy returnis in pane."   20

" Evirmair unto this warldis joy
As nerrest air succeidis noy ;
Thairfoir, quhen joy ma nocht remane,
His verry air succeidis pane."

" Heir helth returnis in seiknes,   25
And mirth returnis in havines,
Toun in desert, forrest in plane :
All erdly joy returnis in pane."

" Fredome returnis in wrechitnes,
And trewth returnis in dowbilnes,   30
With fenyeit wordis to mak men fane :
All erdly joy returnis in pane."

" Vertew returnis in to vyce,
And honour in to avaryce ;
With cuvatyce is consciens slane :   35
All erdly joy returnis in pane."

" Sen erdly joy abydis nevir,
Wirk for the joy that lestis evir ;
For uder joy is all bot vane :
All erdly joy returnis in pane."   40

Man, sen thy lyfe is ay in weir,
And deid is evir drawand neir,
The tyme unsicker and the place ;
Thyne awin gude spend quhill thow hes space.

Gif it be thyne, thy self it use,   5
Gif it be nocht, thow it refuse,
Ane uthir of it the proffeit hes ;
Thyne awin gud spend quhill thow hes spais.

Thow may to day haif gude to spend,
And hestely to morne fra it wend,   10
And leif ane uthir thy baggis to brais ;
Thyne awin gud spend quhill thow hes spais.

Quhill thow hes space se thow dispone,
That for thy geir, quhen thow art gone,
No wicht ane uder slay nor chace ;   15
Thyne awin gud spend quhill thow hes spais.

Sum all his dayis dryvis our in vane,
Ay gadderand geir with sorrow and pane,
And nevir is glaid at Yule nor Pais ;
Thyne awin gud spend quhill thow hes spais.   20

Syne cumis ane uder glaid of his sorrow,
That for him prayit nowdir evin nor morrow,
And fangis it all with mirrynais ;
Thyne awin gud spend quhill thow hes spais.

Sum grit gud gadderis and ay it spairis,   25
And eftir him thair cumis yung airis,
That his auld thrift settis on ane es ;
Thyne awin gud spend quhill thow hes spais.

It is all thyne that thow heir spendis,
And nocht all that on the dependis,   30
Bot his to spend it that hes grace ;
Thyne awin gud spend quhill thow hes spais.

Trest nocht ane uthir will do the to,
It that thy self wald nevir do,
For gife thow dois, strenge is thy cace ;   35
Thyne awin gud spend quhill thow hes spais.

Luke how the bairne dois to the muder,
And tak example be nane udder,
That it nocht eftir be thy cace ;
Thyne awin gud spend quhill thow hes space.   40

73. NO TRESSOUR AVAILIS WITHOUT GLAIDNES

BE MIRRY, man ! and tak nocht far in mynd
The wavering of this wrechit warld of sorrow ;
To God be humill, and to thy freynd be kynd,
And with thy nychtbouris glaidly len and borrow ;
His chance to nycht it may be thyne to morrow.   5
Be blyth in hairt for ony aventure,
For oft with wysmen hes bene said a forrow,
Without glaidnes availis no tressour.

Mak the gud cheir of it that God the sendis,
For warldis wrak but weilfar nocht availis ;   10
Na gude is thyne saif only at thow spendis,
Remenant all thow brukis bot with bailis ;
Seik to solace quhen sadnes the assailis,
In dolour lang thy lyfe ma nocht indure ;
Quhairfoir of confort set up all thy sailis :   15
Without glaidnes availis no tresour.

Follow on petie, fle truble and debait ;
With famous folkis hald thy cumpany ;
Be charitabill and humyll in thyne estait,
For warldly honour lestis bot a cry ;   20
For truble in erd tak no mallancoly ;
Be riche in patience, gif thow in gudis be pure ;
Quho levis mirry, he levis michtely :
Without glaidnes availis no tresour.

Thow seis thir wrechis sett with sorrow and cair   25
To gaddir gudis in all thair lyvis space,

And quhen thair baggis ar full, thair selfis ar bair,
And of thair riches bot the keping hes ;
Quhill uthiris cum to spend it that hes grace,
Quhilk of thy wynning no labour had nor cure ;　　30
Tak thow example and spend with mirrines :
Without glaidnes availis no tresour.

Thocht all the wraik that evir had levand wicht
Wer only thyne, no moir thy pairt dois fall
Bot meit, drynk, clais, and of the laif a sicht,　　35
Yit to the juge thow sall gif compt of all ;
Ane raknyng rycht cumis of ane ragment small ;
Be just and joyus and do to non injure,
And trewth sall mak the strang as ony wall :
Without glaidnes availis no tresure.　　40

74. OF MANIS MORTALITIE

Memento, homo, quod cinis es !
Think, man, thow art bot erd and as !
Lang heir to dwell na thing thow pres,
For as thow come sa sall thow pas ;
Lyk as ane schaddow in ane glas　　5
Hyne glydis all thy tyme that heir is.
Think, thocht thy bodye ware of bras,
Quod tu in cinerem reverteris.

Worthye Hector and Hercules,
Forcye Achill and strong Sampsone,　　10
Alexander of grit nobilnes,
Meik David and fair Absolone,
Hes playit thair pairtis, and all are gone
At will of God that all thing steiris :
Think, man, exceptioun thair is none,　　15
Sed tu in cinerem reverteris.

Thocht now thow be maist glaid of cheir,
Fairest and plesandest of port,
Yit may thow be, within ane yeir,
Ane ugsum, uglye tramort ;　　20

And sen thow knawis thy tyme is schort,
And in all houre thy lyfe in weir is,
Think, man, amang all uthir sport,
Quod tu in cinerem reverteris.

Thy lustye bewte and thy youth   25
Sall feid as dois the somer flouris ;
Syne sall the swallow with his mouth
The dragone Death that all devouris.
No castell sall the keip, nor touris,
Bot he sall seik the with thy feiris ;   30
Thairfore, remembir at all houris
Quod tu in cinerem reverteris.

Thocht all this warld thow did posseid,
Nocht eftir death thow sall posses,
Nor with the tak, bot thy guid deid,   35
Quhen thow dois fro this warld the dres.
So speid the, man, and the confes
With humill hart and sobir teiris,
And sadlye in thy hart inpres
Quod tu in cinerem reverteris.   40

Thocht thow be taklit nevir so sure,
Thow sall in deathis port arryve,
Quhair nocht for tempest may indure,
Bot ferslye all to speir is dryve.
Thy Ransonner with woundis fyve,   45
Mak thy plycht anker and thy steiris,
To hald thy saule with him on lyve,
Cum tu in cinerem reverteris.

75. OF THE WARLDIS VANITIE

O WRECHE, be war ! this warld will wend the fro,
    Quhilk hes begylit mony greit estait ;
Turne to thy freynd, beleif nocht in thy fo,
    Sen thow mon go, be grathing to thy gait ;
    Remeid in tyme and rew nocht all to lait ;   5
Provyd thy place, for thow away man pas
    Out of this vaill of trubbill and dissait :
Vanitas Vanitatum, et omnia Vanitas.

Walk furth, pilgrame, quhill thow hes dayis lycht,
   Dres fra desert, draw to thy duelling place ;   10
Speid home, for quhy anone cummis the nicht,
   Quhilk dois the follow with ane ythand chaise ;
   Bend up thy saill and win thy port of grace ;
For, and the deith ourtak the in trespas,
   Than may thow say thir wourdis with " allace ! "   15
Vanitas Vanitatum, et omnia Vanitas.

Heir nocht abydis, heir standis nothing stabill,
   This fals warld ay flittis to and fro ;
Now day up bricht, now nycht als blak as sabill,
   Now eb, now flude, now freynd, now cruell fo ;   20
   Now glaid, now said, now weill, now in to wo ;
Now cled in gold, dissolvit now in as ;
   So dois this warld transitorie go :
Vanitas Vanitatum, et omnia Vanitas.

76. OF LYFE

Quhat is this lyfe bot ane straucht way to deid,
   Quhilk hes a tyme to pas, and nane to duell ;
A slyding quheill us lent to seik remeid ;
   A fre chois gevin to Paradice or Hell ;
   A pray to deid, quhome vane is to repell ;   5
A schoirt torment for infineit glaidnes,
Als schort ane joy for lestand hevynes.

77. A GENERAL SATYRE

Doverrit with dreme, devysing in my slummer,
How that this realme, with nobillis owt of nummer,
Gydit, provydit, sa mony yeiris hes bene ;
And now sic hunger, sic cowartis, and sic cummer
Within this land was nevir hard nor sene.   5

Sic pryd with prellattis, so few till preiche and pray ;
Sic hant of harlettis with thame bayth nicht and day,
That sowld haif ay thair God afoir thair ene ;
So nyce array, so strange to thair abbay,
Within this land was nevir hard nor sene.   10

So mony preistis cled up in secular weid,
With blasing breistis casting thair clathis on breid,
It is no neid to tell of quhome I mene ;
So quhene to reid the deirgey and the beid
Within this land was nevir hard nor sene.   15

So mony maisteris, so mony guckit clerkis,
So mony westaris to God and all his warkis,
So fyry sparkis of dispyt fro the splene,
Sic losin sarkis, so mony glengoir markis,
Within this land was nevir hard nor sene.   20

Sa mony lordis, so mony naturall fulis,
That better accordis to play thame at the trulis,
Nor seis the dulis that commonis dois sustene ;
New tane fra sculis sa mony anis and mulis
Within this land was nevir hard nor sene.   25

Sa mekle tressone, sa mony partiall sawis,
Sa littill ressone to help the commoun cawis,
That all the lawis ar not sett by ane bene ;
Sic fenyeit flawis, sa mony waistit wawis
Within this land was nevir hard nor sene.   30

Sa mony theivis and mycharis weill kend,
Sa grit relevis of lordis thame to defend,
Becawis thai spend the pelf thame betwene ;
So few till wend this mischief till amend,
Within this land was nevir hard nor sene.   35

This to correct thay schoir with mony crakkis,
Bot littill effect of speir or battell ax,
Quhen curage lakkis the cors that sowld mak kene ;
Sa mony jakkis, and brattis on beggaris bakkis,
Within this land was nevir hard nor sene.   40

Sic vant of vostouris with hairtis in sinfull staturis,
Sic brallaris and bosteris degenerat fra thair naturis,
And sic regratouris the peure men to prevene ;
So mony tratouris, sa mony rubeatouris,
Within this land was nevir hard nor sene.   45

Sa mony jugeis and lordis now maid of lait,
Sa small refugeis the peur man to debait,
Sa mony estait, for commoun weill oa quhene,
Ouir all the gait sa mony thevis sa tait,
Within this land was nevir hard nor sene.   50

Sa mony ane sentence retreitit, for to win
Geir and acquentance or kyndnes of thair kin,
They think no sin, quhair proffeit cumis betwene ;
Sa mony ane gin to haist thame to the pin,
Within this land was nevir hard nor sene.   55

Sic knavis and crakkaris to play at cartis and dyce,
Sic halland schekkaris, quhilk at Cowkelbyis gryce
Ar haldin of pryce, quhen lymmaris dois convene ;
Sic stoir of vyce, sa mony wittis unwyce,
Within this land was nevir hard nor sene.   60

Sa mony merchandis, sa mony ar mensworne,
Sa peur tennandis, sic cursing evin and morne,
Quhilk slayis the corne and fruct that growis grene ;
Sic skaith and scorne, so mony paitlattis worne,
Within this land was nevir hard nor sene.   65

Sa mony rakkettis, sa mony ketchepillaris,
Sic ballis, sic nackettis, and sic tutivillaris,
And sic evill willaris to speik of king and quene ;
Sic pudding fillaris, discending doun frome millaris,
Within this land was nevir hard nor sene.   70

Sic fartingaillis on flaggis als fatt as quhailis,
Facit lyk fulis with hattis that littill availlis,
And sic fowill tailis, to sweip the calsay clene,
The dust upskaillis ; sic fillokis with fucksailis
Within this land was nevir hard nor sene.   75

Sa mony ane Kittie, drest up with goldin chenye,
So few witty, that weill can fabillis fenye,
With apill renye ay schawand hir goldin chene ;
Off Sathanis senyie sic ane unsall menyie
Within this land was nevir hard nor sene.   80

78. ANE ORISOUN

SALVIOUR, suppois my sensualitie
Subject to syn hes maid my saule of sys,
Sum spark of lycht and spiritualite,
Walkynnis my witt, and ressoun biddis me rys,
My corrupt conscience askis, clips, and cryis   5
First grace, syn space, for to amend my mys,
Substance with honour doing none suppryis,
Freyndis, prosperite, heir peax, syne hevynis blys

79. OF THE NATIVITIE OF CHRIST

Rorate celi desuper!
Hevins distill your balmy schouris,
For now is rissin the bricht day ster,
Fro the ros Mary, flour of flouris :
The cleir Sone, quhome no clud devouris,   5
Surminting Phebus in the est,
Is cumin of his hevinly touris ;
Et nobis Puer natus est.

Archangellis, angellis, and dompnationis,
Tronis, potestatis, and marteiris seir,   10
And all ye hevinly operationis,
Ster, planeit, firmament, and speir,
Fyre, erd, air, and watter cleir,
To him gife loving, most and lest,
That come in to so meik maneir ;   15
Et nobis Puer natus est.

Synnaris be glaid, and pennance do,
And thank your Makar hairtfully ;
For he that ye mycht nocht cum to,
To yow is cumin full humly,   20
Your saulis with his blud to by,
And lous yow of the feindis arrest,
And only of his awin mercy ;
Pro nobis Puer natus est.

All clergy do to him inclyne, 25
And bow unto that barne benyng,
And do your observance devyne
To him that is of kingis King ;
Ensence his altar, reid and sing
In haly kirk, with mynd degest, 30
Him honouring attour all thing,
Qui nobis Puer natus est.

Celestiall fowlis in the are
Sing with your nottis upoun hicht ;
In firthis and in forrestis fair 35
Be myrthfull now, at all your mycht,
For passit is your dully nycht,
Aurora hes the cluddis perst,
The son is rissin with glaidsum lycht,
Et nobis Puer natus est. 40

Now spring up flouris fra the rute,
Revert yow upwart naturaly,
In honour of the blissit frute
That rais up fro the rose Mary ;
Lay out your levis lustely, 45
Fro deid tak lyfe now at the lest
In wirschip of that Prince wirthy,
Qui nobis Puer natus est.

Syng hevin imperiall, most of hicht,
Regions of air mak armony ; 50
All fishe in flud and foull of flicht
Be myrthfull and mak melody :
All *Gloria in excelsis* cry,
Hevin, erd, se, man, bird, and best,
He that is crownit abone the sky 55
Pro nobis Puer natus est.

80. OF THE PASSIOUN OF CHRIST

AMANG THIR freiris, within ane cloister,
   I enterit in ane oritorie,
And knelit doun with ane pater noster,
   Befoir the michtie king of glorie,

Haveing his passioun in memorie ;   5
Syn to his mother I did inclyne,
    Hir halsing with ane *gaude flore ;*
And sudandlie I sleipit syne.

Methocht Judas with mony ane Jow
    Tuik blissit Jesu, our Salvatour,   10
And schot him furth with mony ane schow,
    With schamefull wourdis of dishonour ;
    And lyk ane theif or ane tratour
Thay leid that hevinlie prince most hie,
    With manassing attour messour,   15
O mankynd, for the luif of the.

Falslie condamnit befoir ane juge
    Thai spittit in his visage fayr ;
And, as lyounis with awfull ruge,
    In yre thai hurlit him heir and thair,   20
    And gaif him mony buffat sair,
That it was sorrow for to se ;
    Of all his claythis thay tirvit him bair,
O mankynd, for the luif of the.

Thay terandis to revenge thair tein,   25
    For scorne thai cled him in to quhyt ;
And hid his blythfull glorious ene,
    To se quham angellis had delyt ;
    Dispituouslie syn did him smyt,
Saying, " Gif sone of God thow be,   30
    Quha straik the now, thow tell us tyt ? "
O mankynd, for the luf of the.

In tene thai tirvit him agane,
    And till ane pillar thai him band ;
Quhill blude birst out at everie vane,   35
    Thai scurgit him bayth fut and hand :
    At everie straik ran furth ane strand,
Quhilk mycht have ransonit warldis thre ;
    He baid in stour quhill he mycht stand,
O mankynd, for the luif of the.   40

Nixt all in purpyr thay him cled,
    And syne with thornis scharp and kene,

His saikles blude agane thai sched,
  Persing his heid with pykis grene;
  Unneis with lyf he micht sustene   15
That crounc, on thrungin with crucltie,
  Quhill flude of blude blindit his ene,
O mankynd, for the luif of the.

Ane croce that wes bayth large and lang
  To beir thai gaif this blissit Lord ;   50
Syn fullelie, as theif to hang,
  Thay harlit him furth with raip and corde ;
  With blude and sweit was all deflorde
His face, the fude of angellis fre ;
  His feit with stanis was revin and scorde, 55
O mankynd, for the luif of the.

Agane thay tirvit him bak and syd,
  Als brim as ony baris woid ;
The clayth that claif to his cleir syd,
  Thai raif away with ruggis rude,   60
  Quhill fersly followit flesche and blude,
That it was pietie for to se ;
  Na kynd of torment he ganestude,
O mankynd, for the luif of the.

Onto the crose of breid and lenth,   65
  To gar his lymmis langar wax,
Thai straitit him with all thair strenth,
  Quhill to the rude thai gart him rax :
  Syne tyit him on with greit irne takkis,
And him all nakit on the tre   70
  Thai raissit on loft be houris sax,
O mankynd, for the luif of the.

Quhen he was bendit so on breid,
  Quhill all his vanis brist and brak,
To gar his cruell pane exceid   75
  Thai leit him fall doun with ane swak,
  Quhill cors and corps all did crak ;
Agane thai rasit him on hie,
  Reddie mair turmentis for to mak,
O mankynd, for the luif of the.   80

Betuix tuo theiffis the spreit he gaif
  On to the Fader most of micht;
The erde did trimmill, the stanis claif,
  The sone obscurit of his licht;
  The day wox dirk as ony nicht,   85
Deid bodiis rais in the cite:
  Goddis deir Sone all thus was dicht,
O mankynd, for the luif of the.

In weir that he was yit on lyf,
  Thai ran ane rude speir in his syde,   90
And did his precious body ryff,
  Quhill blude and watter did furth glyde:
  Thus Jesus with his woundis wyde
As martir sufferit for to de,
  And tholit to be crucifyid,   95
O mankynd, for the luif of the.

Methocht Compassioun, vode of feiris,
  Than straik at me with mony ane stound,
And for Contritioun, baithit in teiris,
  My visage all in watter drownd,   100
  And Reuth into my eir ay rounde,
" For schame, allace! behald, Man, how
  Beft is with mony ane wound
Thy blissit Salvatour Jesu!"

Than rudelie come Remembrance   105
  Ay rugging me, withouttin rest,
Quhilk crose and nalis scharp, scurge and lance,
  And bludy crowne befoir me kest;
  Than Pane with passioun me opprest,
And evir did Petie on me pow,   110
  Saying, " Behald how Jowis hes drest
Thy blissit Salvatour Chryst Jesu!"

With greiting glaid be than come Grace,
  With wourdis sweit saying to me,
" Ordane for Him ane resting place,   115
  That is so werie wrocht for the:
  That schort within thir dayis thre
Sall law undir thy lyntell bow,
  And in thy hous sall herbrit be
Thy blissit Salvatour Chryst Jesu."   120

Than swyth Contritioun wes on steir,
   And did eftir Confessioun ryn ;
And Conscience me accusit heir,
   And kest out mony cankerit syn ;
   To rys Repentence did begin   125
And out at the yettis did schow ;
   Pennance did walk the house within,
Byding our Salvatour Chryst Jesu.

Grace become gyd and governour,
   To keip the house in sicker stait   130
Ay reddy till our Salvatour,
   Quhill that he come, air or lait ;
   Repentence, ay with cheikis wait,
No pane nor pennence did eschew
   The house within ever to debait,   135
Onlie for luif of sweit Jesu.

For grit terrour of Chrystis deid,
   The erde did trymmill quhair I lay ;
Quhairthrow I waiknit in that steid
   With spreit halflingis in effray ;   140
   Than wrayt I all without delay,
Richt heir as I have schawin to yow,
   Quhat me befell on Gud Fryday
Befoir the Crose of sweit Jesu.

81. ON THE RESURRECTION OF CHRIST

Done is a battell on the dragon blak,
Our campioun Chryst confountet hes his force ;
The yettis of hell ar brokin with a crak,
The signe triumphall rasit is of the croce,
The divillis trymmillis with hiddous voce,   5
The saulis ar borrowit and to the blis can go,
Chryst with his blud our ransonis dois indoce :
Surrexit Dominus de sepulchro.

Dungin is the deidly dragon Lucifer,
The crewall serpent with the mortall stang ;   10

The auld kene tegir with his teith on char,
Quhilk in a wait hes lyne for us so lang,
Thinking to grip us in his clows strang ;
The mercifull Lord wald nocht that it wer so,
He maid him for to felye of that fang :   15
Surrexit Dominus de sepulchro.

He for our saik that sufferit to be slane,
And lyk a lamb in sacrifice wes dicht,
Is lyk a lyone rissin up agane,
And as gyane raxit him on hicht ;   20
Sprungin is Aurora radius and bricht,
On loft is gone the glorius Appollo,
The blisfull day depairtit fro the nycht :
Surrexit Dominus de sepulchro.

The grit victour agane is rissin on hicht,   25
That for our querrell to the deth wes woundit ;
The sone that wox all paill now schynis bricht,
And dirknes clerit, our fayth is now refoundit ;
The knell of mercy fra the hevin is soundit,
The Cristin ar deliverit of thair wo,   30
The Jowis and thair errour ar confoundit :
Surrexit Dominus de sepulchro.

The fo is chasit, the battell is done ceis,
The presone brokin, the jevellouris fleit and flemit ;
The weir is gon, confermit is the peis,   35
The fetteris lowsit and the dungeoun temit,
The ransoun maid, the presoneris redemit ;
The feild is win, ourcumin is the fo,
Dispulit of the tresur that he yemit :
Surrexit Dominus de sepulchro.   40

82. ANE BALLAT OF OUR LADY

Hale, sterne superne ! Hale, in eterne,
    In Godis sicht to schyne !
Lucerne in derne for to discerne
    Be glory and grace devyne ;

Hodiern, modern, sempitern,
 Angelicall regyne !   5
Our tern inferne for to dispern
 Helpe, rialest rosyne.
  Ave Maria, gracia plena !
 Haile, fresche floure femynyne !   10
Yerne us, guberne, virgin matern,
 Of reuth baith rute and ryne.

Haile, yhyng, benyng, fresche flurising !
 Haile, Alphais habitakle !
Thy dyng ofspring maid us to syng   15
 Befor his tabernakle ;
All thing maling we doune thring,
 Be sicht of his signakle ;
Quhilk king us bring unto his ryng,
 Fro dethis dirk umbrakle.   20
  Ave Maria, gracia plena !
 Haile, moder and maide but makle !
Bricht syng, gladyng our languissing,
 Be micht of thi mirakle.

Haile, bricht be sicht in hevyn on hicht ! 25
 Haile, day sterne orientale !
Our licht most richt, in clud of nycht,
 Our dirknes for to scale :
Hale, wicht in ficht, puttar to flicht
 Of fendis in battale !   30
Haile, plicht but sicht ! Hale, mekle of mycht !
 Haile, glorius Virgin, haile !
  Ave Maria, gracia plena !
 Haile, gentill nychttingale !
Way stricht, cler dicht, to wilsome wicht, 35
 That irke bene in travale.

Hale, qwene serene ! Hale, most amene !
 Haile, hevinlie hie emprys !
Haile, schene unseyne with carnale eyne !
 Haile, ros of paradys !   40
Haile, clene, bedene, ay till conteyne !
 Haile, fair fresche flour delyce !
Haile, grene daseyne ! Haile, fro the splene,
 Of Jhesu genetrice !

Ave Maria, gracia plena!   45
Thow baire the prince of prys;
Our teyne to meyne, and ga betweyne
  As humile oratrice.

Haile, more decore than of before,
  And swetar be sic sevyne,   50
Our glore forlore for to restore,
  Sen thow art qwene of hevyn!
Memore of sore, stern in Aurore,
  Lovit with angellis stevyne;
Implore, adore, thow indeflore,   55
  To mak our oddis evyne.
    Ave Maria, gracia plena!
  With lovingis lowde ellevyn.
Quhill store and hore my youth devore,
  Thy name I sall ay nevyne.   60

Empryce of prys, imperatrice,
  Brycht polist precious stane;
Victrice of vyce, hie genetrice
  Of Jhesu, lord soverayne:
Our wys pavys fra enemys,   65
  Agane the feyndis trayne;
Oratrice, mediatrice, salvatrice,
  To God gret suffragane!
    Ave Maria, gracia plena!
  Haile, sterne meridiane!   70
Spyce, flour delice of paradys,
  That baire the gloryus grayne.

Imperiall wall, place palestrall,
  Of peirles pulcritud;
Tryumphale hall, hie trone regall   75
  Of Godis celsitud;
Hospitall riall, the lord of all
  Thy closet did include;
Bricht ball cristall, ros virginall,
  Fulfillit of angell fude.   80
    Ave Maria, gracia plena!
  Thy birth has with his blude
Fra fall mortall, originall,
  Us raunsound on the rude.

To THE, O mercifull Salviour, Jesus,
My King, my Lord, and my Redemar sweit,
Befoir thy bludy figor dolorus
I repent my synnys, with humill hairt contreit,
That evir I did unto this hour compleit,   5
Baith in werk, in word, and eik intent ;
Falling on face, full law befoir thy feit,
I cry The mercy, and lasar to repent.

To The, my sweit Salviour, I me schirryve,
Committing me in thy mercy excelling,   10
Off the wrang spending of my wittis fyve,—
In hering, seing, gusting, twiching, and smelling,
Ganestanding, greving, moving, and rebelling
Aganis The, my God and Lord omnipotent ;
With teiris of sorrow frome my ene distilling,   15
I cry The mercy, and lasar to repent.

I wretchit synner, vyle, and full of vyce,
Off the Sevin Deidly Synnys dois me schirryve,—
Off pryd, off yre, invy, and covetyce,
Off lichery, gluttony, with slewth ay to ourdryve,   20
Exercing vycis evir in all my lyve,
For quhilk, allace ! I servit to be schent :
Rew on me, Jesu, for thy woundis fyve !
I cry The mercy, and lasar to repent.

I confes me, Lord ! that I abusit haif   25
The Sevin Deidis of Mercy Corporall,—
To hungre meit, nor drynk to thristy gaif,
Nor veseit the seik, nor did redeme the thrall,
Harbreit the wolsome, nor naikit cled att all,
Nor yit the deid to bury tuke I tent :   30
Thow, that put mercy aboif thy workis all,
I cry The mercy, and lasar to repent.

In the Sevin Deidis of Marcy Spirituall,—
To ignorantis nocht gaif I my teiching,

Synnaris correctioun, nor destitut counsall,   35
Na unto wofull wretchis conforting,
Nor to my nychtbouris support of my praying,
Nor was to ask forgifnes penitent,
Nor to forgif my nychtbouris offending ;
I cry The mercy, and lasar to repent.   40

Lord ! I haif done full littill reverence
To thy Sacramentis excellent of renoun,—
Thy Haly Supper for my syn recompence,
And of my gilt the holy satisfactioun,
And Bapteme als, quhilk all my syn wesche doun ;   45
Heirof, als far as I was negligent,
With hairt contreit, and teiris falling doun,
I cry The mercy, and lasar to repent.

The Ten Commandis,—ane God for till honour,
Nocht tane in vane his name, no sleyar to be,   50
Fader and moder to wirschep at all hour,
To be no theif, the haly day to uphie,
Nychtbouris to lufe, fals witnes for to fle,
To leif adultre, to covet no manis rent ;
Aganis thir preceptis culpable knaw I me ;   55
I cry The mercy, and lasar to repent.

The Articulis of Trewth,—in God to trow,
The Fader that all thingis wrocht and comprehendit,
And in his haly blissit Sone, Jesu,
Of Mary borne, on croce deit, to hell discendit,   60
The thrid day rysing to the Fader ascendit,
Off quick and deid to cum and hald jugement ;
In to thir poynttis, O Lord ! quhair I offendit
I cry The mercy, and lasar to repent.

I trow in to the blissit Haly Spreit,   65
And in the Kirk, to do as it commandis,
And to thy dome that we sall rys compleit
And tak our flesche agane, baith feit and handis,
All to be saiff in stait of grace that standis ;
Plane I revoik in thir quhair I miswent,   70
Befoir The, Juge and Lord of see and landis,
I cry The mercy, and lasar to repent.

I synnyt, Lord ! that nocht being strong as wall,
In howp, in faith, in fervent cheretie ;
Nocht with the Foure Vertewis Cardenall,   75
Aganis vycis seure enarming me,
With fortitude, prowdence, and temperance, thir thre
With justice evir [in] work, word or intent ;
To The, Chryst Jesu, casting up myne e,
I cry The mercy, and lasar to repent.   80

The sevin commandis of the Kirk, that is to say,
Thy teind to pay, and cursing to eschew,
To keipe the festuall and the fasting day,
The mess on Sonday, the parroche kirk persew,
To proper curat to mak confessioun trew,   85
Anis in the yeir to tak the sacrament ;
In thir pointis, quhair I offendit, sair I rew ;
I cry The mercy, and lasar to repent.

Off syn als aganis the Haly Spreit,
Of vertew postponyng, and syn aganis nateur,   90
Off contritioun confessour indiscreit,
Of ressait sinfull of The my Salviour,
Of non repentance, and satisfaction seur,
Of the Sevin Giftis the Haly Gaist me sent,
Of Sex Petitionis in Pater Noster peur ;   95
I cry The mercy, and lasar to repent.

Nocht thanking The of gratitud nor grace,
That thow me wrocht, and bocht with thy deid ;
Of this schort lyfe remembring nocht the space,
The hevenis blis, the hellis hiddous feid,   100
But moir trespas, my synnis to remeid,
Concluding evir all thruch in myne entent ;
Thow, quhois blude on rude for men ran reid,
I cry The mercy, and lasar to repent.

I knaw me vicious, Lord, and richt culpable   105
In aithis sweiring, leising, and blaspheming,
Off frustrat speiking in court, in kirk, and table,
In wordis vyle, in vaneteis expreming,
Preysing my self, and evill my nichtbouris deming,
And so in ydilnes my dayis haif spent ;   110

Thow that was rent on rude for my redeming,
I cry The mercy, and lasar to repent.

I synnit in consaving thochtis jolie,
Up to the hevin extolling myne ententioun,
In he exaltit arrogance and folye,   115
Prowdnes, derisioun, scorne, and vilipentioun,
Presumptioun, inobedience, and contemptioun,
In fals vane gloir and deidis negligent;
O Thow, that deit on rud for my redemptioun,
I cry The mercy, and lasar to repent.   120

I synnit als in reif and in oppressioun,
In wrangus gudis taking and posseding
Contrar gud ressoun, conscience, and discretioun,
Of prodigall spending but rewth of peure folkis neiding,
In fowll disceptionis, in fals inventionis breiding,   125
To conqueis honor, tresor, land, and rent,
In fleschly lust aboif mesur exceding;
I cry The mercy, and lasar to repent.

Off mynd dissymulat, Lord! I me confes,
Of feid undir freindly countenance,   130
Of parciall jugeing, and perves wilfulnes,
Off flattering wourdis and fenyeing for substance,
Of fals solisting for wrang deliverance
At Counsale, Sessioun, and at Parliament;
Of every gilt, and wicket govirnance,   135
I cry The mercy, and lasar to repent.

I schryve me of all cursit cumpany,
All tymes both witting and unwitting me,
Off criminall caus, off deid of fellony,
Of tyranny, and vengeable crewaltie,   140
In hurt or slawchter, culpable gif I be,
Be ony maner, deid, counsale, or consent,
O deir Jesu! that for me deit on tre,
I cry The mercy, and lasar to repent.

Thocht I haif nocht thy pretious feit to kis,   145
As had the Magdalene, quhen scho did mercy craif,
I sall, as scho, weip teiris for my mis,
And every morrow seik The at thy graif;

Thairfoir, forgif me, as Thow hir forgaif,
That seis my hart as hiris penitent !   150
Thy pretious body in breist or I ressaif,
I cry The mercy, and lasar to repent.

To mak me, Jesu, on The to remember !
I ask thy Passioun in me so to habound,
Quhill nocht unmenyeit be in me ane membir,   155
Bot fall in wo, with The, of every wound ;
And every straik mak throw my hart a stound,
That evir did stenyie thy fair flesche innocent,
So that no pairt of my body be sound,
Bot crying The mercy, and lasar to repent.   160

Off all thir synnis that I did heir expreme,
And als foryhet, to The, Lord ! I me schryif,
Appeling fra thy justice court extreme
Unto thy court of mercy exultyif ;
Thow mak my schip in blissit port to arryif,   165
That sailis heir in stormis violent,
And saif me, Jesu ! for thy woundis fyve,
That cryis The mercy, and lasar to repent.

84. THE MANER OF PASSING TO CONFESSIOUN

O SYNFULL man, thir ar the fourty dayis
    That every man sulde wilfull pennence dre ;
Oure Lorde Jhesu, as haly writ sayis,
    Fastit him self oure exampill to be ;
    Sen sic ane michty king and lorde as he   5
To fast and pray was so obedient,
We synfull folk sulde be more deligent.

I reid [the,] man, of thi transgressioun,
    With all thi hert that thow be penitent ;
Thow schrive the clene and mak confessioun,   10
    And se thairto [that] thow be deligent,
    With all thi synnes into thi mynde present,
That every syn be the selfe be schawin,
To thyne confessioun it ma be kend and knawin.

Apon thi body gif thow hes ane wounde   15
   That causis the gret panis for to feill,
Thair is no leiche ma mak the haill and sounde,
   Quhill it be sene and clengit every deill;
   Rycht sua thi schrift, bot it be schawin weill,
Thow art nocht abill remissioun for to get   20
Wittandlie, and thow ane syn foryhet.

Off tuenty woundis and ane be left unhelit
   Quhat avalis the leiching of the laif ?
Rycht sua thi schrift, and thair be oucht concelit,
   It avalis nocht thi sely saule to saif;   25
   Nor yit of God remissioun for to haif :
Of syn gif thow wald have deliverance,
Thow sulde it tell with all the circumstance.

Sa that thi confessour be wys and discreit,
   Than can the discharge of every doute and weir,   30
And power hes of thy synnes compleit :
   Gif thow can nocht schaw furth thi synnes perqueir,
   And he be blinde, and can nocht at the speir,
Thow ma rycht weill in thi mynde consydder
That ane blynde man is led furth be ane uther.   35

And sa I halde that ye ar baith begylde ;
   He can nocht speir, nor thow can nocht him tell,
Quhen, nor how, thi conscience thow hes fylde ;
   Thairfor, I reid, that thow excuse thi sell,
   And rype thi mynde how every thing befell,   40
The tyme, the place, and how, and in quhat wyis,
So that thi confessioun ma thi synnes pryce.

Avys the weill, or thou cum to the preist,
   Of all thi synnes and namelie of the maist,
That thai be reddy prentit in thi breist ;   45
   Thow sulde nocht cum to schryfe the in haist,
   And syne sit doun abasit as ane beist :
With humyll [hart] and sad contrytioun,
Thow suld cum to thine confessioun.

With thine awin mouth thi synnes thow suld tell ;   50
   Bot sit and heir the preist hes nocht ado,

Quha kennes thi synnes better na thi sell ?
   Thairfor, I reid the, tak gude tent thairto ;
   Thow knawis best quhair bindis the thi scho ;
Thairfor, be wys afor or thow thair cum,   55
That thow schaw furth thi synnes all and sum.

Quhair seldin compt is tane, and hes a hevy charge,
   And syne is rekles in his governance,
And on his conscience he takis all to large,
   And on the end hes no rememberance,   60
   That man is abill to fall ane gret mischance :
The synfull man that all the yeir our settis,
Fra Pasche to Pasche, rycht mony a thing foryhettis.

I reid the, man, quhill thow art stark and young,
   With pith and strenth into thi yeris grene,   65
Quhill thow art abill baith in mynde and toung,
   Repent the, man, and kepe thi conscience clene ;
   Till byde till age is mony perrell sene :
Small merit is of synnes for to irke
Quhen thow art ald and ma na wrangis wyrke.   70

85. THE BALLAD OF KYND KITTOK

My Gudame wes a gay wif, bot scho wes ryght gend,
   Scho duelt furth fer in to France, apon Falkland Fell ;
Thay callit her Kynd Kittok, quhasa hir weill kend :
   Scho wes like a caldrone cruke cler under kell ;
Thay threpit that scho deit of thrist, and maid a gud end.   5
   Efter hir dede, scho dredit nought in hevin for to duell,
And sa to hevin the hieway dreidles scho wend,
   Yit scho wanderit and yeid by to ane elriche well.
      Scho met thar, as I wene,
         Ane ask rydand on a snaill,   10
         And cryit, " Ourtane fallow, haill ! "
         And raid ane inche behind the taill,
    Till it wes neir evin.

Sa scho had hap to be horsit to hir herbry
   Att ane ailhous neir hevin, it nyghttit thaim thare ;   15

H

Scho deit of thrist in this warld, that gert hir be so dry,
  Scho never eit, bot drank our mesur and mair.
Scho slepit quhill the morne at none, and rais airly ;
  And to the yettis of hevin fast can the wif fair,
And by Sanct Petir, in at the yet, scho stall prevely :   20
  God lukit and saw hir lattin in and lewch his hert sair.
    And thar, yeris sevin
      Scho levit a gud life,
      And wes our Ladyis hen wif :
      And held Sanct Petir at strif,   25
    Ay quhill scho wes in hevin.

Sche lukit out on a day and thoght ryght lang
  To se the ailhous beside, in till ane evill hour ;
And out of hevin the hie gait cought the wif gaing
  For to get hir ane fresche drink, the aill of hevin wes sour.   30
Scho come againe to hevinnis yet, quhen the bell rang,
  Saint Petir hat hir with a club, quhill a gret clour
Rais in hir heid, becaus the wif yeid wrang.
    Than to the ailhous agane scho ran the pycharis to pour,
    And for to brew and baik.   35
      Frendis, I pray yow hertfully,
      Gif ye be thristy or dry,
      Drink with my Guddame, as ye ga by,
    Anys for my saik.

86. THE MANERE OF THE CRYING OF ANE PLAYE

    HARRY, Harry, hobbillschowe !
    Se quha is cummyn nowe,
    Bot I wait nevir howe,
      With the quhorle wynd ?
    A soldane owt of Seriand land,   5
    A gyand strang for to stand,
    That with the strenth of my hand
      Beres may bynd.
    Yit I trowe that I vary,
    I am the nakit Blynd Hary,   10
    That lang has bene in the fary
      Farleis to fynd :

And yit gif this be nocht I,
I wait I am the spreit of Gy,
Or ellis go by the sky,   15
    Licht as the lynd.

The God of most magnificence
Conserf this fair presens,
And saif this amyable audiens
    Grete of renoune.   20
Provest, baillies, officeris,
And honorable induellaris,
Marchandis and familiaris
    Of all this fair towne.
Quha is cummyn heir bot I,   25
A bauld, bustuos bellamy,
At your cors to mak a cry
    With a hie sowne ?
Quhilk generit am of gyandis kynd,
Fra strang Hercules be strynd ;   30
Off all the Occident of Ynd,
    My eldaris bair the croune.

My foregrantschir hecht Fyn McKowle,
That dang the Devill and gart him yowle,
The skyis ranyd quhen he wald scowle   35
    And trublit all the aire :
He gat my grantschir Gog Magog ;
Ay quhen he dansit, the warld wald schog ;
Five thousand ellis yeid in his frog
    Of Hieland pladdis of haire.   40
Yit he was bot of tender youth ;
Bot eftir he grewe mekle at fouth,
Ellevyne ell wyde met was his mouth,
    His teith was tene myle sqwaire.
He wald apone his tais stand,   45
And tak the sternis doune with his hand,
And set tham in a gold garland
    Abone his wyfis haire.

He had a wyf was lang of clift,
Hir heid wan heiar than the lift ;   50
The hevyne rerdit quhen scho wald rift ;
    The las was no thing sklender :

Scho spittit Lochlomond with hir lippis ;
Thunner and fyreflaucht flewe fra hir hippis ;
Quhen scho was crabit the son tholit clips ;   55
   The Fende durst nocht offend hir.
For cald scho tuke the fever cartane,
For all the claith of Fraunce and Bertane
Wald nocht be till hir leg a gartane,
   Thocht scho was ying and tender ;   60
Apon a nycht heire in the north,
Scho tuke the gravell and stalit Cragorth,
Scho pischit the mekle watter of Forth,
   Sic tyde ran eftirhend hir.

A thing writtin of hir I fynd :   65
In Irland quhen scho blewe behynd,
At Noroway costis scho rasit the wynd,
   And gret schippis drownit thare.
Scho fischit all the Spanye seis,
With hir sark lape befor hir theis ;   70
Sevyne dayis saling betuix hir kneis
   Was estymit and maire.
The hyngand brayis on athir syde
Scho poltit with hir lymmis wyde ;
Lassis micht leir at hir to stryd,   75
   Wald ga to lufis laire.
Scho merkit syne to land with myrth ;
And pischit fyf quhalis in the Firth,
That cropyn war in hir count for girth,
   Welterand amang the waire.   80

My fader, mekle Gow MakMorne,
Out of that wyfis wame was schorne ;
For litilnes scho was forlorne
   Sic a kempe to beire :
Or he of eld was yeris thre,   85
He wald stepe oure the occeane se ;
The mone sprang never abone his kne,
   The hevyn had of him feire.
Ane thousand yere is past fra mynd,
Sen I was generit of his kynd,   90
Full far amang the desertis of Ynde,
   Amang lyoun and beire :

Baith the King Arthour and Gawane,
And mony bald berne in Brettane,
Ar deid and in the weiris slane, 95
   Sen I couth weild a speire.

I have bene forthwart ever in feild,
And now so lang I haf borne scheld,
That I am all crynd in for eild
   This litill, as ye may se. 100
I have bene bannist under the lynd
Full lang that no man couth me fynd,
And now with this last southin wynd,
   I am cummyn heir parde.
My name is Welth, thairfor be blyth, 105
I come heire comfort yow to kyth ;
Suppos that wretchis wryng and wryth,
   All darth I sall gar de ;
For sekerly, the treuth to tell,
I come amang yow heire to duell, 110
Fra sound of Sanct Gelis bell
   Nevir think I to fle.

Sophea and the Soldane strang,
With weiris that has lestit lang,
Furth of thar boundis maid me to gang, 115
   And turn to Turky tyte.
The King of Frauncis gret army
Has brocht in darth in Lombardy,
And in ane cuntre he and I
   May nocht baith stand perfyte. 120
In Denmark, Swetherik, and Noroway,
Na in the Steidis I dar nocht ga,
Amang thaim is bot tak and sla,
   Cut thropillis and mak quyte.
Irland for evir I have refusit, 125
All wichtis suld hald me excusit,
For never in land quhar Erische was usit,
   To duell had I delyte.

Quharfor in Scotland come I heire
With yow to byde and perseveire,
In Edinburgh quhar is meriast cheire, 130
   Plesans, disport, and play,

Quhilk is the lampe and A *per se*
Of this regioun in all degre,
Of welefaire and of honeste   135
   Renoune and riche aray.
Sen I am Welth cummyn to this wane,
Ye noble merchandis everilkane
Addres yow furth with bow and flane
   In lusty grene lufraye,   140
And follow furth on Robyn Hude,
With hartis coragious and gud,
And thocht that wretchis wald ga wod,
   Of worschipe hald the way.

For I and my thre feres aye,   145
Weilfaire, Wantones, and Play,
Sall byde with yow in all affray,
   And cair put clene to flicht,
And we sall dredles us addres
To bannis derth and all distres   150
And with all sportis and merynes
   Your hartis hald ever on hicht.
I am of mekle quantite
Of gyand kynd, as ye may se,
Quhar sall be gottin a wyf to me   155
   Siclyke of breid and hicht ?
I dreid that thair be nocht a maide
In all this towne may me abyd,
Quha wait gif ony heir besyd,
   Micht suffir me all nycht.   160

With yow sen I mon leid my lyf,
Gar sers baith Louthiane and Fyf
And wale to me a mekle wyf,
   A gret ungracious gan,
Sen scho is gane, the Gret Forlore.   165

     .   .   .

Adow, fair weill ! for now I go,
Bot I will nocht lang byd yow fro ;
Chryst yow conserve fra every wo,
   Baith madin, wyf, and man ;
God bliss thame, and the Haly Rude,   170
Givis me a drink sa it be gude ;
And quha trowis best that I do lude,
   Skynk first to me the can.

87. ROS MARY: ANE BALLAT OF OUR LADY

Ros MARY, most of vertewe virginale,
    Fresche floure on quhom the hevinlie dewe doun fell;
O gem joynit in joye angelicall,
    In quhom Jhesu rejosit for to duell;
    Rute of refute, of mercy springand well,   5
Of ladyis chose as is of letteris A,
    Emprys of hevyne, of paradys, and hell,
O *mater Jhesu, salve Maria!*

O sterne that blyndis Phebus bemes bricht,
    With cours abone the hevynnis circulyne;   10
Abone the speir of Saturn hie on hicht,
    Surmonting all the angell ordouris nyne;
    Haile, lamp lemand befoir the trone devyne,
Quhar cherubim sweit syngis Osanna,
    With organe, tympane, harpe, and symbalyne;   15
O *mater Jhesu, salve Maria!*

O cleir conclaif of clene virginite,
    That closit Crist but curis criminale;
Tryumphand tempill of the Trinite,
    That torned us fra Tarter eternale;   20
    Princes of pes and palme imperiale,
Our wicht invinsable Sampson sprang the fra,
    That with ane buffat bure doune Beliale;
O *mater Jhesu, salve Maria!*

Hayle! Davydes doughter, depured Ave,   25
    Fulfylled withe all plenytude of grace;
Suche salutation due unto thee,
    And to none other in suche soveraigne case,
    The Prynce, cheeif of all, in thee to take place,
Boarne ere begynnyng in moste merveylous waye,   30
    And boarne heere of thee, after nyne months space,
Oh mater Jesu, salve Maria!

Hayle, indistinguyble sterre celestiall!
    Illumynous Ladye, in lune lucyferat;
Of gloryous Jesus, King imperiall,   35
    Hayle! genetrix, of Jesse germynat,

Of Adonay liayle annule illibat.
Buche in combuste of Moses, brennyng aye,
  Trynaunte tryumphante, Rose intemerat,
Oh mater Jesu, salve Maria!   40

Thy blissit sydis bure the campioun,
  Quhilk, with mony bludy woundis, in to stour,
Victoriusly discomfit the dragoun
  That redy wes his pepill to devoure ;
  At hellis yettis he gaf tham no succour,   45
Syne brak the barmekyn of that bribour bla,
  Quhill all the feyndis trymblit for raddoure :
O mater Jhesu, salve Maria!

O madyn meike, most mediatrix for man,
  O moder myld, full of humilite !   50
Pray thy sone Jhesu, with his woundis wan,
  Quhilk denyeit him for oure trespas to de,
  And as he bled his blude apon a tre,
Us to defend fra Lucifer oure fa,
  In hevyne that we may syng apon our kne :   55
O mater Jhesu, salve Maria!

Hail, purifyet perle !   Haile, port of paradys !
  Haile, redolent ruby, riche and radyus !
Haile, clarifyet cristale !   Haile, qwene and emperys !
  Haile, moder of God !   Haile, Virgin glorius !   60
  O gracia plena tecum Dominus !
With Gabriell that we may syng and say,
  Benedicta tu in mulieribus :
O mater Jhesu, salve Maria!

Hayle, patryarkes pleye !   Hayle, potestates plesaunce ! 65
  Hayle, virgins' queen !   Hayle, apostles' princesse white !
Hayle, martyrs' myrthe !   Hayle, angels' observaunce !
  Hayle, fyndys foe !   Hayle, Goddes owne cheeif delyte !
  Hayle, Chrystys love !   Hayle, Lucyfer's despyte !
Hayle, spiritu sancto obumbrata !   70
  Hayle, confessors' queen !   Hayle patryarkes cleare endyte !
O mater Jesu, salve Maria !

When Deathe shall crushe mee in his armes stronge,
  And vyolant peyne shall reave me my naturall sight,

And thynfernall dragon wolde hale me his emonge,   75
  Into that storme, O sterre ! caste uppe thye light,
  And me recomforte withe thye beamys bright ;
The fearfull sight of dyvlles, dearre Ladye, dryve awaye,
  Rescue thye servaunte, sweet Mayde, with all thye myght,
O mater Jesu, salve Maria.   80

88. TO THE CITY OF LONDON

London, thou art of townes A *per se*.
  Soveraign of cities, semeliest in sight,
Of high renoun, riches, and royaltie ;
  Of lordis, barons, and many goodly knyght ;
  Of most delectable lusty ladies bright ;   5
Of famous prelatis in habitis clericall ;
  Of merchauntis full of substaunce and myght :
London, thou art the flour of Cities all.

Gladdith anon, thou lusty Troy Novaunt,
  Citie that some tyme cleped was New Troy,   10
In all the erth, imperiall as thou stant,
  Pryncesse of townes, of pleasure, and of joy,
  A richer restith under no Christen roy ;
For manly power, with craftis naturall,
  Fourmeth none fairer sith the flode of Noy :   15
London, thou art the flour of Cities all.

Gemme of all joy, jasper of jocunditie,
  Most myghty carbuncle of vertue and valour ;
Strong Troy in vigour and in strenuytie ;
  Of royall cities rose and geraflour ;   20
  Empresse of townes, exalt in honour ;
In beawtie beryng the crone imperiall ;
  Swete paradise precelling in pleasure :
London, thow art the floure of Cities all.

Above all ryvers thy Ryver hath renowne,   25
  Whose beryall stremys, pleasaunt and preclare,
Under thy lusty wallys renneth down,
  Where many a swanne doth swymme with wyngis fare ;

Where many a barge doth saile, and row with are,
Where many a ship doth rest with toppe-royall.   30
　　O ! towne of townes, patrone and not-compare :
London, thou art the floure of Cities all.

Upon thy lusty Brigge of pylers white
　　Been merchauntis full royall to behold ;
Upon thy stretis goth many a semely knyght   35
　　In velvet gownes and cheynes of fyne gold.
　　By Julyus Cesar thy Tour founded of old
May be the hous of Mars victoryall,
　　Whos artillary with tonge may not be told :
London, thou art the flour of Cities all.   40

Strong be thy wallis that about the standis ;
　　Wise be the people that within the dwellis ;
Fresh is thy ryver with his lusty strandis ;
　　Blith be thy chirches, wele sownyng be thy bellis ;
　　Riche be thy merchauntis in substaunce that excellis ; 45
Fair be thy wives, right lovesom, white and small ;
　　Clere be thy virgyns, lusty under kellis :
London, thow art the flour of Cities all.

Thy famous Maire, by pryncely governaunce,
　　With swerd of justice the rulith prudently.   50
No Lord of Parys, Venyce, or Floraunce
　　In dignytie or honoure goeth to hym nye.
　　He is exampler, loode-ster, and guye ;
Principall patrone and roose orygynalle,
　　Above all Maires as maister moost worthy :   55
London, thou art the flour of Cities all.

89. TO THE PRINCESS MARGARET

Now FAYRE, fayrest off every fayre,
Princes most plesant and preclare,
The lustyest one alyve that byne,
　　Welcum of Scotland to be Quene !

Younge tender plant of pulcritud,   5
Descendyd of Imperyalle blude ;

Freshe fragrant floure of fayrehede shene,
    Welcum of Scotland to be Quene !

Swet lusty lusum lady clere,
Most myghty kyngis dochter dere,   10
Borne of a princes most serene,
    Welcum of Scotland to be Quene !

Welcum the Rose bothe rede and whyte,
Welcum the floure of oure delyte !
Oure secrete rejoysyng frome the sone beme,   15
Welcum of Scotland to be Quene ;
    Welcum of Scotlande to be Quene !

90. GLADETHE THOUE QUEYNE OF SCOTTIS REGIOUN

Gladethe thoue Queyne of Scottis regioun,
    Ying tendir plaunt of plesand pulcritude,
Fresche flour of youthe, new germyng to burgeoun,
    Our perle of price, our princes fair and gud,
    Our chairbunkle chosin of hye Imperiale blud,   5
Our Roys Riale, most reverent under Croune,
    Joy be and grace onto thi Selcitud !
Gladethe thoue Queyne of Scottis regioun.

O hye triumphing peradiss of joy,
    Lodsteir and lamp of eivry lustines,   10
Of port surmounting Pollexen of Troy,
    Dochtir to Pallas in angellik brichtnes,
    Mastres of nurtur and of nobilnes,
Of fresch depictour princes and patroun,
    O hevin in erthe of ferlifull suetnes :   15
Gladethe thoue Queyne of Scottis regioun.

Of thi fair fegour natur micht rejoiyss,
    That so the kervit withe all hir curiys slicht ;
Sche has the maid this verray wairldis chois,
    Schawing on the hir craftis and hir micht,   20
    To se quhow fair sche couthe depant a wicht,
Quhow gud, quhow noble of all condicioun,
    Quhow womanly in eivry mannis sicht :
Gladethe thoue Queyne of Scottis regioun.

Roys red and quhit, resplendent of colour,   25
   New of thi knop, at morrow fresche atyrit,
One stalk yet grene, O ! ying and tendir flour,
   That with thi luff has all this Regioun firit ;
   Gret Gode us graunt that we have long desirit,
A plaunt to spring of thi successioun,   30
   Syne with all grace his spreit to be inspirit :
Gladethe thoue Queyne of Scottis regioun.

O precius Mergreit, plesand, cleir, and quhit,
   Moir blith and bricht na is the beriall schene,
Moir deir na is the diamaunt of delit,   35
   Moir semely na is the sapheir one to seyne,
   Moir gudely eik na is the emerant greyne,
Moir riche na is the ruby of renowne,
   Fair gem of joy, Mergreit of the I meyne :
Gladethe thoue Queyne of Scottis regioun.   40

91. TO THE QUEEN DOWAGER

O lusty flour of yowth, benying and bricht,
   Fresch blome of bewty, blythfull, brycht, and schene,
Fair lufsum lady, gentill and discret,
   Yung brekand blosum, yit on the stalkis grene,
   Delytsum lilly, lusty for to be sene,   5
Be glaid in hairt and expell havines ;
   Bair of blis, that evir so blyth hes bene,
Devoyd langour, and leif in lustines.

Brycht sterne at morrow that dois the nycht hyn chase,
   Of luvis lychtsum lyfe and gyd,   10
Lat no dirk clud absent fro us thy face,
   Nor lat no sable frome us thy bewty hyd,
   That hes no confort, quhair that we go or ryd,
Bot to behald the beme of thi brychtnes ;
   Baneis all baill, and into blis abyd ;   15
Devoyd langour, and leif in lustines.

Art thow plesand, lusty, yoing, and fair ;
   Full of all vertew and gud conditioun,
Rycht nobill of blud, rycht wyis, and debonair,
   Honorable, gentill, and faythfull of renoun,   20

Liberall, lufsum, and lusty of persoun,
Quhy suld thow than lat sadness the oppres ?
   In hairt be blyth and lay all dolour doun ;
Devoyd langour, and leif in lustines.

I me commend, with all humilitie,   25
   Unto thi bewty blisfull and bening,
To quhome I am, and sall ay servand be,
   With steidfast hairt and faythfull trew mening,
   Unto the deid, without depairting ;
For quhais saik I sall my pen addres   30
   Sangis to mak for thy reconforting,
That thow may lcif in joy and lustines.

O fair sweit blossum, now in bewty flouris,
   Unfaidit bayth of cullour and vertew,
Thy nobill lord that deid hes done devoir,   35
   Faid nocht with weping thy vissage fair of hew ;
   O lufsum lusty lady, wyse, and trew,
Cast out all cair and comfort do incres,
   Exyll all sichand, on thy servand rew !
Devoyd langour, and leif in lustines.   40

92. TO THE GOUVERNOUR IN FRANCE

WE LORDIS hes chosin a chiftane mervellus,
That left hes us in grit perplexite
And him absentis, with wylis cautelus,
Yeiris and dayis mo than two or thre,
And nocht intendis the land nor peple se,   5
Faltis to correct nor vicis for to chace.
Our Lord Governour, this sedull send we the :
In lak of justice this realme is schent, allace !

Is nane of us ane uddir settis by,
Bot laubouris ay for utheris distructioun ;   10
Quhilk is grit plese to our auld innamy
And daly causis grit dissentioun
Amang us now and als divisioun,
Quhilk to heir is ane drery cacc
To the, our lord and gyd under the croun ;   15
In lak of justice this realme is schent, allace !

Thy prudent wit we think thow hes abusit,
Absentand the for ony warldly geir ;
We yarne thy presens, bot oft thow hes refusit
Till cum us till, or yit till merk us neir,　　　　　　20
Quhilk is the caus of theft, slawchtir, and weir.
Approch in tyme our freindschip to purchace ;
Thy leiges leill thy byding byis full deir ;
In lak of justice this realme is schent, allace !

Covatyce ringis in to the spirituall state,　　　　　25
Yarnand banifice the quhilk ar now vacand ;
That, but thy presens, will caus rycht grit debait,
And contraversy to rys in to this land ;
And thy bidding we trest thay sall ganestand,
Without thow cum and present thame thy face.　　30
Addres the sone, fulfill thy will and band ;
In lak of justice this realme is schent, allace !

Grit wer and wandrecht hes bene us amang,
Sen thy depairting, and yit approchis mair ;
Thy tardatioun causis us to think lang,　　　　　35
For of thi cuming we haif rycht grit dispair.
Off gyd and govirnance we ar all solitair,
Dependand ay upoun thy stait and grace ;
Speid the thairfoir, in dreid we all forfair ;
In lak of justice this realme is schent, allace !　　40

93. THE FREIRIS OF BERWIK

As it befell, and happinnit in to deid,
Upoun a rever, the quhilk is callit Tweid.

At Tweidis mowth thair standis a nobill toun,
Quhair mony lordis hes bene of grit renoune,
Quhair mony a lady bene fair of face,
And mony ane fresche lusty galland was,
In to this toun, the quhilk is callit Berwik,　　　　5
Upoun the sey thair standis nane it lyk,
For it is wallit weill abowt with stane,
And dowhill stankis castin mony ane ;

And syne the castell is so strang and wicht,
With strait towris and turattis he on hicht ;   10
The wallis wrocht craftely withall ;
The portcules most subtelly to fall,
Quhen that thame list to draw thame upoun hicht,
That it micht be of na maner of micht
To win that hous be craft or subteltie.   15
Quhairfoir it is maist gud allutirly
In to my tyme, quhair evir I haif bene,
Moist fair, most gudly, most plesand to be sene ;
The toune, the wall, the castell, and the land,
The he wallis upoun the upper hand,   20
The grit croce kirk, and eik the Masone Dew,
The Jacobene freiris of the quhyt hew,
The Carmeleitis, and the Minouris eik ;
The four ordouris wer nocht for to seik,
Thay wer all in this toun dwelling.   25
So appinnit intill a Maij morning,
That twa of the Jacobyne freiris,
As thay wer wont and usit mony yeiris
To pass amang thair brethir upaland,
Wer send of thame best practisit and cunnand,   30
Freir Allane, and Freir Robert the uder.
Thir silly Freiris with wyffis weill cowld gluder ;
Rycht wondir weill plesit thai all wyffis
And tawld thame tailis of haly sanctis lyffis,
Quhill on a tyme thay purposit to pas hame.   35
Bot verry tyrit and wett wes Freir Allane,
For he wes awld, and micht nocht wele travell,
And als he had ane littill spyce of gravell ;
Freir Robert wes young and verry hett of blude,
And be the way he bure both clothis and hude   40
And all thair geir, for he wes strong and wicht.
Be that it drew neir towart the nicht,
As thay wer cumand to the toune full neir ;
Freir Allane said than, " Gud bruder deir,
It is to lait, I dreid the yettis be closit,   45
And we ar tyrit, and verry evill disposit
To luge owt of the toun, bot gif that we
In sume gud hous this nycht mot herbryt be."
Swa wynnit thair ane woundir gude hostillar,
Without the toun, in till a fair manar,   50
And Symon Lawrear wes his name ;

Ane fair blyth wyf he had, of ony ane,
Bot scho wes sumthing dynk and dengerous.
The silly Freiris quhen thay come to the hous,
With fair hailsing and bekking courteslye,   55
To thame scho anserit agane in hye ;
Freir Robert sperit eftir the gud man,
And scho agane anserit thame thane,
" He went fra hame, God wait, on Weddinsday,
In the cuntre for to seik corne and hay,   60
And uthir thingis quhairof we haif neid."
Freir Robert said, " I pray grit God him speid
Him haill and sound in to his travell,"
And hir desyrit the stowp to fill of aill,
" That we may drink, for I am wondir dry."   65
With that the wyfe went furth richt schortly,
And fillit the stowp, and brocht in breid and cheis ;
Thay eit and drank, and satt at thair awin eis.
Freir Allane said to the gudwyf in hye,
" Cum hiddir, deme, and sett yow doun me bye,   70
And fill the cop agane anis to me ; "
Freir Robert said, " Full weill payit sall ye be."
The Freiris wer blyth, and mirry tailis cowld tell,
And even with that thay hard the prayer bell
Off thair awin abbay, and than thay wer agast,   75
Becaus thay knew the yettis wer closit fast,
That thay on na wayis micht gett entre.
Than the gudwyfe thay prayit for cheritie
To grant thame herbrye that ane nicht ;
Bot scho to thame gaif anseir with grit hicht,   80
" The gudman is fra hame, as I yow tald,
And God it wait, gif I durst be so bald
To herbry Freiris in this hous with me,
Quhat wald Symon say, ha, benedicite,
Bot in his absence I abusit his place ?   85
Our deir Lady Mary keip [me] fra sic cace,
And keip me owt of perrell and of schame."
Than auld Freir Allane said, " Na, fair dame,
For Godis saik, heir me quhat I sall say,
In gud faith we will both be deid or day ;   90
The way is evill, and I am tyrit and wett,
Our yettis ar closit that we may nocht in gett,
And to our abbay we can nocht win in ;
To caus us perreis but help ye haif grit syn ;

Thairfoir of verry neid we mon byd still,   95
And us commit alhaill in to your will."
The gudwyf lukit unto the Freiris tway,
And, at the last, to thame this can scho say,
" Ye byd nocht heir, be Him that us all coft ;
Bot gif ye list to lig up in yone loft,   100
Quhilk is weill wrocht in to the hallis end,
Ye sall fynd stray, and clathis I sall yow send ;
Quhair, and ye list, pass on baith in feir,
For on no wayis will I repair haif heir."
Hir madin than scho send hir on befoir,   105
And hir thay followit baith withowttin moir ;
Thay war full blyth, and did as scho thame kend,
And up thay went in to the hallis end,
In till a loft wes maid for corne and hay ;
Scho maid thair bed, syne past doun but delay,   110
Closit the trop, and thay remanit still.
In to the loft thay wantit of thair will ;
Freir Allane lay doun as he best micht ;
Freir Robert said, " I hecht to walk this nicht,
Quha wait perchance sum sport I ma espy ? "   115
Thus in the loft latt I thir Freiris ly,
And of the gudwyf now I will speik mair.
Scho wes richt blyth that thay wer closit thair,
For scho had maid ane tryst that samyn nicht
Freir Johine hir luvis supper for to dicht ;   120
And scho wald haif none uder cumpany,
Becaus Freir Johine that nicht with hir sowld ly,
Quha dwelland wes in to that samyne toun,
And ane Gray Freir he wes of grit renown.
He govirnit alhaill the abbacy ;   125
Silver and gold he had aboundantly ;
He had a prevy posterne of his awin,
Quhair he micht ische, quhen that he list, unknawin.
Now thus in to the toun I leif him still
Bydand his tyme ; and turne agane I will   130
To this fair wyfe, how scho the fyre cowld beit,
And thristit on fatt caponis to the speit ;
And fatt cunyngis to fyre did scho lay,
Syne bad the madin, in all the haist scho may,
To flawme, and turne, and rost thame tenderly.   135
And to hir chalmer so scho went in hy ;
   [*Omission of four lines expanded to eight in M.*]

·

Scho cleithis hir in a kirtill of fyne reid,
Ane fair quhyt curch scho puttis upoun hir heid ;
Hir kirtill wes of silk and silver fyne,
Hir uther garmentis as the reid gold did schyne ;   140
On every finger scho weiris ringis two ;
Scho was als prowd as ony papingo.
The burde scho cuverit with clath of costly greyne,
Hir napry aboif wes woundir weill besene.
Than but scho went, to se gif ony come,   145
Scho thocht full lang to meit hir lufe Freir Johine.
Syne schortly did this Freir knok at the yett ;
His knok scho kend, and did so him in lett.
Scho welcomit him in all hir best maneir ;
He thankit hir, and said, " My awin luve deir,   150
Haif thair ane pair of bossis, gud and fyne,
Thay hald ane gallone full of Gascone wyne ;
And als ane pair of pertrikis richt new slane,
And eik ane creill full of breid of mane ;
This I haif brocht to yow, my awin luve deir,   155
Thairfoir, I pray yow, be blyth, and mak gud cheir ;
Sen it is so that Semon is fra hame,
I wilbe hamely now with yow, gud dame."
Scho sayis, " Ye ar full hertly welcome heir
At ony tyme, quhen that ye list appeir."   160
With that scho smylit woundir lustely ;
He thristit hir hand agane richt prevely,
Than in hett luve thay talkit uderis till.
Thus at thair sport now will I leif thame still,
And tell yow off thir silly Freiris two   165
Wer lokit in the loft amang the stro :
Freir Allane in the loft still can ly ;
Freir Robert had ane littill jelosy,
For in his hairt he had ane persaving,
And throw the burdis he maid with his botkin   170
A littill hoill, on sic a wyiss maid he
All that thay did thair doun he micht weill se,
And every word he herd that thay did say.
Quhen scho wes prowd, richt woundir fresche and gay,
Scho callit him baith hert, lemmane, and luve ;   175
Lord God, gif than his curage wes aboif,
So prelat lyk sat he in to the chyre :
Scho rownis than ane pistill in his eir ;
Thus sportand thame and makand melody :

And quhen scho saw the supper wes reddy,   180
Scho gois belyfe and cuveris the burde annon,
And syne the pair of bossis hes scho tone,
And sett thame doun upoun the burde him by.
And evin with that thay hard the gudman cry,
And knokand at the yett he cryit fast :   185
Quhen thay him hard then wer thay both agast,
And als Freir Johine wes in a fellone fray,
He stert up fast, and wald haif bene away,
Bot all for nocht, he micht no way win owt.
The gudwyfe spak than, with a visage stowt,   190
" Yone is Symone that makis all this fray,
That I micht tholit full weill had bene away ;
I sall him quyt, and I leif half a yeir,
That cummert hes us thus in sic maneir,
Becaus for him we may nocht byd togidder ;   195
I soir repent and wo is ye come hidder,
For we wer weill gif that ye wer away."
" Quhat sall I do, allace ? " the Freir can say,
" Hyd yow," scho said, " quhill he be brocht to rest,
In to yone troich, I think it for the best ;   200
It lyis mekle and huge in all yone nuke,
It held a boll of meill quhen that we buke."
Than undir it scho gart him creip in hy,
And bad him lurk thair verry quyetly ;
Scho closit him, and syne went on hir way.   205
" Quhat sall I do, allace ? " the Freir can say.
Syne to hir madin spedyly scho spak,
" Go to the fyre, and the meitis fra it tak ;
Be bissy als, and slokkin out the fyre ;
Ga clois yone burd, and tak away the chyre,   210
And lok up all in to yone almery,
Baith meit and drink with wyne and aill put by ;
The mayne breid als thow hyd it with the wyne ;
That being done, thow sowp the hous clene syne,
That na apperance of feist be heir sene,   215
Bot sobirly our selffis dois sustene."
And syne, withowttin ony mair delay,
Scho castis of haill hir fresch array ;
Than went scho to hir bed annone,
And tholit him to knok his fill, Symone.   220
Quhen he for knoking tyrit wes and cryid,
Abowt he went unto the udir syd,

And on Alesone fast cold he cry,
And at the last scho anserit crabitly,
" Ach, quha be this that knawis sa weill my name ?   225
Go hens," scho sayis, " for Symon is fra hame,
And I will herbry no gaistis heir perfey ;
Thairfoir I pray yow to wend on your way,
For at this tyme ye may nocht lugit be."
Than Symone said, " Fair dame, ken ye nocht me ?   230
I am your Symone and husband of this place."
" Ar ye my spous Symone ? " scho sayis, " allace !
Be misknawlege I had almaist misgane,
Quha wenit that ye sa lait wald haif cum hame ? "
Scho stertis up and gettis licht in hy,   235
And oppinit than the yet full haistely ;
Scho tuk fra him his geir at all devyis,
Syne welcomit him on maist hairtly wyis.
He bad the madin kindill on the fyre,
" Syne graith me meit, and tak ye all thy hyre."   240
The gudwyf said schortly, " Ye may trow
Heir is no meit that ganand is for yow."
" How sa, fair deme, ga gait me cheis and breid,
Ga fill the stowp, hald me no mair in pleid,
For I am verry tyrit, wett, and cauld."   245
Than up scho rais, and durst nocht mair be bauld,
Cuverit the burde, thairon sett meit in hy,
Ane sowsit nolt fute and scheipheid haistely ;
And sum cauld meit scho brocht to him belyve,
And fillit the stowp. The gudman than wes blyth ;   250
Than satt he doun, and swoir, " Be all hallow
I fair richt weill, and I had ane gud fallow :
Dame, eit with me and drink, gif that ye may."
Said the gudwyf, " Devill inche cun may I ;
It wer mair meit in to your bed to be,   255
Than now to sit desyrand cumpany."
Freir Robert said, " Allace, gud bruder deir,
I wald the gudman wist that we wer heir,
Quha wait perchance sum bettir wald he fair ;
For sickerly my hairt will ay be sair   260
Gif yone scheipheid with Symon birneist be,
Sa mekill gud cheir being in the almerie : "
And with that word he gaif ane hoist anone.
The gudman hard, and speirit, " Quha is yone ? "
The gudwyf said, " Yone are Freiris tway."   265

Symone said, " Tell me quhat Freiris be thay."
" Yone is Freir Robert and silly Freir Allane,
That all this day hes travellit with grit pane ;
Be thay come heir it wes so verry lait,
Houris wes rung, and closit wes thair yait,   270
And in yone loft I gaif thame harbrye."
The gudman said, " Sa God haif pairt of me,
Tha Freiris twa ar hairtly welcome hidder,
Ga call thame doun, that we ma drink togidder."
The gudwyf said, " I reid yow latt thame be,   275
Thay had levir sleip nor sit in cumpanye.
The gudman said unto the maid thonc,
" Go, pray thame baith to cum till me annone."
And sone the trop the madin oppinit than,
And bad thame baith cum doun to the gudman.   280
Freir Robert said, " Now be sweit Sanct Jame,
The gudman is verry welcome hame,
And for his weilfair dalie do we pray ;
We sall annone cum doun to him, ye say."
Than with that word thay start up baith attone,   285
And doun the trop delyverly thay come,
Halsit Symone als sone as thay him se,
And he agane thame welcomit hairtfullie,
And said, " Cum heir, myne awin bredir deir,
And sett yow doun sone besyd me heir,   290
For I am now allone, as ye may se ;
Thairfoir sitt doun and beir me cumpanye,
And tak yow pairt of sic gud as we haif."
Freir Allane said, " Schir, I pray God yow saif,
For heir is now annuch of Godis gud."   295
Than Symon anserit, " Now, be the Rud,
Yit wald I gif ane croun of gold for me,
For sum gud meit and drink amangis us thre."
Freir Robert said, " Quhat drinkis wald ye craif,
Or quhat meitis desyre ye for to haif ?   300
For I haif mony sindry practikis seir,
Beyond the sey in Pareis did I leir,
That I wald preve glaidly for your saik,
And for your demys, that harbry cowd us maik.
I tak on hand, and ye will counsale keip,   305
That I sall gar yow se, or ever I sleip,
Of the best meit that is in this cuntre ;
Off Gascone wyne, gif ony in it be,

Or, be thair ony within ane hundreth myle,
It salbe heir within a bony quhyle."   310
The gudman had grit mervell of this taill,
And said, " My hairt [will] neir be haill
Bot gif ye preve that practik, or ye pairte,
To mak ane sport."   And than the Freir upstart ;
He tuk his buk, and to the flure he gais,   315
He turnis it our, and reidis it a littill space,
And to the eist direct he turnis his face,
Syne to the west he turnit and lukit doun,
And tuk his buk and red ane orisoun ;
And ay his eyne wer on the almery,   320
And on the troch quhair that Freir Johine did ly.
Than sat he doun, and kest abak his hude,
He granit, and he glowrit, as he wer woid ;
And quhylis still he satt in studeing,
And uthir quhylis upoun his buk reding ;   325
And [quhylis] with baith his handis he wald clap,
And uthir quhylis wald he glour and gaip ;
Syne in the sowth he turnit him abowt
Weill thryis, and mair than lawly cowd he lowt,
Quhen that he come neir the almery.   330
Thairat our dame had woundir grit invy,
For in her hairt scho had ane persaving
That he had knawin all hir govirning.
Scho saw him gif the almery sic a straik,
Unto hir self scho said, " Full weill I wait   335
I am bot schent, he knawis full weill my thocht ;
Quhat sall I do ?   Allace, that I wes wrocht !
Get Symon wit, it wilbe deir doing."
Be that the Freir had left his studeing,
And on his feit he startis up full sture,   340
And come agane, and seyit, " All haill my cure !
Now is it done, and ye sall haif playntie
Of breid and wyne, the best in this cuntre ;
Thairfoir, fair dame, get up deliverlie,
And ga belyfe unto yone almerie,   345
And oppin it ; and se ye bring us syne
Ane pair of boissis full of Gascone wyne,
Thay hald ane galloun and mair, that wait I weill ;
And bring us als the mayne breid in a creill ;
Ane pair of cunyngis, fat and het pypand ;   350
The caponis als ye sall us bring fra hand ;

Twa pair of pertrikis, I wait thair is no ma ;
And eik of pluveris se that ye bring us twa."
The gudwyf wist it wes no variance ;
Scho knew the Freir had sene hir govirnance ; 355
Scho saw it wes no bute for to deny ;
With that scho went unto the almery,
And oppinnit it, and than scho fand thair
All that the Freir had spokin of befoir.
Scho stert abak, as scho wer in a fray, 360
And sanyt hir, and smyland cowd scho say,
" Ha, banedicitie, quhat may this bene ?
Quha evir afoir hes sic a fairly sene ?
Sa grit a mervell as now hes apnit heir,
Quhat sall I say ?   He is ane haly Freir, 365
He said full suth of all that he did say."
Scho brocht all furth, and on the burd cowd lay
Baith breid and wyne, and uthir thingis moir,
Cunyngis and caponis, as ye haif hard befoir ;
Pertrikis and pluveris befoir thame hes scho brocht. 370
The Freir knew weill and saw thair wantit nocht,
Bot all wes furth brocht evin at his devyis.
Fra Symone saw it appinnit on this wyis,
He had grit wondir, and sweris be the mone
That Freir Robert weill his dett had done ; 375
" He may be callit ane man of grit science,
Sa suddanly maid all this purviance
Hes brocht us heir, throw his grit subteltie
And throw his knawlege in filosophie :
In ane gud tyme it wes quhen he come hidder ; 380
Now fill the cop that we ma drink togidder,
And mak gud cheir eftir this langsum day,
For I haif riddin ane woundir wilsome way.
Now God be lovit, heir is suffisance
Unto us all throw your gud govirnance : " 385
And than annone thay drank evin round abowt
Of Gascone wyne ; the Freiris playit cop owt.
Thay sportit thame, and makis mirry cheir
With sangis lowd, baith Symone and the Freir ;
And on this wyis the lang nicht thay ourdraif ; 390
No thing thay want that thay desyrd to haif.
Than Symon said to the gudwyf in hy,
" Cum heir, fair dame, and sett yow doun me by,
And tak pairte of sic gud as we haif heir,

And hairtly I yow pray to thank this Freir 395
Off his bening grit besines and cure,
That he hes done to us upoun this flure,
And brocht us meit and drink haboundantlie,
Quhairfoir of richt we aucht mirry to be."
Bot all thair sport, quhen thay wer maist at eis, 400
Unto our deme it wes bot littill pleis,
For uther thing thair wes in to hir thocht ;
Scho wes so dred, hir hairt wes ay on flocht,
That throw the Freir scho sowld discoverit be,
To him scho lukit oft tymes effeiritlie, 405
And ay disparit in hart was scho,
That he had witt of all hir purveance to.
Thus satt scho still, and wist no udir wane ;
Quhat evir thay say, scho lute him all alane,
Bot scho drank with thame in to cumpany 410
With fenyeit cheir, and hert full wo and hevy.
Bot thay wer blyth annuche, God wait, and sang,
For ay the wyne was rakand thame amang,
Quhill at the last thay woix richt blyth ilk one.
Than Symone said unto the Freir annone, 415
" I mervell mikill how that this may be,
In till schort tyme that ye sa suddanlye
Hes brocht to us sa mony denteis deir."
" Thairof haif ye no mervell," quod the Freir,
"I haif ane pege full prevy of my awin, 420
Quhen evir I list, will cum to me unknawin,
And bring to me sic thing as I will haif ;
Quhat evir I list it neidis me nocht to craif.
Thairfoir be blyth, and tak in pacience,
And trest ye weill I sall do diligence ; 425
Gif that ye list or thinkis to haif moir,
It salbe had and I sall stand thairfoir,
Incontinent that samyn sall ye se ;
Bot I protest that ye keip it previe,
Latt no man wit that I can do sic thing." 430
Than Symone swoir and said, " Be hevynnis king,
It salbe kepit prevy as for me ;
Bot, bruder deir, your servand wald I se,
Gif it yow pleis, that we may drynk togidder,
For I wait nocht gif ye ma ay cum hidder, 435
Quhen that we want our neidis sic as this."
The Freir said, " Nay, so mot I haif hevynis blis,

Yow to haif the sicht of my servand
It can nocht be ; ye sall weill undirstand,
That ye may se him graithly in his awin kynd,   440
Bot ye annone oowld go owt of your mynd,
He is so fowll and ugly for to se ;
I dar nocht awnter for to tak on me
To bring him hidder heir in to our sicht,
And namely now so lait in to the nicht ;   445
Bot gif it wer on sic a maner wyis
Him to translait or ellis dissagyis
Fra his awin kynd in to ane uder stait."
Than Symone said, " I mak no moir debait,
As pleisis yow so lyk is it to me,   150
As evir ye list, bot fane wald I him se."
Freyr Robert said, " Sen that your will is so,
Tell onto me withouttin wourdis mo,
In till quhat kynd sall I him gar appeir ? "
Than Symone said, " In liknes of a Freir,   455
In quhyt cullour, richt as your self it war,
For quhyt cullour will na body deir,"
Freir Robert said that swa it cowld nocht be,
For sic causis as he may weill foirse,
That he compeir in to our habeit quhyt ;   460
" Untill our ordour it wer a grit dispyte,
That ony sic unworthy wicht as he
In till our habeit men sowld behald or se.
Bot sen it pleisis yow that ar heir,
Ye sall him se in liknes of a Freir ;   465
In habeit gray it was his kynd to weir,
Into sic wys that he sall no man deir.
Gif ye so do, and rewll yow at all wyis
To hald yow clois and still at my devyis,
Quhat evir it be ye owdir se or heir,   470
Ye speik no word, nor mak no kynd of steir,
Bot hald yow clois, quhill I haif done my cure."
Than said he, " Semon, ye mone be on the flure,
Neirhand besyd with staff in to your hand ;
Haif ye no dreid, I sall yow ay warrand."   475
Than Symone said, " I assent that it be swa ; "
And up he start, and gat a libberla
Into his hand, and on the flure he stert,
Sumthing effrayit, thocht stalwart was his hart.
Than to the Freir said Symone verry sone,   480

"Now tell me, maister, quhat ye will haif done."
"No thing," he said, "bot hald yow clois and still;
Quhat evir I do, tak ye gud tent thairtill,
And neir the dur ye hyd yow prevely,
And quhen I bid yow stryk, strek hardely,   485
In to the nek se that ye hit him richt."
"That sall I warrand," quod he, "with all my micht."
Thus on the flure I leif him standand still,
Bydand his tyme; and turne agane I will,
How that the Freir did take his buke in hy,   490
And turnit our the levis full besely,
Ane full lang space, and quhen he had done swa,
Towart the troch withowttin wordis ma
He gois belyfe, and on this wyis sayis he,
"Ha, how, Hurlybas, now I coniure the,   495
That thow uprys and sone to me appeir
In habeit gray in liknes of a freir;
Owt of this troch, quhair that thow dois ly,
Thow rax the sone, and mak no dyn nor cry;
Thow tumbill our the troch that we may se,   500
And unto us thow schaw the oppinlie;
And in this place se that thow no man greif,
Bot draw thy handis boith in to thy sleif,
And pull thy cowll doun owttour thy face;
Thow may thank God that thow gettis sic a grace;   505
Thairfoir thow turs the to thyne awin ressett,
Se this be done and mak no moir debait;
In thy depairting se thow mak no deray
Unto no wicht, bot frely pas thy way;
And in this place se that thow cum no moir,   510
Bot I command the, or ellis the charge befoir;
And our the stair se that thow ga gud speid;
Gif thow dois nocht, on thy awin perrell beid."
With that the Freir, that under the troch lay,
Raxit him sone, bot he wes in a fray,   515
And up he rais, and wist na bettir wayn,
Bot of the troch he tumlit our the stane;
Syne fra the samyn quhairin he thocht him lang,
Unto the dur he preisit him to gang,
With hevy cheir and drery countenance,   520
For nevir befoir him hapnit sic a chance.
And quhen Freir Robert saw him gangand by,
Unto the Gudman full lowdly cowd he cry,

" Stryk, stryk herdely, for now is tyme to the."
With that Symone a felloun flap lait fle,   525
With his burdoun he hit him on the nek ;
He wes sa feice he fell owttour the sek,
And brak his heid upoun ane mustard stane.
Be this Freir Johine attour the stair is gane
In sic wyis, that mist he hes the trap,   530
And in ane myr he fell, sic wes his hap,
Wes fourty futis of breid undir the stair ;
Yeit gat he up with clething nothing fair ;
Full drerelie upoun his feit he stude,
And throw the myre full smertly than he yude,   535
And our the wall he clam richt haistely,
Quhilk round abowt wes laid with stanis dry :
Off his eschaping in hairt he wes full fane,
I trow he salbe laith to cum agane.
With that Freir Robert stert abak and saw   540
Quhair the Gudman lay sa woundir law
Upoun the flure, and bleidand wes his heid ;
He stert to him, and went he had bene deid,
And clawcht him up withowttin wordis moir,
And to the dur delyverly him bure ;   545
And fra the wind wes blawin twyis in his face,
Than he ourcome within a lytill space ;
And than Freir Robert franyt at him fast,
Quhat ailit him to be so soir agast.
He said, " Yone Freir hes maid me thus gait say."   550
" Lat be," quod he, " the werst is all away ;
Mak mirry, man, and se ye murne na mair,
Ye haif him strikin quyt owttour the stair.
I saw him skip, gif I the suth can tell,
Doun our the stair, in till a myr he fell ;   555
Bot lat him go, he wes a graceles gaist,
And boun yow to your bed, for it is best."
Thus Symonis heid upoun the stane wes brokin,
And our the stair the Freir in myre hes loppin,
And tap our taill he fyld wes woundir ill ;   560
And Alesone on na wayis gat hir will.
This is the story that hapnit of that Freir,
No moir thair is, bot Chryst us help most deir.

NOTES

Print C. and M. = Chepman and Myllar's printed issue of 1508. The MSS. are distinguished thus : A. = Asloan ; B. = Bannatyne ; M. = Maitland ; R. = Reidpeth. Other sources are specified in their place. References to Laing are to the first collected edition of the poems prepared by David Laing, 2 vols., Edinburgh, 1834 ; to Schipper for *The Poems of William Dunbar*, edited by J. Schipper, Ph.D., LL.D., Vienna, 1894. S.T.S. = Scottish Text Society, and particularly its edition of Dunbar. E.E.T.S. = Early English Text Society.

I

MS. B. only. Cf. *The Compleynt of Chaucer to his Purse* and Lydgate's *Application to the Duke of Gloucester for Money*. 1. *Sanct Salvatour* or Saint Saviour, a late mediaeval form of dedication. Of examples known in Scotland all but two were chapels, and of the two much the most important was the College of St. Salvator at St. Andrews founded by Bishop Kennedy in 1450, the church of which still survives. On this point see *Introd.*, p. xx, *sorrow*. Here an imprecation. Cf. Stevenson's *Catriona*, ii, " and their pleas—a sorrow of their pleas." 22. *cors*: a coin, so called from the "cross' on one side.

2

MS. B. 14. *fleis of Spenyie*. The " Spanish fly," *cantharides*, or the " blister fly." On *Spenyie* see *Introd.*, p. xxxvii (4).

3

MS. R. only.

4

MS. B. MS. M. omits ll. 20-25. In l. 49 *hous end* is from M. for *houshend* in B. 2. *Sanct Francis* (1182-1226) of Assisi was founder of the Grey Friars. 34. *Kalyce* : Calais. " Calice " in *Maitland Folio MS.* (S.T.S.), p. 30. 38. *Derntoun* : not identified.

5

MS. M. only. In l. 18 *ressoun* has been altered on the margin to *seasoun*. 2. *Muris*. Mure is not otherwise known. 9. *salpeter*. It was used medicinally. Cf. " For ij pund salt petir to the leich (doctor) " (*Accts. Lord*

High Treas., ii, p. 139). 12. *servis ded*: "deserves death." 24. *Cuddy Rig.* "Cuddy" is short for Cuthbert. 26. *yallow and reid.* These were later the colours of the royal livery.

On the subject of this poem see Appendix B.

6

MS. B. to l. 315. Thereafter C. and M. On this composition see *Introd.*, p. xxxii. With regard to it Prof. Schipper came to the conclusion that "the succession of the different parts . . . is wholly confused." He therefore took in hand to rearrange the stanzas in a more logical and chronological order, and considered that the result came, in some degree, nearer to the original form of the composition. This involved a division into six instead of four separate pieces. Apart from the assumptions made as to the way in which such a work would be done, it may be pointed out that we have two complete versions of it in MSS. B. and M., with that of M. repeated in MS. R., while what is left of the Print of 1508 preserves ll. 316 to the end. Save for a difference in one part of M., which is due to a displacement of certain pages, the MSS. and the Print, as far as it goes, agree in the order of the verses, which is that followed here. It is all very well to claim, as Schipper does, that Dunbar and Kennedy ordinarily "worked on artistic principles," but it does not follow that these necessarily apply to a composition of this type, which could have its own "principles." Moreover, if Dunbar had thought that his work had been mishandled in the Print, it is unlikely that he would not have resented the fact, as he did the interference of John Mure in such a case (No. 5). It is further unlikely that, if there had been a version in existence so different in its presumed arrangement from the one we have, no trace of it should appear in either MSS. It is therefore unsafe to alter, on possibly irrelevant grounds, the order of verses common to all the sources. It was not a composition serious in character—MS. B. describes it in the title as "jocound and mirrie"—or necessarily prolonged and deliberate in output, but merely a piling up of heterogeneous abuse.

It may further be noted that, while in the earliest surviving printed editions (1629) of the *Flyting of Montgomerie and Polwart* the different portions alternate for each author, in the MS. of over forty years earlier those of Montgomerie come first and then those of Polwart (see *Poems of Alexander Montgomerie, Supplementary Volume*, S.T.S.). One inference, therefore, seems to be that logical coherence was not regarded as essential to this strange species of amusement, that its effect did not depend upon its qualities as dialectic but upon the immediate impression. Genuine quarrels on these lines in real life, which in fact are here imitated, show just that characteristic.

As the piece stands, it will be observed that each of the long sections ends in a corresponding verse-firework of abusive terms in short or internal rhyming lines. Schipper's rearrangement misses this effect.

1. *Schir Johne the Ros.* Not certainly identified. See note on No. 7, l. 83. 2. *Kennedy.* Walter Kennedy, son of Gilbert, first Lord Kennedy, and in 1478 a Master of Arts of Glasgow University. He may well have

been, as Laing suggested, the son of Lord Kennedy who was made Provost of the Collegiate Church of Maybole in 1494. Poems by him are in the *Bannatyne MS.* and the *Maitland MS. Quinting.* Quentin Shaw. See note on No. 7, l. 86. 26. *skaldit skrowis* : " libellous " or " scurrilous scrolls." Cf. l. 322 ; and Montgomerie's *Flyting,* l. 112 : " Thy scrows obscure are borrowed fra some buike." 51. *Denseman on the rattis* : " Dane on the wheels," being the " wheel " on which a criminal was executed and on which his dead body was exposed. Cf. ll. 355, 424. 59. *haltane in thy harlotrie* : " haughty [O.Fr. *hautailn*] in thy rascality." One sense of " harlot " was that of a buffoon who told coarse stories. It was still used mostly of a male person. 62. *Quytclame clergie* : " Give up learning " or " literature." 78. *In Paislay, with ane poysone.* The note in the S.T.S. edition explains this as a charge connected with the rebellion by the Earl of Lennox and Lord Lyle in 1489, when Lyle was besieged in Duchal Castle. The laird of Hillhouse was in charge of the royal artillery, and the king visited Paisley in connection with the operations (*Treasurer's Accts.,* i, pp. 112, 116). *Poysone* is taken to be a metaphor for rebellion. But something more definite seems to be in question. 79. *thoill a breif* : " suffer " or " answer to a writ or indictment." 97. *rethory with thy golden lippis.* This is taken by Schipper to be Dunbar's retort to Kennedy's description of himself as *of Rethory the Rose* (l. 500) and he reverses the order of the stanzas accordingly. But the expressions are not identical, and the first is quite general. 99. B. *gluntoch.* M. *gluntow* : Gaelic=" black-knee " (*glùn,* " knee " and *dubh,* " black "), *i.e.* " bare-knee " or wearing Gaelic dress. Used in the phonetic Gaelic in the *Buke of the Howlat,* l. 794. 102. *lathand* (M. *lauchtane*) *as ane leik* : " pale-coloured or livid as a leek." Cf. " lauchtane *as the leid* " (*Maitland MS.,* i, p. 206, l. 14). 121. *lisk and lonye.* For " flank (groin) and back (loin)." Cf. Douglas, " At his left flank or leisk " (*Aeneid,* X, x, l. 103). 123. *rostit Lawarance.* St. Lawrence was martyred by being roasted on a gridiron. 124. *Sanct Johnis ene.* Incident unknown. 125. *Sanct Augustine.* The story is thus summarised by Bellenden in his translation of Boece, who, however, does not himself give it, Bellenden here drawing upon the *Scotichronicon* (IX, xxxii), " Quhen this haly man, Sanct Austine, wes precheand to the Saxonis in Miglintoun, thay were nocht onlie rebelland to his precheing, but in his contemptioun thay sewit fische talis on his abilyements. Otheris alliegis thay dang him with skait rumpillis [tails] ... God tuke on thaim sic vengeance, that thay and thair posteritie had lang talis mony yeris eftir." The story appears first on record in the second half of the eleventh century, is located in different places, and developed into the favourite mediaeval gibe that all Englishmen had tails. On the whole matter see *Caudatus Anglicus,* by Dr. G. Neilson, and " The Story of the Long-Tail Myth," in *Byways of Scottish History,* by Louis A. Barbé. Cf. here below, l. 351. 126. *Bartilmo.* St. Bartholomew was martyred by being flayed with a knife. 172. *Spreit of Gy.* See note on 86. 13. 184. *carrybald.* " Caribal," a native of the " Carib " or Carribee Islands, a people reputed by their discoverers—the Spaniards—to eat human flesh, hence=monster. " Cannibal " is a variant name. *in saphron.* " saffron " here apparently as a liniment, whether as treatment against vermin or

lues venerea. But the Highland body garment was dyed with saffron—
"the yellow shirt," (cf. l. 171). 192. M. *of no clowse.* 199. *gulsoch gane* :
"jaundiced face." *Gule* = yellow + O.E. *suht* = sickness. Cf. *gule snowt* in
l. 52. 241. *byt.* From M. B. *byle* . . . *air to Hilhous.* Sir John Sandi-
lands of Hillhouse appears in the *Treasurer's Accts.*, i, particularly in con-
nection with the artillery, but the allusion is obscure. Cf. note on 78.
242. *the flet* : " the inner part of the house." Cf. Henryson of flax which
was "hekkillit (heckled) in the flet " (*Fables*, S.T.S., l. 1821). B. *foule*
fleggaris. 249-250. *Dathane . . . Abiron.* Rebels. See *Numbers*, chap. 16.
258. *Cokburnispeth* : " Cockburnspath," Berwickshire. 260. *Dewlbeir* :
454. *Deulbere* = " De'il-bear " for " Devil-bear." Cf. *Introd.*, p. xxxviii (8).
261. *a meir of Mar.* " Many Scots are wont privately to compare the
Stewarts to the horses of Mar, which are good when they are young but
bad when they are old " (Major, *Historia Maj. Brit.* (1740), vi, 14). 262.
Corspatrik. Properly " Gospatrick," who was deprived of his earldom of
Northumbria by William the Conqueror and received Dunbar from
Malcolm Canmore, founding the line of the Earls of March or Dunbar.
In the verses following Dunbar proceeds to confuse him with Earl Patrick,
the contemporary of Wallace, who is " Corspatrik " in *The Wallace*, Bk. viii,
" the Cornicle " (l. 272) from which the material here used has been taken.
Spottismuir (l. 269) is east of Haddington. 299. *the house of Hailis.* " Hailes "
on the Tyne, East Lothian. In 1446 Archibald Dunbar seized the House of
Hailes, but shortly after had to surrender it to James Douglas (Pitscottie,
xviii., chap. xii). Dunbar's action was apparently in retaliation for the part
played by Adam Hepburn of Hailes in capturing the Castle of Dunbar in
the previous reign, when the eleventh Earl of March was forfeited by
James I. Hepburn had custody of the place for some years (l. 300). 319.
trentalis. A " trental " was a service of thirty masses for the dead, occupying
thirty days. Here simply " a great number." 321-322. *fals Eustace* and
Alathya. These are almost certainly to be identified with the *Pseustis* and
Alathya, that is " Falsehood " and " Trust ", who appear in the Latin *Ecloga*
Theoduli, as was shown by the American scholar H. M. Ayres in a paper entitled
" Theodulus in Scots" and published in 1918 in *Modern Philology* xv, 539-548.
A juxtaposition of *Alathya* and *Eustace*, the monk, outlaw and " magician "
who was killed at sea in the reign of King John, is decidedly less probable.
328. *Dereliquisti quia.* Apparently the reading of M., " because thou hast
forsaken me " (Ps. xxii, 1). C. and M. reads *deliquisti quia*, " because thou
hast sinned." 331. *Stobo.* Cf. No. 7, l. 86 and note. 337. *Pernaso* : " Par-
nassus." 345. Irisch : Gaelic. 351. *Inglise rumplis* : " English tails."
See note on l. 125. 355. *the rattis.* See on l. 51. 368. *Mount Falcoun* :
Montfauçon in Paris, where criminals were hanged. 388. *Dunbar of*
Westfelde. The first Dunbar Earl of Moray (l. 386) was a grandson of
Thomas Randolph, Earl of Moray. The fourth and last Dunbar earl had
a natural son, who became Sir Alexander Dunbar of Westfield, an estate
in the parish of Spynie, Morayshire. Sir Alexander died 1497/8. 394. *cor*
mundum : " a clean heart " (Ps. li, 10). 397. *of thy greis* : " from thy posi-
tion." *Greis*, literally " steps " (Fr. *degré*), as in " turngreis " for " turnpike,"
a winding stair. 400. *trone the to the treis.* M. reads *for tresone . . . thrunit.*
But " with " can also be used to mean " on account of," " by reason of,"

as " for " is used instead of " with " in " For battering at the studdy "
(38. 52). A " tron(e) " was a weighing-machine, utilised on occasion for a
pillory, and the word was also used as a verb to mean " weigh." Thus it
might come to bear the derived sense of " to pillory," as it seems to do here.
Cf. " Than trasoun man be thrunit to ane tre " (*M. Folio MS.*, p. 354, l. 49).
" Tre " or " treis "=timber or timbers. 417. *the kingis blude*. Kennedy's
grandfather married a daughter of Robert III. 431. *clamschellis . . .
burdoun*. A large hat adorned with scallop shells and a long staff or *burdoun*
were parts of the costume of the professional pilgrim. Cf. l. 509. 432.
wolroun. See note on No. 47, l. 90. 433. *Mount Barnard, etc.* Swiss
mountains over which were passes for the pilgrims to Rome. 450. *doun fra
starn to stere* : " from rudder to helm," *i.e.* over the ship's stern. *Starn* and
stere were often used for either rudder or helm. Cf. No. 74, l. 46. 446. *in
Danskyn . . . of my tailye* : " in Denmark to my account." 449. *the
Kutryne*. Cf. *Introd.*, p. xxii. 475. *hors marschall*, " horse attendant " or
veterinary surgeon. Cf. " to the Inglis hors marschael to hele the broune
geldin, 18/-" (*Treas. Accts.*, i. p. 330). 489. *the grete eclips*. See *Introd.*,
p. xix. 513. *Caym*. " Cain." This form occurs, *e.g.*, in the Miracle Plays.
Tutivillus. A demon whose business was to collect all cases of words
mispronounced, mumbled, or curtailed by the priest in reading or singing.
(Cf. *The Myroure of Oure Ladye*, E.E.T.S., p. 54.) The name might also
be applied to the Devil, " *Titivillus . . . princeps tenebrarum* " (see Leh-
mann's *Parodie im Mittelalter*, p. 15). In the *Towneley Mysteries* (Surtees
Soc., p. 311) he is a demon. Thus applicable to any one of a devilish
nature. 515. *Hillhouse*. See on l. 241. 528. *Gog and Magog*. See on
No. 86, l. 37. 530. *Egipya* or *Egyptia* (M.), the name given to Potiphar's
wife in *Testamentum Josephi* (see note in S.T.S.). 532. *Termygantis*. " Ter-
magant," one of the gods of the Saracens, according to the *Chanson de
Roland* : " lur deus Tervagan e Nahun E Apollin " (ll. 2696-7). Used
in a secondary application in No. 57, l. 115. 532. *Vaspasius*. ? Aspasius
(see Addenda). 537. *Egeas*. The proconsul who martyred St. Andrew
(see S.T.S. *Legends of the Saints*, 1, 63 - 96. 538 *Marciane*. Probably
Marcion of Sinope (see Addenda). *Maxencius*. Maxentius, a rival of the
Emperor Constantine, by whom he was defeated. He had an evil reputa-
tion and was responsible for the martyrdom of St. Catharine. 539. *Antenor*.
He persuaded the Trojans to admit the wooden horse within the walls of
Troy. 540. *Throp*. M. *Ethroup*. According to the poet Lydgate in his *Fall of
Princes*, Chaucer derived his tale of *Troylus and Criseyde* from an Italian
original entitled " Trophe." By a misunderstanding Kennedy may have
concluded that " Trophe " or, as it could also be written, " Throphe," was
another name for the lady, and so wrote the form " Throp " to signify
" Criseyde " or " Cresseid," who otherwise would suit the context. This
is the ingenious suggestion of Mr. Bruce Dickins in the *Times Literary
Supplement*, July 10, 1924. *Olibrius*. The Roman prefect who caused the
martyrdom of St. Margaret at Antioch (cf. Scottish *Legends of the Saints*,
l. 620). 541. *Eyobulus*. M. *Ezobulus*. Eubulus Aurelius, an official of the
Emperor Elagabalus, who, on the Emperor's death, was torn to pieces by
the soldiers and people (Dio's *Roman History*, lxxx, 21).

I

7

Print C. and M.   A few spellings in MS. M. have been preferred, *e.g.* *hes* for *has*, *nocht* for *nought*, *on* for *one*.   Lydgate has the Latin refrain meaning " The fear of death troubles me " in his poem beginning " So I lay the other night."   But there was a common source in the *Responsorium* to the seventh lesson in the Office for the Dead, where the sentence may be found.   In l. 53 for ' And eik," which is printed " Et eik " (cf. Appendix A), MS. B. has " Ettrik " and MS. M. " Eleik," forms which have been taken as a personal name but really suggest a misreading by the scribes.   MS. M. does not have ll. 85-8.   51. *the monk of Bery.*   John Lydgate (1375-1460).   *Gower.*   John Gower (1320-1402).   53. *Syr Hew of Eglintoun.*   Married a half-sister of Robert II and died about 1375.   Not known as a poet unless he is to be identified with " Huchown of the Awle Ryale," mentioned by Wyntoun with a list of his works.   54. *Heryot.*   Not known.   *Wyntoun.*   Andrew of Wyntoun, author of the *Orygynale Cronykil* written between 1395 and 1424.   58. *Johne Clerk.*   Some poems in the *Bannatyne MS.* are attributed to a " Clerk."   *James Afflek.*   May be a James Auchinleck, but nothing is really known of such a poet.   61. *Holland.*   Sir Richard Holland (fl. 1482), author of *The Buke of the Howlat.*   *Barbour.* John Barbour, author of *The Bruce.*   63. *Schir Mungo Lokert of the Lee.* No Sir Mungo is on record in the genealogy of the Lee family.   A " Sir Mungo Lokkart of the Lee " is in the *Acta Dominorum Concilii* as dead some time before 11th July 1498 (vol. i, p. 263).   65. *Clerk of Tranent.* Unknown.   67. *Sir Gilbert Hay* (fl. 1456).   A prose translator, but as a poet known only as a translator of the *Buik of Alexander*, which was once projected by the S.T.S.   69. *Blind Hary.*   He is usually spoken of as the author of the poem called *The Wallace*, but on the single surviving MS. of 1489 no author's name appears.   John Major, however, in his *Historia Majoris Britanniae* (1521) speaks of a " Henry, blind from his birth," who, in the time of the historian's childhood, " composed (*cudit*) a whole book on William Wallace, writing down (*conscripsit*) in popular verse, in which he was skilled, the stories that were current."   That *The Wallace*, as we have it, depending, as it does, so much on literary sources, answers to Major's description is a debatable proposition, but that it was the work of a man blind from birth is incredible.   There are in the *Lord Treasurer's Accounts* for 1490-1 a few entries of gifts of so many shillings " to Blind Hary," but no particular reason is assigned.   For an assumed reference to this person in another poem see Appendix D.   *Sandy Traill.*   Not known.   71. *Patrik Johnestoun.*   One poem in the *Bannatyne MS.* is attributed to " Patrik Johinstoun."   He was a play-actor and a producer of stage entertainments. See *Treasurer's Accts.*, i, pp. lxxvii, xcii, ccxxxix, ccxliv, covering the years 1476-90.   73. *Merseir.*   Three poems by " Mersar " are in the *Bannatyne MS.* and one more in the *Maitland MS.*   The former deal with love in a sententious not a " lifly " fashion.   77, 78. *Roull of Aberdene, Roull of Corstorphine.*   In the *Bannatyne MS.* is " The cursing of Sir Johine Rowlis/ Upoun the steilaris of his fowlis."   Which, if either, this is cannot be said. 81. *done roune—i.e.* " Death has held converse with, etc."   MS. B. has the reading *tane Broun,* and in the same MS. there is one poem by a " Walter Broun," but the reading of the Print and MS. M. has been preferred. 82. *Robert Henrisoun.* The well-known older contemporary of Dunbar, whose poems have been published by S.T.S. He was schoolmaster at Dunfermline. 83. *Schir Johne the Ros.* Also in *Flyting,* 1. 1 ; probably Sir John Ross of Montgreenan, dead by 12 March 1494/5 (*Scott. Hist. Rev.* xxxiii, 87-88. 86. *Stobo.* John Reid *alias* Stobo was a clerk in the Secretary's office in the time of James III and had a pension of £20 from the customs of Edinburgh (cf. *Exchequer Rolls,* xi, pp. xxix-xxx). He is referred to in *The Flyting,* l. 331. *Quintyne Schaw.* He has one poem in the *Maitland MS.* and is referred to in *The Flyting.* He enjoyed a pension of £10. 89. *Walter Kennedy.* Dunbar's antagonist in *The Flyting* (*q.v.*).

8

MS. B., where the poem is attributed to Dunbar. There are two versions in MS. M., in one of which " Stewarte " is given as the author. There is therefore some doubt as to authorship, and the present editor does not think it was by Dunbar. The verse in ll. 41-5 is not in B. but is taken from the earlier version in M., from which the other version differs somewhat. In l. 8 B. has *I lie.* 13. M. has *set* for *warit.* 27. *createure* : three syllables rhyming with *nature* accented on the final syllable. 34. For *mowth* M. in both versions has *mulls* ; cf. Ger. *maul* = mouth. 46. *James the Ferd.* James the Fourth.

9

MS. M. In neither M. nor B. is the text satisfactory, but M. has a verse omitted in B. and has a few other prints in its favour. The refrain in B. has *sall* throughout instead of *sould,* while M. has *sall* in vv. 3, 4, 5. There are several other variants. 14. B. has *Thus will thay say.* 23. B. *hairt.* 26. B. *Gif I be nocht weill als besene.* 28. B. *That evill he gydis yone man trewlie.* 29. B. *Lo ! be his claithis.* 32. B. *murmour.* 36. From B. M. reads *And gif sum tyme rewarde gif I.* 39. B. *hinder.* 41. B. *I wald my gyding war devysit.* 43. B. *Gif I be nobill, gentill.* 46. *Now juge thay me,* etc. Only the principal variants have been noted.

10

MS. M. only. One version complete, another only from l. 22 to end, while MS. R. has ll. 1-22 and no more. 24. MS. *Quhone.*

11

MS. M. only. There are two versions which differ merely in spelling, and of which the later one is here given. 9. M1. has *for thirst.*

12

MS. M. only. There are two versions which differ mainly in spelling but neither of which is quite perfect. Preference is here given to the later version M2, with some readings corrected from M1.

6. *Sum swelleis swan*, etc. Editors, strange to say, have taken these expressions literally (cf. *Introd.*, p. xxiii). But the occasion is a "feist" of benefices, as in the preceding poem, and here as there the terms denoting food and drink are used metaphorically. "Swan" as a characteristic food of the great (cf. No. 30, l. 51) stands for a rich benefice; "duke" or duck for a lesser one; while to be "fastand" is to be without any. 8. *effec* or *effect* (M2.) = "quantity" or "amount," later "feck." Cf. Burns, "I hae been a Devil the feck o' my life" (*Kellyburn Braes*, v. xiv). 11. *sic hie feistis of sanctis*, etc. Continuing the metaphor, *sanctis in glorie* representing the benefices, known by their dedications. 20. *set* = "seat." Cf. "Seik to the sett that is certane" (*Maitland Fol. MS.*, p. 444, l 100). 26. *warryit*: "cursed," from M1. M2. *variant*.

13

MS. M. only. 7. *The sweit abayd, the slichtfull trane.* "Sweit" in the sense of "clever," "adroit," as in "You never imagined a sweeter schooner —a child might sail her" (*Treasure Island*, chap. vii). Thus, "The adroit delay, the skilful snare." 19. *Spane.* Pronounce the final "e" as in the fuller form *Spenyie* (2. l. 14). 55. *with ane thraif playis passage plane.* A "thraif" or "thrave" was twenty-four sheaves. "Some have freer access to so many." 62. *Calyecot.* See Addenda. *new fund Isle.* America. Cf. Donne's "O my America! my new found land" (*Elegie xix*). 71. *Aphrycane.* Africa. There are several "isles" off the east coast. 78. *unicornis.* Gold coins, value 20s., so called from the figure of a unicorn on one side, first issued by James III. *crownis of wecht.* French crown pieces. Their exchange value had been fixed by Parliament at 13s. 4d. 85-6. Note rhyme : *dd = th.* 99. *crop and grayne* : "foliage and stem or branch " = "altogether." Cf. in Douglas's *Aeneid* the blasts "quhisland (whistling) amang the granys " of an ancient oak tree (ed. Bannatyne Club, i, p. 217). Branches of Border families were known as "graynes" (*The Lord Wardens of the Borders*, Pease, p. 174). Cf. *Ane Ballat of our Lady*, l. 72.

14

MS. B. M. omits ll. 16-20 and is otherwise distinctly inferior. 13. *as braidis of me* : "As is like or akin to me." Cf. Fergusson's *Scottish Proverbs* : "Ye breid of bourtrie [elder-tree], ye ar all heart."

15

MS. B. The versions in B. and M. differ a good deal in detail and neither is quite satisfactory, while M. lacks ll. 30-5. To preserve uniformity with the companion poem (No. 14) B. has been preferred. 1. M. has *giftis*. 8. *in practik for supple* : "habitually as assistance." 11. B. *cheritie*, which is obviously wrong. 28. M. has *Throw want and prodigalitie*. 37. M. *will not pay auld servandis fee*. 41. B. *can ask and plenyie*. 51. B. *gud kowis*, which is unintelligible. 53. B. *knaw his*. 59. B. *That he na wit hes thume to'gyd*.

16

MS. B. Ll. 16-20, 36-40 are additional verses from M. but seem to be intrusions. In l. 16 Schipper alters *Thir* to *The*, while he rejects the second set. As to the change of reading it may be noted that M. also begins the preceding verses with *Thir clarkis* and *Thir baronis*, so that Schipper's substitution is quite arbitrary. In l. 26 M. reads, *Pairt takis be sey and part*, etc. 27. *And part fra taking can not hald his hand*. 36. M. reads, *And not yit can be satisfeid*.

1, 2. These lines are obscure in meaning. 13. *mailis and gersomes*. "Money-rents and fines," the latter being paid, in addition to the rent, on entering upon or renewing the lease of a holding. The "gersom" or "grassum" was usually equal to a year's rent.

17

MS. M. only. The inclusion of *pryntouris* in l. 16 suggests that this poem was written after 1507, when the first printing-press was set up in Scotland. That is, if "printers" be not stampers or impressers of a design upon metal or fabric and so comparable with "painters" and "potters." Cf. "to prent fals plakkis [coins]" (Douglas, *Aeneid*, Prol. viii, 93), and No. 57, l. 66. Many terms, specially among the abusive ones, are quite obscure. 42. *clarat-cunnaris* : "claret-drinkers." See note on 93, 254. 43. *of Yrland kynd*. In the *Treasurer's Accounts* are many entries of payments to "Irland" friars, priests, performers, etc. See vols. i, ii, iv *passim*. 48. *kennis*, etc. : people "no man knows good of." 55. *In quintiscence*. Cf. *The Fenyeit Freir of Tungland*, l. 58. 58. *evill—deidie*. MS. "diedie," but cf. "evil deidie" in Lindesay's *Thrie Estaitis*, l. 4028 := "given to evil deeds," and see *Introd.*, p. xxxviii (8). 66. *Cokelbeis gryce*. An allusion to the contemporary *Tale of Colkelbie* (or *Cowkelbie*) *Sow* printed in Laing's *Early Popular Poetry of Scotland*. Colkelbie sold a sow for three pennies. One was lost and the finder bought with it "a pig sum callis a gryss." This pig was made the occasion of a feast, to which all sorts of rascals were invited. The character of the company is the point of the present reference. 85. MS. has *And lat*. 87. *tryackill*. A medicinal compound or salve reputed as a protection against or antidote to poison, etc. Cf. 50, l. 26.

18

MS. M. only. 4. *Johne Thomsounis man*. For "Johan" or "Joan" Thomson, to whom, proverbially, her husband was wholly complaisant,

19. *vowit to the Swan*. In mediaeval times solemn vows were made over the swan or the peacock, which was the chief dainty of a feast. Matthew of Westminster relates how in 1306, before setting out for Scotland, Edward I gave a feast at which two ornamented swans were brought to the table, whereupon he vowed " to God and the swans " that he would avenge the death of Comyn and the breach of faith by the Scots.

19

MS. M. only. The theme of this poem is the offence and injustice done to men of noble birth and men of learning who see people of the kind described in a long list of abusive epithets promoted to positions far above their station or qualifications. Most of these abusive terms are now beyond explanation. Prof. Gregory Smith speaks of them as a " quagmire of verbal eccentricities, in which a modern philologer might well lose himself " and as " in all probability . . . a study in fifteenth-century nonsense " comparable to one composed by Lewis Carrol (*The Transition Period*, p. 55). But then he thinks the whole poem " eminently lacking in seriousness " (*Ibid.*). On this judgment see *Introd.*, p. xxvi. Such an attitude affects his philological conclusions.

21. R. *mastyf*, which is adopted by Schipper and S.T.S. But M. has what is apparently the older form of the word, of Provençal origin, as it is also in Douglas's *Aeneid*, Prol. Bk. ix, l. 49 : " The cur, or mastys, he haldes at smal availl."

20

MS. M. Editors have usually printed the version in MS. B. with some imperative readings from M. But the latter gives evidence throughout of more careful transcription, though this is most obvious in the first four verses and particularly in the third verse, which has been printed from B. as follows :

> Fforsett is ay the falconis kynd,
> Bot evir the mittane is hard in mynd,
> Of quhome the gled dois prettikis preif ;
> The gentill goishalk gois undynd :
> Excess of thocht dois me mischeif.

Schipper, however, adopts *foryhet* from M. with the " yok " letter for " yh " (cf. *Introd.*, p. xxxvi (2)), while Laing reads *forfett*, but in the S.T.S. edition it is as above. These " ghost-words " then call for some exercise in the way of explanation. Obviously " forgot " is the word required. *Mittane* occurs also in No. 38, l. 90, but *myttell*, as it is in M., is the " mittall " mentioned in an Act of Parliament of James II (1457, cap. 32) as one of the birds of prey. The third and fourth lines are incomprehensible in B., but an ingenious, if wholly unsatisfactory, explanation derived from falconry has been devised by Dr. Gregor for the S.T.S. edition, where it appears in the Notes to the poem, and has been accepted by Prof. Schipper. But the reading in M. is perfectly clear. *Peirtrikis* are " partridges," *Preiff* is " taste " or " eat," as in Lindesay's *Dialog*, etc., l. 932, " That plesand fruct gyf he [*i.e.* Adam] wald preve." The lines then mean that, while the vulgar gled eats part-ridges, the noble goshawk has no meal ; carrying on the contrast in the preceding lines to the effect that the falcon is forgotten, while the " myttell " is remembered.

1. Reading from B. M. has *ye*. Cf. " I charge the yit as of befoir " (*Philotus*, v. 125). 18. *corchat cleif* : apparently for " reach the high note." 23. *at cheif* : " in the place of honour." M. has *but greif*, which is weak. 33. *Rauf Coilyard . . . Johnne the Reif*. Ralph the Collier entertained Charlemagne unawares and in the end was knighted and made Marshal of France. John the Reeve did a similar service to Edward I, and his two daughters were wedded to squires, while one son was made a knight and the other a parson. Both tales are included in Laing's *Early Popular Poetry of Scotland*. This line in M. runs *Raf Coilyearis kynd*, etc. 74. *totum . . . nychell*. In playing with a teetotum, he whose side shows T (*totum*) gets the stake, while with N (*nihil*) he gets nothing.

21

MS. M. In verses 4, 5, 7, 8, 9, 10, 12, 17 MS. B. opens the last line with *In to*, in 6 with *So*. 13. *laik of spending* : " lack of money to spend." 46. *quhite quhale bone*. Ivory. 48. *blew asure*. " Blue lapis-lazuli." Cf. " Ther gold and sylvyr wase spred / And asur that wase blo [blue] " (*Torrent of Portyngale*, E.E.T.S., ll. 350-1). Editors have treated the expression as tautological and preferred the mistaken *blyth asure* from B., just as they have missed the point of *quhale bone*. In each case a hard substitute is in question. 71-2. " Where souls in fire are ever crying, ' Woe ! Woe ! ' " 74. " Oh, how great is that darkness." 82. " I am to rise from the earth."

22

MSS. M., R. In M. are only five verses and two lines (ll. 23-53). These appear in one place in R., while the rest is found in the same MS. in two other places.

6. *ane Youllis* (or *Yowllis*) *yald*. The expression is explained in the Notes to the S.T.S. version as follows : " It was a custom that every one should wear a piece of new dress at Christmas. The name of ' Yeel's Jade ' was given to the one that was not fortunate enough to enjoy such a piece of dress. The name bore a little reproach in it. The name is still in use in Banffshire." *Yald* or *yaud* (O.N. *jalda*), originally a " mare," and especially an old one, came to signify any old worn-out horse. In the sense of " mare," cf. *The Flyting*, l. 246. 27. M. has *Streneverne*, which does not rhyme. *Strenever* may be for " Strathnaver " in Sutherland, but the point of the allusion is quite obscure. 58. *uglie gumes*. Apparently in reference to the cobblers (*soutteris*) biting the leather. Cf. *seme bytaris* for tailors in No. 58, l. 10 ; and of the dogs in *The Gyre-Carling*, l. 18, " Thay gnew [gnawed] doun with thair gomes mony grit stane."

23

MS. R.   Versions in B. are defective and inferior to that in R., which represents the lost version in M.   In R. the poem is attributed to Dunbar, as it would have been in M., but in B. it is anonymous, for which reason it has been omitted from the S.T.S. edition.

15. *vane* in R. seems to be a mistake for *wame* as in B.

24

MS. R. only.   The Lord Treasurer made miscellaneous payments on the royal account, including alms, pensions, liveries, etc.   5. *raik.* Can this be for *rike*, " rich, powerful " ?   Cf. *Golagros and Gawane*, l. 15.

25

MS. R. only.   The Lords of Exchequer held an audit of state expenditure once a year.   Dunbar is, of course, only stating his personal grievance in a humorous way.

26

MS. R. only.   18. *Fraunce crownes* : " the croune of France havand a crownit flowre delice on ilk syde of the schield " (*Acts Parl. Scot.*,1451, cap. 8).   The gold coin most current in Scotland, worth 14s. (*Treas. Accts.*, iv, p. 401).

27

MS. B.   12. *lowrit* : " bowed, bent."   Cf. " Unto his law then quhy suld I not lowre " (*Philotus*, v. 58).   12, 58. *on growfe* : " downwards, prone."   Cf. Chaucer : " And gruf he fell, al plat (l. 58) upon the grounde " (*Prioress's Tale*, l. 222).   66. *bell*, from M.   B. *tod*, an obvious blunder.

28

MS. M.   In B. attributed to " Clerk " (? John Clerk.   Cf. 7. 58), but in a hand later than that of the MS. text.   Many of the terms of endearment seem to be invented after the fashion of " baby language."

23. *tuchan.*   " Tulchains, that is, calffs' skinnes stuffed with stra, to cause the cow giff milk " (*Autobiography of James Melville*, Wodrow Society, p. 31).   28, 42. *Fow leis*, etc., from B.   M. reads *Full leifis me your*, etc. *Fow*, " full " : *leis*, " lief, *i.e.* dear is."   Cf. Burns : " Leeze me on thy bonie craigie [neck] " (*The Highland Balou*, l. 5).   51. *golk of Marie land.* *Golk* is the " gowk " or cuckoo.   The allusion is to the story of King Berdok, who wooed " Mayiola " or " Mayok the golk of Maryland." Mayok's father was " the King of Fairy " (poem in Laing's *Early Popular*

Poetry of Scotland).   *Marie* is for O.E. *mere* or *mera*, "goblin" or such like, the word preserved in "nightmare." Cf. O.E. *wudu-mær*, nymph. Hence *Marie land* is "elf-land" or "fairy-land." 58. *cowhubye* : "booby," a term of contempt used affectionately. Cf. Douglas, "Knychtis ar kow hubeis, and commonys plukkyt crawis" (*Aeneid*, viii, Prol., l. 86).

29

MS. M.   Two versions, of which this is the earlier.
7. *Sum singis, sum dances, sum tells storyis.* On these see *Treas. Accts.,*
passim, e.g. "Wallass that tellis the taylis" (i, p. 183) : "Watschod the tale tellar" (*Ib.*, p. 378).   23. *humill.* M1. has *hummble.*

30

MS. B.   *Dregy* or "Dirge" from Dirige, the first word of the antiphon at Matins in the Office for the Dead according to the Latin rite, and so used as a name for that service or for a song ("dirge") in commemoration of the dead.   In later Scots it signified also the refreshment given at a funeral, as of the hoodie-crow in *Hamewith*, "waitin' for his share o' the dregie," where the accent is on the last syllable (*A Green Yule*).   The Responses are in French "triolet" form, *i.e.* eight lines (here printed as four double lines) with two rhymes, the first line repeated as the fourth, and the first pair as the seventh and eighth.
8. Reading from M.   B. *thus ane Apostill.*   9. *hanker saidilis* with intrusive "h," M. *ankersadillis*, "anchorets" or "anchorites." "Anchor-settle" or "-saidell" was strictly the anchorites' cell but was also applied to its occupant.   Cf. "Thow nayther girne, gowl, glowme, nor gaip, Lyke Anker-saidill" (*Philotus*, 1603, Bann. Club, v, 124).   13. B. *Bot aill and.*
17. *your allone.*   "One" intensified by "all" and preceded by a pronoun, generally in the possessive case, was a construction analogous to "self" with a pronoun, *e.g.* "yourself."   Cf. in *The Mourning Maiden*, "walkand your alone" (MS. M., l. 60).   56. Angers.   On the Loire, below Orleans. 59, 62. *Sanct Jeill* or *Geill.*   St. Giles, to whom was dedicated the parish church of Edinburgh.   61. *sonce and seill* : "abundance and happiness." Cf. "Away wes sons off ale and brede" (*Wyntoun*, VII, x, 3621), and "he was worth na seyle That mycht of nane anoyis fele" (*Bruce*, i, 303).   101. *A porta tristitie de Strivilling.*   Possibly an allusion to the name for Stirling Castle, recorded by Boece, *Mons Dolorum,* "the Dolorous Montane."   These Latin sections are free adaptations of the actual words of the service.   The first two lines are from the Paternoster : "Lead us not into the temptation of Stirling, but deliver us from its evil."   Then follows : "Give them the rest of Edinburgh and let its light shine upon them."   (Cf. *Requiem eternam dona eis, Domine, et lux perpetua luceat eis*).   Next : "From the gate of dolour of Stirling deliver, Lord, their souls and bodies" (cf. *A porta inferi erue, Domine, animas eorum*).   Thereafter : "I believe that they will yet taste the wine of Edinburgh in the land of the living."   (Cf. *Adeo videre bona Domini in terra viventium.*)   The last verse is a prayer : "O God,

who deignest to free the just and humble of heart from all their tribulation, liberate thy children who live in the town of Stirling from its pains and sorrows, and bring them to the joys of Edinburgh, that Stirling may be at rest."

31

MS. M. only. 2. *Fasterrennis*: "Fastern's een," the "day" or "evening" before the "fast" of Lent, *i.e.* Shrove Tuesday, an occasion of feasting before the long abstinence. 4. *betteis som*. The latter word may also be read *soin*. The S.T.S. version reading *soun* explains as "the sound of Betty's voice—*i.e.* their wives voice." This is not satisfactory, and there may be a scribal misreading. MS. R. has *son*.

32

MS. M. only. 1. *Sir Jhone Sinclair*. One of the king's household, frequently mentioned in the *Treas. Accts.* from 1490 onwards.

8. *Robert Scha*. Apparently practised as a physician, figuring in the *Treas. Accts.*, 1502-8 ; at the latter date he became a priest. 13. *Stranaver*. Strathnaver in Sutherland ; according to Boece, "the outmaist boundis of Scotland" (Bellenden). 15. *Almaser*. "Almoner" or official distributor of charity. Cf. "to Maister William Prestoun, Almesar to my lord Prince, to dispone [give away]" (*Treas. Accts.*, iii (1507), p. 290). 19. *John Bute*. First mentioned in *Treas. Accts.* for 1506. 29. *Maesteres Musgraeffe*. Has been claimed (S.T.S.) to be the wife of Sir John Musgrave, an Englishman, and "the Lady Maistres" of the Queen, so styled but not named in the *Treas. Accts.* The identification is not certain. 36. *Dame Dounteboir*. The latter term, of unknown origin, signified a lady-in-waiting. Cf. "Madame Baylie, Maistres to the Quenis Dountibouris (for Maides that Court could not then weill beir)" (Knox, *Historie of the Reformatioun*, 1732, p. 335). 43. *Dog*. "Jame" or James Dog, on whom see No. 33.

33

MS. M. only. James or "Jame" is first mentioned in connection with the king's clothing in 1488 (*Treas. Accts.*, i, p. 146). He became the queen's "wardrober," as such having charge not only of apparel but also of furniture, etc., not in use. He appears last in 1527, apparently still in this office (*Accts.*, v, p. 314).

3. *ane futt syd frog*. A "frock" as a wide-sleeved garment, or in the sense of "mantle," reaching (*syd*=long) to the feet. Cf. "With blak froggis all helit [covered] thai The armouris at thai on thame had" (*Bruce*, x, 375-6).

34

MS. M. only.

35

MS. M. only. 2. *Sir Thomas Norny.* So with spelling *Norne(e)* in *Treas. Accts.*, iii, 166, 375, varying, however, to *Norrie.* MS. R. *Nory.* He was one of the king's many fools or jesters. 4. *giand keyne.* From R., meaning a "savage or ferocious giant." Cf. "Nero, that tyrane kene" (*Paulus*, l. 647, in *Scottish Lives of the Saints*). M. reads *grand keyne*, which has been explained as "Great Khan." 16. *Clen Quhettane.* Clan Chattan. 25. *Robein under bewch.* Robin Hood, "under the greenwood tree," as in the Ballads. 26. *Roger of Clekniskleuch.* Unidentified, but see next note. 28-29. *Gy off Gysburne . . . Allan Bell . . . Simonis sonnes.* These men, apparently, are grouped as great archers. Guy, according to the Ballad, set out to slay Robin Hood and was slain by him ; "Guy was an archer good enough," which means a very good one. Allan is the "Adam" of the Ballad, one of the outlawed yeomen :

> "The one of them hight Adam Bel
> The other Clym of the Clough," etc.

The second may be for the personage in l. 26. *Simonis sonnes* are unknown, but a dance in *Cokelbie Sow* (cf. No. 17, l. 66) was called "Symon Sonis of Quhynfell." *Sir Bevis.* Hero of a fourteenth-century romance.

36

MS. B. The S.T.S. transcript not having been published, the text has been checked from the MS. Donald Odhar (*Gael.* "brown" or "dun"), or Donald Dubh ("black") or Donald of Islay or the Isles, was a grandson of John, last Lord of the Isles. His mother was a daughter of the Earl of Argyll, but the Scottish Government held that he was illegitimate, though his supporters in the Western Isles would not accept the allegation. He was imprisoned while still a boy, but escaped in 1501, and became leader in a formidable insurrection of most of the island clans against the severe measures of the king, which broke out in 1503. This rising took two years to suppress, and by 1507 Donald was again a prisoner (*Treas. Accts.*, iii. p. 415). The poem, therefore, is of about that time. Dunbar takes the extreme royalist view of *the fell strong tratour*, who lived to get out of prison forty years later, when he headed another rising. But the whole tone of the poem is unnecessarily malignant towards one who had known no personal freedom save for the few years he was "out" against the Government. He was partly the victim, partly the instrument of higher powers (cf. Gregory, *History of the Western Highlands and Islands*, pp. 98-103). 22. *suppleis.* Usually glossed "supports" but surely = Fr. *supplice*, punishment, suffering.

37

MS. M. only. Elaborate and costly provision was made in 1506-7 for the spectacle of "the justing of the wild knycht for the blak lady" (*Treas.*

Accts., iii, pp. 365, 258. On the whole matter see pp. xlviii, lii). This may have been the occasion of the poem. In 1512, however, clothing was being supplied for " the twa blak ladeis " (*Ibid.* iv, p. 401). There were Moors at Court (*Ibid.* iii, p. 94), but the *blak moir* was obviously a negress.

6. *tute mowitt*, etc. : with a projecting mouth. 7. *lyk a gangarall onto gaep*. The MS. has *graip*, but of the various explanations of the phrase none is in the least satisfactory. But *gangarall* or " gangrel " = " wanderer " is, among other things, a toad, and *graip* is apparently a scribal error for *gaep* or " gape." *Onto gaep* would then be for " on-gape " or " agape " or " opened," and the comparison would run, " a mouth when opened like that of a toad."

38

MS. B. Ll. 1-69 are in the *Asloan MS*. The story is best told in the words of Bishop Leslie. " This tyme ther wes ane Italiane with the King, quha wes maid Abbott of Tungland and wes of curious ingyne. . . . This Abbot tuik in hand to flie with wingis, and to be in Fraunce befoir the saidis ambassadours ; and to that effect he causet mak ane pair of wingis of fedderis, quhilks beand fessinit apoun him, he flew of the castell wall of Striveling, bot schortlie he fell to the ground and brak his thee [thigh] bane ; bot the wyt [blame] thairof he asscryvit to that thair was sum hen fedderis in the wingis, quhilk yarnit [yearned for] and covet the mydding and not the skyis " (*Historie of Scotland* (Bannatyne Club), p. 76). The " Italiane " in question is called in the *Treas. Accts.* of 1501, where he first appears, and subsequently " Maister John the French leiche " or " medicinar," and the various parts he played at court can be followed in the entries down to 1513, after which year he is not mentioned. In 1504 he was made Abbot of Tongland, a house of Canons in a parish of that name in the Stewartry of Kirkcudbright, and in an entry of 8th Sept. 1508 he is " Damian, Abbot of Tungland."

3. *A swevyng*: " a dream." B. has *swenyng*, but cf. *The Goldyn Targe*, l. 244. 5. *a Turk of Tartary*. The Ottoman Turks arrived in Europe from the East about the middle of the fourteenth century. 16. *Lumbard leid*: " the learning (*leid*=O.E. *leden*, for ' Latin ') of Lombardy, famous in mediaeval times on that account because of the University of Bologna, particularly its school of medicine." 58. *the quintessance*. " He [*i.e.* Damian] causet the King to believe that he, be multiplyinge and utheris his inventions, wold make fine gold of uther mettall, quhilk science he callit the quintassence ; quhairupon the King maid greit cost, bot all in vaine " (Leslie, as cited). 67. B. *Martis smyth*. A. *Mertis blak smyth*. 123. *skrymming* : " scudding, darting." Cf. " Of fowlys . . . Quhilk on thar weyngis . . . Skrymmis heir and thar " (Douglas, *Aeneid*, XII, v, 66-8). 126. *beir* : " noise, crying." Cf. " The commonis makis ane hiddous beir," etc. (*Bannatyne MS.*, S.T.S., ii, p. 246).

39

MS. B. Line 40 has been omitted and is here supplied from M. The *abbot* is John Damian of the preceding poem.

40

Print C. and M. MS. M. for *Andro* has " Walter " and the colophon, " Finis quod Kennedie." But the Print rules out Walter and with it probably the attribution to the poet of that name. MS. B. has the colophon :

> " Heir ends the tesment [*sic*] of Mr. Andro Kennedy
> Maid be Dunbar when he was lyk to de."

In l. 10 the Print and M. after *de* read *man that is done* ; the text is from B. After l. 40 M. adds the following superfluous stanza :

> Thair wald I be bereit, me think,
> Or beir my bodie ad tabernam,
> Quhair I may feill the savour of drink,
> Syn sing for me requiem eternam.

Poems written in alternating lines from two or three languages, one of them Latin, were a favourite exercise in western Europe in the fifteenth, sixteenth and seventeenth centuries. In the present example this mode is applied to a " Testament " or " Will," a form developed in France, where it was given high poetic value by François Villon, who died probably *c*. 1484. Villon's *Petit* and *Grand Testament* were followed by many imitations and parodies, one of the latter class being *Testament de Tastevin roy des Pions* or " King of the Topers," who expresses the desire that after burial

> Aupres de taverne la belle
> Qu'on plante sur sa servelle [*cervelle* = head]
> Un sep [branch] de la meilleure vigne.

This has the savour of Dunbar's poem (cf. ll. 110-115). Details of funeral and burial arrangements are a feature of actual wills of the period, and so have their place in such poems. The " Testament " in the hands of Chaucer and Henryson was treated seriously, but in his use of it Dunbar would seem to have been influenced by such French examples as the one quoted above, though here again he follows a line of his own in adapting to it a style of verse not hitherto associated with this content.

1. *Andro Kennedy*. Most probably the person of that name to whom payments are recorded in the *Treasurer's Accounts*, 1502-3. On 18th September of the latter year a payment was made on his behalf " to pas to Wigtown to the King with ane Relique of Sanct Niniane." Line 57, *omnia mea solacia*, " all my remedies," suggests that he was one of the numerous practising physicians at Court. 3. *Gottin with sum incuby* : having a demon (*incuby*) for father. 12. *blind Allane*, etc. A proverbial expression occurring also in Lindesay's *Tragedie of the Cardinall*, l. 396.

50. *caupe*. Explained in previous line as the *best aucht* or "best piece of property" as to a gift to one's superior or chief, usually, however, in his lifetime. 60. *Sanct Antane*. The "Preceptory" better known as the "Hospital of St. Anthony," founded near Leith in 1430. 68. Psalm cxii, 19. 92. *Ade* : "Adam" as a diminutive = "Addy." 110. *ail wosp*. A bunch of straw or hay as the sign of an ale-house.

41

MS. B. only. 15. *The Psalme* : xviii, 26. 21. *chakmait* : "checkmate." Chess was introduced into Europe in the eleventh century and was the favourite indoors recreation till the fourteenth century, when card games began to take its place. Card-playing was a feature of the court of James IV. 25. Something has gone wrong with this line, as it extends into an Alexandrine of twelve syllables instead of being of the normal ten.

42

MSS. M. and B. On this poem see Appendix B.
3. *aithis of crewaltie* : "painful or harsh oaths." 73. *syisis thre*. Three sixes, the highest throw in dice.

43

MS. B. In some lines M. reverses the order of the words, *e.g.* reading in l. 25 *Off parcialite sum complenis*.
5. *undir·confessioun*. As if at confession to a priest, who, of course, would not repeat what was said. According to an Act of Council of 1530, which would regularise earlier practice, the general public was not allowed to hear the proceedings of the Court, none being admitted "bot Advocats and sic able men to leir practik as sall pleis the Chancelare" (cited S.T.S.). Further, such persons as were permitted to be present were sworn not to reveal the opinions and arguments of the Lords in giving their decisions, and, if they did so, were to be excluded for the future. 13. *a futher* : see Note on 57. 62. 30. *skaild law keppis* : "catch the incidental utterances on law," and so "leir practik," as explained in the previous note. 41. *the Sait*. The Court of Session, as in "the Seite of Sessioun" (*Register of Privy Council*, i, p. 5). Cf. "A lord of seat—a lord of Sessioun—I fash mysel' little wi' lords o' state" (*Heart of Midlothian*, chap. iii). 45. *Carmeleitis and Cordilleris*. The "Carmelites" or "White Friars," so called from the colour of their body garment, professed to trace their Order to a foundation by the prophet Elijah on Mount Carmel. The "Cordeliers" were the Franciscans or "Grey Friars," owing the first name to the knotted cord they wore as a girdle to their frock, which by the fifteenth century was no longer grey but brown.

44

MS. R. only. In the MS. the last line lacks the word or words between *to* and *yow*. Neither Laing's conjecture " reconqueis " nor Small's (S.T.S.) " win back to " is satisfactory.

15. *Scull*. Altered in MS. from *style*. Not identified. 16. *parroche kirk*. St. Giles. 22. *hie Croce*. The Market Cross on the north side of the east end of St. Giles. It was rebuilt in 1555 and again in 1617, but appears to have retained its " old long stone, about fortie foots or thereby in length " (Calderwood's *Historie of the Kirk of Scotland*, Wodrow Society, vii, pp. 273-4). The present Cross is a restoration after that of 1617. 29, 30, 31, 34. *tone . . . Joun . . . Cloun . . . moyne*. These words " tune," " June," " Clown," " moon " rhyme together, the common sound being a modified " u " or " o " = ü or ö. *Sanct Cloun* is canonically unknown, but appears again in Lindesay's *Thrie Estaitis* (S.T.S.), l. 1371, " be Sanct Clone," where the spelling is to be explained as above. 38. *the Stinkand Styll* or " Old Kirk Style " was a passage through the block of building known as the Luckenbooths on the north side of St. Giles. In London there was a " Stinking Lane," where the Franciscan Friars had a house, and in or near which prelates and nobles had residences.

45

MS. B. Title from colophon in M. 26. M. reads *sic a fule*, making Dunbar commit a pun, *fowll* and *fule* (" fool ") being pronounced in the same way. But Dunbar does not pun.

46

MS. B. This poem is found also, written in a contemporary hand, on a blank page of a Minute Book of Sasines of 1503-4 in the Town Clerk's office, Aberdeen. As there transcribed, it corresponds closely with the version in B., except for the closing line, which is that of the text from M. The last MS., however, in many places differs verbally from the other two, and does so particularly in the form of the refrain, which in vv. 2, 3, 4, 5 there reads *That lentrune sall* (3, *suld*) *nocht mak us lene*. In the last line B. simply repeats the refrain of the other verses.

1. *Ask Weddinsday*. " Ash Wednesday," the first day of Lent, the time of abstinence from flesh meat lasting forty week-days (cf. No. 84, l. 1). 14. *mavasy*. " Malmsey," a strong, sweet, expensive wine first made at Napoli de Malvasia, the Morea, Greece. Cf. 1493, " bocht [in] Medylburgh and laid in the L. Marye [a ship] 2 bottis [butts] of mavyssye, ilk bot cost £6. 16/- " (*Ledger of A. Halyburton*, p. 17). Middleburgh in Holland was the Scottish " staple " port. The wine at this date probably came from the Canaries. 26. *ane choppyne stowp*. A " chopin " was half a pint Scots or 1½ imperial pint. 28. B. *constrene*.

47

MS. M. to line 103 ; thereafter Print C. & M., which lacks the preceding portion.

9. *in derne*: " in secret." Cf. " My dule in dern," *i.e.* " my secret sorrow " (Henryson's *Robene and Makyne*, l. 7). *to dirkin eftir mirthis*: " to lurk or lie in wait for anything amusing." Cf. " But derkon evon down on a depe slomur [slumber] " (*Destruction of Troy*, ll. 13, 285). 10. *donkit . . . dynnit*: " made damp " . . . " made a din." Cf. " the fresche den . . . hed maid dikis and dailis verray donc . . . the dyn that the foulis did " (*Complaynt of Scotland*, E.E.T.S., pp. 38-9). 32. *heynd*. Substantive use of adjective meaning " gracious," " gentle." Cf. " hende men " (*Morte Arthure*, 167). 36. *wlonkes*. The alliteration indicates that the " *w* " was pronounced. 38. *sindry*. Reading faded and uncertain. 65. *we war*. Concluding word lost. S.T.S. inserts " we may be fre," a contribution by Pinkerton. 73. *makdome* : " comeliness." Cf. Henryson, " This yung man . . . mervellit mekle of his makdome maid " (*The Ressoning betwix Aige and Yowth* (B.), l. 18. 90. *wolroun*. Strictly the wild boar, but also as signifying " mongrel " or some such epithet of abuse. Less generally in Alexander Scott, " The wolf the wilrone usis," etc. (*Ye blindit Luvaris*, l. 106). 106. M. *chowis . . . chevill*. 113. *smy*. Usually glossed as " sneak," but apparently also " weakling " or " poor creature." Cf. Douglas, " Ya, smy, quod he, wald thou eschape me swa " (*Aeneid*, Prol. xiii, l. 131). In the *Flyting of Montgomerie and Polwart*, l. 565, " Sathanis slavish smy." 124. " How by some trick he will catch me in a meeting [*trist*] with another." 139. *engranyt* : " dyed," " tinted." Cf. 1455 *Acts Parl. Scot.*, ii, p. 43 (11), " that all Erlis sall use mantillis of brown granyt opyn befor," etc. 142. *Johne Blunt*. A proverbial personage, figuring as a term of abuse in *The Flyting of Montgomerie and Polwart*, l. 770, " Jock Blunt, thrawn frunt." 162. *a ragment*. Usually of a document, here apparently " a discourse " or " statement." Cf. Douglas,

> " Of my bad wit perchance I culd have fenit
> In ryme or ragmen twise als curious " (*Aeneid*, Prol. i, ll. 294-5).

192. *into derne* : see on l. 9. 218. *be sie sevin* : " seven times as much," or " as many " in No. 4, l. 27. 272. M. *hachart*. 275. C. & M. *kewt*. 292. *cheif chymys* : " principal mansion." O.Fr. *chefmez*=Lat. *caput mansi*. Cf. *principale messuagium quod* " le chemis " *Scotice dicitur* (*Reg. Mag. Sig.*, 1511, No. 3664). 338. *hie burrow landis* : " houses in a high or principal burgh." Cf. " The Buildings here, elsewhere called Houses, are denominated Lands " (Maitland's *History of Edinburgh*, 1753, p. 140). This use [of land] is specifically Scots. 346. *or the band makin* : " before the compact or conveyance was completed." 352. *mensk* : " manliness," M. *mens*, the more regular Scottish form, as " buss "=" busk " (bush). 362. *lumbart*= " Lombard," *i.e.* " banker," so called from the country which produced so many bankers. The pawnbroker's three balls are the arms of Lombardy. 374. *prunya*, M. *prein* : " preen," " adorn." Cf. Alexander Scott of ladies,

" Bot prowdly thay will prounye " (*Poems*, S.T.S., p. 88).   The termination
a is for the French " é."   392. " graceless to look at."   418. *caerfull* : " sad."
Cf. " Comfourthes the carefull with knyghtly wordez " (*Morte Arthure*,
l. 3131).   *blynis of devotioun* : " stop my devotions."   Cf. " For blode, said the
bolde kynge, blyn sall I never " (*Morte Arthure*, l. 3981).   449. " We set our-
selves to conceal the truth from the sight of men."   465. *Hutit be the halok las*,
etc.   The significance of this line is obscure.   *Hutit* occurs twice in Douglas's
Aeneid, VII, ix, 65, and VIII, iv, 33.   In the first case " hutit goddes " trans-
lates *invisum numen*, giving the meaning " hateful " or " odious."   *Halok* is
found in the " Postscript " added to Rutherford's *Letters*, ed. 1738, p. 525 :
" a well-meaning kind of harmless, tho' half-hallocked persons," where it
is taken to mean " foolish " or " thoughtless."   473. *personis mony* : " when
there are many people present."   502. *sely* : see Note on No. 93, l. 32.

48

MS. B.   Line 40 from M.   In B. it is *Thair seilis are to pendit*.   47. B. reads
not.   *suppryis* : " crush," " harm."   Cf. " Practikis of weir, the Troianys
to supprys " (Douglas's *Aeneid*, XI, x, heading).

49

MS. M. only.   4. Two syllables lacking in this line.   David Laing
suggested " held most."

50

MS. M. only.   6. *your man*, *i.e.* " your lover."   Cf. " Quhen sall your
merci rew upon your man " (*The Kingis Quair*, l. 63).   10. Syllable lacking.
Laing suggests *suld*.   26. *tryacle*.   Cf. note on No. 19, l. 87.

51

MS. B. only.   Constructed on two rhyme-sounds.   17. *pount*.   Cf. note
on No. 44, l. 29.   20. *creature*.   Three syllables, as in No. 8, l. 27, etc.

52

MS. B. only.   56. *hir denger* : " her influence or dominion."   Cf.

> " Narcisus was a bachelere
> That Love had caught in his daungere "
> > (*Romaunt of the Rose*, 1469-70).

53

MS. M. only.   It is not possible to fix any date for Dunbar's visit to
Oxford.

54

MS. B. only complete, without any attribution, but in MS. R. are the first two verses, which, " *et quae sequuntur*," are assigned to " Dumbar." 60. *the great gyn*. A war-engine (Fr. *engin*) for throwing heavy missiles. Cf.

> " Gert bend the gyne in full gret hy
> And the stane smertly swappit out " (*The Bruce*, xvii, ll. 682-3).

95. *lanis*: "conceals." Cf. "layne noghte the sothe [truth] " (*Morte Arthure*, l. 2593).

55

MS. B. only. The poem was written on 9th May (l. 189) to celebrate the marriage of James IV and the Princess Margaret Tudor, which took place on 8th August 1503. 2. *Appryll*. To be pronounced as a trisyllable in the usual manner of the time. Cf. " The soft morow ande the luster Aperill " (*Lancelot of the Laik*, l. 1). 12. *fro the splene* = "from the heart." Cf. "And craftie musick, singing from the splene" (Lyndsay's *Deploratioun of the Deith of Quene Magdalene*, l. 171). 37. *do thy observance*. Cf. "Arys, and do thyn observaunce " (Chaucer, *Knight's Tale*, l. 1045). 46. *eftir hir*. Inserted in a defective line by Lord Hailes. 57. *blisfull sonne of cherarchy*. Sir David Lyndsay in *The Dreme* (ll. 519-32) describes the " Hierarcheis three " . . . " the quhilkis excellentlye

> Makis lovyng [praise], with sound melodious."

73. *flour of vertew*: "flower of power," *i.e.* "medicinal." 96-8. *Reid of his cullour*, etc. The Royal Arms of Scotland. Scott's "ruddy lion ramped in gold." 119. *parcere prostratis*: "to spare the vanquished." The MS. reads *proceir*, but the reference is clearly to the motto cited, in connection with the armorial bearings of the kings of Scotland, in *Le Simbol Armorial*, etc., Paris, 1455: *Parcere prostratis scit nobilis ira leonis*, which is almost the line in the text (see Note in S.T.S. edition). The scribe has probably expanded wrongly a sign of abbreviation. 142. *reid and quhyte*. Lancaster and York, united in the Tudors. 150. *Aboif the lilly*, *i.e.* superior to France. 183. *Than all the birdis song*, etc. Another reminiscence of Chaucer, who so ends *The Parlement of Foules*:

> " And with the showting whan the song was do
> That foules maden at hir flight awey,
> I wook."

56

Print C. and M. 1. *the stern of day*: "the star of day," *i.e.* the sun. 2. *Lucyne*: the moon. *Luna a lucendo nominata sit, eadem est enim Lucina* (Cicero, *De Natura Deor.*, Lib. II, cap. xxvii). 7 *purpur*: "purple," used loosely in mediaeval times for various shades of red. 10. *sang thair houris*. The church services sung at definite times were called "hours." This was the "matins" of the birds. 21. *Venus chapell clerkis*. Carrying on the idea of a religious service, in the present case connected with the Queen of Love. 26. *in silvir sloppis*. Apparently patches of cloud. 31. *the bruke was full of bremys*. Apparently "breams," a fish not familiar in Scotland, but giving the alliteration. Probably the poet had in mind Chaucer's line about the streams, "That swommen ful of smale fisches light" (*Parlement of Foules*, l. 188). 36. *staneris*. Apparently "pebbles." Cf. "I herd mony hurlis of stannirs and stanis that tumlit doune" (*Complaynt of Scotland*, E.E.T.S., p. 39). 55. *hard on burd*: alongside the shore. 73. Reading in Print and MS. M. Editors have substituted the reading from MS. B., *Nature and als dame Venus quene*, but why ? The two queens came together. The agreement of the Print and the MS. is significant. *Nature* is accented on the second syllable. 85. *gladdith*. A southern not a Scots termination of the present tense. 106. *fro the splene*. See note on No. 55, l. 12. 119. *Phanus*. Faunus. 126. *In cloke of grene*. Green is the colour of fairy clothing, and so proper to "Pluto, that is the kyng of faïrye" (Chaucer, *Merchant's Tale*, l. 2227). 170. *dures*: "injuries." B. reads, *do to me no deirance | For all thair preis*, etc., and M. the same with a slight difference of spelling. But *deirance* is off its proper rhyme. Schipper alters to *deires*, which may be preferable to *dures*. Cf. "That to the Scottis he did full mekill der" (*Wallace*, I, 206 ; cf. 359). 190. *Hamelynes*: "Familiarity" as in Lindesay's *Thrie Estaitis*. 225. *fremyt fare*: "strange" (cf. Ger. *fremd*) and so "unfriendly manner." 262. *morall Gower*. So styled by Chaucer in the dedication of *Troilus and Criseyde*.

57

MS. B. 1, 8. 15th February would make *Fasternis evin* in l. 8 fall on the 16th, a date possible only in 1496, 1507, and 1518 (S.T.S. note). The last year may be disregarded, and the choice for date of composition lies between the other two. 17. *hair wyld bak*. M. reads *bair collit bak*, where *collit*= "clipped," "cut," as in Burns's *Ordination*: "And cowe [=coll] her measure shorter." It is proposed, however, to read *hair* for *bair*, though B. M. and R. all have the latter word. But hair cut short was, at the time, a fashion only among the professional classes and the peasants. A dandy wore it long and loosely flowing. In *Nature*, a play (*c.* 1486-1500) by Henry Medwall, the character "Pride" says of his hair :

> "I knyt yt up all the nyght
> And the day tyme kemb yt down ryght."

18. *waistie wanis*: "empty dwellings.' Douglas has "wasty wanis" translating *relictis . . . castris* (*Aeneid*, XII, viii, l. 6). The implication is the wastefulness of extravagance in dress, on which see on *Superbia* in Chaucer's *Parson's Tale*. In MS. M. an anonymous poem *Of Ladies Bewties* says :

> "Thair beltis, thair brochis, and thair ringis
> Makis biggingis bair at hame."

36. *bodin in feir of war* : " arrayed in accoutrements of war." 62. *a fudder*, or *a futher* (43. 13) signifies generally a great quantity or number, specifically, however, a ton weight. Cf. " 18 tunes or fothers of lead " (Fyfe's *Scottish Diaries*, p. 130). 87. *turkas birnand reid.* A " turkas " was a smith's tongs or pincers, which would be heated red in the fire. Cf. Douglas, *Aeneid*, VIII, vii, l. 185 :

> " And with the grippand turcas oft also
> The glowand lump thai tumyt to and fro."

108. *be breif of richt.* A term of law, *breve de recto*, being the " brieve " or writ determining a right of property. 110. *Makfadyane.* This must be a literary reminiscence from the *Wallace*, vii, ll. 626-7, etc., as the name had been absorbed in the Maclaines of Lochbuie, Mull, and was not specially significant. 115. *tarmegantis* : " savages." Cf. note on No. 6, l. 532. 119. *pot.* M. *pit.* Cf., however, No. 6, l. 543.

58

MS. B. The versions in MSS. A. and M. have many variants from B., but as the poem obviously continues from No. 57, with which, indeed, it is linked in M., it seems desirable to follow the same MS.

11. *stomok steillaris* : " stealers of stomachers," an article of dress. 17. Reading from M., B. has *Greik sie*, familiar in the romances. MS. A. gives *the se flude fillis*. 44. *Sanct Girnega.* Apparently the same as " *Sir Garnega*," who is one of a diabolical company in *Sir John Rowll's Cursing*, l. 95. In *The Flytting betuix the Sowtar and the Tailyour* we get allusions by the latter to " Sanct Garnega, that grym gaist " and " Your girnand god, grit Garnega " (*Bannatyne MS.*, S.T.S., iii, pp. 22, 25). The name can scarcely be for St. Crispin, the patron saint of shoemakers, as Editors assume. 95. B. *still.* A. *style.* M. *styll.*

59

MS. B. M. omits v. 2. The colophon to the latter version reads : " Quod Dumbar quhone he drank to the dekynnis ffor amendis to the bodeis of thair craftis." 30. B. *gude crafty.* M. *gud tailyour.*

60

MS. R. only. 25. *wallowed as the leid* : " pale-coloured or livid like lead." Cf. note on No. 6, l. 92, and *Philotus*, v. 60 : " The rubent Rois bot with the wallowit weid." 26. *in ane trace* : " in a row." A mediaeval " dance " was frequently in the form of a procession or single file with a leader, as *Nobilnes* is here. Cf. No. 57, l. 73. 56. *Weill worth the* : literally, " good be to thee." *Worth*= " be," O.E. *weorthan*, to become.

61

Print C. and M., where it is prefaced by the following paragraph :
" The ballade of ane right noble victorious & myghty lord Barnard stewart
lord of Aubigny erle of Beaumont roger and bonaffre consaloure and
chamerlane ordinare to the maist hee maist excellent & maist crystyn
prince Loys king of france knyght of his ordoure Capitane of the kepyng
of his body Conquereur of Naplis and vmquhile constable general of the
same Compilit be Maistir Willyam dumbar at the said lordis cumyng to
Edinburghe in Scotland send in ane ryght excellent embassat fra the said
maist crystin king to our maist Souuerane lord and victorious prince James
the ferde kyng of Scottis."

Bernard Stewart, third Lord of Aubigny, was a grandson of Sir John
Stewart of Darnley, Renfrewshire, who commanded the Scots in the service
of Charles VII of France and received the fief of Aubigny in Berry. Bernard
led the French auxiliaries who fought on the side of Henry Tudor at Bos-
worth, became Captain of the Scots Guard in France, and was lieutenant-
general of the French forces in Italy, where in 1495 he won the battle of
Seminara against Ferdinand of Spain and his renowned commander Gon-
salvo de Cordova, thus winning, for a time, the kingdom of Naples. In the
reign of Louis XII, the successor of Charles VIII, he again commanded
the French forces in Calabria, and in 1503, at Terra Nuova, again defeated
the Spaniards, but later in the same year suffered defeat at their hands.
He then withdrew to a fortress, where, however, he had to surrender after
making it a condition that all save himself should be set at liberty. Subse-
quently he was released, and on 9th May 1508 arrived in Scotland on an
embassy from the king of France only to die in Edinburgh about a month
later. He was buried in Corstorphine Kirk, but his heart was sent to
St. Ninians, Wigtownshire, he having, when fighting in Italy, made a vow
to go on pilgrimage to that ancient shrine. Brantome includes him among
the great commanders under Louis XII as " D'Aubigné, a great Scot
and great Lord, who did honour to his nation in such a manner that some
of our French annalists have styled him *grand Chevalier sans reproche*."
Dunbar laments his death in the next poem.

62

MS. R. only. 1. *Lodovick*. Louis XII. 21. *crop of curage* : " summit or
utmost reach of courage." Cf. Chaucer, " she that was the sothfast crop
and more of al his lust," etc. (*Troilus and Criseyde*, v, l. 25). 23. MS. *schoiss*.
24. *charbuckell*. A form of " carbuncle " found also in English writers.
It signified a red stone, preferably a ruby, which further was supposed to
emit light in darkness. Cf. Chaucer, *Legende of Good Women*, l. 1119.

63

MS. B. MS. M. omits ll. 17-32. 38. *makis on* : " makes one." 17. *sould
nocht with youth be sene*. 70. *splene* : see note on No. 55, l. 12. 75. M. *sic*

bewtie.   115. *ythand pleid*: "constant or busy argument"; later Scots "eident."

64

MS. R. only.   The decision of the magistrates and community of Aberdeen "to ressave our soverane lady, the Queyne, als honorablie as ony burgh of Scotland, except Edinburgh allanerlie [only]" is dated 4th May 1511.   A sum of £200 was to be raised to meet the expense (*Extracts from the Council Register of Aberdeen*, Spalding Club, p. 81).
3. [*ascendit*].   Blank in MS.   The word is Laing's suggestion.   7. *wall*. Usually explained as "well" but more probably for "wale" in the sense of "choice" and so "the perfection" or "choicest example."   Cf. Montgomerie, "As waill and wit of womanheid" (*Sang on the Ladie Montgomerie*, l. 45).   13. *velves*: "velvet."   "Velvus" and "velvous" are forms in the *Treasurer's Accts*.   15. *artelyie*: "artillery."   Cf. for form Note 56, l. 161.   21-2. *The Salutation of the . . . Virgin*.   A tableau of this favourite scene, familiar in carvings and paintings of the age.   Cf. *Luke*, i, 28.   35. *portratour*: "figure," "shape."   Cf. Barbour's description of Thomas Randolph as "portrait weill at all mesure," *i.e.* having a well-proportioned figure (*Bruce*, x, 281).   37. [*nobill Stewarts*].   Blank in MS. Laing's suggestion.   47. MS. *husband*.   54. [*schene*].   Blank in MS.

65

MS. M.   Dated by title June 1517, when the Regent, the Duke of Albany, returned to France.
12. MSS. M. and R.   *Off*, which Pinkerton amended to *Giff*.

66

MS. M.   Two versions, of which the earlier was copied into MS. R. and is given here.   From R. comes l. 16, which in the original has been trimmed away.

67

MS. B.   20. M.   *Is now bot cair and.*   30. M. *haiff sould* [sold] *thair seill* ("happiness," "prosperity."   Cf. No. 30, l. 60).

68.

MS. B. only.

69

MS. B.   M. omits ll. 16-20.   8. *it* inserted from M., which reads *in turning can it tak rest.*

70

MS. M. Another version with some variant readings is in MS. R., where it has apparently been copied from the lost quire of MS. M.
4. R. *nor yitt.* 17. M. *hunyt hals.* 18. For *maist sall* in R., M. has *sall sonast.* 19. *surcharge.* M. has *subchettis,* which is wrong. A *surcharge* or " subcharge " was an additional course at meals. Cf.

" Till eik their cheir ane subcharge furth scho brocht,
Ane plate of grottis, and ane dische full of meill "

(Henryson, *The Uponlandis Mous and the Burges Mous,* ll. 281-2). 34. M. *he hes.*

71

MS. B. M. omits ll. 17-20. 11. M. *flowrit.* For *grane* see Note on No. 13, l. 99. 27. *plane.* In the sense of a region bare of trees. Cf. " playne feld " with this meaning frequently in the *Bruce.*

72

MS. B. The version in MS. M. has for refrain *Man spend thy gude quhill thow hes space.* It also reverses the order of the second and third and the last two verses. In M., too, the poem is anonymous, but in B. is attributed to Dunbar. To that extent its authorship is doubtful, while it may be added that its theme is scarcely congruous with Dunbar's usual utterances, and that the exposition of it is rather more awkward than we should expect.
5, 6. Readings from M. B. has *it usis . . . the it refusis.* 23. M. *mirrey face.* But the rhyme of the text occurs again in the next poem, l. 31, where again, too, M. alters to *mirrie face.* 28. Here B. begins the refrain with *Man* as in M. throughout. It makes an unnecessary syllable.

73

MS. B. There it has the title " Hermes the Philosopher," after which comes the couplet :

" Be mirry and glaid, honest and vertewous,
Ffor that suffisis to anger the invyous."

This is the scribe's contribution ; nothing of it appears in MS. M.
7. B. reads *it hes.* M. omits *it.* 10. *warldis wrak.* M. has *welth,* which is the same thing but savours of " modernising." Cf. " Now he has gold and warldis wrak " (*The Selie Court Man,* l. 15, Maitland MS., S.T.S., p. 241). In Burns, " The warld's wrack we share o't " (*My Wife's a Winsome Wee Thing*). 11. *at* for " that " from M. B. *bot,* possibly carried up from just below in the next line. 17. M. *peis.* 20. M. *plesour.* 30. M.

tuik bot lytill cure.   31. M. *Thairfor be glaid.*   33. *werk* for M., *wraik* B.
Cf. on l. 10.   37. *Ane raknyng rycht,* etc.   M. reads *ryche.*   The meaning is
that a small list (*ragman* ; cf. note on No. 47, l. 162) gives either a correct
(*rycht*) or a " rich," *i.e.* " favourable " account.

74

MS. B. The opening line and the refrain are an adaptation of the words
spoken by the priest on Ash Wednesday when he lays the blessed ashes on
the heads of the worshippers : " Man, remember you are dust and to dust
will return." Observe the rhymes *steiris, feiris, teiris . . . reverteris.*
6. M. *hyne gais the tyme.*   13. M. *Hes past thair tyme.*   20. M. *ugsum horrible.*
22. M. *thy dait*: " time."   Cf. " O febill age, drawand neir the dait Of
dully deid " (Henryson, *The Three Deid Pollis,* l. 49).   30. M. *sall feche.*
36. M. *fra the cuntre.*   38. M. *Tak this to spur the quhen thow sweiris.*
44. M. *freschlie . . . to spumis dryff. Speir* probably aphetic form of
despeir, " despair."   MS. reads *speiris,* suggested to be for " spars."   45.
woundis fyve : in hands, feet, and heart, as on a bench end at Sutcombe,
N. Devon. The S.T.S. ed. confounds these with the Passion emblems.

75

MS. M. only.   4. *be grathing to thy gait* : " prepare for your journey."
11. *for quhy* : " because," not an interrogative.

76

MS. M. only.

77

MS. B. In this MS. the poem is given to Dunbar, but in MS. M. to Sir
James Inglis, of whose work however, no other known example survives,
though Sir David Lindesay gives the name as that of a writer of " ballatts,
farses and plesand playes " (*Testament of the Papyngo,* l. 40). There are a
good many variations of reading between the versions and a slight difference
in the arrangement of the stanzas. Laing considered that the poem was
" more correctly " attributed to Inglis ; Schipper accepts it as by Dunbar,
but thinks the version in M. the better one. The S.T.S. editor also places
it among the genuine works of the poet. If a choice must be made, the
present editor is more inclined to agree with Laing. It may be pointed
out that (1) Dunbar adopts a brisker metre in all his undoubted satirical
poems and nowhere else uses this particular form of stanza ; (2) he does not
elsewhere write throughout with inner or sectional rhymes such as we have
here ; (3) the expressions " the commoun cawis " and the " commoun
weill " are not found in other poems by him ; (4) the complaint as to
" nobillis out of nummer " is foreign to his general criticism, which is rather

that of the usurpation of nobility by upstarts ; (5) he nowhere else complains of lack of courage in national defence.   These political sentiments appear to be of a later time, resembling those discussed at length in *The Complaynt of Scotlande*, 1549.   It is perhaps worth noting that only in this poem does the word *quhene* (= few) occur.   On the suggested date of the poem see note on l. 46.

   1. *Doverrit*: "sunk in sleep."   B. *Devorit*.   But cf. Douglas, "dovyrrit Nycht" (*Aeneid, VI*, vi, 12).   4. *sic cowartis*: "such cowardice."   Cf. "Sall nevir man this cowartys in me se" (*Wallace*, vi, 31).   14. *to reid the deirgey and the beid*.   From M.   B. has *The Psalme and Testament to reid*, which cannot be right as it misses the sectional rhymes *neid . . . reid . . . beid*.   It is clearly a Protestant emendation.   On *the deirgey* see note on No. 30.   *beid* = "prayer."   16. *maisteris* : "masters of arts" or "graduates."   18. *fyry sparkis*.   Cf. "Hell spark, scabbed dark, etc." (*Flyting, Montgomerie and Polwart*, l. 761).   *the splene* : see note on No. 55, l. 12.   19. *losin sarkis*.   Garments with "lozenge"-shaped insertions or made that way.   Cf. Berner's *Froissart*, Globe edition, p. 286 (note 2) : "some had coats losenged of blue and red."   29. *fenyeit flawis*.   Explained by Lord Hailes and Dr. Gregor (S.T.S.) as pretended defects in title-deeds.   31. *mycharis*, from M.   B. has *murder[er]is*.   But cf. "mychers and thefes" (*Towneley Mysteries*, Surtees Soc., p. 314).   33. *pelf*.   M. reads *spreyth* = "spoil," but for the phrase cf. No. 12, l. 5, etc.   38. "When courage, which should make one bold, is lacking."   39. *jakkis . . . brattis*.   These words have been variously explained, the former in the familiar sense of "defensive coats," the latter as children, M. indeed having the reading *brude* = "brood."   But the first seems to be intended for "low-bred fellows" or "knaves," as in Shakespeare : "Since every Jack became a gentleman" (*Richard III*, I, iii, 72 ; cf. also 73) ; while the second, as "on backs," would be "cloaks."   Cf. Chaucer : "And a brat to walkin inne by day-lyght" (*Canon's Yeoman's Tale*, l. 162).   43. *regratouris*.   Those who bought up food supplies in the market or corn growing in the field in order to re-sell at a higher price, such transactions being criminal under several Acts of Parliament.   46. *maid of lait*.   In this statement has been found allusion to the establishment of the Lords of Daily Council on 11th March, 1503/4, or the institution of the College of Justice or Court of Session in 1532, the former, of course, being preferred by those who hold to Dunbar's authorship.   As 1513 is a lower limit (cf. l. 68) the S.T.S. editor suggests 1507 or 1508 as a "probable date" (*Introd.*, p. clxii).   But this is mainly guesswork.   47. *refugeis*.   M. reads *So mony ane judge . . . So small refuge*.   48. *Sa mony estait*.   Apparently "So many estates," *i.e.* "So many thinking only of their own estate or rank."   M. has *So mony ane stait*.   54. *pin*.   Lindesay has "pin" in the sense of "gallows" (*Thrie Estaitis*, l. 4195).   57. *halland schekkaris*.   Beggars or tramps shaking the "hallan," a screen or short, slight partition cross-wise between the door and the central fire.   So the "mendicant," Edie Ochiltree, in Scott's *Antiquary* remarks : "I and a wheen hallenshakers like mysell" (chap. iv).   *Cowkelbyis gryce* : see note on No. 17, l. 66.   62. *cursing* : "coursing" or hunting over growing crops.   66. *ketche-pillaris* : "tennis-players."   The "caichpule" (Flem. *caetse-speel*, Du. *kaatsspel*) or covered court in which the game was played can still be seen close to Falkland Palace.   67.

tutivillaris : see note to No. 6, l. 513. 74. *fucksailis* : " fore-sails." Cf. Ger. *focksegel,* " fore-sail." 78. *apill renye.* Literally an orange (" apill oreynye "), but why then the golden chain ? Really it was a small casket in the shape of an orange, in which was a mixture of aromatic substances to give a pleasant perfume in smelly surroundings, and which was hung from the neck or the waist by a chain. Such an article came to be known as a " pomander " (Fr. *pomme d'ambre*). Thus it is that Jamieson in his *Dictionary of the Scottish Language* has " appleringie " (the same word ; cf. " ring " = " reign," No. 8, l. 9) = " southernwood," *i.e.* an aromatic plant familiar in old gardens. And therefore the reading of M. *to schaw thair semblance schene,* which Schipper holds is the only one to " yield sense," is plainly a makeshift reconstruction which misses the point.

78

MS. M. only. Because this short piece follows in this MS. and MS. R. a longer poem beginning *The beistlie lust,* etc., which in MS. B. is one of a set of poems entitled *Ballatis Aganis Evill Wemen,* that poem also has been attributed to Dunbar and is included as his in the S.T.S. edition. Laing, however, repudiated it, and Schipper only includes it in his " Supplement " of " Anonymous Poems." The " Orisoun " is subscribed *Quod Dunbar,* but its immediate predecessor, the *Ballate,* only *Explicit,* which means that this is the end of the poem but that the scribe does not know the author. The S.T.S. editor, however, carries forward the attribution to Dunbar to include the *Ballate* and attaches the " Orisoun " as a sort of epilogue after *Explicit.* The *Ballate* is omitted here as plainly not by Dunbar.

2. *of sys.* Possibly should be *oft sys,* the more usual phrase, = " often."

79

MS. B. only. 1. *Rorate celi desuper. Isaiah* xlv, 8. 8. " Unto us a child is born," slightly varied in other verses.

80

MS. M. Ll. 1-96 are in MS. A. 7. *halsing with ane gaude* : Saluting with the expression *Gaude flore virginali* as in the opening of the hymn cited in note in S.T.S. edition. 129. MS. M. *Grudge become.*

81

MS. B. only.

82

MS. A. only. Throughout this poem Dunbar imposes forms of words to serve his rhyme, *e.g.* 6. *regyne* from *regina,* and 8. *rosyne,* from *rosa* on the analogy of the former, are of this kind. Other forms are directly

traceable to the Latin hymns on the Virgin, from which the epithets are
borrowed. Thus three in the first stanza are echoes from as many lines in a
twelfth-century on the same subject :

> *Luce floret hodierna* [" hodiern "]
> *Flore jugi ad superna* [" superne "]
> *Flos devectus et materna* [" matern "]
> *Jura dat in Filio.*

Similar forms appear in *Ane Prayer for the Pest*, attributed to Henryson.

3, 4. " Lamp in darkness to be discerned by glory and divine grace."
14. *Alphais habitakle* : " Christ's dwelling " ; Christ as God who is " Alpha
and Omega, the beginning and the ending . . . the Almighty " (*Rev.* i, 8).
The names are those of the first and last letters of the Greek alphabet.
31. *plicht but sicht.* Apparently " plight " or " principal anchor (cf. No. 56,
l. 187) not to be seen." 43. *grene daseyne.* " Green " probably represents
a Latin adjective, such as *florens*. " Daisy " as " The emperice and floure
of floures all " (Chaucer, *Legend of Good Women*, l. 184). 58. *ellevyn.*
" Eleven " used apparently to serve the rhyme. 59. *store and hore* :
" trouble and old age [hoariness]." 60. *nevyne* : " mention." Cf. " Bot
all thar names to nevyn, etc." (*Buke of the Howlat*, l. 33). Icel. *nefna*, to
name. 72. *grayne* : see note on 13. 99. 75. *trone regall.* Cf. " Tu thronus
es Salomonis " (*In Nativitate B.M.V.*, Adam de S. Victore).

83

MS. B., two copies. In M. ll. 43-8 have been crossed out. The same
has been done in ll. 81-3, where also the rest of the stanza has been omitted,
probably from Reformation scruples, while the whole of it is lacking in B.
The verse as a whole has been supplied from a collection in MS. in the
British Museum.

23. *woundis fyve* : see note on No. 74, l. 45. 91. The point of this line
is not clear, but the reading of M. is scarcely better, *Off incontritioun of
confessioun indiscreit.*

84

MS. British Museum. Bracketed words supplied by David Laing.
1. *the fourty dayis.* The season of Lent.

85

Print C. and M. The poem is found also in MS. B., but in neither source
is it attributed to Dunbar. In the Print it follows immediately on *The Twa
Mariit Wemen*, etc., and the *Lament for the Makaris*, both of which are
subscribed " quod Dunbar," while in the MS. it is followed by *Man, sen
thy Lyfe*, etc., which is similarly subscribed. It seems remarkable, therefore,
that if this poem had been known to be by Dunbar, neither source should
have said so.

1. *gend* : "simple." Cf. " Scho wes so guckit [foolish] and so gend "
(*Peblis to the Play.* M. l. 25). 2. *France.* No district so named is known
near Falkland. 3. *Kyttok.* " Kitty," a common name for a woman. 4.
cler under kell. " Clear," in the sense of " beautiful " under her " head-
dress." " Clear " in this sense appears also as a noun : " I met a cleir
undir kell, a weilfard may [maiden] " (*Bannatyne MS.*, S.T.S., iii, p. 26).
C. and M. has *Fellis . . . kellys,* but the usual expression fixes the reading
as in B. 8. *elriche* : " fairy " or " having a supernatural connection."
Cf. " the alrich Queene of Farie " (Lindesay's *Satyre,* etc., l. 1536). 15.
hevin. From B. ; not in Print.—*it nyghttit thaim* : " night overtook
them." Cf. " Evill lykand was the King it nichtit him sa lait " (*Rauf
Coilyear,* l. 38). 29. *cowth,* from B. Print reads *cought.* 35. B. *Thair for.*
38. B. *quhen.*

86

MS. A. In this MS. the poem ends abruptly at l. 165, and, as ll. 161-5
are not found in MS. B., the only other version, it is impossible to say how
the stanza finished, while the lines composed by Robert Jamieson to fill
the gap may be disregarded. MS. B. continues ll. 166 to the end. Thus
in MS. A. the attribution of the poem, if any such existed, has been lost,
while in MS. B. the poem is anonymous. David Laing was the first to
assign it to Dunbar, basing his conclusion on " the peculiarity of its measure,
and its very close resemblance to the ballad, *Off the Fenyeit Freir of Tung-
land,*" further, and more important, " the style in which it is written."
Schipper agrees, adding what he thinks one of the corroborative details
as follows : " The Genius of Wealth is here represented under the character
of a dwarfish minstrel, who introduces himself, it is true, as the well-known
poet Blind Harry, but who probably was nobody else but Dunbar himself,
whose stature must have been very small." On this argument see *Appendix*
D. and *Introd.,* p. xxiv. There are many differences of readings between
the texts, and ll. 17-24, 113-20, and 137-52 are not in B.

1. *Harry . . . hobbilschowe. Harry,* a cry, usually of distress or for help.
Cf. Chaucer, " Or I wol crie out ' Harrow ' and ' Allas ! ' " (*Miller's Tale,*
l. 100.) *Hobbilschowe,* a confused tumult or uproar. Of both words the
etymology is unknown, but their significance here is apparently a call for
silence. 5. B. *A sargeand out of Sowdoun land,* of which no intelligible
explanation has been given. But *Soldane,* of which *Sowdoun* is a form spelled
as it was pronounced (cf. *Introd.,* p. xxxvii (2)), occurs again in l. 97, and
Seriandland is probably for " Surylande," as in *Morte Arthure,* l. 2657, where
also we have " The Sowdane of Surry " (l. 608). 10. B. *bot ane Blynd Hary.*
See *Appendix* D. 13. *the spreit of Gy.* Referred to again in *The Flyting,*
l. 172. *Gy* or " Guy " was Guido de Corvo, whose " spirit," after his
death, haunted his wife and was interrogated by four Dominican friars, who
ultimately secured a stoppage of the visits. The sound of the " spirit "
crossing the floor was like that of a broom. The story is told in full detail
in the *Scotichronicon,* Lib. XIII, cap. vi-ix. The " spirit " was a favourite
bogy-man of later mediaeval times. Cf. 6. 172 16. *licht as the lynd* : see
Note on l. 101. *Lynd* here as " the leaf on the tree." Cf. Chaucer, " as

light as leef on lynde " (*Clerk of Oxford's Tale*, l. 1211).   27. B. *Among
yow all to cry a cry.* 33. *Fyn McKowle.* Finn mac Coul [Cumhail], Finn, son
of Coul, a legendary hero of the Scottish Gael.   Cf. from Boece in Bellen-
den's translation : " It is said that Fynmakcoule, the sonne of Coelus,
Scottisman, was in these days ; ane man of huge statoure, of xvii cubitis
of hicht. He was ane gret huntar, and richt terribill, for his huge quantitie,
to the pepill : of quhome ar many vulgar fabillis amang us, nocht unlike
to thir fabillis that are rehersit of King Arthure " (*Croniklis of Scotland*,
Bk. vii, chap. 18). The episode in which he *dang the Devill* is not given in
any of the surviving tales. 37. *Gog Magog.*   " Goemagog," a Cornish giant,
is referred to by Wyntoun :

> " He was twelf cubytys large of hycht,
>   Ane half elne is the cubyt rycht "
>   (*Orygynale Cronykil*, Bk. i, cap. vii, ll. 345-6).

Cf. *Rev.* 20, 8. 40. B. *und mair.* 43. B. *myle.* In 44 *tene myle* is in A.
and B. The one dimension is as absurd as the other. 49. *lang of clift* :
" long in division," *i.e.* long-legged. B. *mekle.* 57. *cartane*, " quartane," *i.e.*
coming every fourth day. Lyndesay refers to " the fever quartane " in the
Satyre, etc., l. 2188. 62. *Craigorth.* Craigforth near Stirling, so called in
Exch. Rolls, *e.g.* vi, lxxv. 64. A. *eftir hender.* 81. *Gow Mak Morne.* The
genealogy, of course, is absurd. Gow or Goll mac Morna was the slayer of
Finn's father, Cumhal. 84. *Kemp* : " a very big fellow." The word occurs in
early literature in the sense of a " Great Warrior " or " Champion," and is
used of the *Feinne* or followers of Finn (cf. l. 33), *e.g.* in a gloss to a 13th-
century Charter : " The Grett or Kempis men called Fenis " (*Registrum
Moraviense*, App. No. 4). 93. B. *Worthie king.* 101. *under the lynd.* As
of Robin Hood, " Under the grene-wode lynde," where " lynde "=tree
[O.E. *lind*, used poetically for any tree]. Cf. No. 6, l. 196. Schipper
explains " lynd " as " The line, equator." 103. *southin.* B. *eistin.*
Schipper prefers the former as the wind " by which he could only come
from the equator." But *southin* may be for " soughing," *i.e.* " whistling "
or " humming." Cf. Burns, " We'll sit an' sowth a tune " (*Epistle to
Davie*, v. 4). 107. B. *waill and wryth.* 111. B. *curphour* [curfew] *bell.*
112. B. *To dwell thinkis nevir me.* 113. *Sophea* or *Sophie* (B.) was a title
of the Shah of Persia. 117. *The King of Frauncis gret army.* The allusion
is to the invasion of Lombardy by Louis XII either in 1499 or in 1509
or in 1512. That by Francis I in 1515 is too late, as the Asloan MS. is of
the same year. The *gret army* would suggest the campaign of 1509, when
the famous Bayard was the French commander. 120. B. *Can nocht dwell
baith perfyte.* 121. *Swetherik* : Sweden. 122. *the Steidis* : The (Hanseatic)
States (see Addenda). 123. B. *Thair is nocht thair.* 124. *mak quyte* :
" make quit," *i.e.* " get rid of "=slay. Cf. " Maid quyt of him, syne
slew all at thai fand " (*Wallace*, vii, 504). 133. *A per se* : " A in itself," *i.e.*
first-class=A1. It may be observed that this expression occurs only here
and in No. 88, both of them poems in the anonymous group attributed by
editors to Dunbar. The phrase occurs in *The Wallace*, ii, 170, in Henry-
son, Douglas, etc. 141. *Robyn Hude.* The favourite summer pageant-play,
usually in May, in all the burghs. On 26th June, 1503, King James

gave four French crowns " to Robin Hude of Perth " (*Treas. Accts.*, ii, p. 377). 157-9. These lines are quite differently expressed in B., though to the same effect. 176. *skynk*. Usually in the sense of " pour out " as in Douglas, " Thai skynk the wine and wauchtis [quaff] cowpis full " (*Aeneid*, VII, ii, 99). Here in the secondary sense of " give " or " pass." Cf. Ger. *schenken*.

87

MSS. A, F. This poem, as far as l. 40, also appears, with some variant readings, in the Makulloch MS. in Edinburgh University Library. These were the only versions known to previous editors. Another [F] has since been found " in a book probably written in the hand of William Forrest, priest and poet, not earlier than 1581, since this date occurs in the early part of the book " (see *Modern Language Notes*, vol. xxiv, No. 4, April 1909, pp. 110-1). It omits two verses given in the other texts, but adds four previously unknown, attributing the piece to " a devoute Scotte." As the language has obviously been anglicised in spelling and in some grammatical forms (*e.g.* " springinge " for *springand* (5), " singethe " for *syngis* (14), " withoute " for *but* (18)), these new stanzas are printed in italics. In each of the three sources the poem is anonymous.

5. *refute* : " refuge " [O.Fr. *refuite*]. F. reads *truyt* = " truth." 6. *chose*. F. has *cheeif*. 10. *circulyne*. F. like Mk. has *chrystallyne*. 18. *curis*. Mk. and F. *crymes*. 20. *Tartar*. F. *terrour*. 22, 23. These two lines in F. read :

" Illustrat lyllye, to thee Ladye I saye,
Withe infynyte Aveis, Hayle, floure of women all ! "

25. *depured Ave* : " depured," the anglicised form of *depurit* = " purified " (cf. No. 56, l. 5) with the first word of *Ave Maria*. 34. *in lune lucyferat*. " Lune " is an anglicisation of Lat. *luna* in the sense of " silver," while *lucy-ferat* is for " light-bringing." 36. *of Jesse germynat* : " sprung from Jesse " in allusion to the " Tree " or " Stem of Jesse," a pictorial subject showing a tree rooted in the sleeping figure of the father of David, the branches holding representations of the ancestors of Jesus and culminating in the figures of the Mother and Child. 37. *Of Adonay*, etc. *Adonay* or *Adonai*, " Lord " ; *liayle*, " loyal " or " true " ; *annule*, apparently " ring " for " bride " ; *illi-bat* [Lat. *illibata*], " unblemished." 38. *Buche in combuste* : " burning bush." Cf. *Exodus* iii, 2. 62. *Gabriell*. See *Luke* i, 28. 69. *spiritu sancto obumbrata* : " overshadowed with the Holy Spirit." See *Luke* i, 35.

88

MS. British Museum, also printed from another MS. in the Museum in *Reliquae Antiquae*, Wright and Halliwell, vol. 1, pp. 205-7, and in an unprinted MS. of Balliol College, Oxford. From the former *thy* has been substituted for *their* in l. 46, and *fyne* has been inserted from the latter in l. 36. See Schipper's edition, p. 388. On this poem see *Appendix* C.

1. *A per se*. See note on No. 86, l. 117. 9. *Troy Novaunt* : " New Troy " as in l. 10, having been founded, according to Geoffrey of Monmouth, as a

second Troy by Brutus, grandson of Aeneas ! 22. *crone*. All the MSS. read *trone*, but this scarcely fits the context, while " t " and " c " are easily confused in MS. For the form " crone " = " crown " see *N.E.D.*

89

MS. British Museum. Above the words are the notes of a musical setting, but only of one of several parts and that part not the melody (Laing). The poem is anonymous. Line 15 is both unmetrical and obscure, but, as the first two words have also their musical notes, Schipper is not justified in leaving them out in order to preserve the metre. S.T.S., after Laing, reads *beine*, without making any improvement in the sense.

90

MS. Aberdeen. Cf. No. 46. No name attached.
1. *Gladethe*. A Southern, not a Scots imperative. 50. *chairbunkle* : see note on 62. 24.

91

MS. B., where it is anonymous. Laing suggested, as an inference from l. 35, that it was written by Dunbar after Flodden. The less reason why no name should have been attached. Line 10 is rhythmically defective. Schipper suggests *the lamp* after *lyfe* ; Laing *day the* after *lychtsum*.

92

MS. B. Anonymous. The date must be between 1517, when Albany left for France (cf. No. 65), and 1521, when he returned. The opening *We lordis* is improbable for Dunbar, and no fewer than eight words in this short poem are not found in his genuine works. These words are : 2. *perplexite*, 3. *cautelus*, 10. *distructioun*, 12. *dissentioun*, 20. *merk*, 28. *contraversy*, 33. *wandrecht*, 35. *tardatioun*. Schipper says " there can be no doubt that the poem was not written by Dunbar."

93

MS. B. Also in M. but tinkered at in both. There is no textual warrant for attributing this poem to Dunbar, as was first done by Pinkerton in his edition of 1786. In neither MS., B. or M., nor in the printed issue of 1622—of that of 1603 nothing is known—is any author named. The MSS. differ very greatly, and the sole surviving copy of the 1622 print had disappeared before 1894, when Schipper published his edition of the poet's works (p. 393). Laing, however, who had examined it, was able to say that it corresponded very closely with MS. B. and did not contain the additional lines found in MS. M. These, in any case, read like scribal expansions and generally fit but awkwardly into their places. They have, therefore, not been inserted in the present text, while only a few preferable readings have been taken from M., the divergencies being too numerous to record here. Schipper supplies a conflate text which " differs considerably from each of the two MSS. copies," but which he hopes to have brought " somewhat nearer to its original shape." The latter claim, in certain instances at least, cannot be accepted. For example, he says of l. 303 that it " should have been printed *for your demy's* [=for your dame's] to make it somewhat intelligible." In M., however, which he takes as the basis of his text, he finds : *And for our dame*, etc., which he sees to be obviously wrong. He therefore substitutes for both the conflate expression " for your dame." But as the reading in B. is perfectly clear, " for your sake and for your dame's sake," no apostrophe being needed where the possessive case is fully written out [*demys*], we have neither a better reading nor one nearer the original form of the poem, but only a blend which can confidently be rejected. One other example, of a different type, may be added. A reading in M., *he yeid the hous about Weill twys or thrys* (cf. ll. 328-9), he rejects as " very suspicious, as all this takes place in the room, which the company has not left." That is, he is unaware of the fact that in Scots " house " could just mean " room," so that the scribe of M. was not suggesting what he supposes. A Border lady in the late sixteenth century complained to the Privy Council of the burning of her dwelling " twa hous [*i.e.* rooms] hicht with a laich hall " (*Reg. Pr. Co.*, vi, p. 115).

It may be noted here that such words as *allutirly* (l. 18) and *manar* (" manor," l. 52) do not occur elsewhere in Dunbar's certain works.

Further, it is surely obvious that the first couplet is a sub-title and not the opening lines of the poem. It is accordingly so printed here. Curiously, in B. the real opening couplet appears with its lines in reverse order.

The central theme and incidents of the story have been handled in various ways and combinations by several writers in different countries. A Latin prose version, in MSS. of the thirteenth century, largely written in expressions taken from the Vulgate Bible, is given in Lehmann's *Parodistische Texte*, pp. 50-7. An early example in vernacular verse, using the same general ideas on other lines, is *Le Povre Clerc* in *Recueil général des fabliaux des XIIIe et XIVe siècles*, Montaiglon et Raynaud, v, pp. 192-200. A much later one is *Der Fahrendt Schuler*, a short dramatic piece (*ein Fassnacht Spil*), by Hans Sachs (1551). A " wandering scholar " is roughly turned away by a peasant's wife [*Bewrin*] and the parson [*der Pfarrer*] in her company. He meets the peasant himself, who invites him back to the house. The parson and the dainty food prepared for him have been hidden in the kiln [*den Ofen*]. At his host's request the scholar undertakes to call up the devil. Left alone in the room to make his preparations, he blackmails the parson into appearing, at his summons, as the devil and bringing out the food. The peasant remarks on the resemblance of the escaping devil to the parson. (*Hans Sachs' Werke*, ed. Arnold, ii, pp. 192-204.) For other references to such material see *Les Fabliaux*, Joseph Bedier, pp. 453-4.

The Scottish version is not directly dependent upon any other and is the longest and most skilfully developed of all.

10. M. *staitlie* 11. M. *With kirnalls closit most craftelie of all.* 13. *upoun hicht.* That is, to close the lower parts and conduct the fighting, as was usual, from the upper works. 14. M. *in to na mannis micht.* 21. *The grit croce kirk.* Not, as it has always been explained, " The Church of the Great Cross," which is absurd, but the " cross-kirk," *i.e.* the church with transepts giving it the form of a cross, a quite usual description in Scotland. *Masone Dew* : *maison Dieu* or hospital. 22. *Jacobene freiris,* or Jacobites, were Dominicans or " Black Friars," so called because their first settlement was in the church of St. Jaques [" James "] in Paris. Their body garment was white [*the quhyt hew*], over which was worn a black gown. 23. This line has gone wrong. B. has *and the monkis eik,* but " monks " were not friars. M. gives *The Carmelitis, Augustinianis, and als the Minouris eik,* which is impossible. The *four ordouris* were these : Dominicans or Jacobins or " Black Friars " ; Carmelites or " White Friars " proper ; Augustinians or Austin Friars ; and Friars Minor or Franciscans or " Grey Friars," whose habit at this time, however, was really brown. 32. *silly Freiris* : " silly " in the sense either of " simple " or " good " or " holy." Cf. " Thy sillie Sancts," etc., in *Ane Godlie Dream,* l. 33 (*Early Popular Poetry of Scotland,* Laing, ed. Hazlitt, ii, p. 285). 45. B. *yet*=" gate," but cf. l. 76. 47. M. *lig*=" lie." 49. *wynnit* : " dwelt." Cf. Henryson, " And now my wynning is in Hevin for ay " (*The Lyoun and the Mous, Prolog.,* S.T.S. ed., ii, p. 103). 64. *the stowp to fill,* etc., but the next line is direct address, as happens again at l. 375. In this section, ll. 50-78, the verbal differences in the MSS. are very numerous. 94. M. omits and adjusts the other lines to rhyme. 124. *Gray.* B. has " black " here and in the other references (ll. 465, 496), which would make him a Dominican like the other friars, while the suggestion in l. 462 and context is surely that he was of a different order. The fact seems to be that neither scribe is clear as to the orders with which he is dealing. 136. After this line come four in B., extended to eight in M., which, from their coarseness and apparent character as an interpolation, are here omitted. 143. *costly greyne.* Table-covers were then always green, the cloth being usually " Inglis [English] green." 145. *but.* The room into which the outer door gave entrance, in contrast with " ben," the inner room. 154. *breid of mayne* or *mayne breid* (ll. 213, 348) : " bread of the finest quality " =*panis dominicus,* " lord's bread." 174-5. Lines in M. quite different. 177. *the chyre.* A chair proper was still an uncommon article of furniture, there being usually only one for the head of the house, others having but stools or benches. The distinction survives in " chairman " and " taking the chair." 210. The dining-table was of boards laid on trestles. It was " closed " by laying the boards against the wall and removing the trestles. 231. *husband* : in the sense of " owner " or " freeholder " [O.E. *húsbonda*]. Cf. " In Awchtirmuchty thair dwelt ane man, Ane husband," etc. (*The Wyf of Auchtermuchty,* ll. 1-2, in MS. B., S.T.S., ii, p. 320). 240. *tak ye all thy hyre.* M. has *tax all my hyre.* *Hyre* apparently in the sense of " hurry," " speed " (cf. Donaldson's *Supplement* to Jamieson's *Dictionary*), and the sentence thus meaning, " be quick about it." In the *Buke of the Howlat* (l. 424) we have : " I sall haist me to hewe [describe] hartlie but hyre," where it may have this meaning as " without [but] hurry." On the other

K

hand, the word may be just " hire," and in the present context simply signify, " act up to the value of your wages." 249. *belyve*. M. *full swyth* (quickly). The expressions have the same meaning, but the word in B. does not rhyme. Originally it was written *belyth*, a ghost-word, probably a confusion with *blyth* of the next line. 251. *all hallow*. Properly " all hallows "=all saints. Curtailed for the sake of the rhyme. 254. *cun* : " taste," " eat." Cf. Montgomerie, " Thay sall not than the cherrie cun " (*The Cherry and the Slae*, l. 626). " Ale cunnaris " were the burgh ale-tasters. Cf. 17. 42. 261. *birneist*=" burnished," *i.e.* cleaned or cleared : *with*=by. 270. B. *curfur* : " curfew," but l. 74 seems to support M. as in the text. 277. *thone*=then. Cf. " quhone "=when. M. has *sone*= soon, but the order was for immediate execution. 286. M. *doun the leddyr*. 297. M. *fra me*. 315-7. B. is not satisfactory here as three successive lines have the same rhyming word. 341. B. *seyit all his cure*. Text from M. 358-9. *thair . . . befoir*. Reading in M. also. R. has *richt yoir*, *i.e.* " right ready," *yoir* being a variant of " yare " with that meaning. Ll. 392-9, 406-7, 410-11, 438-442 not in M. 460-61. Again a sudden transition to direct address. M. has these lines differently but not any more satisfactorily. 495. *Hurlybas*. M. *Hurlbasie*, name of a fiend. Cf. No. 28, l. 38. 505-12. Not in M. 528. *ane mustard stane*. So in both MSS. Apparently a stone mortar for pounding mustard seeds like a " knocking-stane " for husking barley. 560. *tap our taill*=" from head to heel."

APPENDIX A

PROFESSOR SCHIPPER ON THE CHEPMAN AND MYLLAR PRINTS

PROFESSOR SCHIPPER contests the textual value of the early Print in comparison with the MSS. of about half a century later on the ground that the " expert men " who had to be imported as printers, " most probably Englishmen," made changes in the spelling and, occasionally, even in the wording to bring these into conformity with southern usage. The main items are as follows :

(1) That " the English spelling is substituted nearly everywhere . . . for the Scotch one in words containing a long *e*, which sound was represented in the southern counties of Scotland in the sixteenth century by *ei*, together with a final *e* in monosyllables." Schipper lists a number of these forms, supposed to be the work of the printers, of which the following is a representative collection : *suete, bene, dede, wele, lele, fere, chekis, gret, bestis, teris, gretand, lesingis*, etc., to which correspond generally in the MSS. : *sueit, bein, deid, weill, leill, feir, cheikis, greit, beistis, teiris, greitand, leisingis*, etc. But it must be pointed out that, of the presumed Anglicised forms, *lele, fere, chekis, teris* and *gretand* appear in the Edinburgh MS. of *The Bruce*, written by a Scottish scribe twenty years (1489) before the Print, that *clere* appears in *The Wallace*, composed by a contemporary of Dunbar and copied by the same scribe in the year before, while all the others are to be found, some of them many times, in both MSS., where they are accompanied by analogous terms in the same orthography. *Bestis* is in the contemporary *Accounts of the Lord High Treasurer*. Of certain others cited to the same effect, it is to be noticed that *plate* instead of *plait* and *targe* for *terge* occur also in *The Bruce*, while *have (haue)* for *haif*, rhyming with *save (sawe)* for *saif*, is in *The Wallace*, and is actually of frequent occurrence in the

Maitland MS. The fact is that such spelling, with distracting variations, had been domiciled in Scotland long before printers set foot in Edinburgh. They, too, as Professor Schipper brings out, were no more uniform in their practice than the scribes. No conclusion, therefore, can be drawn from the varying proportions of particular spellings as between MSS. and Print. To say that the ending *-es* where we should expect *-is* occurs "not infrequently" in the Print, while *-is* appears "almost exclusively" in the MSS., though MS. M. has "a few forms" in *-es*, is a description that really leads nowhere.

(2) Schipper's next major proposition is this : "Of greater importance than the frequent occurrence of the ending *-ing* as a proof of the English colouring of the orthography of the old Print is the alteration of the indefinite pronoun [*sic*] *ane*, as it is spelt generally in the MSS. M. and B., into the English form *a* before consonants, while *ane* (sometimes written *an*) is preserved before vowels." Examples cited are *a rosere, a ryvir*, etc.

Now the bearing of this is quite the contrary to what Schipper affirms. The more ancient usage of the indefinite article was *a* before consonants, as in a line from Dunbar's older contemporary, Robert Henryson : "No mervell is a man be lik a best." In *The Wallace*, too, *a* is the prevailing form. The adoption of the standardised *ane* in all positions was a literary development of the sixteenth century, just beginning to take hold in Dunbar's later years. And so in the line quoted above from the earliest MS. version of Henryson's poem the articles in the printed texts of 1570 and 1571 become *ane*. When, therefore, it is pointed out that while in *The Tua Mariit Wemen*, ete., and *The Flyting* the printed versions have " nearly in every instance . . . *a* before consonants," where " the usual form of the MSS. is *ane*," the inference is, not that the printers have made a southern change, but that the writers of the MSS. have introduced a fashion which by their time had been adopted in literary circles. And the corollary is that the Print in this respect and, by further inference, in general is nearer the original form of the poems in question than are the MSS. But, whether or not we go so far, it is clear that the data of Professor Schipper do not bear out his argument as to the alleged inferiority of the Print. In the judgment of Professor Gregory Smith, " Chepman & Myllar's English craftsmen dealt honestly with their Scots ' copy,' but they at

times betray their Southern habit." [1]   This qualification, how-
ever, is quite a different issue from that raised by Dr. Schipper
and may amount to very little, probably a few spellings of *gh*
for *ch* and similar lapses, though, in view of the Anglicising
tendency of authors themselves, even so much cannot safely be
claimed.

But, after all, the statement that the "expert men" were
English printers is not proved.   The fact that in so many cases
we get "et" for "and" suggests that the printers were thus
lettering the sign " & " and perhaps giving not the Latin form
but that in their own language, in which case they would be
Frenchmen.   Myllar acquired his practical knowledge of
printing at Rouen, and may well have brought over craftsmen
from that city.   But various characteristics point to the Dunbar
poems having actually come from a foreign, probably French,
press,[2] though published in Edinburgh.   If so, then the whole
argument about Anglicising the language fails to make even a
start.

[1] *The Poems of Robert Henryson*, S.T.S., vol. i, p. lxxxi.
[2] *Annals of Scottish Printing*, Dickson and Edmond, pp. 44, 72-3 ; *The Chepman and Myllar Prints*, S.T.S., p. xviii.

APPENDIX B

THE VERSIONS OF "THE DEVILS INQUEST," No. 42

THIS POEM in M. consists of 13 stanzas, in B. of 17. Moreover M. has 5 which are not in B., and B. 9 which are not in M. Out of this medley the S.T.S. editor has framed a version of 21 stanzas, thus drawing upon both texts while dropping one of the verses which has the same subject in the two MSS. but is expressed quite differently in each. Schipper restricts himself to 18 verses, refusing the last one from B. and the last two from M. He points out, what is pretty clear, that the poem has been retouched and added to by later admirers. That Dunbar himself did this would seem to be barred by the fact that it has been thereby robbed of symmetry and coherence. Now if we take the version in M., less the last three verses, it will be observed that we have a self-contained little poem on a definite subject, the oaths of the " commone people," followed by examples from the different crafts and ending with a comprehensive inclusion of the " rest of craftis." We may then presume that some poetical copyist, taken with the general idea, considered how it might be extended to bring in other classes equally reprehensible with the common people. Thereupon to the version in M. are added a stanza introducing a thief, who is quite out of keeping with the other characters and the drift of the poem, and then two more embracing a " court man," the " clargie," and everybody else. This version may have been known to the scribe of B., as he, too, has the stanza on the thief, though not exactly in the same position. This scribe, however, carries out a more drastic " improvement." He saw, we may assume, the impropriety of dragging in " courtier " and " clergy " at the close and accordingly transfers their parts to new verses written in at the beginning. This meant the dropping of the corresponding stanzas in M., but brought the rewritten ones into direct conflict with the subject as stated in the first verse—

the oaths of " the common people." Neither courtiers nor
clergy were in that category, and the writer accordingly is forced,
for the sake of consistency, to make a fresh start and not a very
happy one. Thereafter he proceeds to amplify the list by
introducing a goldsmith, a maltman, a baker, a smith, and a
dicer, the second, third, and fourth being further betrayed as
insertions by a difference in the introduction of the refrain,
which is simply tagged on. The whole is finally rounded off
with a verse which, in its new motive of " devillis . . . as beis
thik," abruptly departs from the central conception of the poem.

All this, of course, is hypothetical, but will serve to suggest
how the piece was brought to its present condition. To exhibit
this probable sequence of rehandling, the version in M. is printed
in roman type, the two final added stanzas being enclosed in
brackets. The additional matter from B. is given in italics.
In B., too, the " merchant " verse appears in this form :

> " Ane merchand, his geir as he did sell,
>   Renuncit his pairt of hevin and hell ;
>   The Devill said, ' Welcum mot thow be,
>   Thow salbe merchand for my sell,
>   Renunce thy God and cum to me.' "

Obviously the second line is an absurdly strained effort.

One speculative point remains. Dunbar rhymed a *Com-
plaint to the King Aganis Mure* as having interfered with the
text of one of his poems, into which Mure had introduced, in
verses of his own composition, defaming and discordant matter
about lords. All this he had passed off at court as Dunbar's
work. Is it possible that in this obviously reconstructed poem,
with its incongruous reflections on " lords," we have the
composition rehandled by Mure or something based upon it ?

APPENDIX C

POEM TO LONDON, No. 88

THE STANDARD text of this poem is contained in an English *MS. Chronicle*, which explains that the occasion was a reception by the Lord Mayor, in Christmas week 1501, of the Scottish mission to arrange the marriage of James IV with Margaret Tudor, when " sittying at dyner ane of the said Scottis giving attendance upon a Bishop ambassador, the which was reputed to be a Protonotary of Scotland and the servant of the Ld. Bishop, made this Balade." On 31st December, 1501, there is a payment on behalf of Henry VII of £6 13s. 4d. " to the Rhymer of Scotland in reward," repeated on 7th January, 1502, as " to a Rhymer of Scotland."

Now on 20th December, 1501, an entry occurs in the Scottish *Accounts of the Lord High Treasurer* [1] of a payment to Master William Dunbar of £5, " quhilk wes payit to him eftir he com furth of England." This is plainly the amount of pension due to him at the previous Martinmas, and the entry would suggest that this was the later date of payment and that Dunbar by that time was therefore back in Scotland, in which case he could not have been at the Lord Mayor's dinner or been the writer of the poem. But an entry in the *Accounts* [2] for 3rd January, 1501/2, records a payment to Lyon Herald "quhen he cum furth of Ingland," yet " Lyon King of Armes " is recorded among those who received gifts from King Henry on the Thursday after the conclusion of the treaty of marriage on 25th January, 1502. [3] It would seem, then, that the inference as to Dunbar's return suggested by the entry in the *Treasurer's Accounts* does not necessarily follow.

Further questions, however, assert themselves. We have no other notice of Dunbar as a " Protonotary," but the designation

---

[1] ii, p. 95.   [2] p. 132.

[3] Leland, *De Rebus Britannicis Collectanea*, ed. 1770, iv, p. 264.

240

probably means no more than a principal clerk. It is more difficult to account for him as a servant of Bishop Blackader of Glasgow, who is the " Bishop ambassador " referred to. One writer, founding on this reference, posits the bishop as the early patron of Dunbar.[1] Otherwise we know nothing of this connection.

The poem itself is rich in southern verb terminations in *ith*— *restith*, *renneth*, *doth swymme*, etc. These, however, may be due to the English scribe or grammatical concessions on the poet's part to his English hearers.

As regards the latter possibility it may be noted that in his poem to Oxford Dunbar keeps to his native inflection and writes : "As Maii flouris dois, etc." This poem, too, is engrossed by a Scottish scribe as Dunbar's work ; that to London is not.

The proposition that no one but Dunbar *could* have produced this poem is not at all self-evident, since it is clear that other clerkly people of the time were capable of turning out quite tolerable verses. And there, in these puzzling circumstances, the matter must be left.

---

[1] *Étude sur William Dunbar*, by Cécile Steinberger, Dublin, 1908, pp. 23-4.

L

APPENDIX D

"THE BLYND HARY," No. 86

THIS PIECE appears in the *Bannatyne MS*. under the title of ANE LITTILL INTERLUD OF THE DROICHIS PAIRT OF TH[E PLAY], the letters in brackets having been cut by the inlaying of the page. Of what sort of play this monologue could have formed a part one cannot imagine, the only allusion to such being the injunction to the " merchandis " of Edinburgh to " follow furth on Robyn Hude"—that is, the summer-time entertainment explained in the notes. Further, the speaker announces that he has come " at your cors (cross) to mak a cry with a hie sowne"—that is, to announce something. It would seem, there-fore, that the title given in the *Asloan MS*., THE MANERE OF THE CRYING OF ANE PLAY, is the correct one and that we have to do with a " Banns " [1] or " Proclamation " of a play, of which another example occurs in Lyndsay's *Satyre of the Thrie Estaitis*.

Proffering several explanations of what he was, who had come with the whirlwind—a Sowdane or Sultan from the East, a giant strong enough to bind bears, etc.—the performer continues:

> " Yet I trow that I vary ;
> I am the nakit Blynd Hary
> That lang has bene in the fary
> Farleis to fynd."

Be it noted that the *Bannatyne MS*. significantly gives for the second line the reading : " I am bot ane Blynd Hary." The pronunciation of the name is fixed by the rhymes as = " hairy."

On this passage all editors have commented with entire confidence, finding an allusion to the " Blind Hary " of the *Lament for the Makaris* and the " Blind Hary " who had occasional gifts of money from the king. To none has it

---

[1] See *The Mediaeval Stage*, E. K. Chambers, ii, 454-5, where this poem is so described.

seemed incongruous that a real person, probably familiar in appearance to many, should thus be conjoined with a semi-mythical entity like a Sultan or a supernatural one like the Spirit of Guy. From the epithet *nakit*, Professor Schipper draws the desperate inference that " it would appear that the old minstrel lived in needy circumstances during the later years of his life, when the infirmities of old age may have hindered him from continuing his occupation." As to what the " Blind Hary " of the records had to do with *fary* or *farleis*, there is no explanation.

The truth is that the " Blynd Hary " of the poem is to be sought farther afield than the *Lord Treasurer's Accounts*. It was the name, with variants, of a figure in folk-tale. " By the Lord Harry, I'll stay no longer," says a character in Congreve's *Old Bachelor*, using a familiar adjuration. The servant-girl in *Redgauntlet*, seeing the horse-shoe frown upon Darsie Latimer's face and immediately connecting him with the Squire, exclaimed : " If you want a third, there is none but ould Harry, as I know of, that can match ye for a brent broo ! " " Ould Harry " is a name for the Devil, who here, as is regularly the case (cf. Apollyon = Apollo), represents a pagan god—in the present case Odin under his epithet of " Har," the high one. Odin bartered an eye for wisdom and in the later popular tales is a mysterious visitor gifted with knowledge and great skill. To Olaf Tryggvason he came as "a very old man, clever of speech, one-eyed, and weak-sighted." In this guise he is *Gestr* or " the stranger," and as *Gestr blindi* he solved the riddles of King Heidrik in the *Herverar Saga*.[1] In Saxo Grammaticus he is " one-eyed " or " bereft of his eyes " (*orbus oculis*) or just " blind." [2] But the loss of one eye alone was popularly sufficient for the general description. In the present poem, indeed, the performer gives as his father " Gow Makmorne," where " Gow " is for Gaelic *goll*, " one-eyed or blind," who in Ireland, says Gavin Douglas, was a god, and who according to the legend had another name before he lost an eye and came to be known

---

[1] Ed. 1847, Copenhagen, p. 31, § 12.

[2] The references in Saxo and the sagas are collected by Grimm in *Deutsche Mythologie* (1854), i, pp. 133-4. The personal appearance of the god is a feature of the northern mythology but receives little notice in the German versions.

as " the blind." Similarly the " Bellie Blin " of certain ballads
has been identified with Odin by Professor Childs.[1] In Scotland
the game of "Blind-man's buff" was known as "Blind Harry."
We are told in the song *The Humble Beggar* how

> " Some were blyth, and some were sad
>   And some they play'd at blind Harrie." [2]

We have thus the mysterious old personage, a degenerate god,
who has been in " fary " or the other-world,[3] brings " farleis "
or wonders,[4] and in the tales appears in a wide mantle and broad
hat. Without this mantle he could be described as " naked,"
as even a man-at arms could be if he threw off his armour [5] or
an ordinary person if he discarded his cloak or gown. And the
conception as a whole is in its proper company with the other
weird personages, which a living man could not be. We also
see that there is a great deal to be said for the reading in the
Bannatyne MS.: " I am bot ane Blynd Hary." It shows at
least that the scribe took the reference as to a stock figure not
a real man.

[1] *English and Scottish Popular Ballads*, vol. i, p. 67.

[2] Herd's *Ancient and Modern Scottish Songs*, ii, p. 29.

[3] Cf. Lyndsay's *Papyngo*, l. 1133, and *Ane Satyre of the Thrie Estaitis*
(S.T.S.), l. 3247.

[4] Thus in the *Volsungasaga* it is Odin as the one-eyed man in mantle and
hat who brings the sword—Wagner's *Nothung*—to the Volsungs.

[5] Cf. " baith the parties war unarmet, or as we use to speik, naked men,"
The Historie of Scotland, a translation by Father James Dalrymple of Leslie's
De Origine, etc. Scotorum, by Bishop Leslie, 1596, ed. S.T.S., vol. i, p. 186.
Cf. also St. John xxi, 7, where the Greek for " naked " is taken by the
American revisers to mean " had on his under garment only."

GLOSSARY

(1) The more familiar words slightly disguised in spelling are not included. It is impossible to give all varieties of spelling, a typical case being *cler, cleir, clere*. Further, *i* and *y* are interchangeable, so that we have *perfit, perfyt*[*t*], etc. The same holds of *u* and *w*, e.g. *bourd, bowrd*.

(2) Only a few numbered references to the text have been given in cases of special significance or where the meaning is obscure. The first number is that of the poem, the second of the line.

(3) *n.*=noun ; *a.*=adjective ; *v.*=verb ; *adv.*=adverb ; *p.*=pronoun ; *prep.*=preposition. A. Fr.=Anglo-French. Other abbreviations will be understood.

(4) For personal names see Notes.

A *per se*, the best.
A, *n.* awe.
A, *a.* one : all.
Abayd, delay.
Ab(b)eit, Abyte, habit, dress.
Aboif, Abone, above, high.
Aboucht, bought.
Abufe, above.
Abusioun, abuse.
Abyd(e), stay, remain, submit to, endure.
Address, *v.* prepare, make ready.
Adew, adieu.
Adir, either.
Adjutorie, -ory, helper, help.
Ado=to do.
Adore, beg, plead.
Affeir, manner.
Afferit, afraid.
Affray, Affrey, *n.* fear, distress ; *v.* frighten.
Affy, trust.
Afo(i)r, before.
Aforrow, before.
Air, *n.* heir ; *n.* court of justice, 24. 19 ; *adv.* early.
Aithis, oaths.
Aits, oats.
Aild, Auld, old.

Aix, axe.
Alhaill, *adv.* wholly.
Allevin, (?)alleged, admitted, 4. 26.
All hallow, all saints.
Allowit, praised.
Allther=of all.
Allutirly, completely.
Allya, ally (Fr. allié).
Almery, "aumbry," locker.
Almous, alms.
Als, as, also.
Alyt, *v.* ailed, hurt.
Amene, pleasant.
An(n)amalit, enamelled ; *n.* Anamalyng.
Anarmit, armed.
And, and, if.
Anewch, Annuch(e), enough.
Anis, asses.
Annule, ring=bride, 87. 37.
Antecessouris, ancestors.
Anterus, Aunterus, adventurous.
Apill renye, pomander : see note, 77. 78.
Apill rubye, (?)red apple, 28. 57. But cf. preceding entry.
Apon, upon.
Appelle, *v.* charge.
Apperrall, apparel.

245

Appinnit, Apint, happened.
Applyit, inclined, brought round.
Arbe(i)r, arbour.
Are, oar, 88. 29.
Argh, timid.
Argone, Argown, argue.
Arryif, arrive.
Artilye, artillery, missiles.
As, ashes.
Ask, newt.
Astrologgis, astrologers.
Asure, lapis lazuli, 21. 48.   See note.
At, that, 65. 24.
At(t)our, over, above.
Atteir, attire.
Attircop, *n.* spider ; hence a repulsive person, 6. 523.
Attone, Attonis, together.
Aucht, *n.* possession, 40. 49 ; *a.* eight ; *v.* ought.
Austern, " austere," harsh.
Availl, value.
Aventeure, aventur, chance.
Aver, Avoir, cart-horse or old horse.
Averill, old horse.
Aune, *p.* own.
Aw, *a.* all.
Awalk, *v.* awake.
Awin, Awne, *p.* own.
Awnter, *v.* adventure.
Awppis, whaups, curlews, 55. 122.
Ayrtis, " airts," directions.

Bace, bass.
Bad, Baid, *v.* asked for, 40. 34 ; ordered ; endured, 81. 39 ; *n.* waiting, 47. 143.
Bagit hors, stallion, 57. 80.
Bailfull, sorrowful.
Baill, bale, grief, trouble.
Bair, beir, boar.
Baird, bard.
Bakstar, baker.
Ballingaris, small ships.
Bandoun, dominion.
Bane, bone.
Banesoun, " benison," blessing.
Bar(r)at, Bar(r)et, trouble, strife, vexation.

Barkit, hardened, tanned.
Barmekyn, wall.
Barres, *n.* lists, tilting enclosure.
Bartane, Britain.
Batalrus, warlike, 61. 89.
Bath, Baith, Baythe, both.
Bauchles, documents, 47. 347.
Bausy, big, coarse.
Bawch, feeble, 47. 143.
Bawis, balls.
Baxstar, baker.
Be, *prep.* by.
Beclip, embrace.
Bedene, soon, quickly.
Bedrait, Bedret, covered with dirt.
Bedroppit, spattered.
Beft, *v.* struck, beat.
Begouth, Begowth(e), began.
Behechtis, *n.* promises.
Behud, behoved.
Behufe, purpose, 63. 57.
Beild, *n.* shelter, refuge.
Beild, *v.* suppurated, swollen, 47. 164, etc.
Beir, barley, 6. 133.
Beir, noise, outcry, 38. 126. See note.
Beiris, *v.* roars, 29. 15.
Beist knapperis, biters of basting-thread, 58. 10.
Beit, *v.* supply, amend.
Bekis, ? teeth, 22. 40.
Bellamy, good friend (Fr. *bel ami*).
Belly huddroun, glutton.
Belyf(f), Belyve, at once.
Bendit, inflated, extended, 6. 6.
Bening, benign.
Berand, neighing ; cf. *v.* Beiris.
Beriall, beryl.
Berne, child ; man, 47. 237, etc.
Bertan, Britain.
Beschate, Beschittin, covered with excrement.
Beseik, beseech.
Beswakkit, struck forcibly, 6. 188.
Beswik, beguile, 47. 226.
Betrasit, Betrasd, betrayed.
Betteis : see note on 31. 4.
Beuche, Bewch, bough.
Bewis, boughs.

Bewrie, reveal.
Bicker, a drinking-cup.
Bickert. See Bikkerit.
Bid, must, 6. 137.
Biggingis, buildingo.
Biggis, builds.
Bikkerit, Bickerit, Bikkrit, assaulted.
Bikkir, n. assault, 56. 144.
Billie, comrade.
Binkis, n. banks.
Birkis, birches.
Birneist, cleaned, 93. 261.
Birs, bristles.
Bissart, buzzard.
Bla, livid.
Bladyeanes (epithet), 19. 23.
Blait, abashed.
Blait-mowit, stupid-spoken (?), 19. 23.
Blandit, soothed (?), 20. 77.
Blawe, n. blow.
Ble, complexion, 6. 165.
Bleir eit, blear-eyed.
Blenk, v. glance ; Blenkit ; Blenkand.
Blent, glanced.
Bler, deceive.
Blinkis. See Blenk.
Blynis, cease, 47. 428.
Bodin, arrayed.
Bogane, bogle, 6. 334.
Bollokis, testicles.
Bordour, Bourdour, jester : border, 56. 197.
Borrow, lay in pledge, and thus forego, 1. 4 ; redeem, 81. 6.
Bossis, Boissis, leather bottles.
Bosterus, Busterus, boisterous, violent.
Bot. See But : Bot gif (that), unless.
Botingis, boots.
Botwand (obscure), 6. 474.
Boun, Bown, a. ready ; v. prepare, go.
Bourd(e), Bowrd, n. and v. jest.
Bowdyn, swollen, 47. 345.
Bowgle, wild ox.
Bowk, body, 28. 25.
Brace, Brais, embrace.

Braid, Bred, n. start, spring ; braids of, resembles, 14. 13. See note.
Brand, brawned, 47. 429.
Brankand, showing off, swaggering.
Brattis, children ; cloaks, 77. 39. See note.
Breif, write, tell.
Breik, breeches.
Bremys, (?) breams, 56. 35.
Brennyng, burning, 87. 38.
Bribour, Brybour, beggar, robber, the devil, 87. 46 (O. Fr. brib*eur*).
Brim, brym, fierce.
Brist, burst.
Broddit, spurred.
Brow (obscure), 6. 458.
Browstar, brewer.
Bruik, Bruke, use, enjoy.
Bruikit, streaked with black, 38. 51.
Brukill, brittle.
Brybrie, beggary, thieving.
Brylyoun (obscure), 28. 44.
Buche, bush, 87. 38.
Buddis, bribes.
Bugrist, sodomite.
Buke, baked, 92. 212.
Bumbart, drone.
Bune, bottom.
Burd, board.
Burdoun, pilgrim's staff.
Bure, v. bore.
Buriawe, hangman (Fr. *bourreau*).
Busk, dress, deck.
Bussis, bushes.
But, n. in the outer room.
But, *prep*. without, 13. 30.
By, *adv*. besides, in addition, 23. 4.
Byd(e), stay ; bydand.
Byding, n. staying away.

Caa, crow.
Cabeld, haltered.
Cabroch, lean.
Caff, chaff.
Cahute, cabin (Fr. *cahute*).
Cale, broth.
Calsay, causeway.
Came, n. comb.
Capirculyoun, (?) capercaillie.

Cappill, horse.
Caprowsy, a cape with a hood, 6. 202.
Carle, man.
Carlich, clownish.
Carlingis, old women.
Carp, v. talk, discourse.
Car(r)ybald, monster, 6. 185. See note.
Catherein, cateran, Highland reiver.
Cawandaris, (obscure), 17. 10.
Cawkit, defecated.
Cedull, schedule, writing.
Celicall, heavenly.
Celsitud(e), greatness.
Certis, certain.
Chaftis, jaws.
Chaip, escape.
Chalmer, Chalmir, chamber.
Chalmirleir, chamberlain.
Char, on = " ajar," open.
Charbuckell, chairbunkle, carbuncle. See note 62. 24.
Chaumir. See Chalmer.
Cheis, choose.
Cheny(i)e, n. chain ; v. Chenzeit, clad in chain-armour.
Cherarchy, hierarchy, the heavenly host.
Chessone, v. to accuse.
Chevist, assigned by deed.
Chitirlilling, n. (obscure).
Choip, chap or jaw.
Choll, jowl.
Chose, choice, 6. 504 ; 87. 6.
Chuf, churl.
Chuff-midding, a. chaff-dungheap.
Chymys, mansion, 47. 292. See note.
Chyre, chair.
Clais, Clayis, n. clothes.
Cla(i)th, Cla(i)this, n. cloth, clothes.
Clam, climbed.
Clarat-cunnaris, claret-tasters or drinkers, 17. 42. See note.
Clarefeid, " clarified," polished.
Claver, clever, clover.
Clawcht, caught.
Cleik, n. catch, clutch ; v. seize, lay hold of.

Cleith, Cled, v. clothe, clothed.
Clek, v. hatch.
Cleke, v. fasten, 6. 510.
Clenge, cleanse.
Cleped, called.
Cler, " clear " = beautiful, 85. 4. See note.
Clergie, Clergy, learning, clergy.
Clerk, learned man, clergyman.
Clething, n. clothing.
Clewch, cliff ; pl. Clewis.
Clipis, v. calls.
Clippis, n. eclipse.
Cloddis, pelts.
Clok(e), cloak.
Closet, womb, 82. 78.
Clour, bruise, bump.
Cloutit, patched.
Clows, Cluvis, claws.
Clowttar, mender. See Cloutit.
Clucanes (obscure), 19. 24.
Cluik, claw.
Clype, a big soft fellow.
Coclinkis, harlots.
Coft, bought.
Collapis, collops.
Collep, flagon.
Colleveris = coal-avers (q.v.), horses for carrying coals. Cf. 6. 229.
Collum, ship, 6. 468.
Combuste, burning, 87. 38.
Commirwald, a. henpecked, 6. 129.
Compasand, compassing, devising.
Composition, settlement by mutual arrangement.
Compt, n. account ; v. reckons, values.
Concedring, Conciddering, considering.
Conclaif, closet, a private room,
Condampnit, condemned.
Counyng, Cunning, Cunnand, skilled, learned ; n. learning.
Conqueis, Conquys, acquire.
Conquestis, acquisitions.
Consaif, conceive ; Consaving.
Contemptioun, contempt.
Continuation, succession, inheritance, 54. 106.

Contra(i)r, contrary (O. Fr. *contraire*).
Convickit, convicted.
Cop, cup.
Corce. See Cors.
Corchet, crotchet (music).
Correnoch, coronach, lament for the dead.
Cors, cross; body, 77. 38.
Cought = " could," did, 47. 281, 85. 29.
Couhirttis, cowards.
Counyie (obscure), 57. 78.
Cout, colt.
Couth(e), could.
Covan, company.
Cowhubye, booby.
Cowit, cropped, 47. 275.
Cowkin-kenseis, (obscure) 19. 16.
Cradoun(e), Crawdoun, coward.
Crakkaris, Craikaris, boasters.
Crakkis, boasts.
Cramase, crimson.
Crap, crept.
Crauche, cry = admit defeat, 6. 245.
Craw, *n.* crow.
Creddens, credence, trust, belief.
Creill, wicker basket.
Creische, grease.
Croapand, croaking harshly.
Crok, old ewe.
Croppis, young growths.
Crowdie-mowdie (obscure), 28. 46.
Crows, briskly, elated.
Croynd, bellowed.
Cruddis, curds.
Cruke, hook.
Crya, cry, 6. 325.
Crynit, wasted, shrivelled.
Cuk, defecate.
Culroun, rascal.
Cumbir, encumbrance.
Cummer, *n.* care.
Cummer, *n.* gossip; *adv.* Cummer-lik.
Cummerans, *n.* encumbrance, distress, 47. 118.
Cun, taste, 93. 254. See note.
Cunning. See Connyng.
Cuntbittin, infected.

Cunyngis, rabbits.
Cunyie, Cunyeitt, Cunyouris, coin, coined, coiners.
Curche, kerchief.
Curio(u)s(e), Curiouslie, with care.
Curldodie, a plant.
Cutis, ankles.

Dagone, Dagon = devil, 6. 66.
Daill. See Deill; dale.
Dainte, denty, esteem.
Damys, makes water.
Dandillie, " darling," a pet name, 20. 62.
Dane, haughty.
Dantis, subdue.
Darett, *v.* address, 19. 2.
Dautit, petted.
Daw, slattern.
Dawing, dawning.
Dearch, dwarf.
Debait, defend.
Decore, becoming.
Ded, Dede, Deid, death; dead.
Defamous, derogatory.
Deflorde, disfigured.
Degest, calm, settled, considered.
Deidie, active in doing, 17. 58. See note.
Deidis, " deeds " in " almous deidis " = alms giving, 15. 1.
Deill, part, bit.
Deir, injure.
Dele, *v.* have to do with.
Delyverly, Deliverlie, smartly.
Demane, treat.
Demar, one judging.
Deming, the act of judging or being judged.
Dennar, dinner.
Denty. See Dainte.
Depant, Depeint, paint, painted.
Depictour, *n.* painting.
Depurit, purified; Depured in 87. 25.
Deray, disorder.
Derene, *v.* disorder, 52. 56 (O.F. *derener*).
Derne, *n.* darkness; *a.* dark, secret.

Descryve, Discrive, describe.

Detressit, hanging in tresses.

Devis, Deiff, deafen.

Devoid(e), *v.* remove.

Devoir, Devore, devour.

Devyce, counsel, skill ; at all devyis, completely ; evin at his devyis, 93. 372, according to his wish (O. Fr. *à devise*).

Deyne, *n.* disdain.

Dicht, made ready, treated.

Digne. See Ding.

Ding, *a.* worthy (Fr. *digne*).

Ding, Dang, Dungin, *v.* beat.

Dink, neatly dressed, trim.

Dirk, dark.

Dirkin, listen secretly, 47. 9.

Discry, describe, 61. 87.

Discure, make known.

Disdenyie, *n.* disdain.

Dises, Diseis, discomfort, trouble.

Disheris, disinherit.

Disjone, breakfast (O. Fr. *disjune*).

Dispern, disperse.

Dispitous, contemptible.

Dispone, dispose, lay out.

Dispulit, despoiled.

Dispyt, *n.* scorn, spite ; *v.* despise.

Dissymlit, Dissymulat, *a.* dissembling, hypocritical.

Disteynit, stained.

Diurn, of day.

Dogonis, worthless fellows.

Dok, the fundament.

Dollin, buried.

Dolly. See Dully.

Dompnationis, dominions.

Dong, dung.

Donk, dank, moist.

Dothit. See Dow.

Dotit, foolish.

Dow, dove.

Dow, is able ; *pt. t.* dotht ; M. docht.

Dowbart, blockhead.

Dowcare, diver.

Dowsy, stupid fellow.

Dram, sorrow.

Drawkit, drenched.

Dre, endure, suffer.

Drevellis, lazy or dirty fellows.

Drublie, wet.

Drug, drag, 22. 32.

Drup(e), feeble, useless.

Dryte, excrete.

Duddron, (?) sloven.

Duerch(e), dwarf.

Duke, Duik, duck.

Dule, *n.* sorrow ; *a.* sad ; *v.* grieve.

Dully, doleful, dismal.

Dungin, beaten.

Dures, injuries, 56. 170. See note.

Dwawmes, feelings of faintness.

Dynnit, made noise, 47. 10.

Dysour, player at dice.

Dyt, *n.* writing ; *v.* write.

Dyvour, bankrupt.

E, eye ; *pl.* Ene, Eyn(e).

Eddir, adder ; -stangit, adderstung.

Effec. See Effek.

Effeir, manner, behaviour, quality.

Effeiritly, in fear.

Effek, effect, truth, avail, result ; Effec, amount, 12. 8. See note.

Efferay, terror.

Eftir, Efter, after ; Eftirhend, behind, 86. 64.

Eik, eke, also.

Eild. See Eld.

Eird. See Erd.

Eith, easy.

Eld, eild, age.

Eldning, jealousy.

Elrich(e), elvish, fairy.

Elyk, alike.

Eme, uncle.

Enbrast, embraced.

En(s)ches(s)oun, blame.

Endite, Endyte, *n.* writing, literature ; *v.* write.

Endlang, along.

Engranyt, "grained," *i.e.* dyed a fast colour, 47. 139. See note.

Engyne, disposition, talent.

Erd(e), Eird, *n.* earth, the earth.

Erd, *v.* to bury.

Ernis, eagles.

Ersch(e), "Irish"=Gaelic, Highland.
Eschame, to be ashamed.
Eschaping, escaping.
Escheve, eschew, avoid.
Ess, ace in dice, something of little value.
Everilk, each.
Evirmair, evermore.
Excusationis, excuses.
Exeme, examine.
Exerce, Exers, exercise, practise.
Expreme, express.
Exultyf, (?) glorious.

Fa, foe.
Fader, father.
Fa(i)lye, v. fail; Failyeit, Falyeid, failed; Failyeand, failing.
Fair, v. go.
Fairheid, Fayrehede, beauty.
Fairly. See Ferly.
Fald, fold, enclosure.
Falis, false, 36. 31.
Falsate, Falsatt, Falsett, falsehood, falsity.
Falt, fault, lack, evil deed.
Familiaris, servants.
Fand, v. found.
Fang, n. booty, prize.
Fang, v. seize, take.
Fannoun, maniple, a band hanging from the left arm of a priest celebrating Mass.
Fant, weak.
Farcy, suffering from that disease.
Fare, n. manner, expression, 56. 225.
Farleis. See Ferly.
Farne, fared, 47. 153.
Fary, Phary, "fairy," marvel, 60. 11, 111; fairyland, other world, 87. 11; tumult, 69. 39.
Fasert, coward, 6. 517.
Fasso(u)n, fashion.
Faucht, fought.
Fautis, faults.
Fawd. See Fald.
Fe, property.
Feche, fetch.

Fecht, fight.
Feddir, feather; Fedderis.
Fed(d)rem(e), Fethreme, plumage, or coat of feathers.
Feid, n. enmity.
Feill, n. knowledge, understanding.
Feill, a. many.
Feir, mate, comrade; Feiris, Feres; but feir, without equal, 55. 94.
Feir, fere, company.
Feir, manner; feirris.
Feir, active.
Fek, company.
Fell, a. cruel; v. befall. 6. 246.
Felloun, fellone, fierce, dreadful.
Felye, fail. Cf. Failye.
Fene, Fenye, feign; Fenyeing.
Fensum, offensive.
Fenyeouris, pretenders.
Feppillis, fidgets.
Ferde, fourth.
Ferily, boldly.
Ferleit, wondered, 38. 63.
Ferliful, wonderful.
Ferly, Fairly, n. wonder; Farleis; a. wonderful; adv. wonderfully.
Fers(e), a. fierce; adv. Ferslye.
Fessoun. See Fasson.
Fest(i)nit, fastened.
Festuall, festival.
Feure, furrow.
Fewte, fealty.
Feyrse, fierce.
Firit, fired.
Firmance, imprisonment.
Firthe, wild or wooded country.
Flane, arrow.
Flay skinnis, (?) flea skins, 6. 445.
Flawme, baste.
Flayn. See Flane.
Fle, frighten; fly.
Fleggar, flatterer.
Fleichit, fawned.
Fleichouris, fawners.
Flemis, banish.
Flend, silly.
Flet, 6. 242. See note.
Fleyit, frightened.
Flingaris, dancers.

Flit, change place, waver.

Flocht, on=a-flutter, fluttering.

Flode. See Flude.

Flong, flung.

Floyt, flute.

Flour delyce, " fleur de lis."

Flude, flood.

Flure, floor.

Flurest, Flurist, covered with flowers, blooming.

Flyrdis, *v.* gibe, mock.

Flyrdom, mocking.

Flyrit, looked lustfully.

Flyrok, deformed person.

Flyt(e), scold, quarrel ; Flyt(t)ing.

Fog, coarse grass.

Foirfaltour, forfeiture.

Foirse, foresee.

Foirstairis, outside stairs.

Folie, foolish.

Fon, to be foolish, 47. 274.

Fond, (?) stupid fellow, 6. 518.

Force, care.

Forcy(e), forsy, powerful ; *adv.* Forcely.

For'd=for it, 19. 62.

Forder, farther.

Fordir, fore, 27. 9.

Forfair, perish, 92. 39.

Forfairn, overcome, worn-out.

Forflittin (obscure), 6. 239.

Forgeit, moulded.

Forky [Forcy], full of force, strong.

Forlane, useless.

Forleit, *v.* abandon.

Forloir, *v.* weaken, perish ; Forlore, lost ; Forlorne.

Forloppin, *a.* fugitive.

For quhy, because.

Forridden, overdriven.

Forrow, before.

Forthy, therefore.

Forvayit, went astray.

Forworthin, worthless.

Foryhet, forget, forgotten.

Fouth, abundance, size, 86. 42.

Fow, full.

Fowmart, polecat.

Fra, from.

Frackar, more active.

Frak, *v.* rush, move quickly.

Frane, ask.

Fratour, monastic dining-hall, 36. 11.

Frawart, froward.

Fray, *n.* alarm ; *v.* Frayit.

Freke, Freik, fellow, man.

Fremyt, Fremmit, strange.

Frog, upper garment, coat.

Fruct, fruit.

Frustar, Fruster, vain, useless.

Frustir, *v.* lay waste.

Frustrat, *a.* vain, foolish ; *v.* frustrated.

Fucksailis, fore-sails, 77. 74. See note.

Fudder, a great amount, 57. 62. See note.

Fullelie, foully.

Fulyeit, exhausted.

Fumyll, fumble.

Funling, foundling.

Fur(e), fared, went.

Fure, person, 47. 85.

Fure, furrow.

Furth(e), forth ; Furght, 47. 481.

Furth bering, bearing, carriage.

Furtheyst, poured forth.

Fut, foot.

Futher. See Fudder.

Fyle, *v.* defile, dirty ; Fyld(e), Fyling.

Fyne, end, 53. 7.

Fyrefla(w)cht, lightning.

Ga, go ; Gaid, went ; Gane.

Gadderaris, gatherers.

Gadderis, gathers ; Gadderit.

Gaff. See Gif.

Gaist, ghost ; Ghaistly.

Gaistis, guests, 92. 239.

Gait way ; Gaittis.

Gait, get ; Gaittis, gets.

Gallow, *a.* gallows.

Gam, game, sport ; Gammis, 31. 19.

Gammaldis, Gamountis, capers.

Gamis, Gammys, gums.

Ganand, fitting, suitable.

Gane, face.

Gane, v. suit ; Ganis ; Ganyt.

Ganest, most suitable.

Ganestand, stand against, oppose ; Ganestude.

Gang, walk.

Gangarall, toad, 37. 7. See note.

Ganyie, Genyie, arrow, dart.

Gar, Ger, v. force ; Gert.

Gardeyance, trunk or portable box.

Garesoun, company.

Gartane, garter.

Gast, scared.

Gaufe, guffaw.

Gaw, gall-bladder.

Geangleiris, janglers.

Geir, goods.

Geist, tale, talk (Fr. geste).

Geit, jet.

Gekkis, mocking gestures.

Gend, simple, 85. 1.

Genetrix, mother.

Genner, engender, beget ; Generit.

Gent, beautiful.

Gentrice, Gentrise, noble birth ; a. Gentryce, ladylike.

Geraflour, gillyflower.

Germyng, sprouting.

Germynat, " sprouted," descended, 87. 36.

Gersone (Fr. garçon).

Gers, grass ; Gris, Gres.

Gest, guest.

Gest, v. jest, 6. 507.

Gett, offspring.

Gib, tom-cat.

Gif(f), v. give ; Gaif(f), Gevin.

Gif(e), conj. if.

Gild, noise, 6. 225.

Gillot, mare.

Giltin, gilded.

Girnall, meal-store.

Girnis, looks cross, grimaces ; Girnand.

Girth, refuge.

Gladderit, besmeared, 47. 98.

Glaiking, folly.

Glaykis, Glaikis, fooling, 6. 497.

Glangoir, Glengoir, venereal disease.

Glar, mud.

Glaschane (obscure), 19. 59.

Glaschow-hedit (obscure), 19. 26.

Gled, kite.

Gledaris (obscure), 19. 41.

Glemys, glances.

Glete, glitter ; Gletering.

Gleyd, ember, 6. 108.

Glod (obscure), 6. 343.

Gloir, glory.

Glour, stare ; Glowrit, Glowrand.

Gluder, talk flatteringly, 93. 32.

Gluntow, " black-knee," 6. 99. See note.

Goif, gaze ; Govit.

Goishalk, goshawk.

Golk, " gowk," cuckoo.

Goreis, filth, 47. 98.

Gorgeit, stuffed.

Gorge-millaris (obscure), 19. 26.

Gormaw, cormorant.

Goulis, " gules," red in heraldry.

Graith, make ready ; Grathit, grathing.

Graithly, (?) dressed, 93. 439.

Grandschir, grandsire.

Gra(y)ne, n. branch. See note 13. 99.

Grane, v. groan ; Granit, Graneand

Grayth, possessions, 13. 85.

Gre, n. prize.

Gree, v. agree.

Greif, Greve, v. sadden.

Greis, steps, and so position, 6. 397.

Grephoun, griffin.

Grete, weep.

Grewhound, greyhound.

Gris. See Gers.

Grome, Grume, man.

Groukaris (obscure), 19. 41.

Growfe, on = prostrate, 27. 12. See note.

Grund, n. ground.

Grundyn, v. ground, sharpened.

Gruntill, snout.

Grunyie, snout.

Gryce, pig.

Guberne, v. govern, 82. 11.

Guckit, Gukit, foolish.

Gudame, grandmother.
Gudschir, grandfather.
Gukkis (obscure), 6. 497.
Gule, yellow.
Gulsoch, jaundiced, 6. 199. See note.
Gusting, tasting.
Guye, n. guide.
Gy, v. guide.
Gyane, n. giant ; Gyan(d)is.
Gymp, Jimp, neat, graceful.
Gyn, siege-engine.
Gyng, Gang, company.
Gyngill, jingle.
Gyrnd. See Girnis.

Habitakle, abode.
Hable, able.
Habound, abound.
Hache, ache, 47. 224.
Hadder, heather.
Haggeis, haggis.
Haif(f), have.
Hail(l), a. whole, sound.
Haill, adv. wholly.
Hailsing, salutation.
Haire, hoary, grey.
Hait, hot ; Hett.
Hald, Hawd, hold.
Halk, hawk.
Halok, foolish, 47. 465. See note.
Hals, throat, neck.
Halsit, embraced.
Halsum, wholesome.
Haltane, Hautand, Hawtane, haughty, proud.
Hamperit, confined.
Hankersaidilis, anchorites, 30. 9.
Hansell, first gift.
Hanyt, spared, unspent.
Happit, covered.
Hap schackellit, tied leg and head to prevent straying.
Harbry, Herbry, lodging.
Hard, heard.
Hardyment, courage.
Harlis, drags about.
Harlot, low fellow ; Harlotrie, vileness.

Harnis, brains.
Harskness, harshness.
Harth, hard, 6. 181.
Haschbaldis (obscure), 19. 18.
Hatrent, hatred.
Having, manner.
Haw, livid.
Hawd, hold.
Hawkit, streaked, 38. 103.
He, Hie, high.
Hechar, higher.
Hecht, promised.
Hef(f). See Haif.
Heft, haft, handle.
Hege, hedge ; Hegeis ; Hegeit, hedged.
Heggirbald, Haggarbaldis (obscure), 6. 149.
Heich, high.
Heildit, covered.
Heilie, disdainful.
Heill, health.
Heklis, rubs as with a heckle.
Helit, healed.
Hely, highly.
Henches, haunches.
Hend. See Eftir.
Hende, skilful.
Hepit, heaped.
Herbryie, lodge, shelter ; Herbr(e)it.
Herle, heron.
Heryit, Herreit, harried, robbed.
Hest, n. wish.
Het, hot.
Hewd, Hewit, hued.
Heylis, Hals, throat, neck.
Heynd, n. person.
Heynd, a. pleasant, sheltering, 6. 14.
Hicht, height.
Hiddill, secrecy.
Hie, a. high ; v. raise.
Hie gate, highway.
Hing, hang ; Hingand, hanging.
Hint, n. clutch, 38. 88 ; v. caught.
Hirklis, contract, 6. 181.
Hirpland, limping.
Hobbell, shoe.

Hobbill schowe, confused noise, 86. 1.

Hobland, hobbling.

Hodiern, of to-day.

Hog, year-old sheep.

Hogeart (obscure), 47. 272.

Hoist, cough.

Holkand, digging, piercing, 6. 186.

Holkit, hollow.

Holl, hull.

Holyn(e), holly.

Hommilty jommeltye, (?) awkward.

Hony, honey ; Hony came, honey-comb.

Hoo, halt.

Hoppir, a. shaped like a mill-hopper.

Hore, n. age (" hoar ").

Hos, hose.

Hospitall, hostelry, 82. 77.

Hostand, coughing.

Hostillar, innkeeper.

Hostit, coughed.

Houris, prayers, 55. 5, 56. 10.

Hous, Housing, horse-cloth, 22. 21.

Hous menyie, household.

Howffing, clumsy senseless fellow.

Howis, houghs.

Howlat, owl.

Howp, Houp, hope.

Huidpyk, miser.

Hukebanis, haunch bones.

Humill, Homill, humble.

Hummellis, (?) lazy fellows.

Hunder, Hundir, Hundreth, hun-dred.

Hurcheon, hedgehog.

Hurdars, hoarders.

Hurde, v. hoard.

Hure, whore.

Hurkland, crouching, coming to-gether, 6. 186.

Hurle, diarrhœa.

Hurle bawsy (epithet).

Hursone, whoreson.

Hutit, hooted (?), 47. 465.

Hy, n. haste.

Hyne, hence.

Hynting, seizing.

Huny, n. honey ; a. Hunyt.

Hunygukkis (epithet), 28. 39.

Ilk, same, 44. 27.

Ilk, each.

Ilka, each of two.

Ilkane, each one.

Illibat, pure, unblemished, 87. 37. See note.

Illustare, Illuster, illustrious.

Incluse, shut.

Incuby, incubus.

Indeficient, unfailing.

Indistinguyble, (?) outstanding, 87. 33.

Indoce, endorse ; Indo(i)st, Indor-sit, endorsed.

Indyt, v. write, compose.

Indyte, Indytting, n. literary work, poetry.

Infeck, v. be infected ; Infectit, infected.

Infecking, infection.

Infek, made incapable, 7. 57.

Inglis, English.

Ingure. See Injure.

Ingyne, mind, intelligence.

Ingynouris, contrivers.

Injure, Ingure, injury, injustice.

Innis, Innys, lodging, house.

Insensuat, senseless.

Intemerat, pure, 87. 39 (Lat. intemerata).

Inthrang, pushed in.

Intill, into, in.

Irke, tire.

Ische, v. issue.

Ja, jay.

Jaipit, seduced.

Jakkis, jacks, wadded sleeveless coats for protection ; low-bred fellows. See note, 77. 39.

Jalous, jealous.

Janglar, wrangler.

Jemis, gems.

Jevellis, low fellows, 19. 15.

Jevellouris, jailers.

Jolie, pretty, spirited, amorous.

Josit, enjoyed, 47. 201.

Jow, Jew.

Jowellis, jewels.

Jowrdane-hedit, with head like a jordan or chamber-pot.

Joyis, enjoys.

Juffler, shuffler.

Juge, judge ; Jugeing ; Jugement.

Jurdane, Jordan, chamber-pot.

Jupert, jeopardy.

Jure, law.·

Justing, tilting.

Karlingis, old women.

Katherane.   See Catherein.

Kayis, jackdaws.

Keik, peep.

Keild, killed, 6. 271.

Kelde, coloured.

Kell, coif, woman's head-dress.

Kemm, v. comb ; Kemmyng.

Kemp, gigantic person, champion, 86. 84.   See note.

Ken, know ; Kend.

Kene, keyn(e), bold, brave ; sharp.

Kenrik.   See Kinryk.

Kepit, protected, defended, 55. 130.

Keppis, catches.

Kerffis, carves.

Kerse, cress.

Kersp.   See Kirsp.

Ketch pillaris, tennis-players, 77. 66.   See note.

Kethat, a garment, 57. 21.

Kevellis (obscure), 19. 16.

Kinryk, Kenrik, kingdom.

Kirsp, Kersp, a delicate textile fabric.

Kist, chest.

Knaiff, servant ; Knaiffis, knaves.

Knaip, lad, 47. 125.

Knapparis, biters.

Knaw, know.

Knitchell, small burden.

Knowll, knobbed.

Knyp, nibble.

Knyt, joined, 47. 215.

Kokenis, (?) coquins, 17. 48.

Koy, quey, young cow.

Kynd, natural disposition.

Kyth, show ; Kythit, shown.

La, law.

Laeffe.   See Laif.

Laif, the rest, remainder.

Laik, lack.

Laip, lap.

Lair, learning.

Laith, n. evil, harm, 40. 28 ; a. loath, unwilling.

Laithly, loathsome.

Lait(t)is, manners.

Lak, n. blame, disparagement, 45. 11, 22 ; v. Lakkis.

Lak, lack.

Lake, (?) water surface, 56. 30.

Lang, long.

Langit, longed, 39. 5 ; belonged, 47. 407.

Langsum, tedious, tiresome.

Lanis, conceals.

Lap, leaped.

Lape, tucked up, 86. 70.

Lapidaris, lapidaries.

Larbar, n. impotent person ; a. weak, impotent.

Lasar, Laseir, leisure.

Lat, allow, let ; hinder. Cf. Lete.

Lathand, pale-coloured, 6. 102.   See note.

Lathit, loathed ; Lathlyit.

Lauch, v. laugh ; Leuch, Luche, laughed ; Lauchand.

Lauchter, Lawchtir, laughter.

Law, low.

Lawboring, labouring.

Lawd, "lewd," of lower orders, 22. 4.·

Lawd, loud.

Lawliness, lowliness.

Lawry(r), laurel.

Lawte, loyalty.

Le, lie.

Lecheing, Leiching, healing, cure.

Led, Leid, Leyd, person.

Ledder, ladder, 6. 174, 240.

Ledder, leather.

Lede, Leid, language. See note on
    38. 16.
Leg(g)is, Legeis, Leigis, lieges, sub-
    jects.
Leich, Leische, leash.
Leiche, doctor ; Lechis.
Leichecraft, art of healing.
Leichis, leeches, 6. 45.
Leid. See Led.
Leid, learning, 38. 16. See note.
Leif, n. leaf.
Leif, v. leave.
Leif, v. live.
Leik, dead body.
Leill, Lele, loyal, faithful.
Leir, Leyr, v. learn ; lerit.
Leische, leash.
Lelely, faithfully.
Leme, light, 6. 536.
Leme, v. gleam, shine ; Lemand.
Lemmane, sweetheart.
Lemys, rays.
Len, lend.
Lendis, loins, 6. 45.
Lene, lean.
Lerit, educated, 19. 41.
Lern, teach.
Lesing, Leising, lying.
Lessing, lessening.
Lest, last.
Lestand, lasting.
Lete, Leit, Let(t), allow, let.
Lettis, pretends, 47. 228.
Leuket, looked.
Levefell, lawful, becoming.
Lever, rather.
Levis, loaves, 42. 45.
Ley, lie (speak falsely), 57. 51.
Liayle, " loyal," true, 87. 37. See
    note.
Lib. v. geld ; Libbing.
Licht, Lycht, n. light ; v. alight.
Lichtlyit, Lichtleit, despised.
Lifly, lively.
Lift, sky.
Lig, v. to lie ; Liggit.
Lik schilling, chaff-licker.
Lind, Lynd, tree.
Lippinit, trusted.

Lippir, leper.
Lisk, flank, 6. 121. See note.
List, v. wish.
Listly, deftly, cleverly.
Lob, clumsy.
Lodsteir, lodestar.
Loffit, Lovit, praised.
Loft, apon, =loudly ; on=aloft.
Loik hertit, warm (luke) hearted.
Loikman, hangman.
Lonye, Lunyie, loin, back.
Loppin, leapt.
Losingeris, deceivers.
Louket, looked.
Loungand, lounging.
Lounry, rascality.
Lous, let loose, discharge.
Louse, a. loose.
Lout(t), Lowt, bow down.
Lovery, " livery "=allowance. Cf.
    Lufraye.
Loving,   praise ;   Lovingis.   Cf.
    Loffit.
Low, flame.
Lowis. See Lous.
Lowrit, cowered, bent down, 27. 12.
    See note.
Lowry, fox.
Lucern, lantern, light.
Luche. See Lauch.
Lucyferat, light-bearing, 87. 34.
Lude, (?) love, be fond of, 86. 175.
Luf blenk, love-glance.
Lufraye, " livery," dress.
Lug, ear.
Luge, lodge ; Lugeing.
Luk(e), look.
Lumbart, banker, 47. 362.   See
    note.
Lune, silver, 87. 34. See note.
Lurdane, lazy fellow.
Lushbald (obscure), 6. 501.
Lut, a. bent. Cf. Lout.
Luttaird, bowed, stooping.
Lume, tool.
Lyand,   " laying "=building,   17.
    13.
Lyart, grey.
Lychour, lecher.

Lyflett, means of living.

Lymare, Lymmer, rascal ; Lymmer-full.

Lym(m)is, limbs.

Lyne, lain, 82. 12.

Lynning, linen.

Lyntall, lintel.

Lyre, body, skin.

Lyte, small.

Lyth, Lythis, *imp*. listen, 47. 257, 35. 1.

Ma, *a*. more.

Ma(i), *v*. may.

Macull, Makle, stain.

Magellit, mangled, spoiled.

Magryme, migraine.

Mahoun(e), " Mahomet," the devil.

Maik, mate.

Maikles, matchless.

Mailis, rents.

Mair, Mare, more.

Mais, makes.

Maist, most.

Mak, *n*. make.

Makdome, form, figure.

Maling, *a*. malign.

Man, *v*. must ; also Mon.

Manar, *n*. house.

Manas(s)ing, menacing.

Mandrag, mandrake.

Mane, Mayne, of bread = finest. See note 93. 154.

Mangit, bewildered, silly.

Manheid, manhood.

Mank, flaw (Fr. *manque*).

Mannace, menace.

Mard, marred, confounded.

Marleyonis, merlins.

Marrit, frightened, 4. 7.

Martir, *v*. torment.

Mastev-lyke, like a mastiff.

Mastis, mastiff, 19. 21.

Matern, as mother.

Matutyne, *a*. morning.

Mauch, 6. 241. See note.

Maugre, displeasure (Fr. *malgré*), 52. 33.

Maws, sea-gulls.

Mayit, celebrated May, *i.e.* sported.

Meid, reward, 52. 33 ; merit, 67. 2.

Mein, means.

Meir, mare.

Mekill, Mekle, much.

Mell, meddle.

Melle, conflict.

Mell-heidit, mallet-headed.

Mellifluat, mellifluous.

Memore, mindful.

Mene, mayne, *n*. complaint, 48. 8.

Mene, *v*. complain, 52. 64 ; take pity on, 47. 501 ; meyne, lessen, 82. 47.

Mensk, manliness, dignity.

Menskit, honoured.

Mensweir, forswear.

Mensworne, perjured.

Menyie, company.

Menyie, *n*. stain, spot, 2. 12.

Menyie, *v*. pain, 3. 3.

Merciabill, merciful, 19. 68.

Merk, mirk, darkness.

Merk, approach ; Merkit.

Merrens (obscure), 47. 57.

Merse, round top on mast, 56. 52.

Messan, lap-dog.

Mes(o)ur, measure.

Meter, matter, 19. 68.

Methis, *v*. neighbours, adjoins.

Mett, *n*. measure.

Micht, might ; Mycht.

Misdemyng, misjudging.

Misfassonit, ill-shaped.

Misgane, made a mistake.

Misma(i)d, ill-made.

Mismakkis, *v*. makes wrongly.

Miss, *n*. wrong ; Myss.

Misteris, business, 47. 362; needs.

Misteris, *v*. needs, 8. 34.

Mittanis. See Myttane.

Mo, more.

Moir, more ; Moist.

Molet, bridle-bit, 47. 349.

Mon, must ; also Man and Most.

Moreis, morris-dancers.

Morgeownis, grimaces.

Morthour, Murthour, murder.

Most. See Mon.

Mot, may.
Moweris, jesters.
Mowis, *n*. jests.
Mowlis, chilblains.
Moy, mild.
Muk, clean out.
Muldis, mould, ashes of dead.
Munyoun, minion.
Murdris, *v*. murder ; Murdreist.
Mute, court.
Mutis, utters.
Myance, means, resource.
Mychane (obscure), 28. 37.
Mycharis, pilferers, 77. 31. See note.
Mylne, mill.
Mymmerkin (obscure), 6. 29, 514.
Mynnye, mother.
Myntyng, attempt.
Myrit, bemired.
Myten, diminutive creature, dwarf, 6. 494.
Myttane, Myten, kind of hawk.
Myttell, kind of hawk, 20. 12. Cf. Myttane.

Na, *a*. no ; *adv*. no ; *conj*. nor, than.
Nachettis, ball-boys at tennis (Fr. *naquet*), 77. 67.
Nagus, a miserly person.
Namelie, particularly.
Nanis, nonce.
Nar. See Neir.
Naught=nocht, no, 7. 94.
Ne, than ; also Na.
Neichtbouris. See Nychtbour.
Neiff, fist.
Neir, never, 39. 21.
Neir, *adv*. nearly ; *prep*. near ; Nar.
Neis, nose.
Nemmyt, named.
Nevow, nephew.
Nevyne, *v*. name, 82. 60. See note.
Nichell, nothing (*nihil*).
Nigirtnes, niggardliness.
Nigromansy, necromancy.
Nill, do not wish, 13. 85.
Nipcaik, a mean person.

Nocht, Noucht, Nought, *adv*. not ; *n*. nothing.
Nolt, cattle.
None, (?) noon, 85. 18. Cf. 1. 19.
Nor, than.
Nothir, nother. See Nowthir.
Nowthir, neither ; Nowdir, Nowder, No(u)ther, nother.
Noy, *n*. annoyance.
Noyis, *v*. annoys.
Nuke, nook, corner.
Nureis, nurse's.
Nureist, nourished.
Nurissing, *n*. nourishing ; Norising.
Nybbillit, pecked.
Nyce, strange, extraordinary ; Nyse.
Nychtbour, neighbour ; Neichtbour.
Nye, nigh.
Nyghttit, benighted.
Nyse. See Nyce.

Ocht, aught, anything.
Ockeraris, usurers.
Ombesett, besett.
On burd, alongside.
Ondir, under.
Onis, once.
Onone, anon, immediately.
Onrycht, wrongly.
Onsair, not-sore, happy.
Ontill, On(e)to, to ; on=a, 37. 7. See note.
Ony, any.
Opunyoun, opinion.
Or, ere, before.
Oratrice, female pleader.
Oritorie, oratory.
Ost, host, army.
Ostir dregar, oyster-dredger.
Ouirgane, overrun.
Ouir-word, refrain.
Our, Ouir, over, too.
Ourcast, turn over, 58. 30.
Ourcome, revived, 93. 546.
Ourcowerd, covered over.
Ourcum, Overcome ; ourcumin.
Ourdryve, spend time ; Ourdraif, spent, 93. 389.

Ourgane, overrun.
Ourgilt, gilded over.
Our helit, covered over.
Ourhie, over high.
Ourlaiden, overladen.
Our scailit, poured out, 56. 26.
Our sett, overcome.
Our settis, sets aside.
Ourstred, bestrode.
Ourtak, overtake ; Ourtane.
Ourthort, across.
Ourthrow, Ourthruch, through.
Owdir, Owther, either.
Ower slyd, pass.
Owk, week ; Oulkis.
Owsprang, out-sprang, 38. 111.
Owttour, over.
Oxstar, armpit.
Oyis, grandchildren.

Padok rod, frog-spawn, 6. 342.
Padyane, pageant ; Padgeanes.
Paikis, blows, punishment.
Paill, pall, canopy, 64. 13.
Pairte, depart, 93. 312.
Pais. See Pasche.
Paitlattis, neckerchiefs or loose collars.
Pako, peacock.
Palestrall, palatial.
Pallatt, head.
Pamphelet, a wench.
Panence, penance.
Paṅs, think (Fr. *pense*).
Pansches, tripe.
Panting, assuming, 19. 50.
Pantoun, slipper.
Papingo, Papingay, parrot.
Parage, rank.
Paralous, perilous.
Parfyt, perfect.
Parrell, peril.
Parrochynnis, parishes, 15. 56.
Pasche, Easter ; Pais.
Pastance, pastime.
Pastours, pastures.
Patrone, pattern, 88. 31.
Patroun, Patrone, patron.
Patryarkes, patriarchs, 87. 41.

Payis, large shield, 82. 65.
Peax, Peis, peace.
Pechis, laboured breathings.
Pedder, pedlar.
Peild. See Pelit.
Peip, very slight noise.
Pe(i)lit, plucked bare ; Peild.
Pelo(u)r, thief.
Pennis, feathers.
Percaice, perchance.
Perdie, certainly (Fr. *par Dieu*).
Perfay, by my faith, verily (Fr. *par foi*).
Perfit, Perfyt(e), perfect.
Perfurneis, accomplish.
Permansible, lasting.
Peronall, wanton, young woman.
Perqueir, by heart (Fr. *par cœur*).
Perreis, perish.
Pers(e), pierce ; Pers(i)t.
Persaving, thought, 93. 169, 331.
Persew, pursue, *i.e.* continue, frequent, assail.
Pert, pretty, lively, 47. 305.
Pertlyar, more lively.
Pe(i)rtrik, partridge.
Peteous, Petewous, Petous, piteous.
Peur, poor.
Phane, vane (fane).
Phary=fairy, *n.* marvel, illusion.
Phisnom(y), face.
Pietie, Petie, pity.
Pik, pitch.
Pillie wanton (obscure), 32. 25.
Pin, bolt.
Pingill, *v.* quarrel, 6. 114.
Piscence, power.
Pistill, discourse.
Plack, a coin of small value.
Plane, Pleyne, Plenyie, complain.
Ple(i)d, plea, dispute, lawsuit.
Pleid, *v.* contend, debate.
Pleis, pleasure, 93. 400.
Pleny(i)e. See Plane.
Ple(a)sance, pleasure.
Plesere, Ple(s)sour, pleasure.
Pleuch, Pluch, plough.
Plever, plover ; Pluveris.
Pley, *n.* dispute.

Plicht, support, 83. 31.
Plicht anker, principal anchor.
Plukkis, steals.
Ply, condition.
Polk, *a.* of sacking, 6. 145 ; *n.* bags,
6. 147.
Poltit, knocked against.
Port, gate, 64. 17, 87. 41.
Portratour, figure, 64. 35.   See
note.
Posseid, possess.
Possodie, sheep's-head broth.
Potestatis, powers.
Potingaris, apothecaries.
Pottingry, administration of drugs.
Pount, point, mark.
Pow, *v.* pull, 80, 110.
Practicianis, skilful, 7. 41.
Practik, practice, policy.
Prattelie, prettily.
Precelling, excelling.
Preclare, Preclair, famous.
Preif(f), *n.* proof, taste, 20. 13 (*q.v.*);
v. prove ; Preve, Preveit.
Preis, press, strive.
Prenecod, pin-cushion.
Prent, print, impression.
Prese, praise, 47. 475.
Presome, presume.
Prestyt, made a priest.
Preve.   See Preif.
Prevene, get before.
Prickill, Pricliss, prickles, annoys.
Prick lous, term for a tailor, 58. 5.
Prochin (parrochin), parish, 12.
24.
Prodissioun, treachery.
Prolixitness, prolixity.
Promyt, *v.* promise.
Pronunciate, pronounced.
Propois, propose.
Propyne, *v.* present.
Prouvait, provided.
Prowdence, prudence.
Prunya, preen, dress, 47. 374.   See
note.
Pryce, Prys, value.
Pulder, powder.
Punes, punish.

Purchas, Purches, Purchace, pro-
cure.
Purgation, purgative.
Purifit, Purifyet, made pure.
Purpest, purposed.
Purpour, purple.
Purspyk, pickpocket.
Purteth, poverty.
Purviance, Purveance, provision.
Puscence, puissance, power.
Put, *n.* push.
Pycharis, pitchers.
Pyet, Pyot, magpie.
Pykis, prickles, thorns.
Pykpuirs, pickpocket.
Pykthank, sycophant.
Pylers, pillars.
Pyne, *n.* pain.
Pynit, shrivelled.
Pypand (het), piping hot.

N.B.   Quh=wh.
Quair, book.
Quhasa, whoso.
Quhatt rak, Quhat rek, what matter.
Quhene, " wheen,"=few, 77. 14.
Quhilk, which.
Quhill, till.
Quhillelillie, penis.
Quhilum, at times.
Quhinge, whine.
Quhone, when.
Quhow, how.
Quhrync, squeal, 40. 87.
Quhynnis, stones.
Quintessance, 38. 57.   See note.
Quod, quoth.
Quyt(e), *v.* pay ; after " mak "=do
away with, 86. 124.   See note.
Quytclame, give up.

Rad, afraid.   Also Red.
Radius, Radyous, radiant.
Raeff, tore.   Cf. Raif.
Ragment, *n.* list ; discourse, 47. 162.
See note.
Raid, rode.
Raif, rave.

Raif, tore.

Raik, (?) rich, powerful, 24. 5. See note.

Raip, rope.

Rair, *v.* roar.

Raird, resound, 60. 113.

Rak, *n.* crack. See also under Quhatt rak.

Rak, *v.* stretch ; rak sauch, stretch-the-withy, gallows-bird, 6. 245.

Rakit, went ; rakand, going.

Rakit, reckoned, thought.

Rakles, reckless.

Rakyng, gathering.

Ralyeis, *v.* jest ; Ralyeit.

Rame, scream ; Ramand ; Ramys, obtains by clamour, 19. 33.

Ramowd, Raw-mowit, raw-mouthed, abusive, 6. 27, 401.

Rane, rigmarole.

Rang. See Ring.

Rangat, disorder.

Rankild, rankled, 47. 163.

Rattis, wheels.

Raucht, Rawcht, reached.

Rawchter, rough beam, rafter.

Rax, stretch ; Raxit.

Reboytit, repulsed.

Rebute, *n.* repulse.

Recryat, recant.

Red, frightened : *v.* arrange, 19. 44.

Rede-wod, quite mad, furious.

Redly, readily.

Redomyt, wreathed, adorned (L. *redimitus*).

Red(d)our, fear.

Refute, refuge, 87. 5.

Regratouris, retailers.

Regyne, queen (*regina*).

Rehator, enemy, 6. 244, 401.

Re(i)d, *v.* advise.

Reif, robbery.

Reik, Reke, *n.* smoke.

Reikit, *v.* smoked.

Re(i)rd, noise, uproar ; Reirdit, *v.* roared.

Reistit, dried up.

Relevis, supports.

Remord, remember with regret.

Remuffit, removed.

Reny(i)e, *n.* rein ; Renyeis.

Repet, disturbance, 47. 193.

Repreif, reprove.

Rere, roar.

Reskewit, captured.

Ressait, reception ; Ressett, abode, 93. 505.

Rethoris, eloquent writers.

Rethory, Rethorie, rhetoric, eloquence.

Retreitit, reversed.

Revest, clothed.

Revis, Revin. See Rif.

Rif, Ryve, *v.* tear.

Rigbane, backbone.

Rilling, raw-hide shoes.

Ring, reign ; *v.* Rang, Rong.

Rise. See Ryce.

Rispis, sedges.

Roch, *n.* rock.

Rocht, wrought.

Rod, spawn.

Roist, (?) encounter, 6. 27.

Rokkat, rochet.

Rokkis, Rockis, distaffs.

Rolpand, crying hoarsely ; cf. Rowp.

Rong. See Ring.

Rosere, rose garden.

Rosyne, *n.* rose.

Roun, Round. See Rownis.

Round, (?) trim, 6. 399 ; Roundit.

Roundar, whisperer. Cf. Rownis, Rownaris.

Roust, (?) disturbance, 47. 163.

Rowis, rolls.

Rowme, " room," space ; Rowmis, farms, 6. 301.

Rownaris, whisperers.

Rownis, *v.* whispers ; Round ; *infin.* Roun.

Rowp, *v.* croak.

Rowt, *n.* blow.

Rowttit, ranged, passed.

Royis, ravest, 6. 54.

Rubeatouris, scoundrels.

Ruch, rough.

Rude, cross : extent, space, 13. 42.

Ruffie, ruffian.

Ruffill, ruffling.

Rug, *v.* tug, pull ; *n.* Ruggis, pulls.

Ruge, roar.

Rumple, tail ; Rumplis.

Runsyis, horses.

Ruse, *n.* boast, 47. 431 ; *v.* Ruse, 20. 37.

Ryall, Ryell, etc., royal.

Ryce, Rise, brushwood.

Ryne, rind, 83. 12. See note.

Ryn(e), *v.* run ; Renneth, 88. 27.

Ryfe. See Rif.

Rype, search.

Sa, so.

Sacrand, sacring.

Saep, soap, 37. 9.

Sailyeit, assaulted.

Sair, sore ; Sarar.

Sairis, savours.

Sa(i)kles, blameless, innocent.

Salbe, shall be.

Sall, shall.

Sals, sauce.

Salt, *n.* assault.

Saluand, saluting.

Saluse, *v.* salute ; Salust.

Salvatour, Saviour ; *fem.* Salvatrice, 82. 67.

Sam, samyn(e), same.

Sane, *v.* bless ; Saynit.

Sanyne, *n.* blessing.

Sary(e), sorry.

Sauch, willow (as halter), 6. 245.

Saule, Saull, soul.

Savrand, savouring.

Saw, utterance ; Sawis.

Saying, essaying, 19. 49.

Sayn, *v. infin.*, say.

Scaffaris, beggars.

Scaile, Scale, dismiss, scatter.

Scaith, loss, hurt.

Scamelaris, spongers, 17. 45.

Scart, *v.* scratch.

Scart, scarred, 58. 74.

Scarth, monster, hybrid, 6. 58, 47. 92.

Scawpe, "scalp," head.

N.B. Sch=sh.

Schalk, churl, 47. 105.

Schawand, showing.

Scheild, (obscure), 6. 30.

Schell, (?) target, 2. 13.

Schene, bright, beautiful.

Schent, destroyed.

Schevill, wry.

Schew, Schewin, *v.* showed, shown.

Schewre, tore off.

Schill, shrill, 47. 516.

Schilling, husks. Cf. 6. 243.

Schir, " sheer," utter, 6. 496.

Schit (abuse), 6. 496.

Scho, schou, she.

Scho, shoe ; *pl.* Schone.

Schog, shake.

Schoir, *v.* threaten ; *n.* threatening ; Shore.

Schomd, (?) shorn, 22. 3.

Schou=scho (*q.v.*), 34. 15, 18.

Schoud (obscure), 22. 52.

Schow, shove, " shoo."

Schrenk, shrink.

Schrew, *v.* curse.

Schroud, covered.

Schrowd, dress.

Schup(e), shaped, undertook.

Schyre, clear, 47. 2.

Scippis, *v.* skips.

Sclander, Sklander, slander (Fr. *esclandre*).

Scorde, cut.

Scunner, disgust.

Scutarde, evacuator.

Sectour, executor.

Sedull, " schedule," writing.

Sege, man, 6. 13, 47. 469.

Sege, *v.* talk, 47. 196.

Seill, happiness, prosperity, 57. 61. See note.

Seir, various.

Seis, cease.

Sekir. See Sicker.

Selcitud, highness (Lat. *celsitudo*).

Seldin, seldom.

Sely. See Silly.

Sempill, simple.

Sempitern, everlasting.

Sen, since.
Sence, *n.* incense.
Sene, 54. 31. See Sayn.
Sensyne, since then.
Senyeour, lord (Fr. *seigneur*).
Senyie, war-cry, 6. 139; company, court, 77. 79.
Serf, *v.* serve.
Serk, shirt.
Sers, *v.* search.
Servis, deserves; Servit.
Sessioun, Court of Session.
Ses(s)one, season.
Set(t), *v.* sit; *n.* seat, 12. 20. See note.
Sett by, value, esteem.
Settis him, becomes him.
Sew, sue.
Shew, should.
Sib, related.
Sic, Sik, such.
Sich, Sych, sigh.
Sicker, Sic(k)ir, safe, sure.
Sickerly, certainly, surely.
Signakle, sign.
Sile, mislead.
Silly, Sillie, simple, good, poor.
Single, handful of grain, 6. 116.
Singular, personal, 44, 71.
Sith, since.
Skaffis, *v.* collects shabbily.
Skailed. See Scaile.
Skaitbird (abuse), 6. 37.
Skald, *n.* scold, 6. 322.
Skaldand, scalding.
Skaldit, (?) libellous, 6. 26, 37.
Skamelar, sponger.
Skar, *v.* scare; Skarrit.
Skarth, cormorant.
Skeich, shy.
Skeilis, pails or basins. (?) Scale =cup.
Skellat, bell.
Sker, scared, 47. 357.
Skerche, niggardly.
Skillis, baskets, 6. 231.
Skippis, leaps, turns (up), 37. 8.
Skirle, scream.
Sklender, Sklendir, slender.

Skolderit, scorched.
Skomer, defecate (scumber) applied to foxes, 6. 113.
Skowry, shabby.
Skrippit, mocked.
Skrowis, scrolls (A.Fr. *escrowe*, a scroll).
Skrumple, wrinkle.
Skryke, screech.
Skrymming, scudding, darting.
Skynk, *v.* pass, reach, 86. 176.
Skyre, (?) " score," scratch, 16. 122.
Skyttand, excreting.
Slawsy (obscure), 28. 41; Slawsy gawsy, 6. 39.
Sleikit, " sleek," sly.
Slewth, sloth.
Slie, Sle, *a.* sly, cunning, clever.
Slokkin, Slokyn, extinguish; Slo-knyt.
Sloppis, *n.* bands.
Slute, sluttish.
Smake, wretched.
Smoch, (?) snatch, 6. 364.
Smolet (obscure), 47. 113.
Smorit, Smord, smothered.
Smowk, Smuke, smoke; Smowking.
Smy, wretch, 47. 113. See note.
Snawe, snow.
Snevellis, snivels.
Socht, sought.
Soik, suck; Sowkand.
Soldan(e), Sultan.
Solist, solicit; Solistand, solisting.
Solistaris, suitors.
Solistationis, requests.
Sonce, plenty, 57. 61. See note.
Sondir, in, into=asunder.
Sonkin, sunk.
Sonyie, excuse, hesitation (O.Fr. *soigne*).
Sort, company.
Sossery, sorcery.
Soukaris, suckers.
Sould, should.
Soun(e), sound.
Sounder, Sowndir. See Sondir.
Sounyie, *n.* care, 57. 72 (Fr. *soigner*).

Southin, humming, 86. 103. See
  note. Cf. Sowch.
Souttar. See Sowtar.
Sowch, sighing.
Sowdan. See Soldan.
Sowp, *v.* sweep, 93. 214.
Sowsit, soused.
Sowtar, Souttar, cobbler, shoe-
  maker.
Spald, limb, joint, 22. 64.
Spane, *v.* wean ; Spanit.
Sparhalk, sparrow-hawk.
Speir, Spere, *n.* sphere ; spear.
Speir, *v.* ask.
Speir, (?) despair, 74, 44. See note.
Speit, *n.* spit.
Spelunk, cave.
Spirling, a smelt (fish).
Spolyeit. See Spulyeit.
Spousage, marriage.
Sprent, sprang.
Spruning, (=sprungin), sprung,
  sticking out.
Spynist, blown, opened out.
Stackerit, staggered ; Stackarand.
Stafische, stubborn.
Staggis, young horses.
Staiffis, *v.* stuffs.
Stailit, urinated.
Stald, " stalled," stabled.
Stanchell, kestrel.
Stang, sting.
Stanneris, gravel.
Stant, *v.* stand, 87. 11.
Staw, *n.* stall.
Steid, " stead," place.
Steik, shut.
Steir, stir ; *v.* steer.
Stent, *v.* stretch.
Stenyie, *v.* stain.
Sterand, stirring.
Stere, helm ; also Steiris, 74. 46. See
  note.
Stern, star.
Stevin, *n.* voice, sound.
Stew (obscure), 47. 339.
Stirk, young ox.
Stoppell, stopper.
Store, *n.* trouble.

Storkyn, stiffen.
Stound, sudden sharp pain.
Stour(e), conflict.
Stowin, stolen.
Stra(i)k, *n.* stroke.
Straitit, drew tight.
Stramp, trample.
Strand, *n.* stream, 80. 37, 88. 43.
Straucht, straight.
Stray, Strae, Stro, straw.
Streiche, stiff, affected.
Strekouris (obscure), 19. 17.
Strene, *v.* bind.
Strenewite, Strenuytie, strength.
Strenth, strength.
Stro. See Stray.
Strumbell, *n.* (obscure) ; *a.* Strumill.
Strynde, race, kind.
Stryppis, bands of steel as armour.
Studeing, studying.
Study, anvil.
Stuffettis, (?) lackeys (Fr. *estafette*).
Stunyst, astonished.
Sture, stern, sternly.
Sturt, discord.
Stychling, rustling, 54. 78.
Styng, pole.
Sua, Swa, so.
Sueir, Sweir, lazy, unwilling.
Suelly, *v.* swallow ; swelleis.
Sueving, Swevyng, dreaming.
Sugeorne, delay.
Sunyie, *v.* hesitate, 61. 31. See
  Sonyie.
Superne, high.
Supple, help.
Suppryis, *v.* do violence to, harm,
  48. 47. See note.
Surrigianis, surgeons.
Suth, truth ; South.
Suthfast, true.
Swage, assuage.
Swaittis, small beer, 6. 130.
Swak, *n.* dash.
Swalme, swelling.
Swanking, Swanky, (?) big or idle
  fellow.
Swanquhit, swan-white, 47. 243.
Swapit, *v.* quaffed.

Swappit (obscure), 6. 130.

Swentyouris, rogues.

Swerf, *n.* faint.

Sweyrd, Sueird, sword.

Swirk, *v.* dash, move quickly, 55. 84.

Swyr, a pass in the hills.

Swyth, quickly.

Syd, *a.* long, 33. 3 ; *adv.* Syde, at large, 47. 196.

Sysis, Sise, six (in dice).

Symbilyne, cymbal.

Symmer, Somer, summer.

Syn(e), then, afterwards.

Syng, sign, 82. 23.

Synk, five (Fr. *cinque*).

Sypharrit, separated, 6. 253.

Syphir, cipher, of no value, 12. 20.

Syre, *n.* man.

Sys(e), times.

Ta.   See Tane.

Taidis, toads.

Taikinis, tokens.

Taiklit, rigged.

Tailis, trains, skirts.

Tailye, tally.

Tailyeour, Telyour, tailor.

Taingis, tongs.

Tais, toes.

Tait, confident.

Takaris, thieves.

Takkis, leases, and so farms.

Tald, Tauld, Tawld, told.

Tane, the one ; Ta.

Tarsall, male peregrine falcon.

Tauch, tallow.

Tedder, *n.* tether.

Tegir, tiger ; Tygris.

Teme, Tume, *v.* empty : Temit ; Tomit, 57. 69.

Tempand, tempting.

Temptise, tempt.

Te(y)ne, anger ; misery, 83. 47. *v.* enrage.

Tent, heed.

Tern(e), (?) trouble, 83. 7 ; fierce, 47. 261.

Tersis : terse=penis.

Test, (?) trial, 54. 7.

Teuch, tough.

Theis, thighs.

Thewis, habits.

Thir, Ther, Thar, these.

Thocht, thoght, *n.* thought ; *conj.* though.

Thoill, Thole, suffer ; Tholit.

Thone, then.

Thra, boldly.

Thraif, number, 13. 55.   See note.

Thraip, allege ; Thre(i)pit.

Thrang, throng.

Thraward, perverse.

Thrif, Thryff, thrive.

Thrimlaris, jostlers.

Thring, press ; Thrungin.

Thrissil, Thirsill, thistle.

Thrist, *n.* thirst ; Thristy.

Thrist, *v.* thrust.

Thropillis, throats.

Thruch(t), Throucht, through.

Thyne, thence.

Till, *prep.* to.

Tinsale, Tynsall, loss.

Tint.   See Tyne.

Tirvit, stripped.

Tit, pulled.

Tod, fox.

Todlit, played.

Tome, Tume, *a.* empty ; cf. Teme.

Tone, Toun, tune, 44. 29.   See note.

Tone, fundament, 6. 502, 520.

Tone, "tune," agreement.

Tone, *v.* taken.

To-schuke, shook.

Totum, all.

Towdie (obscure), 28. 48.

Towis, ropes.

Townage, Townysche, townish.

Trace, *n.* row.

Traikit, harassed.

Traist, trust.

Trak, roar.

Tramort, dead body.

Tra(y)ne, *n.* snare.

Trappours, trappings.

Tratlar, chatterer.

Trattlis, *v.* gossips, talks ; Tratling.

Travall, Travaill, labour.

Trawe, device, trick, 47. 124.

Trechour, traitor.

Treit, draw, 15. 14.

Trentalis, a great number, 6. 319.

Trest, ? = Trist, *v.* meet with, 52. 34.

Trest, *v.* trust ; Traistand.

Tretable, tractable.

Tribbill, treble.

Trigide, tragedy.

Trimmill. See Trymble.

Troch, Troiche, trough.

Trone, weighing-machine. Cf. note on 6. 400 ; throne.

Trow, believe ; Trowd, Trowit, Trovand.

Trowane, vagabond, 6. 513.

Trulis, (?) bowls, 77. 22.

Trumpir, Trumpour, deceiver.

Tryackill, Tryacle, medicinal mixture. See note on 17. 87.

Tryit, tried, convicted, 6. 513.

Trymble, Trymmyle, tremble ; Trymlit, Trymbillit.

Tryst, assignation, appointment.

Tuchane = tulchan, stuffed calf-skin, 28. 23. See note.

Tuichand, touching.

Tuke, Tuk, Tuik, took.

Turkas, pincers, 57. 87. See note.

Turs(e), " truss," carry.

Turtour, turtle-dove.

Tute-mowitt, with protruding mouth or thick lips.

Tutivillaris, tattlers. See note on 6. 513.

Tuyse, twice.

Twich, touch.

Tydis, befalls.

Tyit, " tied," fastened.

Tympane, drum.

Tyne, lose ; Tynt, Tint.

Tyrlie myrlie (epithet), 28. 46.

Tys, entice.

Tyt, quickly.

Tythingis, " tidings," news.

Ud(d)er, ud(d)ir, other.

Ugsum, repulsive.

Uly, oil.

Umbrakle, shade.

Umquhile, lately.

Unabaisitly, unabashed.

Unaspyit, unobserved.

Uncouth, strange.

Uncow, (?) remote, unknown, 2. 13.

Uncunnandly, unknowingly.

Undemit, unjudged.

Undought, worthless person.

Uneis, scarcely, 80. 45.

Unfulyeit, unspoiled.

Unkend, unknown.

Unlesum, unlawful.

Unmenyeit, unmaimed.

Unmerciable, unmerciful.

Unplane, deceitful.

Unquit, unrewarded.

Unsall, unholy.

Unsicker, uncertain.

Unsoupit, without food.

Unspaynit, unweaned.

Upaland, Uplandis, countrified, up-country.

Updost, dressed, 6. 384.

Uphie, exalt.

Upwith, upward course, 47. 401.

Vacandis, free creatures.

Vakit, were vacant.

Vaneist, vanished.

Vardour, verdure, 47. 30.

Variand, Variant, varying.

Varite, verity.

Vengeable, bitter, persistent.

Vennim, venom.

Vilipentioun, vilifying.

Visar, visor.

Vissy, *v.* visit ; Veseit.

Voce, voice.

Vode, void, destitute, 80. 97.

Vostouris, braggarts.

Wa, woe.

Wa, wall, 29. 11 ; Wawis.

Wachemanis, outlaw's, 6. 143. Cf. Waithman.

Waik, Waek, weak.

Waiknit. See Walkins.

Waire, sea-weed.
Wairis, spends ; Warit.
Waistie, empty, desolate.
Waistles, fat, 57. 97.
Wait, wet.
Wait, at the=in wait. Also " in a wait."
Wait(t), know, knows ; Wat.
Waithman, outlaw, 38. 8.
Wald, wood ; Wold.
Wale, Waill, choose.
Wal(l)idrag, Wallydrag, sloven.
Walk, wake, be awake ; Walkis, Walkand, Walking.
Walkins, awakens ; Walknit, Waiknit, Walkand.
Wallie gowdye (epithet), 28. 45.
Wallowed, faded, pale-coloured.
Walteris, toss.
Wanderit, lost the way.
Wandrecht, trouble.
Wane, waggon, 13. 33.
Wane, dwelling ; Wanis, 57. 18. See note.
Wan fukkit (obscure), 6. 38.
Wan thryvin, badly grown, 6. 493.
War, aware.
War, worse ; Wer(s).
Ware, was.
Wareit, accursed.
Waris, spend, lay out ; Warit, 8. 13.
Warlo, warlock.
Warly, warily or warlike, 56. 201.
Warpit, uttered.
Warsill, wrestle.
Wary, v. curse ; Warit, Wariand ; pt. p. Warryit.
Wattis, welts.
Wauchtit, quaffed.
Wavill, wry.
Waw, wave, 6. 92.
Wawis, walls.
Weche, watchman.
Wecht, weight.
Wed, mortgage, 43, 22.
Wede, Weid, clothing.
Wedsett, pledged.
Wedy, " withy," halter. Cf. Widdy.
Weild, possess ; Weld.

Weil(l), Wele, well.
Weir, doubt.
Weir, Wer(e), war.
Weird, fate.
Welteris, pours, 6. 439.
Wene, know ; Wend, Wen(i)t.
Wer, worse ; Wers, Werst.
Werslingis, wrestlings. Cf. Warsill.
Wesche, v. wash.
Wey, v. weigh.
Weycht, wight ; Wycht.
Weyng, n. wing.
Wichis, witches.
Wicht, n. wight.
Wicht, wight, strong.
Wichtnes, strength.
Wic(k)ir, willow.
Widdefow, gallows-bird.
Widdis, woods.
Widdy, " withy," rope, halter.
Willing wandis, pliant, 31. 22.
Wilsome, wandering, astray.
Winder, Windir, wonder.
Windis, wounds.
Wirchip. See Wirschip.
Wirker, "worker," creator, 63. 53, 60.
Wirling, puny creature.
Wirriand, worrying.
Wirrok, Wyrok, n. a corn or other lump on the foot ; as adj. having corns, etc., distorted.
Wirschip, Wirchip, honour.
Wise, know ; Wist.
Withoutyn, Withouttin, without.
Wittandlie, knowingly.
Wlonk, fair one, 47. 36, 150.
Wobat, caterpillar.
Wod, woid, mad, fierce.
Wodenes, madness.
Wolroun. See note on 6. 432.
Wolsome, wandering, straying.
Womple, wimple.
Wondit, wounded.
Wosp, " wisp " of straw, 40. 110, see note ; stopper, 47. 335.
Wouk(e), kept awake.
Wowf, wolf.
Wowit, wooed.
Wox, waxed.

Wraiglane, wriggling.
Wraith, rage, violence, 40. 28.
Wrak, wealth, goods. See note on
  73. 10.
Wrangous, Wrangus, wrongful.
Wrayt, wrote.
Wreche, wretch, miser.
Wreik, Wreke, avenge ; Wrokin.
Wrink, trick.
Wrocht, " wrought," caused.
Wrokin. See Wreik.
Wy, man.
Wyice, wise.
Wyld, (?) dressed, combed, 57. 17.
  See note.
Wyning, whining.
Wyppit, tied.
Wyt(e), blame.

Ye, yea, 14. 36.
Yadswyvar, a bestial person, 6. 246 ;
  yad = yald.
Yaid. See Yald.
Yaip, eager, active, 47, 170.
Yak, *v.* ache.

Yald, old mare, worn-out horse ;
  yaid, 22. 25.
Yarne, " yearn," desire ; yarnand.
Yawmeris, loud cries.
Ybent, *pt. p.* bent, 56. 110, 145.
Ycid, went.
Yeild, impotent.
Yemen, yeomen.
Yemit, kept.
Yerd, yard.
Yerne. See Yarne.
Yet(t), gate.
Yfere, in company.
Ying, young.
Yockis. See Yolk.
Yok, yoke.
Yoldin, yielded, relaxed.
Yolk, " yoke," embrace.
Yon(e), yonder, that.
Yowis, ewes.
Yrle, dwarf.
Yrnis, *n.* irons.
Ythand, constant, diligent.
Yude, went. Cf. Yeid.
Yuke, itch.

ADDENDA TO GLOSSARY

Cury, dish of cooked food, 47. 455.
Denger, disdain, coyness, 52. 39, 56.
Forflittin, severely scolded, 6. 239.
Fredome, generous disposition, 47.
  299.
Gentill, of good birth, 47. 316.
Gane, walk, 35. 8.
I-wise, certainly, 47. 414.

Kevellis, low fellows, 19. 16.
Kindly, natural, 47. 546.
Mymmerkin, ? dotard, 6. 29, 514.
Penis, feathers just emerging, 6. 157.
Scheild, ? peeled, 6. 30.
Skaitbird, Richardson's Skua, 6. 37.
Skaldit, scabby, 6. 37.
Trewth, Faith, 83. 57.

INDEX OF FIRST LINES

270